AF633114

The Future of Post-Human Humor

The Future of Post-Human Humor

A Preface to a New Theory of Joking and Laughing

Peter Baofu

Viva Books

New Delhi | Mumbai | Chennai | Kolkata | Bengaluru | Hyderabad | Kochi | Guwahati

Copyright © Cambridge International Science Publishing

First Indian Edition 2012

VIVA BOOKS PRIVATE LIMITED

- 4737/23 Ansari Road, Daryaganj, New Delhi 110 002
  E-mail: vivadelhi@vivagroupindia.net, Tel. 42242200
- 76, Service Industries, Shirvane, Sector 1, Nerul, Navi Mumbai 400 706
  E-mail: vivamumbai@vivagroupindia.net, Tel. 27721273, 27721274
- Jamals Fazal Chambers, 26 Greams Road, Chennai 600 006
  E-mail: vivachennai@vivagroupindia.net, Tel. 28290304, 28294241
- B-103, Jindal Towers, 21/1A/3 Darga Road, Kolkata 700 017
  E-mail: vivakolkata@vivagroupindia.net, Tel. 22836381, 22816713
- 7, Sovereign Park Apartments, 56-58, K. R. Road, Basavanagudi, Bangalore 560 004
  E-mail: vivabangalore@vivagroupindia.net, Tel. 26607409, 26607410
- 101-102 Mughal Marc Apartments, 3-4-637 to 641, Narayanguda, Hyderabad 500 029
  E-mail: vivahyderabad@vivagroupindia.net, Tel. 27564481, 27564482
- Beevi Towers, First Floor, SRM Road, Kaloor, Kochi 682 018, Kerala
  E-mail: vivakochi@vivagroupindia.net, Tel: 0484-2403055, 2403056
- 232, GNB Road, Beside UCO Bank, Silpukhuri, Guwahati 781 003
  E-mail: vivaguwahati@vivagroupindia.net, Tel: 0361-2666386

www.vivagroupindia.com

Published by arrangement with
Cambridge International Science Publishing
7, Meadow Walk, Great Abington
Cambridge CB1 6AZ, UK

All rights reserved. No part of this book may be reproduced or transmitted in any form or by any means now known or to be invented, electronic or mechanical, including photocopying, recording or by any information storage or retrieval system without written permission from the publisher.

This edition is for sale in the Indian Subcontinent only. Not for export elsewhere.

ISBN : 978-81-309-1998-0

Published by Vinod Vasishtha for Viva Books Private Limited, 4737/23, Ansari Road, Daryaganj, New Delhi-110 002. Printed and bound by Syndicate Binders, Noida.

To Those in the Future World Beyond Joking and Laughing

BOOKS ALSO BY PETER BAOFU

Category I: Social Sciences and Related Fields

- 37. *The Future of Post-Human Education* (2011)
- 36. *The Future of Post-Human War and Peace* (2010)
- 35. *The Future of Post-Human Law* (2010)
- 34. *The Future of Post-Human Organization* (2009)
- 33. *The Future of Post-Human Mass Media* (2009)
- 32. *The Rise of Authoritarian Liberal Democracy* (2007)
- 31. *Beyond the World of Titans, and the Remaking of World Order* (2007)
- 30. *Beyond Capitalism to Post-Capitalism* (2005)
- 29. Volume 1: *Beyond Democracy to Post-Democracy* (2004)
- 28. Volume 2: *Beyond Democracy to Post-Democracy* (2004)
- 27. *The Future of Capitalism and Democracy* (2002)

Category II: Formal Sciences and Related Fields

- 26. *The Future of Post-Human Formal Science* (2010)
- 25. *The Future of Post-Human Language* (2009)
- 24. *The Future of Post-Human Geometry* (2009)
- 23. *The Future of Post-Human Mathematical Logic* (2008)
- 22. *The Future of Information Architecture* (2008)

Category III: Natural Sciences and Related Fields

- 21. *The Future of Post-Human Geology* (2010)
- 20. *Beyond Cosmology to Post-Cosmology* (2010)
- 19. *The Future of Post-Human Personality* (2010)
- 18. *The Future of Post-Human Sexuality* (2010)
- 17. *The Future of Post-Human Urban Planning* (2009)
- 16. *The Future of Post-Human Engineering* (2009)
- 15. *The Future of Post-Human Unconsciousness* (2008)
- 14. *The Future of Complexity* (2007)
- 13. *Beyond Nature and Nurture* (2006)
- 12. *The Future of Post-Human Space-Time* (2006)
- 11. *The Future of Post-Human Consciousness* (2004)

Category IV: The Humanities and Related Fields

- 10. *Beyond Ethics to Post-Ethics* (2011)
- 9. *The Future of Post-Human Religion* (2010)
- 8. *The Future of Post-Human Chess* (2010)
- 7. *The Future of Post-Human Martial Arts* (2009)
- 6. *The Future of Post-Human Creative Thinking* (2009)
- 5. *The Future of Post-Human Knowledge* (2008)
- 4. *The Future of Aesthetic Experience* (2007)
- 3. *Beyond Civilization to Post-Civilization* (2006)
- 2. Volume 1: *The Future of Human Civilization* (2000)
- 1. Volume 2: *The Future of Human Civilization* (2000)

CONTENTS

Part Three: Laughing

Part Four: Conclusion

TABLES

Category III: Visions on the Mind

Category IV: Visions on History

Category V: Visions on Methodology

Category VI: Visions on Ontology

Category VII. Visions on Society (Socio-Political)

Category VIII. Visions on Society (Socio-Economic)

Category IX: Visions on Culture

FOREWORD

At the conclusion of this year 2010, I heard a widespread expression of disdain over the preceding twelve months that I perceived to be stronger than at the conclusion of other recent years. Stories about "a horrible year" were prolific in both conversations and the media, and it was credited to many causes, especially to an almost worldwide economic collapse that affected individuals and business enterprises. Concomitantly, I sensed an increase in the popularity of comedians whose jokes were forwarded via the internet and repeated at gatherings to much enjoyment by listeners.

An antidote to feelings of sadness and despair appears to lay in humor. Jokes make light of heavy concerns, evident in labeling Greece's request to the International Monetary Fund for 19 billion Euro as "for cigarettes."

People turn to humor in dire times to laugh and feel good. Humor leads the way to a ray of happiness. And so it is that Dr. Peter Baofu's research underscores the importance of humor for humankind. His examination of the topic allows us to place a significant value on humor as an aid to the serious undertakings that best the human condition.

We are indebted to Dr. Baofu for his unique skills as an observer and analyst of situations that perplex people. He sheds a ray of enlightenment on issues that prompt us to give further thought to everyday happenings and their consequences. May the readers of this volume evaluate humor from a new perspective.

Sylvan Von Burg
School of Business
George Washington University

Acknowledgments

For those who had read any previous books of mine, it is well expected that this book too is written to challenge conventional wisdom and to replace it with an alternative novel way of thinking—or more specifically in the current context, a new theory to understand the future fate of humor.

Thus, it is not surprising that this book receives no external funding nor help from any formal organization or institution, because of its political incorrectness—as this is something that I often emphasized in all my previous books.

My only reward is that joyful wonder about something not thought of before in history.

Besides, I greatly appreciate the foreword by Sylvan von Burg at George Washington University School of Business.

In any event, and as always, I bear the sole responsibility for the ideas presented in this book.

Abbreviations

ALD = Peter Baofu. 2007. *The Rise of Authoritarian Liberal Democracy: A Preface to a New Theory of Comparative Political Systems.* Cambridge, England: Cambridge Scholars Publishing, Ltd.

BCIV = Peter Baofu. 2006. *Beyond Civilization to Post-Civilization: Conceiving a Better Model of Life Settlement to Supersede Civilization.* NY: Peter Lang Publishing, Inc.

BCPC = Peter Baofu. 2005. *Beyond Capitalism to Post-Capitalism: Conceiving a Better Model of Wealth Acquisition to Supersede Capitalism.* NY: The Edwin Mellen Press.

BCOS = Peter Baofu. 2010. *Beyond Cosmology to Post-Cosmology: A Preface to a New Theory of Different Worlds.* Cambridge, England: Cambridge International Science Publishing, Ltd.

BDPD1 = Peter Baofu. 2004. Volume 1. *Beyond Democracy to Post-Democracy: Conceiving a Better Model of Governance to Supersede Democracy.* NY: The Edwin Mellen Press.

BDPD2 = Peter Baofu. 2004. Volume 2. *Beyond Democracy to Post-Democracy: Conceiving a Better Model of Governance to Supersede Democracy.* NY: The Edwin Mellen Press.

BEPE = Peter Baofu. 2011. *Beyond Ethics to Post-Ethics: A Preface to a New Theory of Morality and Immorality.* Charlotte, NC: Infomration Age Publishing.

BNN = Peter Baofu. 2006. *Beyond Nature and Nurture: Conceivng a Better Way to Understand Genes and Memes.* Cambridge, England: Cambridge Scholars Publishing, Ltd.

BWT = Peter Baofu. 2007. *Beyond the World of Titans, and the Renaking of World Order: A Preface to a New Logic of Empire-Building.* Cambridge, England: Cambridge Scholars Publishing, Ltd.

FAE = Peter Baofu. 2007. *The Future of Aesthetic Experience: Conceiving a Better Way to Understand Beauty, Ugliness and the Rest.* Cambridge, England: Cambridge Scholars Publishing, Ltd.

FC = Peter Baofu. 2007. *The Future of Complexity: Conceiving a Better Way to Understand Order and Chaos.* London, United Kingdom: World Scientific Publishing Co.

FCD = Peter Baofu. 2002. *The Future of Capitalism and Democracy.* MD: The University Press of America.

FHC1 = Peter Baofu. 2000. Volume 1. *The Future of Human Civilization.* NY: The Edwin Mellen Press.

FHC2 = Peter Baofu. 2000. Volume 2. *The Future of Human Civilization.* NY: The Edwin Mellen Press.

FIA = Peter Baofu. 2008. *The Future of Information Architecture: Conceiving a Better Way to Understand Taxonomy, Network, and Intelligence.* Oxford, England: Chandos Publishing (Oxford) Limited.

FPHC = Peter Baofu. 2004. *The Future of Post-Human Consciousness.* NY: The Edwin Mellen Press.

FPHCHESS = Peter Baofu. 2010. *The Future of Post-Human Chess: A Preface to a New Theory of Tactics and Strategy.* Cambridge, England: Cambridge International Science Publishing, Ltd.

FPHCT = Peter Baofu. 2009. *The Future of Post-Human Creative Thinking: A Preface to a New Theory of Invention and Innovation.* Cambridge, England: Cambridge Scholars Publishing, Ltd.

FPHE = Peter Baofu. 2009. *The Future of Post-Human Engineering: A Preface to a New Theory of Technology.* Cambridge, England: Cambridge Scholars Publishing, Ltd.

FPHEDU = Peter Baofu. 2011. *The Future of Post-Human Education: A Preface to a New Theory of Teaching and Learning.* Cambridge, England: Cambridge International Science Publishing, Ltd.

FPHFS = Peter Baofu. 2010. *The Future of Post-Human Formal Science: A Preface to a New Theory of Abstraction and Application.* Cambridge, England: Cambridge Scholars Publishing, Ltd.

FPHG = Peter Baofu. 2009. *The Future of Post-Human Geometry: A Preface to a New Theory of Infinity, Symmetry, and Dimensionality.* Cambridge, England: Cambridge Scholars Publishing, Ltd.

FPHGEOL = Peter Baofu. 2010. *The Future of Post-Human Geology: A Preface to a New Theory of Statics and Dynamics.* Cambridge, England: Cambridge International Science Publishing, Ltd.

FPHK = Peter Baofu. 2008. *The Future of Post-Human Knowledge: A Preface to a New Theory of Methodology and Ontology.* Oxford, England: Chandos Publishing (Oxford) Limited.

FPHL = Peter Baofu. 2009. *The Future of Post-Human Language: A Preface to a New Theory of Structure, Context, and Learning.* Cambridge, England: Cambridge Scholars Publishing, Ltd.

FPHLAW = Peter Baofu. 2010. *The Future of Post-Human Law: A Preface to a New Theory of Necessity, Contingency, and Justice.* Cambridge, England: Cambridge Scholars Publishing, Ltd.

FPHMA = Peter Baofu. 2009. *The Future of Post-Human Martial Arts: A Preface to a New Theory of the Body and Spirit of Warriors.* Cambridge, England: Cambridge Scholars Publishing, Ltd.

FPHML = Peter Baofu. 2008. *The Future of Post-Human Mathematical Logic: A Preface to a New Theory of Rationality.* Cambridge, England: Cambridge Scholars Publishing, Ltd.

FPHMM = Peter Baofu. 2009. *The Future of Post-Human Mass Media: A Preface to a New Theory of Technology.* Cambridge, England: Cambridge Scholars Publishing, Ltd.

FPHO = Peter Baofu. 2009. *The Future of Post-Human Organization: A Preface to a New Theory of Communication, Decision-Making, and Leadership.*.Cambridge, England: Cambridge Scholars Publishing, Ltd.

FPHP = Peter Baofu. 2010. *The Future of Post-Human Personality: A Preface to a New Theory of Normality and Abnormality.* Cambridge, England: Cambridge International Science Publishing, Ltd.

FPHR = Peter Baofu. 2010. *The Future of Post-Human Religion: A Preface to a New Theory of Spirituality.* Cambridge, England: Cambridge International Science Publishing, Ltd.

FPHS = Peter Baofu. 2010. *The Future of Post-Human Sexuality: A Preface to a New Theory of the Body and Spirit of Love-Makers.* Cambridge, England: Cambridge Scholars Publishing, Ltd.

FPHST = Peter Baofu. 2006. *The Future of Post-Human Space-Time: Conceivng a Better Way to Understand Space and Time.* New York: Peter Lang Publishing, Inc.

FPHU = Peter Baofu. 2008. *The Future of Post-Human Unconsciousness: A Preface to a New Theory of Anomalous Experience.* Cambridge, England: Cambridge Scholars Publishing, Ltd.

FPHUP = Peter Baofu. 2009. *The Future of Post-Human Urban Planning: A Preface to a New Theory of Density, Void, and Sustainability.* Cambridge, England: Cambridge Scholars Publishing, Ltd.

FPHWP = Peter Baofu. 2010. *The Future of Post-Human War and Peace: A Preface to a New Theory of Aggression and Pacificity*. Cambridge, England: Cambridge Scholars Publishing, Ltd.

• PART ONE •

Introduction

CHAPTER 1
INTRODUCTION—THE FUN OF HUMOR

The gods too are fond of a joke.
—Aristotle (QW 2010a)

Humor to Be, or Not to Be, a Frog Can

Is humor really so desirable that, as Aristotle once wrote in a funny passage, "[t]he gods too are fond of a joke"? (QW 2010a)

This positive idea of humor can be contrasted with other (opposing) views. For instance, as Sigmund Freud once wrote, "[o]ne can't express aggression and sexual drive directly, as it is prohibited in the society, so these desires get sublimated in telling 'jokes.' If you look at jokes, they are either about somebody getting hurt, or they have sexual connotations." (A. Chislenko 2010)

Or listen to what Justin Brooks Atkinson has to say about humor: "The humorous man recognizes that absolute purity, absolute justice, absolute logic and perfection are beyond human achievement and that men have been able to live happily for thousands of years in a state of genial frailty." (QW 2010)

But E. B. White was more skeptical when he once argued that "humor can be dissected as a frog can, but the thing dies in the process and the innards are discouraging to any but the pure scientific mind." (WK 2010)

Contrary to these opposing views (and other ones as will be discussed in the book), humor is neither possible nor desirable to the extent that the respective ideologues (on the opposing sides of the fence) would like us to believe.

Of course, one should not misconstrue this critique of the conventional wisdom about the nature of humor as a suggestion that humor is a joyless endeavor, or that some fields of study (related to humor) like evolutionary biology, psychology, sociology, or even culture studies are to be disregarded. Needless to say, neither of these extreme views is reasonable either.

On the contrary, this book provides an alternative (better) way to understand the future of humor, especially in the dialectic context of joking and laughing—while learning from different approaches in the literature but without favoring any one of them (nor integrating them, since they are not necessarily compatible with each other).

Thus, this book offers a new theory (that is, *the metamorphic theory of humor*) to go beyond the existing approaches in the literature on humor in a novel way.

If successful, this seminal project is to fundamentally change the way that we think about humor, from the combined perspectives of the mind, nature, society, and culture, with enormous implications for the human future and what I originally called its "post-human" fate.

Humor in Relation to Joking and Laughing

At the outset, it is important to define the word "humor," which "derives from the humoral medicine of the ancient Greeks, which taught that the balance of fluids in the human body, known as humours (Latin: *umor*, 'body fluid'), control human health and emotion." (WK 2010)

Thus, in accordance to this old definition by the ancient Greeks, humor is important to good health—and, nowadays, "[s]tudies show that people who laugh more often get sick less." (WK 2010k; G. Meredith 1897) And the reason is that "laughter boosts the immune system, lowers cholesterol and blood pressure, and reduces stress." (A. Angelle 2010: 15)

This old definition aside—humor has two sides to be considered, namely, (a) joking (on the giving end) and (b) laughing (on the receiving end), as explained below and summarized in *Table 1.1*.

Joking

On the giving end of humor is joking, from the word "joke," which refers to "a question, short story, or depiction of a situation made with the intent of being humorous. To achieve this end, jokes may employ irony, sarcasm, word play and other devices. Jokes may have a punchline that will end the sentence to make it humorous." (WK 2010a)

A joke, however, can be either "spoken" or "practical"—and "[a] practical joke or prank differs from a spoken one in that the major component of the humour is physical rather than verbal (for example placing salt in the sugar bowl)." (WK 2010a)

With this distinction (between spoken and practical jokes) in mind, the history of jokes can be traced back to "at least 1900 BC. According to research conducted by Dr Paul McDonald of the University of Wolverhampton, a fart joke from ancient Sumer is currently believed to be the world's oldest known joke." (WK 2010a; J. Joseph 2008)

A good illustration of what a joke in antiquity was like is a funny joke in ancient Greece of the 3rd or 4th century AD, which was described in "a document called *Philogelos* (The Laughter Lover)" by Hierocles and Philagrius, about a bald man, a barber, and an absent-minded professor: "A barber, a bald man and an absent minded professor take a journey together. They have to camp overnight, so decide to take turns watching the luggage. When it's the barber's turn, he gets bored, so he amuses himself by shaving the head of the professor. When the professor is woken up for his shift, he feels his head, and says 'How stupid is that barber? He's woken up the bald man instead of me.'" (WK 2010a)

Funny as jokes are, even when they are from the ancient past, they can be classified into different "subjects" and "styles," as shown below.

Subjects of Jokes

Jokes can first be classified into differnet "subjects"; for illustration, hereafter are some major "subjects" of jokes: (WK 2010a)

- "Political Jokes"—"are usually a form of satire [known as political satire]. They generally concern politicians and heads of state, but may also cover the absurdities of a country's political situation....Two large categories of this type of jokes exist [in political cartoons]....The first one makes fun of a negative attitude to political opponents or to politicians in general. The second one makes fun of political clichés, mottoes, catch phrases or simply blunders of politicians." (WK 2010a)

- "Professional Humour"—"includes caricatured portrayals of certain professions such as lawyers, and in-jokes told by professionals to each other." (WK 2010a)

- "Mathematical Jokes"—"are a form of in-joke, generally designed to be understandable only by insiders. (They are also often strictly visual jokes.)" (WK 2010a)

- "Ethnic Jokes" (or "Race Humor")—"exploit ethnic stereotypes. They are often racist and frequently considered offensive. For example, the British tell jokes starting 'An Englishman, an Irishman and a Scotsman...' which exploit the supposed parsimony of the Scot, stupidity of the Irish or rigid conventionality of the English." (WK 2010a)

- "Black Humour" (or "Black Comedy")—is "the sub-genre of comedy and satire in which laughter arises from cynism and skepticism. Black humour is often a satire on the topic of death." (WK 2010g)

- "Religious Jokes"—can further be subdivided into (a) "jokes based on stereotypes associated with people of religion (e.g. nun jokes, priest jokes, or rabbi jokes)," (b) "jokes on classical religious subjects: crucifixion, Adam and Eve, St. Peter at The Gates, etc.," (c) "jokes that collide different religious denominations," and (d) "letters and addresses to God." (WK 2010a)

- "Self-Deprecating or Self-Effacing Humour"—"is superficially similar to racial and stereotype jokes, but involves the targets laughing at themselves. It is said to maintain a sense of perspective and to be powerful in defusing confrontations." (WK 2010a)

- "Dirty Jokes"—"are based on taboo, often sexual, content or vocabulary. The definitive studies on them have been written by Gershon Legman. Other taboos are challenged by sick jokes and gallows humour; to joke about disability is considered in this group." (WK 2010a)

- "Surrealist or Minimalist Jokes"—"exploit semantic inconsistency, for example: Q: What's red and invisible? A: No tomatoes." (WK 2010a)

- "Anti-Jokes"—"are jokes that are not funny in regular sense, and often can be decidedly unfunny, but rely on the let-down from the expected joke to be funny in itself. A question was: 'What is the difference between a dead bird [and a non-dead one]? The answer came: 'His right leg is as different as his left one.'" (WK 2010a)

- "Non-Sequitur Jokes"—"involv[e] non-sequitur humour, with parts of the joke being unrelated to each other; e.g. 'My uncle once punched a man so hard his legs became trombones,' from the Mighty Boosh TV series." (WK 2010a)

- "Wit"—refers to jokes that tend to be intellectual, so wit is a form of intellectual humor. "Forms of wit include the quip and repartee." (WK 2010q)

Surely, no one seriously says that these are all the subjects of jokes available in the literature, except when the person just wants to make a joke. But these are certainly the major ones often cited in the literature.

In addition, some other jokes cannot be easily classified into clear categories. For instance, "burlesque" is a combination of humor, folk poetry, theater, and even striptease (as in the U.S.). (WK 2010m) "Parody," on the other hand, can combine humor, acting, literature, and even music. (WK 2010n) And "farce" can also mix humor, physicality, drama, and even poetry, often with "rapid speech and rapid movement." (WK 2010o & 2010r)

Styles of Jokes

In addition, jokes can be classified in terms of "styles"; for illustration, hereafter are some major "styles" of jokes: (WK 2010a)

- "Question/Answer Jokes"—are "sometimes posed as a common riddle" and have "a supposedly straight question and an answer which is twisted for humorous effect; puns are often employed. Of this type are knock-knock joke, light bulb joke, the many variations on 'why did the chicken cross the road?,' and the class of 'What's the difference between a ___ and a ___' joke, where the punch line is often a pun or a spoonerism linking two apparently entirely unconnected concepts." (WK 2010a)

- "Double-Act Jokes"—"require a double act, where one respondent (usually the straight man) can be relied on to give the correct response to the person telling the joke. This is more common in performance than informal joke-telling." (WK 2010a)

- "Shaggy Dog Jokes"—require "an extremely long and involved joke with an intentionally weak or completely non-existent punchline. The humour lies in building up the audience's anticipation and then letting them down completely. The longer the story can continue without the audience realising it is a joke, and not a serious anecdote, the more successful it is. Shaggy jokes appear to date from the 1930s, although there are several competing variants for the 'original' shaggy dog story. According to one, an advertisement is placed in a newspaper,

> searching for the shaggiest dog in the world. The teller of the joke then relates the story of the search for the shaggiest dog in extreme and exaggerated detail (flying around the world, climbing mountains, fending off sabre-toothed tigers, etc.); a good teller will be able to stretch the story out to over half an hour. When the winning dog is finally presented, the advertiser takes a look at the dog and states: 'I don't think he's so shaggy.'" (WK 2010a)

Again, no one seriously suggests that these are all the styles of jokes available in the literature, except when the person just wants to be funny. But these are certainly the major ones often cited in the literature.

Laughing

And on the receiving end of humor is laughing, from the word "laughter," which refers to "an audible expression of happiness, or an inward feeling of joy. It may ensue from hearing a joke, being tickled, or other stimuli. It is in most cases a very pleasant sensation." (WK 2010b)

A Confusion with Other Terms

Thus, in accordance to this definition, one should not confuse the term "laughter" with other terms like "smile," "joke," "humor," "play," "tickleness," and "laugh-like vocalization" (in some animals), for instance.

The reason is that human laughter by itself does not necessarily involve any of these, alrhough it can result from being "tickled, or other stimuli" (like joke, play, and so on). (WK 2010b)

This book, as indicated by its title, will focus on laughing in relation to joking in the context of humor, although laughing does not necessarily involve joking (in humor), as it can result from any of other stimuli (as indicated above).

In other words, although this book will address, whenever relevant, other stimuli which can result in laughter, the focus is on laughter in relation to joking in the context of humor.

Laughing and Gelotology

With this clarification in mind—"laughter is found among various animals, as well as in humans. Among the human species, it is a part of human behavior regulated by the brain, helping humans clarify their intentions in social interaction and providing an emotional context to conversations....Laughter is sometimes seen as contagious, and the laughter of one person can itself provoke laughter from others as a positive feedback." (WK 2010b)

Any study of "laughter," especially (though not exclusively) in relation to "its psychological and physiological effects on the human body," is known as "gelotology." (WK 2010b)

Two good features of laughter for illustration hereafter concern its genetics and neurophyiology.

Laughter and Its Genetics

Laughter has its genetic basis, in that "[r]esearchers have shown infants as early as 17 days old have vocal laughing sounds or laughter....Robert R. Provine indicated 'Laughter is a mechanism everyone has; laughter is part of universal human vocabulary. There are thousands of languages, hundreds of thousands of dialects, but everyone speaks laughter in pretty much the same way.' Everyone can laugh. Babies have the ability to laugh before they ever speak. Children who are born blind and deaf still retain the ability to laugh." (WK 2010b; K. Kawakami 2006)

For Provine, "laughter is primitive, an unconscious vocalization" and "probably is genetic. In a study of the 'Giggle Twins,' two happy twins were separated at birth and only reunited 43 years later. Provine reports that 'until they met each other, neither of these exceptionally happy ladies had known anyone who laughed as much as she did.' They reported this even though they both had been brought together by their adoptive parents, whom they indicated were 'undemonstrative and dour.' He indicates that the twins 'inherited some aspects of their laugh sound and pattern, readiness to laugh, and maybe even taste in humor.'" (WK 2010b; J. Davis 2010)

In fact, "[a] very rare neurological condition has been observed whereby the sufferer is unable to laugh out loud, a condition known as aphonogelia." (WK 2010b; M. Levin 1931)

In addition, "[s]cientists have noted the similarity in forms of laughter among various primates, which suggests that laughter derives from a common origin among primate species." (WK 2010b; BBC 2009)

Laughter and Its Neurophysiology

Besides its genetics—laughter can also have its neurophysiology to be understood.

For example, some studies in neurophysiology indicate that "laughter is linked with the activation of the ventromedial prefrontal cortex, that produces endorphins. Scientists have shown that parts of the limbic system are involved in laughter. This system is involved in emotions and helps us with functions necessary for human's survival. The structures in the limbic system that are involved in laughter: the hippocampus and the amygdala." (WK 2010b)

In a report dated December 7, 1984 and published by *The Journal of the American Medical Association,* "the neurological causes of laughter" are described in what follows: "Although there is no known 'laugh center' in the brain, its neural mechanism has been the subject of much, albeit inconclusive, speculation. It is evident that its expression depends on neural paths arising in close association with the telencephalic and diencephalic centers concerned with respiration. Wilson considered the mechanism to be in the region of the mesial thalamus, hypothalamus, and subthalamus. Kelly and co-workers, in turn, postulated that the tegmentum near the periaqueductal grey contains the integrating mechanism for emotional expression. Thus, supranuclear pathways, including those from the limbic system that Papez hypothesised to mediate emotional expressions such as laughter, probably come into synaptic relation in the reticular core of the brain stem. So while purely emotional responses such as laughter are mediated by subcortical structures, especially the hypothalamus, and are stereotyped, the cerebral cortex can modulate or suppress them." (WK 2010b)

The cautious note about "inconclusive speculation" on the neurophysiology of laughter in the citation above then leads us to the theoretical debate about the very nature of humor in the first place, be it in relation to joking or laughing.

The Theoretical Debate

Although there can be many different views on the nature of humor, be it about joking or laughing—there are five main theoretical approaches in the debate to be summarized hereafter, and they can be called, in the absence of better words, namely, (a) the *mental* argument, (b) the *natural* argument, (c) the *societal* argument, (d) the *cultural* argument, and (e) the *metamorphic* argument (which is my original contribution to the debate), to be elabroated hereafter, respectively.

Lest misunderstanding occurs, two clarifications should be made here, as this is something that I regularly emphasize in my previous books, whenever a theoretical debate is summarized for a topic, *almost verbatim*.

Firstly, there can be other arguments (and theories within each) besides the first four here, that is, the "mental," the "natural," the "societal," and the "cultural" arguments (as indicated above). The advantage to select these four here has to do with their illustrative representation of the diverse theories in the literature (which are deemed sufficient for the purpose at hand in this book).

And secondly, the four arguments are not necessarily mutually exclusive. For instance, those who advocate the "mental" argument can also consider the "cultural" argument, although they do not focus on the latter.

And the reverse is also true, in that those who make the "cultural" argument can also consider the "mental" argument, although they do not focus on the latter.

In other words, their disagreement is often one in degree, not in kind.

The Mental Argument

With these two clarifications in mind—the first major theoretical approach is called, in the absence of better words, the *mental* argument, which focuses, relatively speaking of course, more on the biological and psychological sides of humor.

Therefore, the word "mental" in the title of the argument is suggestive, because it refers to the focus on the biological and psychological sides of humor.

But the mental argument has different issues of concern, and different defenders of the argument offer their own distinctive stands on the issues, depending on their own interests.

For illustration, consider these four often cited versions of the mental argument, namely, (a) "the incongruity theory," (b) "the superiority theory," (c) "the computer theory of humor," and (d) "the misattribution theory"—to be summarized in what follows, respectively.

The Incongruity Theory

The first version of the mental argument is "the incongruity theory," which refers to the argument that "humor is perceived at the moment of realization of incongruity between a concept involved in a certain situation and the real objects thought to be in some relation to the concept." (WK 2010c; M. Mulder 2002)

For some scholars, "[t]he first formulation of the incongruity theory is attributed to the Scottish poet Beattie." (WK 2010c; J. Beattie 1776)

However, the incongruity theory is better "called the incongruity-resolution theory" instead, because "the main point of the theory is not the incongruity per se, but its realization and resolution (i.e., putting the objects in question into the real relation)." (WK 2010c)

For instance, "Francis Hutcheson expressed in *Thoughts on Laughter* (1725) what became a key concept in the evolving theory of the comic: laughter as a response to the perception of incongruity. Arthur Schopenhauer wrote that the perceived incongruity is between a concept and the real object it represents. Hegel shared almost exactly the same view, but saw the concept as an 'appearance' and believed that laughter then totally negates that appearance. According to Spenser, laughter is an 'economical phenomenon' whose function is to release 'psychic energy' that had been wrongly mobilized by incorrect or false expectations. The latter point of view was supported also by Sigmund Freud." (WK 2010c; P. Berger 1997)

The Superiority Theory

The second version of the mental argument is "the superiority theory," which refers to the view by "Plato and Aristotle, and Thomas Hobbes' *Leviathan*. This theory explains that a person laughs about misfortunes of others, because these misfortunes assert the person's superiority on the background of shortcomings of others." (WK 2010c; M. Mulder 2002)

For instance, "for Aristotle, we laugh at inferior or ugly individuals, because we feel a joy at being superior to them. Socrates was reported by Plato as saying that the ridiculous was characterized by a display of self-ignorance." (WK 2010c)

The Computer Theory of Humor

The third version of the mental argument is "the computer theory of humor," which refers to "the Computer Model of a Sense of Humor…suggested by [I .M.] Suslov in 1992." (WK 2010c)

The theory is more biological in origin, by learning from the analogy of information processing in computers. For instance, for Suslov, "[i]nvestigation of the general scheme of the information processing show a possibility of a specific malfunction, conditioned by the necessity of a quick deletion from consciousness of a false version. This specific malfunction can be identified with a humorous effect on the psychological grounds: it exactly corresponds to incongruity-resolution theory. However, an essentially new ingredient, a role of timing, is added to a well known role of ambiguity. In biological systems, a sense of humor inevitably develops in the course of evolution, because its biological function consists in quickening the transmission of the processed information into consciousness and in a more effective use of brain resources. A realization of this algorithm in neural networks justifies naturally Spenser's hypothesis on the mechanism of laughter: deletion of a false version corresponds to zeroing of some part of the neural network and excessive energy of neurons is thrown out to the motor cortex, arousing muscular contractions." (WK 2010c; I. Suslov 1992a)

For Suslov, "the humor has a pure biological origin, while its social functions arose later. This conclusion corresponds to the known fact that already monkeys (as pointed by Charles Darwin) and even rats (as found recently) possess the sense of humor." (WK 2010c)

The Misattribution Theory

And the fourth version of the mental argument is "the misattribution theory," which refers to the work by [Dolf] Zillmann and [Jennings] Bryant (1980) in their article titled "Misattribution Theory of Tendentious Humor," which was published in *The Journal of Experimental Social Psychology*. (WK 2010c)

The misattribution theory "describes an audience's inability to identify exactly why they find a joke to be funny," as it is based on "the critical concepts of the theory from Sigmund Freud's *Wit and Its Relation to the Unconscious*, originally published in 1905. Freud declared people incapable of knowing exactly what it is they find amusing due to the complex nature of their conscious and subconscious minds. Jokes are crafted by comedians who have experience with causing laughter but who may themselves be blind to the actual cause of humor." (WK 2010c)

However, for the critics, all these four versions of the mental argument (i.e., "the incongruity theory," "the superiority theory," "the computer theory of humor," and "the misattribution theory") have some major problems in common. For illustration, consider two major criticisms below.

Firstly, all these four versions of the mental argument are too restrictive, in ignoring other dimensions of the mental argument (that is, other than the dimension that each theory focuses on).

And secondly, all these four versions of the mental argument are also too narrow, in excluding other arguments (like the natural, societal, and cultural ones, as will be introduced later in this section).

The Natural Argument

The second theoretical approach is called, in the absence of better words, the *natural* argument, which focuses, relatively speaking of course, more on the natural sides of humor (that is, in relation to nature).

Therefore, the word "natural" in the title of the argument is suggestive, because it refers to the focus on the natural sides of humor so understood.

Like the mental argument—the natural argument has different issues of concern, and different defenders of the argument offer their own distinctive stands on the issues, depending on their own interests.

For illustration, consider the theory of "sexual selection" (in the state of nature) in regard to humor, as described below.

The Theory of Sexual Selection in Nature

The theory of "sexual selection" in the context of humor refers to the work by Geoffrey Miller (2001), who "contends that, from an evolutionary perspective, humor would have had no survival value to early humans living in the savannas of Africa. He proposes that cultural aspects like humor evolved by sexual selection. He argues that humor emerged as an indicator of other traits that were of survival value, such as human intelligence." (WK 2010c)

What is important here, for Miller, is "Darwin's theoretical observation that evolution is driven not just by natural selection, but by the process called sexual selection. In support of his views on sexual selection, he [Miller] has written *The Mating Mind: How Sexual Choice Shaped the Evolution of Human Nature*. This revives and extends Darwin's suggestion that sexual selection through mate choice has been critical in human mental evolution—especially the more 'self-expressive' aspects of human behavior, such as art, morality, language, and creativity." (WK 2010d)

For Miller, "our minds evolved not as survival machines, but as courtship machines, and...the human mind's most impressive abilities are courtship tools that evolved to attract and entertain sexual partners. By switching from a survival-centred to a courtship-centred view of evolution, he attempts to show how we can understand the mysteries of mind." (WK 2010d)

However, for the critics, there are major problems with the theory of sexual selection in nature (in regard to humor). Consider, for illustration, two major criticisms, in what follows.

Firstly, the theory of sexual selection in nature is still speculative, because it is not exactly clear what non-survival values (for example, for courtship) humor is supposed to serve.

It is thus no surprise that there are "competing theories of human mental evolution," and good examples are (a) "selection for generalist foraging ability (i.e., hunting and gathering), as embodied in the work of researchers such as Hillard Kaplan and Kim Hill at the University of New Mexico," and (b) "selection for social intelligence, as argued by Andrew Whiten, Robin Dunbar, and Simon Baron-Cohen." (WK 2010d)

And secondly, the theory of sexual selection in nature, like the four theories in the mental argument, is also too narrow, in excluding other arguments (like the mental, societal and cultural ones, for instance, as introduced above and below in this section).

The Societal Argument

The third theoretical approach is called, in the absence of better words, the *societal* argument, which focuses, relatively speaking of course, more on the societal sides of humor.

In this sense, the word "societal" in the title of the argument is suggestive, because it refers to the societal sides of humor.

Like the mental and natural arguments—the societal argument has different issues of concern, and different defenders of the argument offer their own distinctive stands on the issues, depending on their own interests.

For illustration, consider these two often cited versions of the societal argument about humor, namely, (a) the theory of "social functions" and (b) the theory of "social prohibitons"—to be summarized in what follows, in that order.

The Theory of Social Functions

The first version of the societal argument is the theory of "social functions" in relation to humor, which refers to the social purposes and functions of jokes, which "are typically for the entertainment of friends and onlookers. The desired response is generally laughter; when this does not happen the joke is said to have 'fallen flat.' However jokes have other purposes and functions, common to comedy/humour/satire in general." (WK 2010a)

For instance, "Henri Bergson, in his book *Le rire* (*Laughter,* 1901), suggests that laughter evolved to make social life possible for human beings." (WK 2010a)

Other studies by S. Tracy (2006), K. Myers, C. Scott, O. Lynch (2002), and D. Collinson (2002) looked at jokes in social organizations: "Jokes can be employed by workers as a way to identify with their jobs. For example, 9-1-1 operators often crack jokes about incongruous, threatening, or tragic situations they deal with on a daily basis. This use of humor and cracking jokes helps employees differentiate themselves from the people they serve while also assisting them in identifying with their jobs. In addition to employees, managers use joking, or jocularity, in strategic ways. Some managers attempt to suppress joking and humor use because they feel it relates to lower production, while others have attempted to manufacture joking through pranks, pajama or dress down days, and specific committees that are designed to increase fun in the workplace." (WK 2010a)

The Theory of Social Prohibitions

And the second version of the societal argument is the theory of "social prohibitions" in relation to humor, which refers to the social prohibitions in society which give humor a role to express and behave in an indirect (but safe) way.

For instance, Sigmund Freud argued that "[o]ne can't express aggression and sexual drive directly, as it is prohibited in the society, so these desires get sublimated in telling 'jokes.' If you look at jokes, they are either about somebody getting hurt, or they have sexual connotations." (A. Chislenko 2010)

And Marvin Minsky made a comparable point: "There are not only general social prohibitions. There are also things your mother told you not to do—like stick your finger into your eye. So when you tell a story about something stupid, you attack the rules of common sense, in a safe and socially acceptable manner." (A. Chislenko 2010)

However, for the critics, all these two versions of the societal argument have some major problems in common. For illustration, consider three major criticisms, as shown below.

Firstly, all these two versions of the societal argument are questionable. For instance, Alexander Chislenko (2010) rebuked the theory of social prohibitions by saying that, "[i]n many cases, people are ready to openly express more aggression, sexuality, and disagreement with authorities that they are suggesting in the jokes, so their jokes can hardly be viewed as a suppressed revolt. Peaceful people and innocent children find lots of things funny; children find things funny (such as peek-a-boo) that adults don't and wouldn't teach them; there is hardly any evidence that people with strongly suppressed anger or sexuality have more interest in jokes than people who do not have these interests, or feel free to express them."

Secondly, all these two versions of the societal argument are too restrictive, in ignoring other dimensions of the societal argument (that is, other than the dimension that each theory focuses on).

And thirdly, all these two versions of the societal argument are also too narrow, in excluding other arguments (like the mental, natural, and cultural ones, as introduced above and below in this section).

The Cultural Argument

The fourth theoretical approach is called, in the absence of better words, the *cultural* argument, which focuses, relatively speaking of course, more on the cultural aspects of humor.

Therefore, the word "cultural" in the title of the argument is suggestive, because it refers to the focus on the cultural aspects of humor.

Like the mental and societal arguments—the cultural argument has different issues of concern, and different defenders of the argument offer their own distinctive stands on the issues, depending on their own interests.

For illustration, consider "the onti-epistemic theory of humor," as summarized below.

The Onti-Epistemic Theory of Humor

The first version of the cultural argument is "the onti-epistemic theory of humor" (OETC), which refers to the work by P. Marteinson (2006) , in that "laughter is a reaction to a cognitive impasse, a momentary epistemological difficulty, in which the subject perceives that Social Being itself suddenly appears no longer to be real in any factual or normative sense." (WK 2010c)

In this humorous situation, "material reality, which is always factually true, is the only percept remaining in the mind at such a moment of comic perception. This theory posits, as in Bergson, that human beings accept as real both normative immaterial percepts, such as social identity, and noological factual percepts, but also that the individual subject normally blends the two together in perception in order to live by the assumption they are equally real." (WK 2010c)

This blending of the two percepts, however, is essentially fragile, because "[t]he comic results from the perception that they are not. This same result arises in a number of paradigmatic cases: factual reality can be seen to conflict with and disprove social reality, which Marteinson calls

Deculturation; alternatively, social reality can appear to contradict other elements of social reality, which he calls Relativisation." (WK 2010c)

For Marteinson, "laughter...serves to reset and re-boot the faculty of social perception, which has been rendered non-functional by the comic situation: it anaesthetises the mind with its euphoria, and permits the forgetting of the comic stimulus, as well as the well-known function of communicating the humorous reaction to other members of society." (WK 2010c)

Besides Marteinson, there are also other scholars who have provided different semantic interpretatons about the nature of humor. For instance, another version of the cultural argument is "the general theory of verbal humor" (GTVH), which refers to the model by "Victor Raskin and Salvatore Attardo in 1991 (an extension of the semantic script theory of humour, SSTH which Raskin proposed in 1985)," so as to provide "a semantic model capable of expressing incongruities between semantic scripts in verbal humor." (WK 2010c; S. Attardo 2001 & 1994)

However, for the critics, these different versions of the cultural argument have some major problems in common. For illustration, consider two major criticisms, as shown below.

Firstly, these different versions of the cultural argument are too restrictive, in ignoring other dimensions of the cultural argument (that is, other than the dimension that each theory focuses on, semantically speaking).

And secondly, these different versions of the cultural argument are also too narrow, in excluding other arguments (like the mental, natural, and societal ones, as already introduced above).

The Metamorphic Argument

And fifthly, unlike the previous four arguments (viz., the mental, the natural, the societal, and the cultural)—the fifth one to be introduced here can be called, in the absence of better words again, the *metamorphic* argument, which learns from all other theoretical approaches (which include the previous four arguments and also other examples as will be introduced in the rest of this book), without, however, favoring any of them, nor trying to integrate them (as they are not necessarily compatible with each other, as the introduction of the theoretical debate in the previous sub-sections has shown).

The Metamorphic Theory of Humor

My *metamorphic* argument can be more precisely called *the metamorphic theory of humor*, since it is to propose a new theory of education.

The word "metamorphic" is derived from "metamorphism" in geology, which is defined, in a formal definition, as "a change in the constitution of rock." (MWD 2010)

In the current context of humor, I use the word "metamorphic" for the title of my argument, because it provides an unconventional way to understand humor to account for its endless changes over different historical eras, and my metamorphic theory of humor has four distinctive features to remember.

Firstly, my theory makes good use of all theoretical approaches in the literature on humor, be they about the mental argument, the natural argument, the societal argument, or the cultural argument—especially from the most comprehensive combined perspectives of the mind, nature, society, and culture (as will be clear in Chapter Two and Chapter Three).

Secondly, just like many other theories of mine in my previous books, my theory here does not heavily favor any specific theory over others in the literature, nor trying to integrate them (as they are not necessarily compatible with each other).

Thirdly, my theory treats the issue of humor in the distinctive dialectic context of joking and laughing, such that one is not to be reduced as part of the analysis of the other—even though laughing can exist outside humor (like the situations when one is tickled, playful, and so on).

And fourthly, it contains eighteen major theses, namely, (a) the first thesis: the absoluteness-relativeness principle, (b) the second thesis: the predictability-unpredictability principle, (c) the third thesis: the explicability-inexplicability principle, (d) the fourth thesis: the preciseness-vagueness principle, (e) the fifth thesis: the simpleness-complicatedness principle, (f) the sixth thesis: the openness-hiddenness principle, (g) the seventh thesis: the denseness-emptiness principle, (h) the eighth thesis: the slowness-quickness principle, (i) the nineth thesis: the expansion-contraction principle, (j) the tenth thesis: the theory-praxis principle, (k) the eleventh thesis: the convention-novelty principle, (l) the twelveth thesis: the evolution-transformation principle, (m) the thirteenth thesis: the symmetry-asymmetry principle, (n) the fourteenth thesis: the softness-hardness principle, (o) the fifteenth thesis: the seriousness-playfulness principle, (p) the sixteenth thesis: the regression-progression principle, (q) the seventeenth thesis: the sameness-difference principle, and (r) the eighteenth thesis: the post-human rendition—to be elaborated in the rest of the book, with a summary in the concluding chapter.

Of course, as this is something that I often emphasized in my previous books, other principles (besides the 17 as cited above) are also relevant, but these 17 are the most relevant in the current case study (in terms of the number of citations of each principle in the book).

Even then, in some cases, the difference between any two given principles, for instance, in terms of the number of citations in a book, is rather small, so the reason in those cases is more aesthetic (than otherwise), because it looks nicer to list only 17 theses for 17 principles (than 22 theses for all of the 22 principles) in the Table of Contents.

This is true, even if different studies of the same kind can yield different views about the degree of relevance for each principle, depending on the specific nature of a research in question, needless to say. So, if a different author analyzes the same subject matter in a different way, the relevance of the principles will be different.

With this clarification in mind—the seminal project here, if successful, will fundamentally change the way that we think about humor, from the combined perspectives of the mind, nature, society, and culture, with enormous implications for the human future and what I originally called its "post-human" fate.

Theory and Meta-Theory

The *metamorphic* argument, or *the metamorphic theory of humor*, presupposes some kind of meta-theory, in special relation to methodology and ontology—just as all theories, either explicitly or implicitly, require their own versions of meta-theory.

The Classification of Theory and Meta-Theory

Theory and meta-theory, broadly speaking, can be further classified into different categories, as shown below:

- On Theory
  - —Ex: in relation to the mind
  - —Ex: in relation to nature
  - —Ex: in relation to society
  - —Ex: in relation to culture

• On Meta-Theory
  —Ex: in relation to methodology
  —Ex: in relation to ontology

Each category, in its turn, can then be further sub-divided into different levels of analysis—which will be elaborated in the next two sections (and summarized in *Table 4.43*).

With this reminder in mind, I already proposed (in my previous books) my distinctive contribution to meta-theory, namely, methodology (known as "sophisticated methodological holism") and ontology (known as "existential dialectics").

The next two sections are to introduce my meta-theory—that is, existential dialectics and sophisticated methodological holism, respectively—to be repeated, *often verbatim* (with only a few updated revisions), from my previous works, as this is something that I often do in each new book of mine as an introduction to some background information for the convenience of the readers.

In the process, I shall also introduce my numerous new theories (more than 40 of them so far, as of 2010) in relation to the four categories of the mind, nature, society, and culture in the context of theory (as also summarized in *Table 4.43*).

A Unified Theory of Everything

In the end, my distinctive contribution to both meta-theory and theory serves as a foundation to unify all domains of knowledge for an overarching understanding of all forms of reality (by way of some ontological principles at the meta-theoretical level and the comprehensive perspectives of the mind, nature, society, and culture at the theoretical level—as will be explained in the next two sections).

This is so, without commiting the sins of reductionism and reverse-reductionism (as often seen in many holistic approaches, with the fad of systems approach as a most recent notorious example, as already critically explained in *The Future of Post-Human Formal Science*, or *FPHFS*), since my distinctive contribution makes good use of different schools of thought without favoring any of them nor trying to integrate them (as they are not necessarily compatible with each other), so as to include (or adjust for) heterogeneity, conflict, subjectivity, and complexity, for example.

In this sense, the word "unified" does not have to mean an integrative approach, in a narrow sense, nor a systems approach, in a broad one, both of which I have critically rebuked (in my previous books), while learning from them.

This overarching project (consisting of numerous theories of mine, as will be summarized in the next section), thus, constitutes my grand unifed theory of everything in the world and beyond.

The Logic of Existential Dialectics

To start, the ontology of existential dialectics can be summarized in this section—*often verbatim* (with only a few updated revisions), from my previous works, as this is something that I regularly do in each new book of mine as an introduction to some background information for the convenience of the readers.

After all, this book, like all others of mine, is in conversation with all previous ones of mine, for the final aim to converge all of them into a larger grand project on the future of intelligent life, both here on earth and there in deep space unto multiverses.

The summary can be organized in relation to (a) the conception of existential dialectics (or its ontics), (b) the syntax of existential dialectics (or its ontomethodology and ontologic), (c) the semantics of existential dialectics (or its ontosemantics), and (d) the pragmatics of existential dialectics (or its ontopragmatics), respectively hereafter—again *often verbatim*.

This means that, for those readers who had read some of my previous books, the summary below is really not much new (*almost verbatim*, with only some updated revisions).

But for those who have never read my previous books, it is a good review of them.

The Conception of Existential Dialectics (or Its Ontics)

This ontology was originally designated as "existential dialectics" in *Beyond Capitalism to Post-Capitalism* (herein abbreviated as *BCPC*), although it was already analyzed in other books of mine like the 2 volumes of *The Future of Human Civilization* (*FHC*), *The Future of Capitalism and Democracy* (*FCD*), *The Future of Post-Human Consciousness* (*FPHC*), and the 2 volumes of *Beyond Democracy to Post-Democracy* (*BDPD*).

Lest any confusion occurs, it is important to stress at the outset that the word 'existential' in "existential dialectics" has nothing to do with Existentialism, which I rebuked in *FHC*, *FCD*, and also *FPHC*. Instead, the word here merely refers to the existence of intelligent life (both primitive and advanced) in a broad sense.

Some Basic Concepts

The conception of existential dialectics (or its ontics) makes use of different concepts (like "sets," "elements," "relations," "operations," "functions," "truth values," "axioms," "postulates," and "principles"—as shown in *Table 4.3*), which are important for the understanding of any logic of ontology.

That clarified—existential dialectics, as a language of ontology, can be analyzed in different ways that a language, as an analogy, is often analyzed, namely, in relation to phonology ("the study of patterns of a language's sounds"), phonetics ("the study of the physical aspects of sounds of human language"), morphonology ("the study of the internal structure of words"), syntax ("the study of how words combine to form grammatical sentences"), semantics ("the study of the meaning of words [lexical semantics] and fixed word combinations [phraseology]"), and pragmatics ("the study of how utterances are used…literally, figuratively, or otherwise…in communicative acts"). (WK 2007)

But since my theory of existential dialectics makes use of the English language for communication here, it does not propose a new way to make the patterns of a language's sounds (as in phonology), to study the physical aspects of sounds (as in phonetics), or even to strive for a new organization of the internal structure of words for the English language (as in morphonology).

For this reason, the language of existential dialectics to be analyzed hereafter is not concerned with the phonological, phonetic, and morphonological aspects of the English language. Instead, the analysis will explore the syntax, semantics, and pragmatics of existential dialectics as a language of ontology to improve our understanding of reality.

The Ontic Dispute

But first, there is an ontic dispute to be addressed, which is related to what I called "the dilemma of ontology" as introduced earlier in *Sec. 1.4* of *The Future of Post-Human Knowledge* (*FPHK*).

A good point of departure concerns what I want to call *the ontic dispute*, on how to understand the very nature of ontology.

Traditionally, scholars in the field used to study the conception of ontology in terms of its entities (e.g., material objects, abstract numbers), properties (e.g., duration, plurality), and relationships (e.g., causation).

This is a good starting point, but it suffers from different problems. Consider three examples of bias below, which are quite common in the literature, and the recent version (of treating concepts and principles in ontology on the basis of "plurality," "dynamism," "duration," "interaction," "life," "consciousness," and "volition") by Reginald Firehammer (2005) only constitutes a latest addition to this old (impoverishing) tradition.

Firstly, the classification of entities, properties, and relationships is too material-centric, in often focusing more on the existence of material entities than on non-material ones.

Secondly, the classification is too anthropo-centric, in often favoring the factor of human agency in depicting reality.

And lastly, the classification is too confused among the three categories relating to each other, in often lumping them together without adequate consideration of their intricated interrelationships (both in relation to each and in relation to all).

A good alternative is precisely what I want to offer in this debate, that is, a new classification of ontological entities, properties, and their relationships in terms of *method*, *structure*, *process*, *agency*, and *outcome* instead. Let me explicate what these words mean below.

In relation to "method"—it concerns how ontology is to be studied. In this sense, the word 'method' here should not be confused with the different usage of the same term 'method' as a technique of investigation in the context of methodology (as already introduced in *Sec. 1.2* of *FPHK*).

In relation to "structure"—it concerns what the general patterns of entities, properties, and relationships are.

In relation to "process"—it concerns how these general patterns change over time.

In relation to "agency"—it concerns how agency affects any change of these general patterns over time (without putting, however, too much emphasis on the role of human agency).

And in relation to "outcome"—it concerns what the outputs of this change over time are.

The Syntax of Existential Dialectics (or Its Ontomethodology and Ontologic)

The syntax of existential dialectics, analogously speaking, refers here to the structure of an ontology which can be studied by way of combining ideas into complex relationships like ontological principles to depict reality in the world—and can be analyzed in seven sub-sections, namely,

(a) the selection criteria, (b) further clarifications on classification, (c) ontomethodology, (d) ontologic, (e) the principles as short cuts, (f) the principles as family resemblances, and (g) the dialectic constraints imposed by the principles, respectively hereafter.

The Selection Criteria

To start, not any pair of relationship can be chosen as an ontological principle in existential dialectics; otherwise, there could be billions of them under the sky.

Four illustrations below suffice to clarify this point.

(a) Firstly, an ontological principle cannot *overlap* with other principles, in that it is too closely related with other ones.

Of course, one cannot totally rule out any relationship between two entities, especially in a complex world of everything being linked to everything else—but the comparison here is relative, not absolute.

In this sense, the flexibility-inflexibility pair cannot be an ontological principle, since it has something closely in common with other ones (like the simpleness-complicatedness principle, for instance).

As an illustration, something which is flexible in interpretation is more likely to allow multiple viewpoints and thus makes the overall picture more complicated than otherwise (simple).

(b) Secondly, an ontological principle cannot be *redundant* in relation to other principles, in that it somehow duplicates other principles.

In this sense, for instance, the directness-indirectness pair cannot be an ontological principle, because it somehow duplicates other ontological principles (like the preciseness-vagueness principle, for instance).

As an illustration, something which is direct means to be right to the point and does not need to go to an unnecessarily long loop—so it is less vague, in being clearer about the thing in question.

(c) Thirdly, an ontological principle cannot be *derived* from other ones—as if it is a child-parent relationship.

In this sense, the convenience-inconvenience pair cannot be an ontological principle, because it can be derived from other ones (like the slowness-quickness principle, for instance).

For instance, something which is convenient already implies that it can be obtained quickly (rather than slowly)—all things considered.

(d) And fourthly, an ontological principle cannot be *trivial* (or *parochial*)—as if it is only one component competing with other ones for inclusion in a set.

In this sense, the consistency-inconsistency pair cannot be an ontological principle, because its validity is limited (or parochial), as it can be easily challenged and replaced by opposing major (not minor) theories (e.g., the correspondence theory of truth, the pragmatic theory of truth, the semantic theory of truth, the disclosedness theory of truth, and whatnot), not just in accordance to the consistency (or coherence) theory of truth (for consistency).

In this sense, the consistency argument is only one among different opposing arguments in relation to the logic of what constitutes "truth."

Although these examples are not exhaustive, they illustrative the selectiveness of any ontological principle to be existentially dialectic.

Further Clarifications on Classification

Lest any misunderstanding carelessly occurs, some further clarifications on classification should be made here (and summarized in *Table 4.8*).

(a) Firstly, the total number of ontological principles is unknown, to be discovered later, as our knowledge of the world becomes more advanced.

Consequently, the principles as introduced in my books are not exhaustive, with new ones being added, whenever more of them are discovered in later research.

At least, future generations can pick up where I leave off and continue the discovery.

In this sense, my work should be treated as a pioneering effort for the development of a systematic, comprehensive analysis of a new general ontology for the future of knowledge.

(b) Secondly, the principles are not rigidly classified, as they can be reclassified in a different way.

For instance, the preciseness-vagueness principle is classified under the category of "structure" but can be reclassified under the category of "method," although in so doing, it has a different meaning in the context of method.

The same logic applies to the same-difference principle under the category of "outcome," which can be reclassified under the category of "structure," although in so doing, once more, it has a different meaning in the context of structure.

(c) Thirdly, the principles are to be understood together, not that each prinicple is to be treated independently of others. After all, the principles are mutually constraining, in that they work together as a whole.

(d) Fourthly, the principles are relevant to all subject matters, but some principles are, relatively speaking of course, more useful to some subject matters than others under certain conditions—as implied in the symmetry-asymmetry principle.

(e) And fifthly, the principles constitute only two levels of analysis, this time, at the ontological and methodological levels—while other levels of analysis (from the perspectives of the mind, nature, society, and culture) are also needed, in order to understand reality in its totality (as explained in the section on "sophisticated methodological holism," so as to avoid the dual dangers of reductionism and reverse-reductionism).

Ontomethodology

With these selection criteria and clarifications in mind—the syntax of existential dialectics can be divided into two main smaller sections for analysis, since they are related to each other in the context of some fundamental principles, that is, (a) ontomethodology and (b) ontologic, to be addressed hereafter, respectively.

In the context of ontomethodology, some ontological principles are proposed here in relation to the nature of methodology, which however is tied up with the general issue of ontology in the context of knowledge.

In this sense, ontomethodology (in the context of these ontological principles in the category of method) are related with ontologic in general (in the context of ontological principles in general).

Some good instances of ontological principles involving ontomethodology include the formalness-informalness principle, the predictability-unpredictability principle, the explicability-inexplicability principle, the partiality-totality principle, and the absoluteness-relativeness principle, which will be introduced in conjunction with ontological principles in the ontologic of existential dialectics in general hereafter.

Ontologic

With this clarification of the relationship between ontomethodology and ontologic in mind (which is comparable to the relationship between methodology and ontology as described in *Sec. 1.3* of *FPHK*)—the first three principles in existential dialectics were introduced in *BCPC*. And more principles were later added to the logic in my subsequent books (like *FC*, *FAE*, and others), as explained below.

More specifically, in *BCPC*, I proposed three principles (based on previous works of mine, not just something out of the blue) for the ontological logic, namely, (a) the regression-progression principle on the direction of history, (b) the symmetry-asymmetry principle on the relationships among existents, and (c) the change-constancy principle on the alteration of things—or in a more elegant term, the dynamics of space-time (in *FC*).

In *The Future of Complexity* (*FC*), I added three more principles, on top of the three aforementioned, namely, (d) the partiality-totality principle on the relationships between parts and whole, (e) the order-chaos principle on the pattern of things, and (f) the predictability-unpredictability principle on the occurrence of things—as part of the ontological logic of existential dialectics.

In *The Future of Aesthetic Experience* (or simply *FAE*), another principle is added, namely, (g) the evolution-transformation principle (on the multiple kinds of agency).

Also in *FAE*, I then reclassified the 7 principles into four categories, namely, (i) in relation to method, for the partiality-totality principle and the predictability-unpredictability principle, (ii) in relation to process, for the change-constancy principle and the order-chaos principle, (iii) in relation to agency, for the symmetry-asymmetry principle and the evolution-transformation principle, and (iv) in relation to outcome, for the regression-progression principle.

In *The Rise of Authoritarian Liberal Democracy* (*ALD*), I added two more principles, namely, (h) the softness-hardness principle on the force of agency (which is to be classified under the category about agency) and (i) the same-difference principle on the metamorphosis of change (which is to be classified under the category about outcome).

In *The Future of Information Architecture* (*FIA*), I introduce three additional principles, that is, (j) the simpleness-complicadness principle on the interconnection among things, (k) the preciseness-vagueness principle on the refinement of things, and (l) the slowness-quickness principle on the speed of change—with the first two in relation to structure and the third in relation to process.

In *The Future of Post-Human Unconsciousness* (*FPHU*), I added three more principles, that is, (m) the openness-hidden principle on the detection of things, in relation to structure, (n) the explicability-inexplicability principle on the underlying mechanisms of things, in relation to method, and (o) the expansion-contraction principle on the growth of things, in relation to process.

In *The Future of Post-Human Knowledge* (*FPHK*), I added one more principle, that is, (p) the absoluteness-relativeness principle on the multiplicity of entities, in relation to method.

In *The Future of Post-Human Mathematical Logic* (*FPHML*), I added one more principle, that is, (q) the formalness-informalness principle on the formal requirements of systems, in relation to method.

In *The Future of Post-Human Engineering* (*FPHE*), I added one more principle, that is, (r) the theory-praxis principle on the duality of knowledge, in relation to agency.

In *The Future of Post-Human Creative Thinking* (*FPHCT*), I added one more principle, that is, (s) the convention-novelty principle on the nature of creative thinking, in relation to agency.

In *The Future of Post-Human Geometry* (*FPHG*) here, I added one more principle, that is, (t) the finiteness-transfiniteness principle on the nature of numbers, in relation to structure.

In *The Future of Post-Human Urban Planning* (*FPHUP*), I added one more principle, that is, (u) the denseness-emptiness principle on the distribution of entities in space, in relation to structure.

And in *The Future of Post-Human Humor* (*FPHH*) here, I add one more principle, that is, (v) the seriousness-playfulness principle on the extent of seriousness, in relation to agency.

With this update, there are twenty-two principles so far in existential dialectics, that is, five principles for the category in relation to method (viz., the formalness-informalness principle, the partiality-totality principle, the predictability-unpredictability principle, the explicability-inexplicability principle, and the absoluteness-relativeness principle), five principles for the category in relation to structure (viz., the finiteness-transfiniteness principle, the simpleness-complicatedness principle, the preciseness-vagueness principle, the openness-hiddenness principle, and the denseness-emptiness principle), four principles for the category in relation to process (viz., the change-constancy principle, the slowness-quickness principle, the order-chaos principle, and the expansion-contraction principle), six principles for the category in relation to agency (viz., the theory-praxis principle, the convention-novelty principle, the symmetry-asymmetry principle, the evolution-transformation principle, the softness-hardness principle, and the seriousness-playfulness principle), and two principles for the category in relation to outcome (viz., the regression-progression principle and the same-difference principle).

There are thus twenty-two principles in existential dialectics—so far (as summarized in *Table 4.4*).

The Principles as Short Cuts

Yet, these principles should be treated with caution, lest misunderstanding occurs, since they do not constitute rigid dualities (or dichotomies).

The reason is that each pair in an ontological principle consists of two opposites, which are, however, merely short cuts both for multiple variations and degrees, as well as for different interactions with multiple other entities unlike them.

In this light, each pair can end up having hundred (or even thousand, if not more) different versions, which interact with hundred (or even thousand, if not more) other entities—as summarized in *Table 4.5*.

There are two clarifications here.

Firstly, this conception of shortcuts is not mutually exclusive nor absolute, in that the opposites can come in all shapes and sizes, with different degrees. For instance, by analogy, just as there are different degrees of the two colors "white" and "black"—there are likewise different degrees of the opposites in each ontological pair, to the extent that there can be multiple entities (not only two) interacting with each other in each pair.

And secondly, this conception of shortcuts do not ignore other possible entities in interacting with the two opposites (with their different versions) in each pair. For instance, by analogy, there are not only the two colors "white" and "black" as opposites, since there are other colors too besides them like "yellow," "green," "purple," or else. The same logic can be applied to each ontological pair, in that they also interact with other entities, not with only two of them (with their different versions).

Therefore, with these two clarifications in mind—each pair in an ontological principle serves only as an abbreviation for something more complicated and, therefore, although it contains two opposites, it should not be confused as a duality (dualism).

Existential dialectics rejects any dualism (or dichotomy) as too rigid and instead allows the multiplicity of entities, to the extent that between the two opposites in each pair exist many other alternatives to choose from. They are named in that short form for aesthetic elegance only, instead of listing all possible entities between the two opposites in the title (which would be too cumbersome and sound extremely awkward).

To be dialectic is to go beyond any rigid dichotomy and transcend into something different altogether in the long haul. One may be tempted to call the dialectic logic here with a different name like existential "multilectics" (instead of "dialectics"), but this naming is incorrect (or even misleading), for the two reasons aforestated.

After all, all the possible entities between any two opposites in an ontological pair are still about the two opposites, although each ontological pair come in all shapes and sizes (with different degrees) and do not exist by themselves but also interact with other entities unlike them. The virtue of revealing an ontological pair is to show how they relate within themselves (in multiple versions) and also interact with others unlike them (also in multiple versions).

This will be clear in a later sub-section titled "the dialectic constraints imposed by the principles."

The Principles as Family Resemblances

In addition, each ontological principle is generic, with some other comparable ontological pairs to be put in the same family (like a *family resemblance*)—as summarized in *Table 4.6*.

Ludwig Wittgenstein (1953) once suggested the idea of "family resemblance" in explaining different games classified under the same family called *games*.

Why should, for instance, playing football and chess as playing "games," when it is well understood that football is not the same as chess? The answer is that, although each game is different and has different rules, many of them (though not all) share, more or less, some commonalites (e.g., scoring as necessary for winning).

And this is so, even though some games share more than some others in any given selection of critieria, and no two games are exactly identical. So, Wittgenstein's point here is that there is no essential core which is common to all games, and the best that one can look for is some characteristics which are common to many (but not all) games. (A. Biletzki 2006)

(a) Appropriate Family Resemblances

In the context of existential dialectics, I want to distinguish two types of family resemblances, and, in the absence of better words, let me call them (a) *appropriate* family resemblances and (b) *inappropriate* family resemblances.

In regard to appropriate family resemblances—good examples include some of the pairs as already explained in an earlier section on selection criteria, like the flexibility-inflexibility pair, which can be put in the family resemblance of the simpleness-complicatedness principle, although the two pairs are not exactly identical. Likewise, the directness-indirectness pair can be put in the family resemblance of the preciseness-vagueness principle, although, again, the two pairs are not exactly identical.

In this sense, which specific pair in a family should be used to designate the name of the family can be at times a bit arbitrary, but with good reason.

For illustration, in the context of method, the partiality-totality principle can take the different form like individualisticness-holisticness, just as the explicability-inexplicability principle can take the different form like underlyingness-regularness—although each two pairs are not exactly identical and have slightly different meanings and usages.

A more comprehensive listing of this family resemblance for all other principles is shown in *Table 4.6* on the syntax of existential dialectics.

In fact, this section on family resemblances overlaps with the semantics of existential dialectics, which will be introduced later in the next section (and summarized in *Table 4.11*).

(b) Inappropriate Family Resemblances

However, there are some family resemblances which are not appropriate, and let me distinugish two of them by calling them, in the absence of better words, (b1) *inadequate* family resemblances and (b2) *compound* family resemblances (as summarized in *Table 4.10*).

(b1) In regard to "inadequate" family resemblances—there are some pairs which are not adequate, because they fail the test of selection criteria (as already pointed out in an earlier section), especially in relation to the criterion of not being *trivial* (or *parochial*)—as if it is only one component competing with other ones for inclusion in a set.

For instance, the *consistency-inconsistency* pair is inadequate, because it is only one component competing with other ones for inclusion in the larger set of the formalness-informalenss principle (like the *completeness-incompleteness* pair and the *soundness-unsoundness* pair, as discussed in my book titled *The Future of Post-Human Mathematical Logic*, or *FPHML* in short).

The same is true for the *cognition-noncognition* pair, which overlaps with both the completeness-incompleteness pair and the soundness-unsoundness pair in the larger set of the formalness-informalenss principle.

(b2) In regard to "compound" (or non-atomic) family resemblances—there are some pairs which are not appropriate for a different reason, because they fail the test of selection criteria (as already pointed out in an earlier section), especially in relation to the criterion of not *overlapping* with other principles, in that it is too closely related with other ones.

For instance, the *normality-abnormality* pair is compound (and thus inappropriate), because it overlaps with several other principles, like the symmetry-asymmetry principle, the density-emptiness principle, the convention-novelty principle, and the same-difference principle, for instance (as already discussed in *FPHP*).

The normality-abnormality pair overlaps with the symmetry-asymmetry principle, because being "abnormal" (say, for those with mental illnesses) is often treated not equally by others who are "normal." So, the relationship reveals the symmetry-asymmetry principle.

The normality-abnormality pair also overlaps with the density-emptiness principle, because being "abnormal" (say, for those with mental illnesses) is often not as dense in the overall (not local) distribution of a population as those who are "normal." So, the relationship reveals the density-emptiness principle.

The normality-abnormality pair also overlaps with the convention-novelty principle, because being "abnormal" (say, for those with mental illnesses) often exhibits non-conventional (non-conformist) ideas and behaviors when contrasted with those who are "normal." So, the relationship reveals the convention-novelty principle.

The normality-abnormality pair also overlaps with the same-difference principle, because being "abnormal" (say, for those with mental illnesses) shares some similarities in outcome when compared with those who are "normal" (in that both contribute to the control and regulation of human thoughts and behaviors in society, albeit in different ways). Yet, being "abnormal" also has something different from being "normal," in that abnormal thoughts and behaviors follow a different pattern when contrasted with those which are normal. So, the relationship reveals the same-difference principle.

These illustrations of indequate and compound family resemblances show how difficult it is to come up with an ontological principle in existential dialectics out of the blue, because many of them violate the selection criteria in one way or the other. It is all too easy to join two opposing words and simply make them into a pair, but it is all too difficult to pass the test of the selection criteria to be qualified as an ontological principle in existential dialectics.

Other examples of compound (and inadequate) family resemblances are shown in *Table 4.10* on "The Syntax of Existential Dialectics VII: Types of Inappropriate Family Resemblances."

The Dialectic Constraints Imposed by the Principles

The principles, as they constitute the syntax of existential dialectics, are dialectic in character, such that, when they are applied, they impose dialectic constraints on how reality is to be understood.

Consider, say, the symmetry-asymmetry principle as an illustration here, in order to summarize two main characters of the dialectic constraints in question (as summarized in *Table 4.7*).

Firstly, to be dialectic here is to go beyond the narrow dichotomies (and, for that matter, any rigid multi-dimensional classificatory scheme), be they about "self" vs. "world," "freedom" vs. "unfreedom," "barbarity" vs. "civilization," "individuality" vs. "communality," and so on.

One way to do so (to go beyond) is to consider them all in terms of co-existence (without favoring one over the rest). For instance, my theory of "post-civilization" (to be summarized later in the section on the pragmatics of existential dialectics) is to go beyond barbarity and civilization in terms of understanding barbarity and civilization as being co-existent.

And the same logic can be said in relation to my theories of "post-democracy," "post-capitalsm," and others (also to be introduced later in the section on the pragmatics of existential dialectics), in regard to freedom vs. unfreedom, equality vs. inequality, communality vs. individuality, spirituality vs. materiality, and so on.

But to consider them all (in the dichotomies—and, for that matter, in any rigid multi-dimensional classifactory scheme) as co-existent is not the same as to imply that the opposing categories in any classificatory scheme are all equal, since, in accordance to the symmetry-asymmetry principle (as an illustration here), if they are equal in terms of being considered as co-existent, they are asymmetric in terms of being unequal in dialectic interaction (e.g., X can be more dominant than Y in case A, or Y is more dominant than X in case B), although in some special cases, they can be relatively equal (e.g., X and Y are relatively equal in case C).

For this reason, there are different versions of "post-democracy" and "post-capitalism" in my theories. As an illustration, in version I of the theory of post-democracy, freedom is more dominant than equality, whereas in version II of the theory of post-democracy, equality is more so than freedom.

But this "X more than Y" has to be understood in the context of dialectic logic (not in symbolic logic, as conventionally understood), in that both "X" and "Y" are important in post-democracy (in the context of dialectic logic), but in an asymmetry way.

By contrast, in symbolic logic, it often favors one over the other—be it in regard to privileging freedom over equality (in Fascism), favoring freedom relatively more than equality (in Liberal Democracy), or favoring equality relatively more than freedom (in Socialist Democracy). In regard to the latter two cases (about Liberal Democracy and Socialist Democracy), the difference between dialectic logic and symbolic logic can be one in degree, not in kind—in this sense, albeit not in other senses.

The same reasoning can be said about the relatonships between individuality and communality, between spirituality and materiality, and between formal legalism and informal legalism in the different versions of my theory of "post-capitalism."

Secondly, to be dialectic is to go beyond the narrow dichotomies (and, for that matter, any rigid multi-dimensional classificatory scheme) in another way, this time, in a transcendent way, that is, in exploring other possibilities or even other issues not considered within the narrow confines of narrow dichotomies (and, for that matter, any rigid multi-dimensional classificatory scheme).

As an analogy, in this second meaning, to go beyond the narrow dichotomy of "black" vs. "white" is not just to choose both "black" and "white" (as in the first meaning) but also to explore other options (e.g., "green," "purple," "blue," etc.—and, alternatively, "shade," "line," "curve," etc.).

By the same reasoning, to go beyond "democracy" is to transcend democracy (as in version III of my theory of "post-democracy") and to explore other possibilties of lifeforms (e.g., "floating consciousness," "hyper-spatial consciousness," etc., to live beyond the narrow obsession with freedom and equality).

This dialectic character of the principles in existential dialectics has important implications for the pragmatics of existential dialectics (as will be clear shortly, in the section on the pragmatics of existential dialectics).

The Semantics of Existential Dialectics (or Its Ontosemantics)

The syntax of existential dialectics so understood in terms of ontological principles only gives us the structure of ontology in the world, in an abstract (general) sense. These principles by themselves do not tell us the specific meanings in a given context.

In order to grasp the specific meanings of the principles in a given context, it is necessary to study the semantics of existential dialectics (as summarized in *Table 4.11*).

And the analysis of the ontological principles as family resemblances in the previous section on syntax is only a starting point (and thus overlaps a bit with the semantics of existential dialectics here).

For this reason, I have often gone to great lengths in my previous books on different subjects to explain the specific meanings of the principles when applied in different contexts.

Consider two examples below for illustration, which are not exhaustive.

In *FPHST*, for instance, I used the first three principles (i.e., the change-constancy principle, the regression-progression principle, and the symmetry-asymmetry principle) to propose "the perspectival theory of space-time," for a better way to understand space and time—especially, though not exclusively, in relation to future post-human history (as summarized in *Table 1.3*, *Table 1.4*, *Table 1.5*, and *Table 1.6*).

In so doing, I had to introduce concepts and theories specific to the field of physics and other related fields (e.g., "absolute space" and "absolute time" in "classical mechanics" and "relative space-time" in "the theory of relativity").

And in *BNN*, I also exploited the three principles to propose the "transcendent" approach to the study of genes and memes as a new way to understand the interaction between nature and nurture.

In so doing, I had to explore concepts and theories in the world of evolutionary biology (e.g., "mutation," "variation," "adaptation," "selection," and "inheritance" in classical evolutionary theory) and neural biology (e.g., "chromosome," "gene," "DNA," "RNA," "protein," "neuron," "neural network," and "behavior").

Other examples, besdies these two here, are given in other books of mine on different topics.

Therefore, this semantic dimension of existential dialectics is important, since, in each of my books when the ontological principles are used, each principle becomes relevant in a different meaning when contextualized within a given case study in question.

In this book, for instance, the principles are relevant in relation to a different subject matter (as summarized in the concluding chapter), and they can be shown in all shapes and sizes (since they are also to be treated as "short cuts," as indicated before), without, however, being reduced to "specific ontology" (as opposed to "general ontology"), as explained in *Table 4.9*.

The Pragmatics of Existential Dialectics (or Its Ontopragmatics)

Even the semantics of existential dialectics is not enough to understand reality, since semantics by itself does not tell us the nature of intentionality and interests in relation to the matrix of power formations and conflicting interests when existential dialectics as an ontology is applied.

Surely, one cannot completely separate the pragmatics of existential dialectics from its semantics (and for that matter, its syntax), but the point here is to give each a more elaborated analysis.

For this reason, the pragmatics of existential dialectics needs to be studied too, in special relation to the inclusion of power formation and conflicting interests in the application of the principles of existential dialectics (as summarized in *Table 4.12*).

It is thus no wonder that all my previous books have shown in different ways how and why these ontological principles and their theoretical applications can reveal the future world to come in a way that humans have never known, in a totally different battleground for competing human (and later post-human) interests by myriad groups fighting for their own versions of hegemony.

Perhaps a summary of my previous works in relation to existential dialectics and their contributions to my new theories as proposed over the years is deemed revealing here, for the further understanding of the pragmatics of existential dialectics (in close relation to the semantics of existential dialectics too).

That stressed—the following summary in four sub-sections is something that I often do in my previous books too, as a way to introduce the intellectual background of my ideas.

So, for those readers who had read my previous works, the following sub-sections serve as a reminder, as they are repeated hereafter *often verbatim* (with only some updated changes, with the rest kept intact).

These sub-sections are, namely, (a) the two-way street connecting theory with meta-theory, (b) the theoretical application of existential dialectics, (c) direct and indirect applications of existential dialectics, and (d) multiple applications of existential dialectics—to be summaried herefafter, respectively.

The Two-Way Street Connecting Theory and Meta-Theory

However, lest any misunderstanding occurs, it is important to remember that the pragmatics of existential dialectics is not a one-way street (that is, using the ontological principles for theoretical insights in praxis) but a two-way one, namely, (a) from meta-theory to theory, and (b) from theory to meta-theory.

(a) On one side of the street, the ontological principles can inspire some theoretical insights in praxis, that is, in relation to some specific fields.

(b) On the other (opposing) side of the street, however, the study of a subject matter in the specific fields in turn reveals some more hitherto unknown ontological principles to be discovered and identified.

For this reason, three new principles were added in *FC*, one in *FAE*, two in *ALD*, and three in *FIA*, on top of the original three in *BCPC*, for example (as there are more)—after some research on the specific subject matters.

Both theory and meta-theory enrich each other in all my works over the years.

The Theoretical Application of Existential Dialectics

This two-way street connecting theory and meta-theory has contributed to my original construction of many theories in numerous books of mine on numerous fields in all domains of knowledge, which can be classified in terms of specific "meta-theories" (about epistemology, methodology, logic, ontology, etc.) and specific "theories" (about the mind, nature, culture, society, and the rest—as will be further explained later in the sub-section on "the holistic organization of an inquiry" in the section about "sophisticated methodological holism").

The final aim of my numerous new specific theories (on both theory and meta-theory) is to converge all of them (as proposed in my numerous books) into a grand project about the future of intelligent life, both here on earth and in deep space.

In this sense, all these theories of mine serve as a foundation to unify all domains of knowledge for an overarching understanding of all forms of reality (by way of some ontological principles and the comprehensive perspectives of the mind, nature, society, and culture), while allowing for heterogeneity, conflict, subjectivity, and complexity, for example.

With this grand project in mind—the summary of my specific theories on meta-theory are given in this section (on "existential dialectics") and the next (on "sophisticated methodological holism"), whereas the specific theories on theory will be summarized in the following categories of (a) society, (b) culture, (c) the mind, (d) nature, and (e) the rest, as shown below, in that order.

(a) Society

The category of "society" here can be divided into four sub-categories, i.e., (a1) social organizations, (a2) social institutions, (a3) social structure, and (a4) social systems (or trends).

(a1) Social Organizations

In relation to social organizations, I proposed a new thesis on the ambivalent nature of virtual organizations in the future, known as "the theory of e-civic alienation" in *FCD* (and summarized in *Table 4.19*).

And in *FPHO*, another theory called "the combinational theory of organization" is worked out, although it was first proposed in Ch.6 of *ALD*.

(a2) Social Institutions

There are different social institutions, be they about (a2.1) politics, (a2.2) economics, (a2.3) military affairs, (a2.4) mass media, (a2.5) law, and (a2.6) education, for instance.

(a2.1) In relation to politics, I offered different visions on (a2.1.1) political theory, (a2.1.2) comparative politics, and (a2.1.3) international relations, to cite three main ones.

(a2.1.1) In the context of political theory, my vision of a path-breaking political system in future times concerns the different forms of "post-democracy" to supersede democracy unto the post-human age.

My vision of post-democracy was called "the theory of post-democracy" (as summarized in *Table 4.22*, *Table 4.23*, and *Table 4.24*), whereas *Table 4.25* explains the distinctions among democracy, non-democracy, and post-democracy.

And *Table 4.26* stresses the multiple causes of the emergence of post-democracy, while *Table 4.27* clarifies some possible misunderstandings in regard to post-capitalism and post-democracy.

(a2.1.2) In the context of comparative politics, I also showed, in *ALD*, how and why authoritarianism can be an advanced form of liberal democracy (just as it has its own counterpart in non-liberal democracy), or what I originally called "authoritarian liberal democracy" (as summarized in *Table 4.21*), before it is to be superceded by "post-democracy."

(a2.1.3) In the context of international relations (both at the institutional and structural levels), I provided, in *BWT*, "the theory of cyclical progression of empire-building," for a better way to understand the logic of empire-building on earth and beyond—with the rise of what I originally envisioned as "hyper-empires" (like "the Chinese Union" and "the Indian Union"), "meso-empires" (like "the European Union" and "the North American Union") and "micro-empires" (like "the Middle Eastern Union" and "the Latin American Union") in the coming "post-post-Cold War era" as a visionary illustration, as summarized in *Table 4.20*.

In addition, in *FPHWP*, I proposed "the multifaceted theory of war and peace" to understand war and peace, in a small sense—or aggression and pacificity, in a broad sense.

(a2.2) In relation to economics, I also offered another vision, this time to understand the future forms of economic systems, that is, the different forms of "post-capitalism" to supersede capitalism unto the post-human age.

My vision of post-capitalism was referred to (in *FCD*, *BDPD* and *BCPC*) as "the theory of post-capitalism" (as summarized in *Table 4.28*, *Table 4.29*, *Table 4.30*, *Table 4.31*, and *Table 4.32*). And *Table 4.33* clarifies the differences among capitalism, non-capitalism, and post-capitalism, whereas *Table 4.34* shows multiple causes of the emergence of post-capitalism.

This vision on "post-capitalism" constitutes the third theoretical application of existential dialectics, this time, in that there is no wealth without poverty (or the wealth/poverty dialectics).

(a2.3) In relation to military affairs, I also proposed "the multifaceted theory of war and peace" (in *FCD*, although it was first so labeled in *FPHK*) for a new way to understand the causes of war—and, for that matter, the rise and fall of different forms of warfare over time.

This theory was further expanded in *FPHWP*, where I suggested a new way to understand war and peace, in a small sense—or aggression and pacificity, in a broad sense.

(a2.4) In relation to mass media, I also proposed "the totalistic theory of communication" in *The Future of Post-Human Mass Media* (or in short, *FPHMM*).

(a2.5) In relation to law, I also proposed "the reconstruction theory of law" in *The Future of Post-Human Law* (or in short, *FPHLAW*).

(a2.6) In relation to education, I propose "the heterodox theory of education" in *The Future of Post-Human Education* (or in short, *FPHEDU*).

(a3) Social Structure

In relation to social structure, I proposed two additional theories, that is, "the theory of the cyclical progression of hegemony" in *FCD* (and also in *FPHC* and *BDPD*), and "the theory of the cyclical progression of empire-building" (in *BWT*, as already indicated above)—with important implications for the symmetry-asymmetry princple in existential dialectics, just to cite one example.

Also, in *BNN*, I also proposed "the theory of contrastive advantages" to understand the persistence of social structure by gender, race, ethnicity, or any other groupings.

(a4) Social Systems (or Trends)

In relation to social systems, there are several sub-categories for illustration, which can be about (a4.1) urbanization, (a4.2) technology, (a4.3) demography, (a4.4) the environment, and (a4.5) social trends as a whole (which also include the current phenomenon of globalization).

(a4.1) In relation to urbanization, I proposed "the contingent theory of urban planning" in *FPHUP* for a new way to understand density and void.

(a4.2) In relation to technology, I worked out "the ambivalent theory of technology" in *FPHE* for a new way to understand the nature of technology.

Some other books (like *FPHMM*, *FAE*, *FCD*, and *FHC*) also deal with technology, and a good example concerns "the synthetic theory of information architecture" in *FIA* on taxonomy, network, and intelligence, in conjunction with the rise of technology.

(a4.3) In relation to demography, I proposed, first in *FHC* (and later in other books like *FCD*, *FPHC*, *FPHU*, etc.), "the theory of post-humanity," in relation to the "post-human" age at some distant point of "after-postmodernity," long after human extinction, to be eventually superseded by "post-humans" of various forms.

Some good candidates of the post-human lifeforms include, for instance, "thinking robots," "thinking machines," "cyborgs," "genetically altered superior beings," "floating consciousness," "hyper-spatial consciousness," "unfolding unconsciousness," "the hyper-sexual body," and "the hyper-martial body." This post-human vision of mine was first originally worked out in *FHC* and further elaborated in both *FCD*, *FPHC*, *FPHU*, *FPHS*, and *FPHMA*, for instance.

Lest any confusion occurs, I need to emphasize two clarifications here about the term "post-human" as a neologism in my works.

Firstly, the word "post-human" here should *not* be confused with another term which looks similar but has a totally different meaning in the literature of postmodernism, namely, "post-humanism"—which constitutes a critique of "humanism" as tradionally understood (especially, though not exclusively, in relation to the idea of progress in science and reason in the Enlightenment project). (WK 2008)

And secondly, the word "post-human" here should also *not* be confused with a similar term which is used to champion the ideology of technology for the future co-existence between humans and cyborgs in "trans-humanism." (WK 2008a)

Instead, my term "post-human" in relation to "posthuman-ism" also rejects "transhumanism" (especially, though not exclusively, in relation to the promises of technology) and refers to something else altogether, that is, the future extinction of humans and its post-human successors in deep space and beyond unto multiverses.

Later, in *BEPE*, I went further and provided a more comprehensive critique of "transhumanism," together with other issues.

With these two clarifications in mind (as summarized in *Table 1.31*)—in the end, a most fundamental question about intelligent life now has an answer, in that, if asked, "What is the future of human civilization?"—my answer in *FCD* (89) is thus: "As addressed in Ch.7 of *FHC*, a later epoch of the age of after-postmodernity (that is, at some point further away from after-postmodernity) will begin, as what I called the 'post-human' history (with the term 'post-human' originally used in my doctoral dissertation at M.I.T., which was finished in November 1995, under the title *After Postmodernity*, still available at M.I.T. library, and was later revised and published as *FHC*). The post-human history will be such that humans are nothing in the end, other than what culture, society, and nature (with some luck) have shaped them into, to be eventually superseded by post-humans (e.g., cyborgs, thinking machines, genetically altered superior beings, and others), if humans are not destroyed long before then."

(a4.4) In relation to the environment, I also addressed the issue of sustainability, especially in *FHC*, *FCD*, and *FPHUP*. For instance, in *FPHUP*, I specifically proposed a new theory, "the contingent theory of urban planning," on the need to go beyond the contemporoary obsession with sustainability, in the context of not only the environment but also other issues.

(a4.5) In relation to social trends as a whole, I proposed in Ch.9 of *FCD* (367-8), that "civilizational history will continue into the following cyclical progression of expansion, before it is to be superseded (solely as a high probability, since humans might be destroyed sooner either by themselves or in a gigantic natural calamity) by posthumans at some distant point in after-postmodernity (which I already discussed in *FHC*)" unto multiverses (different constellations of universes):

Local → Regional → Global →Solar →
Galactic → Clustery…→ Multiversal

The current phenomeon of "globalization" lies in the third category on the line above and was extensively analyzed in *FCD*, in close connection with "globalism" at the cultural level—in the context of "postmodernity" (which will be introduced later in the section on history).

In *BDPD*, this thesis of mine was referred to as "the theory of the cyclical progression of system integration and fragmentation," at the systemic level—in close relation to another thesis analyzed in Ch.9 of *FCD*, which was called, in the absence of better words, "the multifaceted theory of war and peace" in *FPHK* (as already indicated above).

In *FC*, I also proposed "the dialectic theory of complexity" to account for the factor of uncertainty, which can have a major role to play in the world.

(b) Culture

The category of "culture" here can also be divided into different sub-categories like (b1) aesthetics, (b2) religion, (b3) popular (mass) culture, (b4), logic, (b5) civilization as a whole, (b6) ethics, (b7) epistemology (methodology), (b8) metaphysics (ontology), and (b9) ideology.

However, (b7) epistemology (methodology), (b8) metaphysics (ontology), and (b9) ideology are already discussed elsewhere, be they about "meta-theory" (e.g., methodology and ontology under the categories of "existential dialectics" here and "sophisticated methodological holism" in the next section) or "theory" (e.g., ideology under the categories of "social institutions," as described earlier, and also of "civilization as a whole," as will be addressed shortly).

(b1) Aesthetics

In relation to aesthetics, I proposed "the transformative theory of aesthetic experience" in *FAE* about some great transformations of aesthetic experience in future history.

(b2) Religion

In relation to religion, I proposed "the comparative theory of religion" in *FHC* (and also in *FCD*, although it was first so labeled in *FPHK*).

And in *FPHR*, I provided a solid foundation of this theory with a better name, that is, "the comparative-substitutive theory of religion" for a new way to understand spirituality.

(b3) Popular (Mass) Culture

In relation to popular (mass) culture, there are some sub-categories for illustration, which can be, for example, (b3.1) mass culture in general and (b3.2) sports (like chess).

(b3.1) In relation to mass culture in general, I proposed, in *FHC*, a new way to understand mass culture in terms of some fundamental dilemmas, which is called, in the absence of better words, "the dualistic theory of mass culture" in *FPHO*.

(b3.2) In relation to sports (like chess), I proposed, in *FPHCHESS*, "the mediative-variative theory of chess" for a new way to understand tactics and strategy (in different traditions).

(b4) Logic

In relation to logic, I also worked out, in *FPHML*, "the contrastive theory of rationality" for a new way to understand rationality and knowledge (in the context of mathematical logic).

(b5) Civilization as a Whole

In relation to civilization as a whole, I also argued, in *FHC*, no freedom without unfreedom (as shown in *Table 4.13*) and no equality without inequality (as shown in *Table 4.14*), especially in relation to the seven dimensions of life existence first worked out in *FHC* (i.e., the technological, the everyday, the true, the holy, the sublime/beautiful, the good, and the just).

Even more interestingly, in *BDPD* and later in *BCIV*, I further revealed a theoretical refinement of existential dialectics, this time, in arguing that there is no civilization without barbarity, with human civilization to be eventually superseded by what I originally analyzed as "post-human post-civilization" (which should not be confused with "post-human civilization"), in the context of the freedom/unfreedom and equality/inequality dialectics.

In the final analysis, civilization cannot live without barbarity and has to learn to co-exist with it in ever new ways. Preposteorus as this may seem to many contemporaries—it is no more imperative to preserve civilization than necessary to destroy barbarity, and the ideal of civilization is essentially bankrupt, to be eventually superseded by "post-civilization" (as summarized in *Tables 4.35-4.43*).

This freedom/unfreedom and equality/inequality dialectics holds in pre-moderny, modernity, postmodernity, and what I orignally called "after-postmodernity" in *FHC* and *FCD*—especially, though not exclusively, in the context of the emergence of "post-humans."

There are two specific theories about "after-postmodernity" here. The first theory about "after-postmodernity" is about the trinity of pre-modernity, modernity, postmodernity, and after-postmodernity at the cultural level—and was called, in *BDPD*, "the theory of the trinity of modernity to its after-postmodern counterpart," although it was first analyzed in *FHC* and later in *FCD* and also *BCIV* (as summarized in *Table 1.34*, *Table 1.35*, *Table 1.36*, and *Table 1.37* and will be elaborated further in the later sub-section on "the rest" about future history).

The second theory about "after-postmodernity" is about pre-modernity, modernity, postmodernity, and after-postmodernity at the historical level. For instance, a conclusion in *FHC*, which is shocking indeed for many contemporaries, is none other than that "[t]he post-human history will therefore mark the end of human history as we know it and, for that matter, the end of human dominance and, practically speaking, the end of humans as well. The entire history of human civilization, from its beginning to the end, can be summarized by four words, linked by three arrows (as already discussed in *FHC*)":

Pre-Modernity → Modernity →
Post-Modernity → After-Postmodernity

In *BDPD*, this thesis of mine was specifically called "the theory of the evolution from pre-modernity to after-postmodernity," at the historical level—as shown in *Table 1.34*, *Table 1.35*, *Table 1.36*, and *Table 1.37* (and will be elaborated further in the later sub-section on "the rest" about future history).

Therefore, "[t]he end of humanity in the coming human extinction is the beginning of post-humanity. To say an untimely farewell to humanity is to foretell the future welcome of post-humanity." (P. Baofu 2002: 89) This thesis of mine was known in *BDPD* as "the theory of post-humanity," at the systemic level—as already indicated in (a4.3) above.

(b6) Ethics

In relation to ethics, I proposed, in *BEPE*, "the theory of post-ethics" for a new way to understand morality and immorality.

(c) The Mind

The important vision about "post-humans" (as summarized earlier) brings us to the category of "the mind" here, which, as is often understood in everyday's usage, refers to the "brain" and the "body" (together with their interactions) and has different levels of consciousness which can be both "spiritual" and non-spiritual.

Therefore, the "mind" already presupposes the "brain," "body," and "spirit" (or "soul"), so that one does not fall into the intellectual trap of the "mind-body dualism" as debunked in modern (and especially, postmodern) philosophy (which I already went to great lengths to explain in *The Future of Human Civilization*).

That said—the category of "the mind" can be divided into two sub-categories, namely, in relation to (c1) biology and (c2) psychology.

(c1) Biology

In relation to biology, there are two concerns here, namely, (c1.1) genes and intelligence and (c1.2) the human body.

(c1.1) In relation to genes and intelligence, I worked out "the theory of contrastive advantages" (which was originally proposed in *FCD* and further worked out in *BNN*, as summarized in *Table 1.24*), to show the nature-nurture interactions of multiple levels in action (e.g., the biological, the psychological, the structural, the systemic, the cultural, and others) for humans and post-humans on earth and beyond, to the extent that different groups, be they on the basis of race, gender, ethnicity, class, age, or else, are not equal, on average, and have not been, nor will they be, even if there can be exceptions.

(c1.2) In relation to the human body, for instance, in *FPHMA*, I suggested "the expansive-contractive theory of martial arts," in which two great future transformations of the martial body were envisioned, that is, both "with the hyper-martial body" and "without the body" (as summarized in *Table 1.32*)—although this issue can also be classified under the category of "culture."

And in *FPHS*, I proposed "the theory of virtual sexuality," in which three great future transformations of the sexual body were envisioned, that is, "virtual pleasure," "the hyper-sexual body," and "the post-sexual floating mind" (as summarized in *Table 1.33*).

(c2) Psychology

In relation to psypchology (which also overlaps with biology too, however), I also proposed some greater transformations of the mind to come in the future, especially though not exclusively in the post-human age.

These greater transformations of the mind in psychology can be further sub-divided into different categories, namely, (c2.1) consciousness, (c2.2) unconsciousness (together with subconsciousness), (c2.3) creativity, (c2.4) learning, (c2.5) aggression (and pacificity), (c2.6) personality, and (c2.7) humor.

(c2.1) In relation to consciousness, I analyzed, in *FPHC*, the nature of consciousness in relation to the conceptual dimensions of consciousness (as shown in *Table 1.12*), the theoretical levels of consciousness (as shown in *Table 1.13*), the thematic issues of consciousness (as shown in *Table 1.14*), the different dimensions of human existence (viz., having-ness, belonging-ness, and being-ness) in relation to consciousness (as shown in *Table 1.15*, *Table 1.16*, *Table 1.17*, and *Table 1.18*).

In *BCPC*, the nature of consciousness was further explored in relation to cognition, emotion, and behavior, which can be in consciousness and other mental states (e.g., subconsciousness and unconsciousness), in the context of existential dialectics, as shown in *Table 1.19*, *Table 1.20*, *Table 1.21*, *Table 1.22,* and *Table 1.23*.

In fact, in *FCD*, I already proposed three different theories in relation to the limits of cognition, emotion, and behavior, namely, "the theory of cognitive partiality," "the theory of emotional non-neutrality," and "the theory of behavioral alteration."

Then, I argued that the existence of human consciousness will be superseded one day with "floating consciousness" (as first proposed in *FCD*) and "hyper-spatial consciousness" (as first proposed in *FPHC*) as a climax of evolution in consciousness, after the future extinction of human consciousness (as shown below):

Primordial consciousness → Human consciousness →
Post-human consciousness (with floating consciousness and hyper-spatial consciousness as a climax in the evolution of consciousness)

In *BDPD*, these latest theses of mine were called "the theory of floating consciousness" and "the theory of hyper-spatial consciousness," both at the cosmological and psychological levels (as summarized in *Table 1.26* and *Table 1.25*).

(c2.2) In relation to unconsciousness, for instance, in *FPHU*, the unconsious mind will undergo tremendous change, to the rise of what I originally called "unfolding unconsciousess" in relation to anomalous experience, as a climax of evolution in unconsciousness, in conjunction with the conscious mind (both human now and post-human later), especially at the psychological level, as shown below:

Primordial unconsciousness → Human unconsciousness →
Post-human unconsciousness (with unfolding unconsciousness
as a climax in the evolution of unconsciousness)

In *FPHU*, this thesis of mine is called "the theory of unfolding unconsciousness" in a small sense, or "the unfolding theory of anomalous experience," in a larger one, as shown in *Table 1.27* and *Table 1.28*.

(c2.3) In relation to creativity, for instance, in *FPHCT*, I also proposed "the comprehensive theory of creative thinking" to explore the role of creative thinking, in relation to technology and other factors, together with my original proposal of important creative techniques and traits (as shown in *Table 1.29*) and its double nature of desirability and undesirability (as shown in *Table 1.30*).

(c2.4) In relation to learning, for instance, in *FPHL*, I worked out "the multilogical theory of learning" for a new way to understand the nature of structure and context in language, in relation to learning and its future development in the context of the mind.

(c2.5) In relation to aggression (and pacificity), I proposed "the multifaceted theory of war and peace" in *FPHWP* (as mentioned above).

(c2.6) In relation to personality, I worked out "the contrarian theory of personality" in *FPHP* for a new way to understand normality and abnormality.

(c2.7) And in relation to humor, I worked out "the metamorphic theory of humor" in *FPHH* for a new way to understand joking and laughing.

(d) Nature

The category of "nature" here refers to the state of nature, which can be divided into some sub-categories like (d1) physics, (d2) cosmology, (d3) biology, (d4) geography, and (d5) geology.

But since biology in (d3) overlaps with biology in (c1)—only phyiscs, cosmology, geography, and geology are addressed hereafter.

(d1) Physics

In relation to physics, I also proposed "the perspectival theory of space-time" in *FPHST* (based on *FPHC*) for a new way to understand space and time, as shown in *Table 1.3*, *Table 1.4*, *Table 1.5*, and *Table 1.7.*

In *FPHG* (based on *FPHC* and *FPHST*), I proposed "the selective theory of geometry" for a new way to understand geometry, with implications for the understanding of space-time in the context of infinity, symmetry, and dimensionality for future lifeforms that our world has never known (as shown in *Table 1.6*, *Table 1.7*, *Table 1.8; Table 1.9*, *Table 1.10,* and *Table 1.11*).

And in *FC*, I proposed "the dialectic theory of complexity" for a new way to understand order and chaos in the state of nature and beyond.

(d2) Cosmology

In relation to cosmology, my theories on physics (as indicated above) already have important implications for understanding the nature and the future of the universe (which was also addressed in *FHC*, among other works aforcited).

I also proposed "the theory of hyper-spatial consciousness" in *FPHC* (and also in *FPHG*) for a new way to understand the future evolution of the mind to enter into different dimensions of space-time that our current world has never known.

In addition, in *BCOS*, I proposed "the theory of post-cosmology" for a new way to understand the beginnings and ends of the cosmos and beyond.

(d4) Geography

In relation to geography, I proposed "the theory of the geopower of nature" in *ALD* for a different way to understand the relationships between geography and other entities (like the mind, culture, and society).

(d5) Geology

And in relation to geology, I proposed "the resettlement theory of geology" in *FPHGEOL* for a different way to understand the relationships between statics and dynamics.

(e) The Rest

The category of "the rest" here refers to what cannot be strictly classified in any of the previous categories (i.e., society, culture, the mind, and nature). A good illustration of "the rest" refers to that which is, namely, (e1) historical.

(e1) Historical

Precisely here, I proposed "the theory of the evolution from pre-modernity to after-postmodernity" (as first worked out in *FHC* and later in *FCD* and *FPHC*), which overlaps—as a reminder from (b5)—with the issue concerning "civilization as a whole" in (b5).

For instance, in both *FCD* and *FPHC*, I worked out the structure of "post-human civilization" in terms of the trinity of after-postmodernity (i.e., "free-spirited after-postmodernity," "post-capitalist after-postmodernity," and "hegemonic after-postmodernity").

Both conceptually and theoretically, the trinity of after-postmodernity is a sequential extension to the trinity of modernity (i.e., "free-spirited modernity," "capitalist modernity,"and "hegemonic modernity") and the trinity of postmodernity (i.e., "free-spirited postmodernity," "capitalist postmodernity," and "hegemonic postmodernity") as first proposed in *FHC*.

And the trinity of pre-modernity (i.e., "pre-free-spirited pre-modernity," "pre-capitalist pre-modernity" and "hegemonic pre-modernity") was later conceived in *BCIV* to complete the historical set from pre-modernity to after-postmodernity.

In *BDPD*, this thesis about the trinity of pre-modernity, modernity, postmodernity, and after-postmodernity was collectively known as "the theory of the trinity of modernity to its after-postmodern counterpart," at the cultural level—as already so mentioned in (b5) earlier, and summarized in *Table 1.34*, *Table 1.35*, *Table 1.36*, and *Table 1.37*.

At the structural level, all these trinities are subject to the existential constraints (e.g., the freedom/unfreedom and equality/inequality dialectics in the context of "the cyclical progression of hegemony"), be the historical epoch in pre-modernity, modernity, postmodernity, or after-postmodernity in future times. Each of the historical epochs has its ever new ways of coming to terms with the ever new (different) mixtures of freedom/unfreedom and equality/inequality.

This is importantly so, not because, as is falsely assumed in conventional wisdom, one certain way is superior (or better) than another in terms of achieving more freedom and less unfreedom, or more equality with less inequality.

On the contrary, indeed, in each of the historical epochs, each increase of unfreedom greets each freedom achieved, just as each increase of inequality welcomes each equality achieved, albeit in ever new (different) ways. In *BDPD*, this thesis of mine was labeled as "the theory of the cyclical progression of hegemony," at the structural level, though it was first analyzed in *FCD*.

In *BDPD*, more theoretical applications of existential dialectics were further examined, in relation to five main features, in the context of the duality of oppression, namely, (a) that each freedom/equality achieved is also each unfreedom/inequality created, (b) that the subsequent oppressiveness is dualistic, both by the Same against the Others and itself and by the Others against the Same and themselves, (c) that both oppression and self-oppression can be achieved by way of downgrading differences (between the Same and the Others) and of accentuating them, (d) that the relationships are relatively asymmetric among them but relatively symmetric within them, even when the Same can be relatively asymmetric towards itself in self-oppression, and the Others can be likewise towards themselves, and (e) that symmetry and asymmetry change over time, with ever new players, new causes, and new forms, be the locality here on Earth or in deep space unto multiverses—as summarized in *Table.4.13*, *Table 4.14*, *Table 4.15*, and *Table 4.16*.

The same logic also holds both in relation to wealth and poverty (as addressed in *BCPC* and summarized in *Table 4.17* on the wealth/poverty dialectics) and in relation to civilization and barbarity (as addressed in *BCIV* and summarized in *Table 4.18* on the civilization/barbarity dialectics).

In *BDPD*, this thesis on existential dialectics was labeled as "the theory of existential dialectics."

Direct and Indirect Applications of Existential Dialectics

A different way to appreciate the usefulness of existential dialectics is by way of the analysis of its (a) direct and (b) indirect applications.

(a) In direct applications, on the one hand, the logic of existential dialectics can shed some theoretical insights on diverse phenomena in the world, and good instances are the usage of the principles of existential dialectics for the theoretical insights on the freedom/unfreedom dialectics, the equality/inequality dialectics, and the wealth/poverty dialectics—as introduced earlier in (b5) and (e) in the previous sub-section.

For instance, my books like *FPHST*, *BNN*, *FAE*, *FC*, *FIA*, *FPHU*, *FPHK*, *FPHML*, *FPHE*, *FPHMM*, *FPHCT*, *FPHG*, *FPHUP*, *FPHL*, *FPHO*, *FPHMA*, *FPHS*, *FPHLAW*, *FPHFS*, *FPHWP*, *FPHP*, *BEPE*, *BCOS*, *FPHGEOL*, *FPHCHESS*, *FPHR*, *FPHEDU*, and *FPHH* use the principles to reveal some theoretical insights on the perspectives of space and time (as in *FPHST*), of nature and nurture (as in *BNN*), of beauty and ugliness (as in *FAE*), of order and chaos (as in *FC*), of taxonomy and network (as in *FIA*), of the unconscious mind (as in *FPHU*), of the nature of knowledge (as in *FPHK*), of mathematical logic (as in *FPHML*), of engineering (as in *FPHE*), of mass media (as in *FPHMM*), of creative thinking (as in *FPHCT*), of geometry (as in *FPHG*), of urban planning (as in *FPHUP*), of language (as in *FPHL*), of organization (as in *FPHO*), of martial arts (as in *FPHMA*), of sexuality (as in *FPHS*), of law (as in *FPHLAW*), of formal science (as in *FPHFS*), of aggression and pacificity (as in *FPHWP*), of normality and abnormality (as in *FPHP*). of morality and immorality (as in *BEPE*), of the beginnings and ends of the universe (as in *BOCS*), of statics and dynamics (as in *FPHGEOL*), of tactics and strategy (as in *FPHCHESS*), of secularness and sacredness (as in *FPHR*), of teaching and learning (as in *FPHEDU*), and of joking and laughing (as in *FPHH*).

(b) In indirect applications, on the other hand, the theoretical insights can further be used to reveal other phenomena directly from them (viz., the theoretical insights) and therefore indirectly from the principles themselves.

A good illustration is of course the use of the theoretical insights on the freedom/unfreedom and equality/inequality dialectics for the understanding of the civilization/barbarity dialectics.

This distinction between direct and indirect applications may sound a bit academic, since even in indirect applications, the phenomena under study can still be directly related back to the principles themselves.

In the previous example, as an illustration, the civilization/barbarity dialectics can be directly related to the principles of existential dialectics without the intermediate role of the freedom/unfreedom and equality/inequality dialectics.

Multiple Levels of Application

There is another issue to be clarified, however. In other words, the theoretical insights can be applied to multiple levels of analysis—even though, in a given example, it may refer to one level or a few only.

For instance, in the example concerning the freedom/unfreedom dialectics, it can be used at the structural level (e.g., in relation to the theory of the cyclical progression of hegemony), but it can also be exploited for other levels (e.g., the theory of post-capitalism at the institutional level).

All these levels of application should not be misleadingly construed, as I stress this before, as a one-way street (that is, to use the ontological principles for theoretical application at multiple levels of specific analysis) but a two-way one, in which theoretical insights in praxis, when studied in more specific contexts, can in turn refine the nature of existential dialectics (for example, with the addition of new principles).

Sophisticated Methodological Holism

The summary of my original meta-theory on methodology is provided below, again, to be repeated *often verbatim* from my previous works—as this is something I regularly do in each new book to introduce my past works, which are in conversation with this current one.

This means that, for those readers who had read some of my previous books, the summary below is really not much new (*almost verbatim*, with only some updated revisions).

That clarified—this original contribution of mine to the study of methodology takes the form of an approach known as "the theory of methodological holism" or "methodological holism" in short, as already worked out in *FPHC* (2004).

I have made good use of this methodological approach of mine for all of my previous works.

The Confusion of Holism with Systems Approach

Yet, it is imperative to stress at the outset, as I often emphasized this in all my previous books, that my approach of "methodological holism" does not oppose or exclude "methodological individualism" (as some readers may be tempted to assume, as is conventionally understood) but actually includes it.

The confusion here has to do with equating holism with systems approach in general (be it about systems theory, chaos theory, complexity theory, or else), which I debunked, while learning something from it, as already elaborated in *The Future of Complexity* (2007)—and *The Future of Post-Human Formal Science* (2010) is another addition to this critique of the intellectual fad of systems approach.

In other words, my meta-theory of holism, or sophisticated methodological holism in short, makes a distinction between doing holistic work and doing systems work, for two reasons.

The first reason is that holism, in my theory, does not imply systems approach, since it rejects systems approach because of the myriad problems that the literature on systems approach has been unable to resolve, while learning something from it.

And the second reason is that my theory is related to the other theory of mine, that is, existential dialectics, which does not exclude methodological individualism (but includes it, because it simply goes beyond both reductionism and reverse-reductionism in a dialectic way).

For these reasons (and others too, as summarized in *Table 4.1*), my version of methodological holism is *sophisticated*—not *vulgar* as sometimes used by inapt scholars employing the same term.

The Ontological Constraints

Sophisticated methodological holism is subject to some ontological constraints, and five good examples include "the partiality-totality principle," "the predictability-unpredictability principle," "the explicability-inexplicability principle," "the absoluteness-relativeness principle," and "the formalness-informalness principle" in existential dialectics.

Of course, there can be more than five ontological principles in relation to method, but the five examples here are sufficient to illustrate the point in question.

With this caveat in mind—the first two were already analyzed in previous books of mine like *FC* and *FAE*, whereas the third one was addressed in *FPHU*, and the last two were accounted for in *FPHK* and *FPHML*, respectively.

For now, it suffices to show that sophisticted methodological holism, because of these ontological constraints on methodology, targets two major sins of methodology, namely, what I call, in the absence of better words, (a) *reductionism* and (b) *reverse-reductionism*—both of which come in all shapes and sizes, to be summarized below (and also shown in *Table 4.2*).

Against the Varieties of Reductionism

There are four versions of reductionism to be summarized here, which sophisticated methodological holism rejects, namely, (a1) conceptual, (a2) theoretical, (a3) methodological, and (a4) ontological forms of reductionism.

(a1) In conceptual reductionism, a good case in point concerns myriad dualities like mind vs. body, self vs. world, democracy vs non-democracy, and the like (as already addressed in *FHC*, *FPHC*, and *BDPD*, for instance).

(a2) In theoretical reductionism, an illuminating case study is best exemplified by what I originally called "the foundation fallacy" in *FPHST*, in any attempt to naively understand space-time from the physical perspective as the foundation and, consequently, to dangerously dismiss (or belittle) other perspectives.

In *FAE*, I elaborated further these versions of reductionism in the literature on aesthetics (e.g., form vs. content, representation vs. expression, critics vs. artists, and externalism vs. internalism).

In *FIA*, I revealed other forms of reductionism in the literature on information architecture (e.g., the constructivist argument and the representational argument).

In *FPHU*, I showed the persistent legacy of reductionism, this time, in the literature on anomalous experience (e.g., the obsession with physics, chemistry, and biology for explaining anomalous experience).

In *FPHE*, I examined another case of reductionism in action, in the context of engineering (e.g., technical constraints vs. normative constraints).

In *FPHMM*, I elaborated one more version of reductionism, in relation to the three domains of communication (e.g., the competing views on sending, connecting, and receiving).

In *FPHCT*, I explored another version of reductionism, in relation to invention and innovation (e.g., the bio-psychological argument vs. the socio-cultural arguments).

In *FPHG*, I identified another version of reductionism, in relation to infinity, symmetry, and dimensionality (e.g., the Euclidean argument vs. the non-Euclidean arguments).

In *FPHUP*, I analyzed another version of reductionism, in relation to density and void (e.g., the engineering argument and the ecology argument).

In *PFHL*, I examined another version of reductionism, in relation to structure and context (e.g., the structuralist argument and the contextualist argument).

In *PFHO*, I explored another version of reductionism, in relation to communcation, decision-making, and leadership (e.g., the rational-system argument vs. the natural-system argument vs. the open-system argument).

In *PFHMA*, I revealed another version of reductionism, in relation to the martial body and spirit (e.g., the spiritual argument vs. the materialist argument vs. the defensive argument).

In *PFHS*, I analyzed another version of reductionism, in relation to the sexual body and spirit (e.g., the naturalist argument vs. the constructivist argument).

In *PFHLAW*, I examined another version of reductionism, in relation to law (e.g., the necessity argument vs. the contengency argument).

In *FPHWP*, I show another version of reductionism, in relation to war and peace (e.g., the aggressivist argument vs. the pacifist argument).

In *BEPE*, I analyzed another version of reductionism, in relation to morality and immorality (e.g., the objectivist argument vs. the non-objectivist argument vs. the skeptical argument).

In *BCOS*, I examined another version of reductionism, in relation to the contested beginnings and speculative ends of the universe (e.g., the scientific argument vs. the religious argument vs. the esoteric argument vs. the metaphysical argument).

In *FPHP*, I showed another version of reductionism, in relation to normality and abnormality (e.g., the natural argument vs. the social argument vs. the cultural argument vs. the mental argument).

In *FPHGEOL*, I scrutinized another version of reductionism, in relation to statics and dynamics (e.g., the catastrophe argument vs. the uniformity argument vs. the revision argument).

In *FPHCHESS*, I showed another version of reductionism, in relation to tactics and strategy (e.g., the natural argument vs. the social argument vs. the cultural argument vs. the mental argument).

In *FPHR*, I revealed another version of reductionism, in relation to secularness and sacredness (e.g., the critical argument vs. the skeptical argument vs. the theist argument).

In *FPHEDU*, I examined another version of reductionism, in relation to teaching and learning (e.g., the teacher-centered argument vs. the student-centered argument vs. the balanced argument).

And in *FPHH* here, I explore another version of reductionism, in relation to joking and laughing (e.g., the natural argument vs. the social argument vs. the cultural argument vs. the mental argument).

(a3) In methodological reductionism, a good illustration can be the debate between different versions of qualitative and quantitative methods (as already analyzed in *FC* and also *FHC*).

In *FPHML*, I examined similar reductionism, this time, in the literature on mathematical logic (e.g., the obsession with consistency, soundness, and completeness).

And in *FPHFS*, I explored the problems of reductionism in the context of formal science (e.g., the analytical argument, as opposed to the synthetic argument).

(a4) In ontological reductionism, an excellent instance involves another debate, this time between emergentism and reductionism in complexity theory (as addressed in *FC*) and also in psychology (as elaborated in *FPHC*, in the context of Being and Belonging).

But to target against the varieties of reductionism constitutes only a side of the same coin, and the other side concerns the varieties of reverse-reductionism.

Against the Varieties of Reverse-Reductionism

The other side of the same coin is the reverse version of reductionism, which is what I want to call, in the absence of better words, *reverse-reductionism*.

My sophisticated version of methodological holism targets against the varieties of reverse-reductionism (just as it also rejects the ones of reductionism).

Perhaps nothing expresses better the popularity of reverse-reductionim than the "anything-goes" mentality in postmodernism of our time, as shown in the following four versions.

(b1) In conceptual reverse-reductionism, any concept of "art" (e.g., fine art, applied art, outsider art, junk art) is welcome in postmodernism (as already analyzed in Ch.4 of *FHC*—and also in *FAE*).

(b2) In theoretical reverse-reductionism, a variety of art and literary theories co-exist. Take the case of literary studies, as there are now Literary Structuralism, Marxist Literary Criticism, New Criticism, Phenomenology, Hermeneutics, Language-Game Literary Criticism, Feminist Literary Criticism, Reception Theory, Reader Response Criticism, Poststructuralism, Semiotics, Pyschoanalytic Literary Criticism, just to cite some well-known ones, with no one being said to be better than any others (as detailedly analyzed in Ch.4 of *FHC*). (S. Raman 1997)

In *BNN*, I even introduced "the compromise fallacy" as another good illustration of theoretical reverse-reductionism, in misleadingly treating both genetic and environmental approaches as equally valid.

(b3) In methodological reverse-reductionism, multiple methodologies are deemed as acceptable in postmodernism (e.g., doing art without praxis, doing art with praxis, and doing art by sublation), as analyzed in Ch.4 of *FHC*.

And in *FPHFS*, I exposed the problems of reverse-reductionism in the context of formal science in relation to systems theory (e.g., the synthetic argument).

(b4) In ontological reverse-reductionism, no privileged ontology is allowed, and the door is open practically for anything in postmodernism (e.g., the equal status of the ontology of Being vs. that of Becoming, as already addressed in Ch.4 of *FHC*—and also in *FPHC*).

In *FAE*, I also introduced another version of reverse-reductionism, that is, "the pluralist fallacy," in the context of understanding aesthetic experience, for instance—although this fallacy has been committed not exclusively in relation to the ontological level (but also at the conceptual, theoretical, and methodological ones).

These dual dangers against reverse-reductionism (in this sub-section) and reductionism (in the previous sub-section) are something that sophisticated methodological holism rejects. And in *FPHFS*, I addressed these two problems further.

This point about the dual dangers is important enough, since many scholars often favor one against the other, but it is vital to target both.

The Holistic Organization of an Inquiry

With these dual dangers against reductionism and reverse-reductionism in mind—sophisticated methodological holism suggests that an inquiry of any given phenomenon is more complete, if treated in the context of a comprehensive analysis at all relevant levels, which challengingly encompass all the fields of human knowledge, ranging from the natural sciences and formal sciences through the social sciences to the humanities.

This section is something that I had already stressed in all my previous books and repeat (*often verbatim*) hereafter. But, for those readers who had read my previous books, this serves as a reminder.

With this reminder in mind—there are multiple ways to engage in a holistic inquiry with all relevent levels of analysis. Over the years, I have proposed different ways to fulfill this holistic methodological requirement, as repeated in my previous books.

Hereafter is a summary of four major ways, namely, (a) by discipline, (b) by domain, (c) by subject, and (d) by meta-analysis—all of which fulfill the holistic requirement of sophisticated methodological holism on a given issue.

(a) In a holistic organization by discipline, a good illustration is the multiple levels of analysis, namely, (a1) the micro-physical, (a2) the chemical, (a3) the biological, (a4) the psychological, (a5) the organizational, (a6) the institutional, (a7) the structural, (a8) the systemic, (a9) the cultural, (a10) the macro-physical (cosmological), and (a11) other relevant levels, which are either a combination of all these levels or the practical applications with a combination of them.

This holistic organization by discipline is used in *FCD* and *BCPC*, for instance.

(b) In a holistic organization by domain, some good candidates include the classification of different perspectives of analysis in relation to (b1) nature, (b2) the mind, (b3) society, and (b4) culture, as already worked out in *BCIV*, *FPHST*, *FC*, *FAE*, *FPHU*, *FPHK*, *FPHE*, and *FPHFS*.

Culture in (b4), in this re-classification, is the same as culture in (a9) and can be further divided into different sub-categories, with good examples like (a9i) epistemology (methodology), (a9ii) aesthetics, (a9iii) ethics, (a9iv) metaphysics (ontology), and (a9v) religion. For clarification, epistemology (methodology) in (a9i) and metaphysics (ontology) in (a9iv) overlap with the category of "meta-theory."

Society in (b3) includes the organizational in (a5), the institutional in (a6), the structural in (a7), and the systemic in (a8).

The mind (b2) has more to do with the chemical in (a2), the biological in (a3), and the psychological in (a4), although it can overlap with (a1), (b3) and (b4), for instance.

It should be stressed that the "mind" here also includes the categories like the "brain," "body," and the "spirit" (or the "soul")—whenever needed in a given context, so that one does not fall into the intellectual trap of the "mind-body dualism" in the history of modern (and especially, postmodern) philosophy, which I already went to great lengths to explain in *The Future of Human Civilization*. After all, in everyday's usage, the "mind" already implies the "brain" and the "body" (together with their interactions) and has different levels of consciousness which can be both "spiritual" and non-spiritual.

And nature in (b1) refers to the micro-physical in (a1) and the macro-physical (cosmological) in (a10), although it can also overlap with (a2), (a3) and (a4).

(c) In a holistic organization by subject, some excellent examples concern the analysis of consciousness in *FPHC* (i.e., on Having, Belonging, and Being); of civilization in *FHC* (i.e., the True, the Holy, the Everyday, the Technological, the Beautiful/Sublime, the Good, and the Just); of international politics in *BWT* (i.e., Hyper-Empires, Meso-Empires, and Micro-Empires); of nature and nurture in *BNN* (i.e., genes and memes); of information architecture in *FIA* (i.e., taxonomy and network); of mathematical logic in *FPHML* (i.e., consistency, soundness, and completeness); of communication in *FPHMM* (i.e., sending, connecting, and receiving); of creative thinking in *FPHCT* (i.e., invention and innovation); of geometry in *FPHG* (i.e., infinity, symmetry, and dimensionality); of urban planning in *FPHUP* (i.e., density and void), of language in *FPHL* (i.e., structure and context), and of organization in *FPHO* (i.e., communication, decision-making, and leadership), in *FPHMA* (i.e., the martial body and the martial spirit), in *FPHS* (i.e., the sexual body and the sexual spirit), in *FPHLAW* (i.e., necessity and contingency), in *FPHWP* (i.e., aggression and pacificity), in *FPHP* (i.e., normality and abnormality), in *BEPE* (i.e., morality and immorality), in *BCOS* (i.e., the beginnings and ends of the universe), in *FPHGEOL* (i.e., statics and dynamics), in *FPHCHESS* (i.e., tactics and strategy), in *FPHR* (i.e., secularness and sacredness), in *FPHEDU* (i.e., teaching and learning), and in *FPHH* (i.e., laughing and joking)—by incorporating all the relevent levels of analysis as cited above in each.

(d) And in a holistic organization by meta-analysis, two good cases in point involve the works on post-capitalism in *BCPC* and on authoritarian liberal democracy in *ALD*, with the classification of analysis in theory and meta-theory.

The essential point to remember here, as I thus stress in all my previous books, is that the multiple levels of analysis can be reorganized in many different ways, insofar as none of the levels (if relevant to an inquiry in question) is ignored or dismissed, to avoid the danger of reductionism (and for that matter, the one of reverse-reductionism, in the opposite direction).

Three Clarifications

Three clarifications are needed here, however, to avoid any hasty misunderstanding.

Firstly, the entities in each classification are not mutually exclusive. For instance, in the holisitc organization by domain, nature in (b1) can also be linked to the chemical in (a2), the biological in (a3), and the systemic in (a8). And the mind (b3) can alternatively be related to the micro-physical in (a1) and the chemical in (a2), for example.

Secondly, there is also the important factor of luck (or uncertainty in conventional usage), but it is already implied or allowed in each of the organizations of an inquiry—especially in relation to the predictability-unpredictability principle and the order-chaos principle in existential dialectics. This topic about uncertainty was already addressed in *FHC*—and more extensively, in *FC*, in the context of order and chaos.

And lastly, the comparison in a classification is not absolute, but relative, as there are often some shades of gray, not exactly black or white (figuratively speaking).

Some further clarifications and qualifications of sophisticated methodological holism are shown in *Table 4.2*.

Some Distinctive Usefulness

In the end, sophisticated methodological holism—when applied, especially though not exclusively, as illustrated in my numerous works—

can enrich the understanding of reality in some distinctive ways. Here are four examples (as revealed in each of my books).

Firstly, it provides a comprehensive analysis of a subject matter, from which much can be learned about reality, both in relation to the perspectives of the mind, nature, society, and culture.

Secondly, it offers a new classification of the subject matter.

Thirdly, it suggests some visions of the future in relation to the subject matter in question.

And fourthly, it proposes some insights on meta-theory (e.g., methodology and ontology) in general—with the clear understanding, however, of the dilemma of specific vs. general ontology (as shown in *Table 4.9* on the syntax of existential dialectics in the context of the dilemma of ontology).

For this very reason, all of these ways are important, without reducing one into the analysis of another. (*FPHCT*)

Chapter Outline

With this summary of my two original meta-theories (on methodology and ontology, *almost verbatim* from my previous works) in mind—this book is organized in four main parts, namely, (a) Part I on the introduction to this book, (b) Part II on joking, (c) Part III on laughing, and (d) Part IV on the conclusion of the book.

The book is thus organized in four chapters.

The introductory chapter here, that is, Chapter One titled "Introduction—The Fun of Humor," starts by first asking whether or not, or to what extent, humor is a frog can, humorously speaking, and then introducing humor in relation to joking and laughing—together with the theoretical debate in the literature, my metamorphic theory of humor, the relationship between theory and meta-theory, existential dialectics, sophisticated methodological holism, and some further clarifications.

Chapter Two titled "Joking and Its Double Faces" examines the nature of joking from the four perspectives of the mind, nature, society, and culture , with a constructive critique of each.

Chapter Three titled "Laughing and Its Dual Facets" explores the nature of laughing from the four perspectives of the mind, nature, society, and culture, with a deconstructive analysis of each.

The last chapter titled "Conclusion—The Future of Humor" summarizes the analysis in the book in the dialectic context of joking and laughing, with eighteen major theses, namely, (a) the first thesis: the absoluteness-relativeness principle, (b) the second thesis: the predictability-unpredictability principle, (c) the third thesis: the explicability-inexplicability principle, (d) the fourth thesis: the preciseness-vagueness principle, (e) the fifth thesis: the simpleness-complicatedness principle, (f) the sixth thesis: the openness-hiddenness principle, (g) the seventh thesis: the denseness-emptiness principle, (h) the eighth thesis: the slowness-quickness principle, (i) the nineth thesis: the expansion-contraction principle, (j) the tenth thesis: the theory-praxis principle, (k) the eleventh thesis: the convention-novelty principle, (l) the twelveth thesis: the evolution-transformation principle, (m) the thirteenth thesis: the symmetry-asymmetry principle, (n) the fourteenth thesis: the softness-hardness principle, (o) the fifteenth thesis: the seriousness-playfulness principle, (p) the sixteenth thesis: the regression-progression principle, (q) the seventeenth thesis: the sameness-difference principle, and (r) the eighteenth thesis: the post-human rendition—to be elaborated in the rest of the book, with a summary in the concluding chapter.

This seminal project is to fundamentally alter the way that we think about humor, from the combined perspectives of the mind, nature, society, and culture, with enormous implications for the human future and what I originally called its "post-human" fate.

Some Clarifications

But some additional clarifications are needed, before a formal analysis of the nature of humor is to begin in Chapter Two.

These clarifications, lest any potential misunderstanding by the readers occurs, refer to (a) the conversation with my previous books, (b) the illustrative selection of case studies and examples, (c) detailed analysis versus overall analysis, (d) two distinctive features of using quotations, and (e) the use of neologisms.

These clarifications are something that I also regularly repeat in my previous books too, so these points are repeated hereafter, *often verbatim*—albeit in a different context this time.

In Conversation with My Previous Books

Firstly, my metamorphic theory of humor is constructed on the theoretical foundation of my previous books (i.e., *FHC*, *FCD*, *FPHC*, *BDPD*, *BCPC*, *BCIV*, *FPHST*, *BNN*, *BWT*, *FC*, *FAE*, *ALD*, *FIA*, *FPHU*, *FPHK*, *FPHML*, *FPHE*, *FPHMM*, *FPHCT*, *FPHG*, *FPHUP*, *FPHL*, *FPHO*, *FPHMA*, *FPHS*, *FPHLAW*, *FPHFS*, *FPHWP*, *FPHP*, *BCOS*,

BEPE, *FPHGEOL*, *FPHCHESS*, *FPHR*, and *FPHEDU*—as explicated in "The List of Abbreviations").

Just consider the following two illustrations, namely, (a) in relation to other related theoretical debates and (b) in relation to different visions as worked out in my previous books.

(a) The first illustration is that the theoretical debate here also involves a few other related theoretical issues.

These other related theoretical issues have to do with some deeply contested theoretical debates, which, however, I had already gone to great lengths to analyze in my numerous (previous) books, as summarized below. It should also be stressed, lest misunderstanding occurs, that each of the theoretical debates (as listed below) does not exhaust the issues covered in the books, as each book covers more issues than what is listed below (for illustration only).

- On Inconsistency
  –Ex: *The Future of Post-Human Mathematical Logic*
- On Ambiguity
  –Ex: *The Future of Post-Human Mathematical Logic*
- On Aesthetics
  –Ex: *The Future of Aesthetic Experience*
  –Ex: 2 volumes, *The Future of Human Civilization*
- On Creativity
  –Ex: *The Future of Post-Human Creative Thinking*
  –Ex: *The Future of Aesthetic Experience*
- On Learning
  –Ex: *The Future of Post-Human Language*
  –Ex: *The Future of Post-Human Education*
- On Communication
  –Ex: *The Future of Post-Human Mass Media*
  –Ex: *The Future of Post-Human Organization*
- On Personality
  –Ex: *The Future of Post-Human Consciousness*
  –Ex: *The Future of Post-Human Personality*
- On Cognition
  –Ex: *The Future of Post-Human Unconsciousness*
  –Ex: *The Future of Post-Human Consciousness*
  –Ex: *The Future of Capitalism and Democracy*
  –Ex: *The Future of Post-Human Creative Thinking*
  –Ex: *The Future of Post-Human Personality*

- On Intuition
  - –Ex: *The Future of Post-Human Unconsciousness*
  - –Ex: *The Future of Post-Human Consciousness*
  - –Ex: *Beyond Capitalism to Post-Capitalism*
  - –Ex: *The Future of Capitalism and Democracy*
- On Emotion
  - –Ex: *The Future of Post-Human Unconsciousness*
  - –Ex: *The Future of Post-Human Consciousness*
  - –Ex: *The Future of Aesthetic Experience*
  - –Ex: *Beyond Capitalism to Post-Capitalism*
  - –Ex: *The Future of Capitalism and Democracy*
  - –Ex: *The Future of Post-Human Personality*
- On Behavior
  - –Ex: *The Future of Post-Human Language*
  - –Ex: *The Future of Post-Human Unconsciousness*
  - –Ex: *The Future of Post-Human Consciousness*
  - –Ex: *Beyond Capitalism to Post-Capitalism*
  - –Ex: *The Future of Capitalism and Democracy*
  - –Ex: *The Future of Post-Human Sexuality*
  - –Ex: *The Future of Post-Human Personality*
  - –Ex: *The Future of Post-Human Martial Arts*
- On Spirituality
  - –Ex: 2 volumes, *The Future of Human Civilization*
  - –Ex: *The Future of Capitalism and Democr acy*
  - –Ex: *Beyond Capitalism to Post-Capitalism*
  - –Ex: *The Future of Post-Human Sexuality*
  - –Ex: *The Future of Post-Human Martial Arts*
  - –Ex: *The Future of Post-Human Unconsciousness*
  - –Ex: *The Future of Post-Human Consciousness*
  - –Ex: *Beyond Ethics to Post-Ethics*
- On No Morality Without Immoralitiy
  - –Ex: 2 volumes, *The Future of Human Civilization*
  - –Ex: *The Future of Capitalism and Democracy*
  - –Ex: *Beyond Democracy to Post-Democracy*
  - –Ex: *Beyond Ethics to Post-Ethics*
- On Being and Belonging
  - –Ex: *The Future of Post-Human Consciousness*
  - –Ex: 2 volumes, *The Future of Human Civilization*
- On Different Dimensions of Human Existence
  - –Ex: 2 volumes, *The Future of Human Civilization*

- On No Freedom Without Unfreedom
  - –Ex: 2 volumes, *The Future of Human Civilization*
  - –Ex: *The Future of Capitalism and Democracy*
  - –Ex: *Beyond Capitalism to Post-Capitalism*
  - –Ex: *Beyond Democracy to Post-Democracy*
  - –Ex: *Beyond Civilization to Post-Civilization*
- On Modernity, Post-Modernity, and After-Postmodernity
  - –Ex: 2 volumes, *The Future of Human Civilization*
  - –Ex: *Beyond Civilization to Post-Civilization*
- On Pre-Modernity
  - –Ex: *Beyond Civilization to Post-Civilization*
- On Uncertainty
  - –Ex: *The Future of Complexity*
  - –Ex: 2 volumes, *The Future of Human Civilization*
- On Religion
  - –Ex: *The Future of Post-Human Religion*
  - –Ex: 2 volumes, *The Future of Human Civilization*

Therefore, those who are interested in these other theoretical issues (and debates) which are related to the current context can consult these other books of mine for more details.

(b) And the second illustration is that one of the major theses of this book concerns the future, be it human and later post-human, which is closely linked with the different visions that I had worked out in my previous books, in relation to the mind, nature, society, and culture.

Of course, for the convenience of the readers, a summary of some of these visions will be provided whenever necessary, as shown in the two sections on meta-theory above (*often verbatim*) and in different tables at the end of this chapter and the concluding chapter, for instance.

Yet, I still expect the readers to read my previous books directly for more details—as this book is written in conversation with my previous ones.

Case Studies and Examples

Secondly, the case studies and examples in the chapters are not exhaustive but solely illustrative. Nor are they necessarily mutually exclusive, as they can be reclassified in a different way. And exceptions are allowed.

One is tempted to assume, however, that, since the case studies and their examples are not exhaustive, more case studies and examples are needed. But the problem here is that just adding more of them does not necessarily change the conclusions to be drawn and may even lead to redundancy.

After all, the case studies and examples used in this book are chosen with care and deemed sufficient for the purpose at hand, even though they are solely illustrative.

Detailed Analysis versus Overall Synthesis

Thirdly, there is a distinction between detailed analysis and overall synthesis, in that the former is, especially though not exclusively, more for the specialized viewpoint of a specific discipline, whereas the latter is, especially though not exclusively, more for the broad horizon of an interdisciplinary approach—relatively speaking, of course.

Or, by analogy, there is a distinction between depicting a "tree" (with tiny details) in a "forest" and viewing the entire "forest" itself (with the broader horizon).

This book, like all previous ones of mine, tries to strike a balance between the two forms of understanding, although this does not imply that the two forms should be exactly equally offered, in an exact 50-50 balance.

Instead, the book, more often than not, does not allow the tiny details to obscure the larger picture in a given case study, because the entire book is inter-disciplinary in nature and tries to look at the entire "forest," not being bogged down with the detailed analysis of an individual "tree" in the forest, by analogy.

In this sense, although detailed analysis can be provided whenever needed for a given case study, the important point to remember is the overall horizon with its broadness of scope.

Two Distinctive Features of Using Quotations

Fourthly, the way that quotes are used in this book (and others of mine) has two distinctive features, as explained below.

The first distinctive feature is that, at the end of each quotation, sometimes there are more than one reference—in which case the first reference is for the original citation, and the rest of the references are for the convenience of the reader for more information about the issue under quotation.

And the second feature is that quotations are used as often as possible, so as to let others speak for themselves, without the nuisance of putting my own words into their mouths. Even more importantly, this allows me to use the original text as an evidence for critical analysis at the end of each section.

The Use of Neologisms

And finally, I use different neologisms in my books, mostly to introduce my original concepts and theories, and good instances include those here or elsewhere in my previous books (e.g., "the metamorphic theory of humor," "post-democracy," "hyper-spatial consciousness," "post-capitalism," and whatnot). Needless to say, they are used here solely for our current intellectual convenience, as they will be renamed differently in different ways in future history.

As I thus wrote in *FCD* (508-9), "all these terms 'post-capitalism,' 'post-democracy'...and other ones as introduced in...[the] project (e.g.,...'posthuman elitists,' and 'posthuman counter-elitists,' just to cite a few of them) are more for our current intellectual convenience than to the liking of future humans and post-humans, who will surely invent more tasteful neologisms to call their own eras, entities, and everything else, for that matter. But the didactic point here is to use the terms to foretell what the future might be like, not that its eras and entities must be called so exactly and permanently. After all, William Shakespeare (1995: Act II, Scene II, Line 47) well said long ago: 'What is in a name? That which we call a rose by any other name would smell as sweet.'"

As I had also stressed time and again before, each of the neologisms can be re-written as a different "X," only to be re-named differently by the powers that be in different eras of future history.

With these clarifications for thought in mind—I now proceed to Chapter Two on joking and its double faces.

Table 1.1. Humor in Relation to Joking and Laughing

- **Humor**
  —Ex the word "humor" is derived "from the humoral medicine of the ancient Greeks, which taught that the balance of fluids in the human body, known as humours (Latin: umor, 'body fluid'), control human health and emotion." (WK 2010)
  —Ex: thus, in accordance to this old definition by the ancient Greeks, humor is important to good health—and, nowadays, "[s]tudies show that people who laugh more often get sick less." (WK 2010k; G. Meredith 1897) And the reason is that "laughter boosts the immune system, lowers cholesterol and blood pressure, and reduces stress." (A. Angelle 2010: 15)

- **Joking**
  —Ex: the giving end of humor
  —Ex: different subjects (e.g., ethnic jokes, black humor, etc.)
  —Ex: different styles (e.g., question/answer jokes, etc.)

- **Laughing**
  —Ex: the receiving end of humor
  —Ex: not to be confused with "smile," "joke," "play," "tickleness," etc.
  —Ex: laughter and its genetic basis
  —Ex: laughter and its neurophysiology

Notes: The examples in the categories are solely illustrative (not exhaustive), and the comparison is relative (not absolute), nor are they necessarily mutually exclusive. And some can be easily re-classified elsewhere. As generalities, they allow exceptions.
Source: From *Sec. 1.2* of *FPHH*. See book for citations.

Table 1.2. Four Great Future Transformation of Humor

- **Virtual Humor**
  —Ex: virtual humor has to do with the use of computers to generate jokes in the future, especially when computers will be developed to the point of artificial intelligence unto what I had already extensively discussed as the "post-human" future (in my numerous books).

- **Novel Humor**
  —Ex: in the post-human era, the post-humans will no doubt create new subjects, styles, and forms of humor which will better suite their tastes and the environments that they encoutner in deep space and beyond unto multiverse—in a way that the human world has never known.

- **Holistic Humor**
  —Ex: in the post-human era, the post-human mind will evolve to a different advanced stage of complexity both in scope and depth, such that humor will be transformed in a different dimension of scope and depth that the human world has never known.

- **Spiritual Humor**
  —Ex: in the post-huamn era, the post-humans will further transform humor in a spiritual direction (as illustrated by my different visions) in a way that the human world has never known.

Notes: The examples in the categories are solely illustrative (not exhaustive), and the comparison is relative (not absolute), nor are they necessarily mutually exclusive. And some can be easily re-classified elsewhere. As generalities, they allow exceptions.
Source: From *Ch.4* of *FPHH.* See text for citations.

Table 1.3. The Theoretical Debate on Space-Time (Part I)

- **Isaac Newton's Absolutist (Substantivist) Theory of Space-Time**
  —space and time are independent from each other. The structure of space-time is $E3 \times E1$ (with the structure of space, *P*, as the set of spatial locations in a three-dimensional Euclidean space, *E3*, and the structure of time as the set of temporal moments, *T*, in the one-dimensional real time, *E1*).
  —space and time are also independent from the effects of matter and events. The existence of space and time is possible even in a world absent of matter (and, for that matter, even in a world absent of events), as if they were material objects but with their total unchangingness thorough time.

- **Albert Einstein's Relativist Theory of Space-Time**
  —space and time are interchangeable (not absolute), just as matter and energy are equivalent (not independent) with the famous equation, $E = mc^2$ (as in the special theory of relativity in 1905).
  —space-time and matter-energy are also relative in a grand union (as in the general theory of relativity in 1915). Thus, each pair affects the other pair, as "matter 'tells' spacetime how to curve [in a non-Euclidean geometry] and curved spacetime 'tells' matter how to behave….Space contracts near mass and dilates away from it. Time dilates near mass and contracts away from it. Clocks positioned farther away from the mass of the earth run faster than clocks closer to the earth." (L. Shlain 1991: 328-330)

(continued on next page)

Table 1.3. The Theoretical Debate on Space-Time (Part II)

- **Peter Baofu's Perspectival Theory of Space-Time**
  —space and time can be understood from multiple perspectives, be they in relation to culture, society, nature, and the mind, with each perspective revealing something about the nature of space-time and simultaneously delimiting its view. This is subject to "the regression-progression principle" in existential dialectics.
  —each perspective of space and time exists in society and culture with good reasons, with some being more successful and hegemonic (dominant) than others. This is subject to "the symmetry-asymmetry principle" in existential dialectics.
  —space and time will not last, to be eventually superseded (altered) by post-humans in different forms (e.g.,stretching/shrinking space-time, engineering more dimensions of space-time, and manipulating multiverses), be they here in this universe or in multiverses. Thus, even the physical existence of space-time cannot last forever, with ever more transformations in the process. This is subject to "the change-constancy principle" in existential dialectics.
  —the conventional wisdom (especially by physicists) of treating the physical perspective of space and time as the foundation of all other perspectives (of space and time) and of regarding them as much less important is a form of reductionism,committing what I call *the foundation fallacy*, in misleadingly dismissing the multiple perspectives of space and time in relation to culture, society, nature, and the mind.

Notes: The examples in each category are solely illustrative (not exhaustive), and the comparison is relative (not absolute), nor are they necessarily mutually exclusive. Some can be easily re-classified elsewhere. As generalities, they allow exceptions.
Source: A summary of *Sec.1.1*, *Sec.1.2*, and *Sec.1.3* of *FPHST*—and, for that matter, the rest of *FPHST*

Table 1.4. Main Reasons for Altering Space-Time

- **The Need to Make New Energy-Matter**
  —Ex: manipulating molecular bonds for new materials
  —Ex: creating nanotechnologies on the atomic scale
  —Ex: engineering the atomic nucleus
  —Ex: restructuring most elementary particles
  —Ex: inventing new forms of matter and energy

- **The Need to Create New Space-Time**
  —Ex: creating "warp drive" (as in science fiction) for space travel
  —Ex: creating "pocket universes"

- **The Need to Conquer the Cosmos unto Multiverses**
  —Ex: spreading floating consciousness and hyper-spatial consciousness, besides other forms that humans have never known, in the cosmos and beyond unto multiverses for ultimate conquest

Notes: The examples in each category are solely illustrative (not exhaustive) nor necessarily mutually exclusive, and the comparison is relative (not absolute). As generalities, they allow exceptions. Also, it should be stressed that the three reasons are all related, in that they all contribute to the evolution of intelligent life in the cosmos unto multiverses in the most distant future beyond our current knowledge.
Sources: A summary of *Sec.6.2* of *FPHST*. See also *FHC*, *FCD*, *FPHC*, *FC*, *FPHU*, and *FPHG*, for example.

Table 1.5. The Technological Frontiers of the Micro-World

- **Type I-Minus**
  —Ex: building structures and mining

- **Type II-Minus**
  —Ex: playing with the genetic makeups of living things

- **Type III-Minus**
  —Ex: manipulating molecular bonds for new materials

- **Type IV-Minus**
  —Ex: creating nanotechnologies on the atomic scale

- **Type V-Minus**
  —Ex: engineering the atomic nucleus

- **Type VI-Minus**
  —Ex: restructuring most elementary particles

- **Type Ω-Minus**
  —Ex: altering the structure of space-time

Notes: As already indicated in *Sec.4.4.2.2* of *FPHC*, the problem with this micro-classification (from Barrow's work) is that the civilization types (with the exception of Type Ω-Minus, for example) are not quite distinct, since many of them can be achieved more or less in a civilization, to the extent that Type II-minus and Type III-minus, just to cite two plausible types, can be historically contemporaneous, relatively speaking, unlike the vast historical distance between, say, Type O and Type I (or Type I and Type II) civilizations. In other words, the micro-classification here is not very useful to understand civilization types but is revealing to see the technological frontiers of the micro-world.
Sources: A reconstruction from J.Barrow (1998:133), as originally shown in *Table 4.7* of *FPHC*. See *FPHC* for more info.

Table 1.6. Finity, Transfinity, and Infinity (Part I)

• **Infinity**

—The term "infinity," which is "symbolically represented with ∞," derives from the Latin *infinitas* (or "unboundedness"), to refer to "several distinct concepts—usually linked to the idea of 'without end'—which arise in philosophy, mathematics, and theology." (WK 2008c)

—In the context of mathematics, "infinity" is often "treated as if it were a number (i.e., it counts or measures things: 'an infinite number of terms') but it is a different type of 'number' from the real numbers. Infinity is related to limits,...large cardinals,...projective geometry, extended real numbers and the absolute Infinite," for instance. (WK 2008c)

• **Transfinity**

—To avoid confusion, my usage of the word "transfinite" (as used here in the ontological principle) is not the same as the one which was originally coined by Georg Cantor to refer to "cardinal numbers or ordinal numbers that are larger than all finite numbers, yet not necessarily absolutely infinite" (in the mind of God), as opposed to "relative" infinity (in the mind of Man). (WK 2008d) In other words, for Cantor, there are two kinds of infinity, "absolute" and "relative"—with "relative" infinity or "transfinity" (in the mind of Man) being dependent on "absolute" infinity (in the mind of God) for its existence.

—By contrast, my usage of the word "transfinite" here differs radically from the one used by Cantor (and other mathematicians) and is more limited, in light of the problems confronting any attempt to understand the idea of infinity, be it by intuition, imagination, and conception (as already shown in the prevous three sub-sections).

—With this clarification in mind, I allow numbers which can be many times larger—or smaller, for that matter—than the finite things that we encounter in daily life, but they do not have to be related to the idea of infinity at all (which may not exist).

(continued on next page)

Table 1.6. Finity, Transfinity, and Infinity (Part II)

- **Transfinity *(cont'd)***
  —Of course, there may be some *borderline* cases, in which it is not clear whether the number in question is transfinite (in my usage) or simply a mathematical convenience. A good example of a borderline case is the Planck unit of length for "the smallest space possibly measured in nature," which is "less than billionths of trillionths of trillionths of an inch" (or something like 1.6×10^{-35} meters). (P. Baofu 2006a; N. McAleer 1987: 219; WKV 2008; D. Corbett 2008)
  —The ideas concerning symmetry and dimensions in the examples above were addressed in Chapter Three and Chapter Four of *FPHG*. For now, it suffices to further add that it is mind-boggling to even conceive or imagine extreme numbers like the Planck unit of length (or others). Does it really exist at all? Or is it merely a mathematical convenience to describe a physical situation that the human mind does not understand properly?
  —In any event, "transfinity" (in my usage) can be used as a further extension (of number) to the finite numbers in daily life—albeit with some borderline cases in mind.

- **Finity**
  —It refers to numbers which are bounded (that is, with an end), especially (though not exclusively) in relation to things in everyday life.

Source: From *Sec. 1.4* and *Sec. 2.2.3* of *FPHG*

Table 1.7. Theoretical Speculations of Multiverses

- **"Baby Universes" (Ex: Andre Linde and others)**
  —Ex: In a flat universe theory, "even if our part of it eventually collapses,...some spots in the cosmos would suddenly start inflating on their own, creating brand-new 'baby universes.'" (P. Baofu 2000: 623)

- **"Parallel Universes" (Ex: Stephen Hawking and others)**
  —Ex: In quantum cosmology, there allows the existence of infinite numbers of parallel universes, with tunneling among them. (M. Kaku 1994: 256) Hawking later revised his views on this.

- **"Pocket Universes" (Ex: Alan Guth)**
  —Ex: "As the pocket universes live out their lives and recollapse or dwindle away, new universes are generated to take their place....While life in our pocket universe will presumably die out, life in the universe as a whole will thrive for eternity." (A. Guth 1997: 248; P. Baofu 2002: 482)

- **"Brane Worlds" (Ex: Warren Siegel, Lisa Randall, and others)**
  —Ex: Our universe is stuck on a membrane of space-time embedded in a larger cosmos, with different brane worlds connecting and/or colliding with each other.

Notes: These examples are solely illustrative (not exhaustive), and some of the items can be reclassified somewhere else. Nor are they always mutually exclusive. Since they are generalities, exceptions are expected.
Source: From *Table 4.8* of *FPHC*

Table 1.8. The Confusion between "Many Worlds" and "Multiverse" (Part I)

- **First Problem**
  - —The first problem in this second confusion concerns a debate between the "many-worlds" interpretation of quantum mechanics by Hugh Everett (1957) and others, and the Copenhagen interpretation by Niels Bohr and Werner Heisenberg on the effects of quantum states after interacting with an external environment (e.g., by a measuring observer).
  - —On the one hand, the Copenhagen interpretation of quantum mechanics is more indeterministic in its concern with the probabilities of the outcomes of a wave function after interacting with an external environment (e.g., by a measuring observer using light to detect, for example, "an electron in a particular region around the nucleus at a particular time." (WK 2008e) Each wave function for the state of a particle refers to "a mathematical representation used to calculate the probability for it to be found in a location, or state of motion." (WK 2008f) And the "wavefunction collapse" means that "the act of measurement causes the calculated set of probabilities to 'collapse' to the value defined by the measurement." (WK 2008f)
  - —On the other hand, the Everett's interrpetation is more deterministic, in rejecting "the objective reality of wavefunction collapse" and "instead explaining the subjective appearance of wavefunction collapse with the mechanism of quantum decoherence." (WK 2008g) The words "quantum decoherence" here refers to "the mechanism by which quantum systems interact with their environments to exhibit probabilistically additive behavior," in such a way that "the quantum nature of the system is simply 'leaked' into the environment." (WK 2008g) For example, "[a]s a result of an interaction, the wave functions of the system and the measuring device become entangled with each other. Decoherence happens when different portions of the system's wavefunction become entangled *in different ways* [italic added] with the measuring device...." (WK 2008g) Thus, for Everett, the appearance of "wavefunction collapse" can be explained by "quantum decoherence" for quantum states to branch out in different independent worlds after interacting with an external environment.

(continued on next page)

Table 1.8. The Confusion between "Many Worlds" and "Multiverse" (Part II)

- **First Problem** ***(cont'd)***
  —Yet, a major criticism against Everett's interpretation is that these different independent worlds in Everett's sense "will never be accessible to us," because of the interference by the measuring observer in an external environment. (WK 2008g)
  —For illustration, "once a measurement is done, the measured system becomes entangled with both the physicist who measured it and a huge number of other particles, some of which are photons flying away towards the other end of the universe; in order to prove that the wave function did not collapse one would have to bring all these particles back and measure them again, together with the system that was measured originally. This is completely impractical, but even if one can theoretically do this, it would destroy any evidence that the original measurement took place (including the physicist's memory)." (WK 2008g)
  —But then, the critics ask, If these independent worlds in Everett's sense are inaccessible to us, how do we know much of anything really about them?

- **Second Problem**
  —What is relevant at the quantum mechanical level may not necessarily apply to the world at the physicsl level.
  —In fact, the persistent inability among contemporoary physicists to unifiy the theory of relativity for large objects at the physical level and quantum mechanics for tiny objects at the quantum mechanical level should warn us about the danger of reductionism, by reducing the understanding of different universes ("parallel universes") at the physical level from a generalization of "many worlds" at the quantum mechanical level.

- **Third Problem**
  —There is no empirical evidence to suggest that there are infinite (or extremely many) possible worlds in the cosmos as the many-worlds model by Everett would have us to believe.

Source: From *Sec.4.4.1* of *FPHG*

Table 1.9. Hyperspace and Its Challenge (Part I)

• **First Problem**

—Hyperspace for intra- and inter-universal travel is assumed to be possible, on the basis of four main assumptions; although there may be others, these are the often cited ones.

—The first assumption concerns the existence of "entry" and "exit" points in hyperspace, which is easier said than done to enter, go through, and then exit hyperspace.

—For instance, using hyperspace "requires complex calculations…of single or multiple hyperspace jumps and the control of the jump….Peturbations such as those experienced by ship in space from the gravitional field around an object such as a planet or even a star are exacerbated in hyperspatial travel, since mass in real space distorts hyperspace in an equal measure. 'Jumping' near to a gravitational mass is likely to make resulting exit from hyperspace to be highly uncertain, with the level of improbability *i* increasing with the square of the distance to the nearest gravitional 'well.'" (WK 2008h)

—Besides, "[o]nly spaceships equipped with a special force field can enter hyperspace, because exposure to hyperspace even for short period of time is hazardous to unprotected humans." (WK 2008h)

• **Second Problem**

—The second assumption concerns the faster-than-light speed. It is well known that Einstein argued for the speed of light as the ultimate limit, but nowadays phyiscists do allow the violation of this limit under certain conditions (like the hypothetical existence of tachyons, as will be explained further in a later sub-section on time travel).

—Even then, there is a challenge to explain in science fiction "why ships can travel faster than light in hyperspace," and two good arguments are that "hyperspace may be smaller than real space and therefore a star ship's propulsion seems to be greatly multiplied, or else the speed of light in hyperspace is not a barrier as it is in real space. Whatever the reasoning, the general effect is that ships traveling in hyperspace seem to have broken the speed of light, appearing at their destinations much more quickly and without the shift in time that the Theory of Relativity would suggest." (WK 2008h)

(continued on next page)

Table 1.9. Hyperspace and Its Challenge (Part II)

• **Third Problem**

—The third assumption concerns the speed of time (to be measured, say, by a clock), but this is elaborated in a different section on the related issue of "time travel" (as shown in a different table on time travel).

• **Fourth Problem**

—The fourth assumption concerns spatial shortcut, as it is possible, because of the curvature of space, in that "the manifold of ordinary three-dimensional space is curved in four or more 'higher' spacial dimensions (a 'hyperspace' in the geometric sense…). This curvature causes certain widely separated points in three-dimensional space to nonetheless be 'adjacent' to each other four-dimensionally. Creating an aperture in 4D space (a wormhole) between these locations can allow instantaneous transit between the two locations; a common comparison is that of a folded piece of paper, where a hole punched through two folded sections is more direct than a line drawn between them on the sheet. This idea probably arose out of certain popular descriptions of General Relativity and/or Riemannian manifolds, and may be the original form from which later concepts of hyperspace arose." (WK 2008h)

—But this does not mean that hyperpsace is always safe. In fact, "in some science fiction, the danger of hyperspace travel is due to the chance that the route through hyperspace may take a ship too close to a celestial body with a large gravitational field, such as a star. In such scenarios, if a starship passes too close to a large gravitational field while in hyperspace, the ship is forcibly pulled out of hyperspace and reverts to normal space. Therefore, certain hyperspace 'routes' may be mapped out that are safe, not passing too close to stars or other dangers." (WJ 2008h)

Source: From *Sec.4.4.1* of *FPHG*

Table 1.10. The Problems of Time Travel into the Future (Part I)

- **First Problem**
  - —The first problem concerns "time dilation under the Theory of Special Relativity" (which separates space-time from mass-energy as special cases). Suppose you are on a moving train and an observer outside the train is watching you along the tracks. As your train moves along at the speed of light (or something close to it), "time, as measured by your watch, ticked along at a slower pace than time measured by the observer. Not only that, distance changed, too. For the observer, a one-foot ruler whizzing by on the train would have measured less than a foot." (NO 2000)
  - —In fact, you may not even notice that this slower clicking of the clock; in fact, everything looks normal to you inside the train as it was before: "The weird thing is that, for you on the train, time wouldn't seem to be moving slower and your ruler wouldn't be shorter—all would appear normal." (NO 2008) By contrast, you instead think that "time on the rest of the Earth would appear to be ticking along slower and its rulers would be shorter." (NO 2000) So, both of you insist that the other clock (not his) is clicking more slowly—assuming, of course, an inertial frame of reference.
  - —Now, change the story a bit, in that, this time, instead of an "inertial reference frame," acceleration is allowed, and you are on your way to board a spaceship. As an illustration, suppose "[y]ou board a spaceship and take off for deep space. The ship approaches the speed of light. Time for you seems to pass as it always has. It takes you about five seconds to tie your shoe. But to an observer on Earth (assuming he or she could watch you), you are moving at a snail's pace. It takes hours to tie your shoe." (NO 2000) In any event, "you continue on your journey. You slow down, stop, and accelerate back to Earth. You arrive home. You have aged two years during your flight. Two hundred years have passed on Earth. You have successfully travelled forward through time." (NO 2000) In this case, both the observer (if he is still alive) and you agree that you have aged less.

(continued on next page)

Table 1.10. The Problems of Time Travel into the Future (Part II)

• **First Problem** ***(cont'd)***

—In other words, when you are back to Earth, a lot of things have changed since, and you may find rather strange to be in a new environment which you hardly recognize, when compared with what you used to think as your city, or the Earth (two years ago, well, in accordance to your time of measurement). This means that you are in the future (two hundred years later), even though you are still relatively young (only two years older). But, can you go back? Well, no. The reason is that "[a]ccording to relativity, you can only move through time in one direction." (NO 2000)

• **Second Problem**

—The second problem concerns "time dilation under the Theory of General Relativity" (which unifies space-time with mass-energy in a general theory), the same result of time dilation occurs.

—For instance, when "one clock is deeper in a gravity well than the other," a result is that "the clock deeper in the well" will "tick…more slowly; this effect must be taken into account when calibrating the clocks on the satellites of the Global Positioning System, and it could lead to significant differences in rates of aging for observers at different distances from a black hole." (WK 2008i)

—More precisely, by way of another example, "it has been calculated that, under general relativity, a person could travel forward in time at a rate four times that of distant observers by residing inside a spherical shell with a diameter of 5 meters and the mass of Jupiter. For such a person, every one second of their 'personal' time would correspond to four seconds for distant observers. Of course, squeezing the mass of a large planet into such a structure is not expected to be within our technological capabilities in the near future." (WK 2008i; R. Gott 2002)

—The point here, however, is that time travel into the future, in this sense, is allowed, theoretically speaking, but in a very limited way, from the theory of relativity. But one can also ask, What if the theory of relativity were wrong? Well, in that case, there would be a need to find a better theory to explain time travel into the future.

Source: From *Sec.4.4.2* of *FPHG*

Table 1.11. The Problems of Time Travel into the Past (Part I)

- **First Problem**
  —The first problem concerns the faster-than-light-speed, since, in accordance to the theory of special relativity, when an object goes faster than the speed of light, something weird can happen, in that, instead of having the clock clicking more slowly, it is moving backward, in relation to some inertial frame of reference—which then raisies the issue of whether time travel into the past is possible at all.
  —But the problem here is about the violation of the law of casuality. In everyday language, an excellent illustration of causality violation is that, suppose you travel back into the past and then kill your parents, this then means that you could not have been born. But this is not true, since you are alive.
  —Yet, "in the case of a hypothetical signal moving faster than light, there would always be some frames in which the signal was received before it was sent, so that the signal could be said to have moved backwards in time." The violation of casuality exists in this case.
  —The first part of the problem is that, in accordance to the theory of special relativity, "it would take an infinite amount of energy to accelerate a slower-than-light object to the speed of light"—let alone the energy needed to propel an object to go faster than the speed of light. (WK 2008i) Although some suggest the possibility of "negative energy," it remains to be seen to what extent this is true.
  —And the second part of the problem is that, "although relativity does not forbid the theoretical possibility of tachyons which move faster than light at all times, when analyzed using quantum field theory it seems that it would not actually be possible to use them to transmit information faster than light and there is no evidence for their existence." (WK 2008i; S. Chase 1993)

(continued on next page)

Table 1.11. The Problems of Time Travel into the Past (Part II)

• **Second Problem**

—The second problem concerns cosmic string and black holes, since it is the theory of general relativity which "extends the special theory to cover gravity, illustrating it in terms of curvature in spacetime caused by mass-energy and the flow of momentum." (WK 2008i)

—On the other hand, "[g]eneral relativity describes the universe under a system of field equations…and there exist solutions to these equations that permit what are called 'closed time-like curves,' and hence time travel into the past….The first of these was proposed by Kurt Gödel, a solution known as the Gödel metric, but his (and many others') example requires the universe to have physical characteristics that it does not appear to have." (WK 2008i; K. Thorne 1994)

—But then, the problem now becomes: "Whether general relativity forbids closed time-like curves for all realistic conditions is unknown." (WK 2008i)

• **Third Problem**

—The third problem concerns wormholes and related ones, and "[w]ormholes are a hypothetical warped spacetime which are also permitted by the Einstein field equations of general relativity, although it would be impossible to travel through a wormhole unless it was what is known as a traversable wormhole." (WK 2008i; M. Visser 1995) In other words, "a wormhole is a hypothetical topological feature of spacetime that is fundamentally a 'shortcut' through space and time. Spacetime can be viewed as a 2D surface, and when 'folded' over, a wormhole bridge can be formed. A wormhole has at least two mouths which are connected to a single throat or tube. If the wormhole is traversable, matter can 'travel' from one mouth to the other by passing through the throat." (WK 2008j)

—But the problem here is three-fold, as shown in what follows.

(continued on next page)

Table 1.11. The Problems of Time Travel into the Past (Part III)

- **Third Problem *(cont'd)***
  —The first part of the problem is that "there is no observational evidence for wormholes." (WK 2008j)
  —The second part of the problem is that it is not clear how exactly wormholes (and black holes, for that matter) could allow time travel into the past at all.
  —And the third part of the problem is that if using wormholes (and black holes, for that matter) to travel into the past requires something to go faster than light too, then this raises another issue concerning the two problems as previously indicated in the sub-section on the faster-than-light-speed.

- **Fourth Problem**
  —The fourth problem is that some physicists have argued that, even should time travel into the past be possible, by way of these three methods, the person still would not return to the same past history that he exactly experienced before, but in a different one. (WK 2008i)
  —In other words, "strictly speaking," time travel into the past is not "really" possible, in light of these criticisms, so there is no need to worry that one could travel into the past and kill one's parent, as a way to violate the law of casuality.

Source: From *Sec.4.4.2* of *FPHG*

Table 1.12. The Conceptual Dimensions of Consciousness (and Other Mental States)

- **On Heredity and Time**
  —Heredity and the Environment
  —The Past and the Present

- **On Layers of Mental States and Abnormality**
  —Consciousness, Unconsciousness, and Preconsciousness
  —Normality and Paranormality

- **On Organicity and Motivation**
  —Mechanicity and Organicity
  —Primary Motivations and Multiple Motivations

- **On Other (Mostly Epistemic) Considerations**
  —Synthesis and Analysis
  —Situation and the Subject
  —Process and Outcome
  —Reasoning and Other Modes of Thinking
  —Meta-Conceptual Nominalism and Realism

Notes:: These examples are solely illustrative (not exhaustive), and some of the items can be reclassified somewhere else. Nor are they always mutually exclusive. Since they are generalities, exceptions are expected.
Sources: From *FPHC*. A re-construction, but with my own contribution, originally from G.Lindzey & C.Hall, *Introduction to Theories of Personality* (NY: John Wiley & Sons, 1985).

Table 1.13. The Theoretical Levels of Consciousness (and Other Mental States) (Part I)

- **At the Micro-Physical Theoretical Level**
  - —Quantum-Mechanics
  - —Electromagnetism

- **At the Chemical Theoretical Level**
  - —Biochemistry

- **At the Biological Theoretical Level**
  - —Evolutionary Biology
  - —Neuroscience
  - —Artificial Intelligence

- **At the Psychological Theoretical Level**
  - —Psychodynamic Psychology
    - Psychoanalytical Psychology
    - Analytical Psychology
    - Socially Oriented Psychology
  - —Experimental (Behavioral) Psychology
    - Operant Reinforcement Theory
    - Stimulus-Response Theory
    - Social Learning Theory
  - —Cognitive (Gestalt) Psychology
    - Humanist Psychology
    - Existential Psychology
    - Field Theory
  - —Psychometric Psychology
    - Idiographics
    - Constitutional Psychology
  - —Social Psychology
    - Symbolic Interactive Theory
    - Social Exchange Theory

(continued on next page)

Table 1.13. The Theoretical Levels of Consciousness (and Other Mental States) (Part II)

- **At the Organizational Theoretical Level**
  - —Managerial-Bureaucratic Theory
  - —Oligarchic Theory
  - —Network Theory

- **At the Institutional Theoretical Level**
  - —Functionalist Theory
  - —Anomic Theory

- **At the Structural Theoretical Level**
  - —Conflict Theory
    - Marxian Theory
    - Critical Theory
    - Weberian Theory
  - —Games Theory (in Formal Theory)
  - —Feminist Theory
    - Feminist Concerns
    - Feminist Hopes

- **At the Systemic Theoretical Level**
  - —Equilibrium Theory
  - —System Theory
  - —Chaos Theory

- **At the Cosmological Theoretical Level**
  - —Superluminal Model
  - —The Theory of Floating Consciousness

(continued on next page)

Table 1.13. The Theoretical Levels of Consciousness (and Other Mental States) (Part III)

- **At the Cultural Theoretical Level**
  - —Substantive Theories
    - Structuralist Theory
    - Post-Structuralist Theory (in Postmodernism)
  - —Meta-Theories
    - Epistemic Objectivism vs. Epistemic Historicism
    - Epistemic Subjectivism vs. Epistemic Non-Subjectivism
      - –Phenomenology
      - –Ethnomethodology
      - –Hermeneutics
    - Epistemic Relativism vs. Epistemic Absolutism
    - Epistemic Reductionism vs. Epistemic Emergencism

- **At Other Levels**
  - —Structuration Theory
  - —Reflexive Socioanalysis

Notes: These examples are solely illustrative (not exhaustive), and some of the items can be reclassified somewhere else. Nor are they always mutually exclusive. Since they are generalities, exceptions are expected.
Source: From many different sources as indicated in *FPHC*

Table 1.14. The Thematic Issues of Consciousness (and Other Mental States)

- **The Factor of History**
  - —Pre-Modernity
  - —Modernity
  - —Postmodernity
  - —After-Postmodernity

- **The Importance of Needs**
  - —Having (e.g., the everyday, the technological)
  - —Belonging (e.g., the just and the good)
  - —Being (e.g., the true, the holy, the sublime/beautiful, and the good)

Notes: These examples are solely illustrative (not exhaustive). Nor are they always mutually exclusive. Since they are generalities, exceptions are expected. Also, some categories overlap with others; for instance, the good is also related with being-ness, just as the everyday can be connected with belong-ness.
Sources: From *FPHC*, based on *FHC* and *FCD*

Table 1.15. Having, Belonging, and Being in Consciousness

- **Having (e.g., About the Everyday and Technological)**
  —Ex: Physiological needs (e.g., thirst, hunger, sex)
  —Ex: Safety (e.g., stability, freedom from fear and anxiety)

- **Belonging (e.g., About the Good and Just)**
  —Ex: Social interaction
  —Ex: Friendship, acquaintance
  —Ex: Love, family
  —Ex: Self-respect, respect from others

- **Being (e.g., About the True, Holy, Beautiful/Sublime, and Good)**
  —Ex: Understanding of reality about self and world
  —Ex: Spiritual quest for holiness, beauty, sublimity, and goodness

Notes: These examples are solely illustrative (not exhaustive), and some of the items can be reclassified somewhere else. Nor are they always mutually exclusive. Since they are generalities, exceptions are expected.
Sources: From *FPHC*, based on *FHC* and *FCD*

Table 1.16. The Having-Ness of Consciousness (and Other Mental States)

- **At the Micro-Physical Level**
  —Ex: The finer physics of nutrition
- **At the Chemical Level**
  —Ex: Food guide pyramid
- **At the Bio-Psychological Level**
  —Ex: The hierarchy of needs
- **At the Institutional Level**
  —Ex: The production of commodity fetishism
- **At the Organizational Level**
  —Ex: Mass standardization (and customization); bureaucratic rationality
- **At the Structural Level**
  —Ex: The divide between the haves and the have-nots
- **At the Cultural Level**
  —Ex: The bondage of greater expectations
- **At the Systemic Level**
  —Ex: The technological transformation of poverty with transvaluations
- **At the Cosmological Level**
  —Ex: Floating consciousness in deep space without the human physiological needs

Notes: These examples are solely illustrative (not exhaustive), and some of the items can be reclassified somewhere else. Nor are they always mutually exclusive. Since they are generalities, exceptions are expected.
Sources: From *FPHC*. See also *FCD* and *FHC*.

Table 1.17. The Belonging-Ness of Consciousness (and Other Mental States)

- **At the Micro-Physical Level**
  —Ex: Statistical physics and social networks

- **At the Chemical Level**
  —Ex: Olfaction and social relations

- **At the Bio-Psychological Level**
  —Ex: Dual human nature on relationships

- **At the Institutional Level**
  —Ex: Private property and social cleavage

- **At the Organizational Level**
  —Ex: Legal formalism and iron cage

- **At the Structural Level**
  —Ex: Class conflicts and social alienation

- **At the Cultural Level**
  —Ex: Ruthless society and the culture of law

- **At the Systemic Level**
  —Ex: Human extinction and post-human relations

- **At the Cosmological Level**
  —Ex: The transcendence of equality in the cosmos and beyond

Notes: These examples are solely illustrative (not exhaustive), and some of the items can be reclassified somewhere else. Nor are they always mutually exclusive. Since they are generalities, exceptions are expected.
Sources: From *FPHC*. See also *FCD* and *FHC*.

Table 1.18. The Being-Ness of Consciousness (and Other Mental States) (Part I)

- **At the Micro-Physical Level**
  —Ex: Space-time and matter-energy in classical mechanics, quantum mechanics, and the theory of relativity

- **At the Chemical Level**
  —Ex: Drugs and well being

- **At the Biological Level**
  —Ex: Neuroscience and mystical experiences

- **At the Psychological Level**
  —Ex: Reductionism and emergencism

- **At the Institutional Level**
  —Ex: The proliferation of cults and sects, and the corporate-art industry

- **At the Organizational Level**
  —Ex: The organization of ideas in the scheme of things

- **At the Structural Level**
  —Ex: Disciplinary power and control in the order of things

- **At the Systemic Level**
  —Ex: Mutualism and ecological psychology

- **At the Cultural Level**
  —Ex: The recurrence of competing spirits, and floating consciousness as a climax of evolution

(continued on next page)

Table 1.18. The Being-Ness of Consciousness (and Other Mental States) (Part II)

- **At the Cosmological Level**
  —Ex: The search for elsewherewhen, and the evolution of other consciousnesses (e.g., the hyper-spatial consciousness)

Notes: These examples are solely illustrative (not exhaustive), and some of the items can be reclassified somewhere else. Nor are they always mutually exclusive. Since they are generalities, exceptions are expected.
Sources: From *FPHC*. See also *FCD* and *FHC*.

Table 1.19. Cognitive Partiality in Different Mental States

- **The Conscious**
  - —*Biased*
    - Ex: Self-overratingness
    - Ex: Self-modesty
    - Ex: Self-fulfilling prophesy
  - —*Shallow*
    - Ex: Attribution error
    - Ex: Heuristics
    - Ex: Illusory thinking
  - —*Short-term*
    - Ex: Deindividuation
  - —*Materialistic*
    - Ex: Hierarchy of needs

- **The Subconscious**
  - Ex: mental reconstruction
  - Ex: stereotyping

- **The Unconscious**
  - Ex: automatic processing
  - Ex: cognitive intuition

Notes: These examples are solely illustrative (not exhaustive), and some of the items can be reclassified somewhere else. Nor are they always mutually exclusive. Since they are generalities, exceptions are expected. And the comparison is relative, not absolute.
Source: From *BCPC*

Table 1.20. Emotional Non-Neutrality and Behavioral Alteration in Different Mental States

- **The Emotional**
  —*Conscious*
  Ex: Feelings
  —*Subconscious*
  Ex: Moods
  —*Unconscious*
  Ex: Empathy
  Ex: Instincts

- **The Behavioral**
  —*Conscious*
  Ex: Foot-in-the-door
  Ex: Role playing
  Ex: Saying-is-believing
  —*Subconscious*
  Ex: Discrimination
  —*Unconscious*
  Ex: Non-Verbal Communication

Notes: These examples are solely illustrative (not exhaustive), and some of the items can be reclassified somewhere else. Nor are they always mutually exclusive. Since they are generalities, exceptions are expected. And the comparison is relative, not absolute.
Source: From *BCPC*

Table 1.21. The Limits of Intuition in Unconsciousness

- **Cognitive Intuition (or Intuitive Thinking)**
  —*Features*
    Ex: mental schemas
    Ex: expertise
    Ex: blindsight
  —*Problems*
    Ex: inaccurate
    Ex: non-explanatory

- **Emotional Intuition**
  —*Features*
    Ex: empathy
    Ex: instincts
  —*Problems*
    Ex: over-generalized
    Ex: non-explanatory

- **Behavioral Intuition**
  —*Features*
    Ex: prosemics
    Ex: kinesics
  —*Problems*
    Ex: unreliable
    Ex: non-explanatory

Notes: These examples are solely illustrative (not exhaustive), and some of the items can be reclassified somewhere else. Nor are they always mutually exclusive. Since they are generalities, exceptions are expected. And the comparison is relative, not absolute.
Source: From *BCPC*

Table 1.22. The Wealth/Poverty Dialectics in Different Mental States: The Case of Cognition

- **The Conscious**
  - —*Biased*
    - Ex: If richer in self-serving bias, then poorer in understanding others
  - —*Shallow*
    - Ex: If richer in heuristic thinking, then poorer in comprehending reality
  - —*Short-term*
    - Ex: If richer in short-term tendency, then poorer in long-term planning
  - —*Materialistic*
    - Ex: If richer in physiological obsession, then poorer in spiritual enlightenment

- **The Subconscious**
  - Ex: If richer in mental reconstruction, then poorer in accuracy of recall
  - Ex: If richer in stereotyping, then poorer in understanding groups

- **The Unconscious**
  - Ex: If richer in automatic processing, then poorer in depth of analysis
  - Ex: If richer in cognitive intuition, then poorer in reliability of judgments

Notes: These examples are solely illustrative (not exhaustive), and some of the items can be reclassified somewhere else. Nor are they always mutually exclusive. Since they are generalities, exceptions are expected. And the comparison is relative, not absolute.
Source: From *BCPC*

Table 1.23. The Wealth/Poverty Dialectics in Different Mental States: The Case of Emotion and Behavior

- **Emotion**
  - —*Conscious*
    - Ex: If richer in relying on familiarity and similarity for social attraction, then poorer in having diverse social relations
  - —*Subconscious*
    - Ex: If richer in moodiness, then poorer in sober thinking
  - —*Unconscious*
    - Ex: If richer in empathy, then poorer in task-oriented efficiency
    - Ex: If richer in instincts, then poorer in critical thinking
- **Behavior**
  - —*Conscious*
    - Ex: If richer in foot-in-the-door technique, then poorer in instant Gratification
    - Ex: If richer in role playing, then poorer in identity stability
  - —*Subconscious*
    - Ex: If richer in discriminating, then poorer in social harmony
  - —*Unconscious*
    - Ex: If richer in kinesics and proxemics, then poorer in verbal skills, relatively speaking.

Notes: These examples are solely illustrative (not exhaustive), and some of the items can be reclassified somewhere else. Nor are they always mutually exclusive. Since they are generalities, exceptions are expected. And the comparison is relative, not absolute.
Source: From *BCPC*

Table 1.24. The Theoretical Debate on Nature vs. Nurture (Part I)

- **The Environmental Approach**
  —*Thesis*: It focuses, relatively speaking, more on the environment (culture and society) in explaining the achievement gap among individuals and for that matter, countries or regions, when contrasted with the natural factors.
  —*Discourse*: Examples include Jose Ortega y Gasset ("Man has no nature; what he has is history"), Ashley Montagu ("Man is man because he has no instincts, because everything he is and has become he has learned from his culture, from the man-made part of the environment, from other human beings"), Stephen Jay Gould ("[The] brain [is] capable of a full range of behaviors and predisposed to none"), and Jesse Jackson (who blames white racism for the failure of blacks to close the achievement gap between whites and blacks in America). The works on dependency theory in international political economy (with a Marxian influence) and on the Protestant work ethic (by Max Weber) also point to this environmental direction.

- **The Genetic Approach**
  —*Thesis*: It focuses instead, relatively speaking again, on hereditory factors (e.g., genes and evolution) in explaining the achievement gap among individuals and for that matter, countries or regions, when contrasted with the envrionmental factors.
  —*Discourse*: Examples are Hans Eysenck and William Sheldon (in constitutional psychology), Konrad Lorenz (in his work on innate aggressive human nature), Gary Marcus (on the complexities of human thought by a tiny number of genes) and Robert Plomin, together with Michael Owen and Peter McGuffin (on the genetic basis of complex human behaviors).

(continued on next page)

Table 1.24. The Theoretical Debate on Nature vs. Nurture (Part II)

• **The Compromise Approach**

—*Thesis*: It seeks the middle-of-the-road argument in regard to nature and nurture and regards all differences among individuals and groups as the result of the mixture of both nature and nurture, more or less equally.

—*Discourse*: Examples include C. Murray and R. Herrnstein ("It seems highly likely to us that both genes and environment have something to do with this issue") and Dan Dennett ("Surely 'everyone knows' that the nature-nurture debate was resolved long ago, and neither side wins since everything – is – a – mixture – of – both – and - it's – all – very -complicated...."

• **The Transcendent Approach**

—*Thesis*: It goes beyond both nature and nurture (without, however, committing the compromise fallacy) in showing their closely intertwined interactions in producing the behavioral differences as often seen in individual human endeavors on the micro scale, and for that matter, in country (or regional) endeavors on the macro one—in the context of my five theses, namely, (a) the compromise fallacy, (b) no oppression without self-oppression, (c) no success without failure, (d) the factor of randomness, and (e) the post-human vision, to be elaborated in Chapter Six.

—*Discourse*: Peter Baofu proposed this approach on the basis of his "theory of contrastive advantages" (as an original theoretical contribution to the debate, which was first proposed and analyzed in *The Future of Capitalism and Democracy*). In the end, the human genes will not last, to be eventually superseded by post-human life forms, so the debate between genes and memes has obscured something profoundly important about the future that the world has never known. And the debate is also misleading and faulty in its dichotomy.

Source: From *BNN*. See the book for citations and details.

Table 1.25. Physical Challenges to Hyper-Spatial Consciousness

- **The Understanding of a Higher-Dimensional World of Space-Time**
  —Ex: 4 for traditional aspects of space-time (e.g., length, width, breadth and time) plus 6 more new dimensions in theory of hyper-space, with profound implications for practical applications to new forms of consciousness.

- **The Mastering of Dark Matter and Dark Energy**
  —Ex: "ordinary matter" (e.g., atoms, molecules) as a mere 4.4% of the universe, with 23% made of "cold dark matter" and the rest (about 73%) of mysterious "dark energy," with fundamental significance to questions about the limit of the speed of energy (or info), the availability of energy for use, and the nature of space-time, just to cite some examples.

- **The Exploration of Multiverses**
  —Ex: theoretical speculation of other universes (e.g., "baby universes," "gateways" in black holes, "wave function of the universe," "many worlds," "brane worlds"), with potentially seminary discoveries of different physical laws in relation to matter-energy and space-time, and vital differences to the future of post-human conquest of other universes (for the emergence of new forms of consciousness).

Notes: These examples are solely illustrative (not exhaustive), and some of the items can be reclassified somewhere else. Nor are they always mutually exclusive. Since they are generalities, exceptions are expected. The point here is to give a rough picture of the evolution of consciousness to the hyper-spatial consciousness and others totally unknown to current earthlings. As a note of clarification, it makes no difference to my argument as to whether or not the hyper-spatial consciousness may emerge before, during, and after floating consciousness.
Source: From *Table 4.5* of *FPHC*

Table 1.26. The Theory of Floating Consciousness (Part I)

- **At the Micro-Physical Level**
  —Ex: intelligent life without the human physical-chemical system

- **At the Chemical Level**
  —Ex: space radiation and toxins

- **At the Bio-Psychological Level**
  —Ex: exo-biological evolution in deep space
  —Ex: genetic engineering of new beings

- **At the Institutional Level**
  —Ex: post-capitalism
  —Ex: post-democracy

- **At the Organizational Level**
  —Ex: less legal-formalistic routines

- **At the Structural Level**
  —Ex: alien forms of violence

- **At the Cultural Level**
  —Ex: transcending freedom
  —Ex: transcending equality

(continued on next page)

Table 1.26. The Theory of Floating Consciousness (Part II)

• **At the Cosmological Level**
—Ex: parallel universes
—Ex: pocket universes

• **At the Systemic Level**
—Ex: space habitats (in zero-gravity)

Notes: Each example draws from the works of different scholars in the field. For instance, at the cosmological level, the idea of parallel universes is from the theoretical speculation in quantum cosmology by Stephen Hawking and others, while the one of pocket universes comes from the theoretical work of Allan Guth at MIT. And at the institutional level, I proposed post-capitalism and post-democracy in *FCD* (and later, from *BDPD* and *BCPC*). In addition, the examples are solely illustrative (not exhaustive), and some of the items can be reclassified somewhere else. Nor are they always mutually exclusive. Since they are generalities, exceptions are expected.
Sources: From *FPHC*—and, originally, from *FCD*

Table 1.27. The Potential of Unfolding Unconsciousness

- **Superior Senses**
  - —*Through space*
    - Ex: clair-sentience (in feeling)
    - Ex: clair-voyance (in seeing)
    - Ex: clair-audience (in hearing)
    - Ex: clair-austance (in tasting)
    - Ex: clair-alience (in smelling)
    - Ex: clair-cognizance (in knowing)
  - —*Through time*
    - Ex: pre-cognition (in knowing), pre-sentiment (in feeling)
    - Ex: retro-cognition (in knowing), retro-sentiment (in feeling)

- **Superior Contacts**
  - —*With living minds*
    - Ex: telepathy
  - —*With the dead*
    - Ex: mediumship
  - —*With other-living entities*
    - Ex: telekinesis

Notes: The categories and examples are solely illustrative (not exhaustive), and the comparison is relative (not absolute), nor are they necessarily mutually exclusive. And some can be easily re-classified elsewhere. As generalities, they allow exceptions.
Source: A summary of Ch.5 of *FPHU*

Table 1.28. The Future Exploration of Unfolding Unconsciousness

- **In the Context of Nature**
  - —Ex: the higher-dimensional space-time in hyperspace theory
  - —Ex: the particle-wave interactions in quantum mechanics
  - —Ex: the study of brain waves in electromagnetic theory

- **In the Context of the Mind**
  - —Ex: the unconscious fantasies in psychoanalysis
  - —Ex: the mind-altering drugs in biochemistry
  - —Ex: the manipulation of neural activity in neurobiology

- **In the Context of Culture**
  - —Ex: the correlation between anomalous experience and moral/religious/aesthetic interests in culture studies
  - —Ex: the role of myths and language in epistemology

- **In the Context of Society**
  - —Ex: different organizational agendas in anomalous research
  - —Ex: the scholarly divide on anomalous study
  - —Ex: interests and propaganda in institutioanl research
  - —Ex: the transformative power of technology in research on social systems
  - —Ex: the natural and non-natural selection of other worlds in exo-biology
  - —Ex: the role of the post-human conscious mind in qualitative demography

Notes: The examples in each category are solely illustrative (not exhaustive), and the comparison is relative (not absolute), nor are they necessarily mutually exclusive. And some can be easily re-classified elsewhere. As generalities, they allow exceptions.
Source: A summary of Chs.2-5 of *FPHU*, in conjunction with the rest of the book

Table 1.29. Creative Techniques and Traits

- **Creative Techniques**
  - —*Comprehensiveness*
    - Ex: Broadness of Scope
    - Ex: In-Depth Analysis
    - Ex: Multifaceted Taxonomy
    - Ex: Numerous Theories
  - —*Arrangement*
    - Ex: Separation (or Subtraction)
    - Ex: Combination (or Addition)
    - Ex: Replacement
    - Ex: Accommodation
    - Ex: Reversal
    - Ex: Stretching
  - —*Serendipity*
    - Ex: Play
    - Ex: Chance

- **Creative Traits**
  - —*Openness / Risk*
    - Ex: Ability to welcome new ideas or to do new things, with risk
  - —*Discipline*
    - Ex: Ability to sacrifice whatever it takes to succeed
  - —*Resilience / Confidence*
    - Ex: Ability to take failures to mind, not to heart
  - —*Trust*
    - Ex: Ability to cooperate with others for team work, if necessary

Notes: The examples in the categories are solely illustrative (not exhaustive), and the comparison is relative (not absolute), nor are they necessarily mutually exclusive. And some can be easily re-classified elsewhere. As generalities, they allow exceptions.
Source: From *Sec.4.2* of *FPHCT*. For more details, also read the rest of the book.

Table 1.30. The Desirability of Creativity, and Its Dark Sides (Part I)

- **In Relation to Instrumental Rationality**
  —*Desirability*
  - Ex: For the sake of efficiency and effectiveness in this capitalist era of our time.

  —*Undesirability*
  - Ex: What Max Weber (1930) called the "iron cage" of capitalism, where live the "sensualists without heart, specialists without spirit"—or something which the Frankfurt School has forcefully asked us to be freed from.

- **In Relation to Substantive Rationality**
  —*Desirability*
  - Ex: For the sake of God, the King, Motherland, or other comparable ideals.

  —*Undesirability*
  - Ex: Domination and oppression of various forms—something which the moderns had struggled to free themselves from in the first place, since the dawn of modernity.

- **In Relation to Autonomous Rationality**
  —*Desirability*
  - Ex: For the sake of itself, the autonomy of creative endeavor.

  —*Undesirability*
  - Ex: The decadence of its own degeneration (e.g., the donwsides of postmodernism in our postmodern times, or what Nietzsche once called the unbearable "unreality" and "falseness" of the autonomous artist's "innermost existence"—and, in other cases, the painful suffering from different mental illnesses for those highly creative individuals).

(continued on next page)

Table 1.30. The Desirability of Creativity, and Its Dark Sides (Part II)

Notes: The examples in the categories are solely illustrative (not exhaustive), and the comparison is relative (not absolute), nor are they necessarily mutually exclusive. And some can be easily re-classified elsewhere. As generalities, they allow exceptions.
Also, I already went to great lenghts to explain the desirability and its dark sides of all these three rationalities (although there may be others too) in the two volumes of *FHC*—and, for that matter, *FCD*.
Source: From *Sec.4.9* of *FPHCT*. For more details, also read the rest of the book.

Table 1.31. Posthuman-Ism, Post-Humanism, and Trans-Humanism

• **Post-Humanism**

—The neologism "post-human" used in my books should *not* be confused with another term which looks similar but has a totally different meaning in the literature of postmodernism, namely, "post-humanism"—which constitutes a critique of "humanism" as tradionally understood (especially, though not exclusively, in relation to the idea of progress in science and reason in the Enlightenment project). (WK 2008)

—My works reject the project of "postmodernism" and propose the future world of what I orignally called "after-postmodernity" in *FHC* and *FCD*, for instance.

• **Trans-Humanism**

—Also, the neologism "post-human" used in my books should *not* be confused with a similar term which is used to champion the ideology of technology for the fturue co-existence between humans and cyborgs in "trans-humanism." (WK 2008a)

—Instead, my term "post-human" in relation to "posthuman-ism" also rejects "trans-humanism" (especially, though not exclusively, in relation to the promises of technology) and refers to something else altogether, that is, the future extinction of humans and its post-human successors in deep space and beyond unto multiverses.

—Chapter Two of my book on ethics (*BEPE*) provides a more comprehensive critique of trans-humanism.

• **Posthuman-Ism**

—With these two clarifications in mind, the "post-humans" (as envisioned in my books) can take different forms, and I proposed, in my different books, some of them, such as "unfolding unconsciousness," "floating consciousness," "hyper-spatial consciousness," "thinking machines," "thinking robots," "genetically altered superior beings," "cyborgs," and others (as already analyzed in my previous works).

—They will evolve in conjunction with other visions of mine in relation to nature, society, and culture.

Sources: From *Sec.1.6* of *FPHE* (and also *BEPE*). For more details, also read the rest of the books (and other books of mine).

Table 1.32. Three Great Future Transformations of the Martial Body (Part I)

- **Virtual Battle**
  —Ex: virtual fight
  —Ex: virtual memory

- **The Hyper-Martial Body**
  —*In relation to the physical dimension*
  - Ex: striking (e.g., punching, kicking, trapping, acupressure-striking, and so on in an amazing way)
  - Ex: grapping (e.g., throwing, pinning, joint-locking, and so on in an amazing way)
  - Ex: running and walking (e.g., on different surfaces)
  - Ex: jumping (e.g., through walls, trees, etc.)
  - Ex: flying (e.g., through space)
  - Ex: enduring pain (e.g., absorbing punches, kicks, and so on in an amazing way)
  - Ex: using extremely advanced hi-tech weapons
  - Ex: healing (e.g., with special energy, etc.)
  - Ex: entering (e.g., into different dimensions of space)
  - Ex: sensing (e.g., in extraordinary ways through space and time, etc.)
  - Ex: wearing hi-tech suits for defensive and offensive purposes (e.g., like a hi-tech armor)

  —*In relation to the mental dimension*
  - Ex: the ability to relax the martial body in a way that current humans cannot.
  - Ex: the ability to concentrate the martial mind in a way that current humans are not accustomed to.
  - Ex: the ability to breathe and be timely in preparing the martial body for fighting in a way that current humans are not good at.

- **The Post-Martial Floating Mind**
  —Ex: the mind without the human body
  —Ex: the quest for spirituality beyond martial arts

(continued on next page)

Table 1.32. Three Great Future Transformations of the Martial Body (Part II)

Notes: The examples in the categories are solely illustrative (not exhaustive), and the comparison is relative (not absolute), nor are they necessarily mutually exclusive. And some can be easily re-classified elsewhere. As generalities, they allow exceptions.
Source: From *Sec. 2.5.1* of *FPHMA*. See text for citations.

Table 1.33. Three Great Future Transformations of the Sexual Body

- **Virtual Pleasure**
  —Ex: virtual Sex
  —Ex: virtual Recall

- **The Hyper-Sexual Body**
  —*In relation to the physical dimension*
  - Ex: the ability to perform differenet sexual positions without the various physical limitations that humans currently have.
  - Ex: the ability to produce unusual amount of sexual energy to endure in sexual acts in a way that humans currently cannot.
  - Ex: the ability to engage in multiple sexual experiences comparable to (but different from) non-human sexuality (e.g., hermaphrodite, monoecious, sex-switching, and many other types) that current humans cannot.

  —*In relation to the mental dimension*
  - Ex: the ability to relax the sexual body in a way that current humans are not accustomed to.
  - Ex: the ability to concentrate the sexual mind in a way that current humans are not good at.
  - Ex: the ability to breathe and be patient in preparing the sexual body for sexuality in a way that current humans are not able to.

- **The Post-Sexual Floating Mind**
  —Ex: the mind without the human body
  —Ex: the quest for spirituality beyond sexuality

Notes: The examples in the categories are solely illustrative (not exhaustive), and the comparison is relative (not absolute), nor are they necessarily mutually exclusive. And some can be easily re-classified elsewhere. As generalities, they allow exceptions.
Source: From *Sec. 3.4.2* of *FPHS*. See text for more info.

Table 1.34. The Trinity of Pre-Modernity

- **Pre-Free-Spirited Pre-Modernity (Pre-Modernism) and Its Internal Split**
  —Competing worldviews and values both within and between linear centric (e.g., Islamic, Christian, Judaic, Imperial Roman) and cyclical-centric (e.g., Confucian, Taoist, Hindu, and Buddhist) orientations
  —Compare modernism with pre-modernism here in relation to the seven dimensions of human existence like the true and the holy (e.g., different versions of epistemic dogmas and religious superstitions), the everyday and the technological (e.g.,different versions of non-technophilism and non-consumerism), the beautiful/sublime (e.g., different versions of aesthetic non-autonomy), and the good and the just (e.g., different versions of moral particularism).

- **Pre-Capitalist Pre-Modernity (Pre-Modernization) and Its Own Discontents**
  —Competing versions of societal arrangements (e.g., feudalism, monarchism, and the holy order)

- **Hegemonic Pre-Modernity and Its Countervailing Forces**
  —Different power centers and their enemies (e.g., the Roman Empire and the "barbarian hordes," the "Holy Crusades" and the Muslims, the Middle Kingdom and the invading tribes, different social castes in India, and warring Greek city-states)

Notes: The examples in each category are solely illustrative (not exhaustive) nor necessarily mutually exclusive, and the comparison is relative (not absolute). As generalities, they allow exceptions. Also, it does not matter what the "base" era is in the analysis of any trinity. And in the present context, the "base" era is modernity (for instance, with its "free-spirited modernity" and the other two parts). So, for pre-modernity, the trinity takes the form of, say, "pre-free-spirited pre-modernity," together with the other two parts.
Sources: From Ch.2 of *BCIV* and also the 2 volumes of *FHC*

Table 1.35. The Trinity of Modernity (Part I)

- **Free-Spirited Modernity (Modernism) and Its Internal Split**

  —*On the True and the Holy*
  - The freedom from the dogmas of the past to the better understanding of, and union with, the world and self (Ch.3 of *FHC*)
  - Alternative discourses: about the true (e.g., anti-science discourses) and the holy (non-mainstream theologies) (Ch.3 of *FHC*)

  —*On the Technological and the Everyday*
  - The freedom from life harshness to the higher technophilic, consumeristic lifeform (Ch.2 of *FHC*)
  - Alternative discourses: about the everyday (e.g., transcendental mindsets) and the technological (e.g., Arcadianism) (Ch.2 of *FHC*)

  —*On the Good and the Just*
  - The freedom from the theo-aristocratic tyranny to the moral universality for a just society (Ch.5 of *FHC*)
  - Alternative discourses: about the just (e.g., Communism, Anarchism) and the good (e.g., Nazism/Fascism, and Zarathustrianism) (Chs.5-6 of *FHC*)

  —*On the Beautiful and the Sublime*
  - The freedom from the external distortion of aesthetic pleasure to the boundless infinity of totality in artistic autonomy (Ch.4 of *FHC*)
  - Alternative discourses: about the beautiful/sublime (e.g., kitsch and historical avant-gardism) (Ch.4 of *FHC*)

- **Capitalist Modernity (Modernization) and Its Own Discontents**

  —*During the Industrial Revolution*
  - Ex: Marx on the institution of inequality (Ch.1 of *FHC*)

  —*During the Modern Rational-Instrumental Epoch*
  - Ex: Weber on the politics of soft liberal institutions (Ch.5 of *FHC*)

  —*During the Great Depression*
  - Ex: Keynes on the myth of the free market (Chs.1-3 of *FHC*)

  —*During the Cold War*
  - Ex: Lasch on the narcissistic culture industry (Chs.2-3 of *FHC*)

(continued on next page)

Table 1.35. The Trinity of Modernity (Part II)

- **Hegemonic Modernity and Its Countervailing Forces**
  —*The Legacies of Colonialism and Imperialism*
    - Ex: European colonization of most of the modern world (Ch.1 of *FHC*)

  —*The Struggle for Decolonialization*
    - Ex: The countervailing forces of resentment, rechantment, and regionalism (Chs.1 & 6 of *FHC*)

Notes: The examples in each category are solely illustrative (not exhaustive) nor necessarily mutually exclusive, and the comparison is relative (not absolute). As generalities, they allow exceptions.
Sources: From the 2 volumes of *FHC*—and also from *FCD*

Table 1.36. The Trinity of Post-Modernity

- **Free-Spirited Postmodernity (Postmodernism) and Its Internal Split**
  —*On the True and the Holy*
    - Postmodern performative turn for knowing and its enemies (Ch.3 of *FHC*)
    - Postmodern comparative theology and its opponents (Ch.3 of *FHC*)

  —*On the Technological and the Everyday*
    - Postmodern corporate technological mindset and its adversaries (Ch.2 of *FHC*)
    - Postmodern postmaterialism and its critics (Ch.2 of *FHC*)

  —*On the Good and the Just*
    - Postmodern politics of difference and its foes (Ch.5 of *FHC*)

  —*On the Beautiful and the Sublime*
    - Postmodern deconstruction and its dissenters (Ch.4 of *FHC*)

- **Capitalist Postmodernity (Postmodernization) and Its Own Discontents**
  —*During the Post-Cold War and Beyond*
    - Ex: post-Fordism and its shortcomings (Ch.6 of *FHC*; Chs.6-7 of *FCD*)

- **Hegemonic Postmodernity and Its Countervailing Forces**
  —*The Debate on the Global Village*
    - Ex: uni-civilizationalism vs. multi-civilizationalism (Ch.6 of *FHC*)

  —*The Resistance Movement*
    - Ex: rechantment and the politics of civilizational claims (e.g., Islamic, Confucian and other ethos in relation to the Same) (Ch.6 of *FHC*; Ch.10 of *FCD*)
    - Ex: resentment and the politics of resurgence (e.g., the rising Chinese superpower, the growing EU, and other players in relation to the U.S. and her allies) (Ch.6 of *FHC*; Ch.8 of *FCD*)
    - Ex: regionalism and the politics of inequality (e.g., trans- or international blocs, the North-South divide, NGO's) (Ch.6 of *FHC*; Ch.5 of *FCD*)

Notes: The examples in each category are solely illustrative (not exhaustive) nor necessarily mutually exclusive, and the comparison is relative (not absolute). As generalities, they allow exceptions.
Sources: From *FCD* and the 2 volumes of *FHC*

Table 1.37. The Trinity of After-Postmodernity

- **Free-Spirited After-Postmodernity (After-Postmodernism) and Its Internal Split**
  —The discourse of naked contingency (Ch.10 of *FCD*; Ch.4 of *FPHC*)

- **Post-Capitalist After-Postmodernity (After-Postmodernization) and Its Own Discontents**
  —Different versions of post-capitalism and post-democracy, and their enemies (Ch.10 of *FCD*; Chs.3-4 of *FPHC*)

- **Hegemonic After-Postmodernity and Its Countervailing Forces**
  —The Cyclical Progression of Hegemony in Multiverses (Chs.9-10 of *FCD*; Ch.4 of *FPHC*)

Notes: The examples in each category are solely illustrative (not exhaustive) nor necessarily mutually exclusive, and the comparison is relative (not absolute). As generalities, they allow exceptions.
Sources: From *FCD* and also *FHC*

• PART TWO •

Joking

CHAPTER 2
JOKING AND ITS DOUBLE FACES

> In every wit there is something of a poet.
> —Henri Bergson (WK 2010a)

The Benignity of Joking

The nature of humor involves both joking (from its giving end) and laughing (from its receiving end)—as already discussed in *Sec. 1.2.*

This close relationship between joking and laughing in humor is true, even when a joke can result in having "fallen flat" and when laughing can exist outside humor (like the situations when one is tickled and, alternatively, playful, for instance).

With this note of caution in mind—any study of humor requires an examination of both joking and laughing, as one cannot be completely separated from the other.

Thus, this book offers a dialectic treatment of joking and laughing in that, if joking has its benignity, it has its malignity too—just as, if laughing has its joy, it likewise has its sorrow.

The inquiry concernng joking is the subject matter of this chapter (Chapter Two), whereas that of laughing will be addressed in the next chapter (Chapter Three).

Because this close relationship between joking and laughing poses a scholarly challenge here, in that one cannot analyze joking separately from that of laughing—an important point to remember here is that the issues concerning joking in this chapter (Chapter Two) and laughing in the next chapter (Chapter Three) often overlap, as each issue on one can be relevant to the other too.

With this qualification in mind—a good way to explore joking and its double faces is by way of the evaluation of the extent to which it (joking) is in fact both possible and desirabe.

This chapter thus accepts the challenging task to provide a comprehensive analysis of joking in the context of humor from the four perspectives of the mind, nature, society, and culture (in accordance to my sophisticated methodological holism, as explained in *Sec. 1.7*).

In this light, this chapter is organized in four main sections, in relation to (2.2) joking and the mind, (2.3) joking and nature, (2.4) joking and society, and (2.5) joking and culture—to be addressed hereafter, in that order (and summarized in *Table 2.1*).

Joking and the Mind

Joking, when explored from the perspective of the mind, can reveal something intriguing about its possibility and desirability, and this can be shown by way of two case studies, namely, (2.2.1) joking, the mind, and the psychology of jokes and (2.2.2) joking, black comedy, and the question about human nature—to be addressed in what follows, in that order.

Joking, the Mind, and the Psychology of Jokes

Joking has much to say about the mind, and the psychology of jokes precisely tries to help us understand its inner working, in that the mind is not always about being serious but can have its playful moments too.

Over the centuries, different scholars have tried to show us the playful nature of the mind by addressing the issue of joking. Consider four major cases below, for illustration.

The Case about Transforming a Tense Expectation into Nothing

Immanuel Kant, for example, in *Critique of Judgement* (1790), argued that "[l]aughter is an effect [of joking] that arises if a tense expectation [in a joke] is transformed into nothing" and that he offered his analysis by way of a "220-year old joke." (WK 2010a)

In this joke, Kant thus wrote: "An Englishman at an Indian's table in Surat saw a bottle of ale being opened, and all the beer, turned to froth, rushed out. The Indian, by repeated exclamations, showed his great amazement—Well, what's so amazing in that? asked the Englishman—Oh, but I'm not amazed at its coming out, replied the Indian, but how you managed to get it all in—This makes us laugh, and it gives us a hearty pleasure. This is not because, say, we think we are smarter than this ignorant man, nor are we laughing at anything else here that it is our liking and that we noticed through our understanding. It is rather that we had a tense expectation that suddenly vanished." (WK 2010a)

But, for the critics, the problem with this claim by Kant is that many jokes do not have anything to do with transforming a tense expectation into nothing, as already shown in the opposing views (in *Sec. 1.3*) and others to be introduced below (and in the rest of the book).

The Case about Putting Stories into Familiar Patterns

Edward de Bono, for another, in *The Mechanism of the Mind* (1990) and *I am Right, You are Wrong* (1991), offered his different take on the nature of joking in relation to the mind, in that "the mind is a pattern-matching machine, and that it works by recognising stories and behaviour and putting them into familiar patterns." (WK 2010a)

For de Bono, "[w]hen a familiar connection is disrupted and an alternative unexpected new link is made in the brain via a different route than expected, then laughter occurs as the new connection is made. This theory explains a lot about jokes. For example":

- "Why jokes are only funny the first time they are told: once they are told the pattern is already there, so there can be no new connections, and so no laughter."
- "Why jokes have an elaborate and often repetitive set up: The repetition establishes the familiar pattern in the brain. A common method used in jokes is to tell almost the same story twice and then deliver the punch line the third time the story is told. The first two tellings of the story evoke a familiar pattern in the brain, thus priming the brain for the punch line."
- "Why jokes often rely on stereotypes: the use of a stereotype links to familiar expected behaviour, thus saving time in the set-up."
- "Why jokes are variants on well-known stories (e.g. the genie and a lamp and a man walks into a bar): This again saves time in the set up and establishes a familiar pattern."

Surely, these examples are illustrative, not exhaustive.

Even then, however, for the critics, the problems with this claim by de Bono are two-fold.

Firstly, the focus on pattern-making and its deviance from it in joking only tells us about the creativeness in joking but not about what makes a joke funny in the first place. After all, not all forms of creativity are funny.

And secondly, the focus on pattern-making also misses a lot of other things about the nature of humor, as already shown in the opposing views (in *Sec. 1.3*) and others to be introduced below (and in the rest of the book).

The Case about Abandoning Rational Thought for Creativity

Arthur Koestler, for still another, in *The Act of Creation* (1964), claimed that "humans are most creative when rational thought is abandoned during dreams and trances." (WK 2010e)

For Koestler, "all creatures have the capacity for creative activity, frequently suppressed by the automatic routines of thought and behavior that dominate their lives. Koestler's basic idea is that the creative act is a 'bisociation' (not mere association) which happens, if two (or more) apparently incompatible frames of thought ('matrices') are brought together by an ingenious mind." (WK 2010e)

In the case of "jokes and humour, these conceptual systems are reversed, in the arts and in ritual, they are juxtaposed, in science, they are fused into a new larger synthesis. This corresponds to a 'self-assertive' tendency in humour and a 'self-transcending' tendency in art, while in science both tendencies are balanced." (WK 2010e; L. Eiseley 1964; J. Comerford 2005; M. Turner 2006)

But, for the critics, the problem with this claim by Koestler is that the focus on treating jokes as abandoning rational thought for creativity does not really say much about the different techniques and viewpoints about humor itself, as already shown in the opposing views (in *Sec. 1.3*) and others to be introduced below (and in the rest of the book).

The Case about Expressing Forbidden Thoughts in a Safe Way

And Sigmund Freud, in *Jokes and Their Relation to The Unconscious* (1960) as well as in "Humor" (1928), interpreted jokes in a different way, in that they "let…in forbidden thoughts and feelings which society suppresses into the conscious mind. Thus, there is an interaction between the unconscious and the conscious thoughts." (WK 2010f; A. Smuts 2006)

More specifically, "jokes happen when the conscious allows forbidden thoughts which society suppresses.The superego allows the ego to generate humor. A benevolent superego allows a light and comforting type of humor while a harsh superego creates a biting and sarcastic type of humor. A very harsh superego suppresses humor all together." (WK 2010f; G. Matte 2001; S. Freud 1928 & 1960)

In the process, Freud (1960) distinguished "humor in three particular forms," namely, (a) "joke," (b), "mimetic," and (c) "comic." (WK 2010f)

The first form of humor, "joke," refers to "letting in forbidden thoughts and feelings which society suppresses into the conscious mind." (WK 2010f; S. Freud 1928 & 1960)

The second form of humor, "mimetic," refers to "a process involving two different representations of the body in our mind. For example, [in] the phrase 'He has his heart in the right place',...[t]he heart has two representations, one which is anatomical, while the other is a metaphorical way of being at peace with one self." (WK 2010f; G. Matte 2001; S. Freud 1928 & 1960)

And the third form of humor, "comic," refers to the application of "two different ideational methods" to "one and the same act of ideation.... William Shakespeare's *Falstaff* would be Freud's best example of the 'comic,' generating laughter by utilizing once repressed inhibition. An upset American says at Sunday School: '(Roosevelt) is my Shepherd; I am in want. He makes me to lie down on park benches; he leads me in the paths of destruction for His party's sake.'" (WK 2010f; J. Kincaid 2001; G. Matte 2001; J. Martin 2006)

But, for the critics, the problems with this claim by Freud are two-fold.

Firstly, as Alexander Chislenko (2010) once thus rebuked the theory of social prohibitions, "[i]n many cases, people are ready to openly express more aggression, sexuality, and disagreement with authorities that they are suggesting in the jokes, so their jokes can hardly be viewed as a suppressed revolt. Peaceful people and innocent children find lots of things funny; children find things funny (such as peek-a-boo) that adults don't and wouldn't teach them; there is hardly any evidence that people with strongly suppressed anger or sexuality have more interest in jokes than people who do not have these interests, or feel free to express them."

And secondly, "[m]odern critics debate that Freud's division [of humor in three different forms] is artificial and not very clear. According to Altman (2006), these three different types of humor are divided more in a semantically way than in a functional one." (WK 2010f; J. Newirth 2006)

Favoring No One

Yet, these criticisms of the four illustrative cases about joking, the mind, and the psychology of jokes do not mean to reject their validity completely but to help us learn from the different opposing sides of the debate, such that the possibility and desirability of joking (from the perspective of the mind with joking, the mind, and the psychology of jokes as a case study here) are not to the extent that the respective defenders would like us to believe.

More importantly, the analysis of joking, the mind, and the psychology of jokes can teach us something equally revealing about the ontological principles in existential dialectics, and good examples include the formalness-informalness principle, the absoluteness-relativeness principle, the predictability-unpredictability principle, the explicability-inexplicability principle, the preciseness-vagueness principle, the simpleness-complicatedness principle, the openness-hiddenness principle, the denseness-emptiness principle, the change-constancy principle, the slowness-quickness principle, the expansion-contraction principle, the convention-novelty principle, the evolution-transformation principle, the symmetry-asymmetry principle, the softness-hardness principle, the seriousness-playfulness principle, the regression-progression principle, and the same-difference principle.

For instance, in relation to the formalness-informalness principle, if there is formalness (e.g., the formal requirement of consistency in a system of ideas, like rational thought in science), there is informalness (e.g., the non-formal allowance of non-rational thought in humor, as shown by Arthur Koestler's work). And the reverse direction also holds true.

In relation to the absoluteness-relativeness principle, if there is absoluteness (e.g., the absolute view by Freud that jokes "let…in forbidden thoughts and feelings which society suppresses into the conscious mind"), there is relativeness (e.g., what is true for Freud in regard to social prohibitions in jokes is not so for Chislenko, who argued that "people are ready to openly express more aggression, sexuality, and disagreement with authorities"). And the reverse direction also holds true.

In relation to the predictability-unpredictability principle, if there is predictability (e.g., the predictable tendency, by those who accept de Bono's view about humor, to show a joke as "an alternative unexpected new link…in the brain via a different route than expected" from a conventional "familiar connection"), there is unpredictabiltiy (e.g., the more difficult task to predict exactly when a given "new link" will necessarily produce a laughter, since not all forms of creativity in new links are humorous). And the reverse direction also holds true.

In relation to the explicability-inexplicability principle, if there is explicability (e.g., the explanation by Kant that a joke "arises if a tense expectation [in a joke] is transformed into nothing"), there is inexplicability (e.g., the lack of sufficient explanation by Kant of why many jokes do not have anything to do with transforming a tense expectation into nothing, as already shown in the opposing views in Ch.1 and others in the rest of the book). And the reverse direction also holds true.

In relation to the preciseness-vagueness principle, if there is preciseness (e.g., the precise identification of humor in terms of three different forms by Freud), there is vagueness (e.g., the vagueness in the three forms of humor as identified by Freud, as the critics pointed out that they are "artificial and not very clear," and for Altman, "these three different types of humor are divided more in a semantically way than in a functional one"). And the reverse direction also holds true.

In relation to the simpleness-complicatedness principle, if there is simpleness (e.g., the relatively simple analysis of jokes in the context of the psychology of jokes), there is complicatedness (e.g., the relatively more complicated analysis of jokes in the context of the psychology of jokes, by challenging the claims and assumptions, as shown in the criticisms by the critics). And the reverse direction also holds true.

In relation to the openness-hiddenness principle, if there is openness (e.g., the open exploration of the relationships "between the unconscious and the conscious thoughts" in jokes by Freud), there is hiddenness (e.g., the hidden bias in Freud's psychoanalysis of jokes, in focusing too much on sexuality and aggression, as pointed out by Chislenko). And the reverse direction also holds true.

In relation to the denseness-emptiness principle, if there is denseness (e.g., the relatively denser concentration of individuals who accept the Freudian interpretation of jokes to focus on sexuality and aggression), there is emptiness (e.g., the relatively less dense, or more empty, concentration of individuals who accept the critique of Freud by Chislenko to focus on sexuality and aggression in their interpretation of jokes). And the reverse direction also holds true.

In relation to the change-constancy principle, if there is change (e.g., the ever new links to disrupt the familiar connections in the brain, when successful jokes are made, according to de Bono), there is constancy (e.g., the ever constant nature of the mind as "a pattern-matching machine," even when new jokes are made over time). And the reverse direction also holds true.

In relation to the slowness-quickness principle, if there is slowness (e.g., the relatively slower speed for a very humorous person to follow rational thoughts in his daily life), there is quickness (e.g., the relatively quicker speed for a very humorous person to abandon rational thoughts for creative imagination in his daily life). And the reverse direction also holds true.

In relation to the expansion-contraction principle, if there is expansion (e.g., the relatively more developed ability of a person who likes to joke a lot to make good use of creative imagination), there is contraction (e.g., the relatively less developed ability of a person who likes to joke a lot to make good use of rational thoughts in science). And the reverse direction also holds true.

In relation to the convention-novelty principle, if there is convention (e.g., the conventional way of expressing things, as shown in the "familiar connections" in the brain, as shown in the work on jokes by de Bono), there is novelty (e.g., the alternatively novel challenge to the "familiar connections" by way of "alternative unexpected new links" in jokes). And the reverse direction also holds true.

In relation to the evolution-transformation principle, if there is evolution (e.g., the natural evolution of humans to be playful in the state of nature), there is transformation (e.g., the technical transformation of human ability to be playful with the invention of language to make elaborated jokes, as shown in the example by Kant). And the reverse direction also holds true.

In relation to the symmetry-asymmetry principle, if there is symmetry (e.g., the co-existence of different views about jokes in history), there is asymmetry (e.g., the popularity of the superiority theory about jokes in ancient Greece—but the acceptance of the theory of social prohibitions about jokes in modern times, especially among those in psychoanalysis). And the reverse direction also holds true.

In relation to the softness-hardness principle, if there is softness (e.g., "a benevolent superego allows a light and comforting type of humor"), there is hardness (e.g., "a very harsh superego suppresses humor all together"). And the reverse direction also holds true.

In relation to the seriousness-playfulness principle, if there is seriousness (e.g., the serious business of rational thoughts in science), there is playfulness (e.g., the playful nature of creative imagnation in humor). And the reverse direction also holds true.

In relation to the regression-progression principle, if there is regression (e.g., the regression made by the Freudian interpretation of jokes in fixating its understanding on sexuality and aggression), there is progression (e.g., the progress made by the Freudian interpretation of jokes in showing the interactions "between the unconscious and the conscious thoughts" in jokes). And the reverse direction also holds true.

And in relation to the same-difference principle, if there is similarity in outcome (e.g., the contribution to the molding and regulation of values and behaviors, regardless of whether this be done by way of humor or by way of rational thought), there is difference in outcome (e.g., the contribution to the molding and regulation of values and behaviors by way of rational thought for a more scientific-technical lifeworld—but the contribution to the molding and regulation of values and behaviors by way of humor for a more happy-go-lucky lifeworld). And the reverse direction also holds true.

Joking, Black Comedy, and the Question about Human Nature

Another way to evaluate the possibility and desirability of joking from the perspective of the mind has to do with joking, black comedy, and the question about human nature (with a summary in *Table 2.2*).

Black Humor vs. Black Comedy

The term "black humour" is "from the French *humour noir*" and refers to "a term coined by Surrealist theoretician André Breton in 1935, to designate the sub-genre of comedy and satire in which laughter arises from cynism and skepticism." (WK 2010g; N. Lezard 2009; EC 2010; FD 2010)

Breton himself edited "the *Anthology of Black Humour* (*Anthologie de l'humour noir*), a 1939 French anthology of 45 writers….In the United States, black comedy as a literary genre came to prominence in the 1950s and 1960s. A later English-language anthology edited by Bruce Jay Friedman, titled *Black Humor*, assembles many examples of the genre." (WK 2010g)

What is distinctive about "black humour is often a satire on the topic of death. Breton identified the originator of Black humour in Jonathan Swift, particularly in his pieces *Directions to Servants* (1731) *A Modest Proposal* (1929), *A Meditation on a Broom-Stick* (1710), and a few aphorisms." (WK 2010g; T. Leclair 1975)

Later, "the terms black comedy or dark comedy have been…derived as alternatives to Breton's term. In black humor, topics and events that are usually regarded as taboo, specifically those related to death, are treated in an unusually humorous or satirical manner while retaining their seriousness; the intent of black comedy, therefore, is often for the audience to experience both laughter and discomfort, sometimes simultaneously." (WK 2010g)

Themes in Black Comedy

Because of the tendency to address the issue of death, there is the word "black" (or "dark") in "black comedy" (or "black humor"), which "employs a form of humor that may be known as...'morbid humor.' The purpose of black humor is to make light of serious and often taboo subject matter, and some comedians use it as a tool for exploring vulgar issues, thus provoking discomfort and serious thought as well as amusement in their audience." (WK 2010g)

For the general public, "[p]opular themes of the genre include murder, suicide, mutilation, war, barbarism, drug abuse, terminal illness, domestic violence, insanity, nightmare, disease, racism, disability (both physical and mental), chauvinism, corruption, and crime. By contrast, blue comedy focuses more on crude topics, such as nudity, sex and bodily fluids." (WK 2010g)

But it must be stressed that "black comedy" is not the same as "obscene humor," because "black comedy is different from straightforward obscenity in that it is more subtle and does not necessarily have the explicit intention of offending people. In obscene humor, much of the humorous element comes from shock and revulsion, while black comedy might include an element of irony, or even fatalism." (WK 2010g)

For instance, "the archetypal black-comedy self-mutilation in English appears in the novel *Tristam Shandy*. Tristam, five years old at the time, starts to piss out of an open window for lack of a chamber pot. The sash falls and circumcises him; his family reacts with both chaotic action and philosophic digression." (WK 2010g)

In addition another popular theme in black comedy is "frustrated suicide. For example, in the play *Waiting for Godot*, a man takes off his belt to hang himself, and his trousers fall down." (WK 2010g)

Authors of Black Comedy

There is no lack of noticeable authors of black comedy. For instance, "Thomas Pynchon, Kurt Vonnegut, Warren Zevon, and Joseph Heller have written novels, poems, stories, plays and songs in which profound or horrific events were portrayed in a comic manner." (WK 2010g; EC 2010)

And comedians like "Lenny Bruce, George Carlin, Bill Hicks, Dylan Moran, Peter Cook, Jack Dee, Frankie Boyle, and the Monty Python team have also helped popularize the genre." (WK 2010g; FD 2010)

Black Comedy in Films

Nowadays, "black comedy is commonly used in dramatic or satirical films, retaining its serious tone. Black comedy is a prevalent theme of many cult films, television shows and video games." (WK 2010g)

For instance, "the 1964 Stanley Kubrick film *Dr. Strangelove* presents one of the best-known mainstream examples of black comedy. The subject of the film is nuclear warfare and the annihilation of life on Earth. Normally, dramas about nuclear war treat the subject with gravity and seriousness, creating suspense over the efforts to avoid a nuclear war, but *Dr. Strangelove* instead plays the subject for laughs. For example, in the film, the fail-safe procedures designed to prevent a nuclear war are precisely the systems that ensure that it will happen. Plotwise, Group Captain Mandrake serves as the only sane character in the film, while Major Kong fills the role of the hero striving for a harmful goal. Internet sensation, Salad Fingers relates to Black comedy." (WK 2010g; EC 2010)

The Debate about Human Nature

Because of the satire on the topic of death in black comedy (or black humor), which "makes light of so called dark or evil elements in human nature"—I would like to create a debate about human nature in regard to black comedy. (WK 2010k)

For instance, to what extent does black comedy (or black humor) appeal to the dark sides of human nature like destruction and violence, especially in relation to its satire on the topic of death (by way of cynicism and skepticism)?

(a) On the Dark Sides

On the negative side of the debate are those who argue for the existence of the dark sides of human nature.

Sigmund Freud (1966), for instance, argued that "men are not gentle creatures who want to be loved, and who at the most can defend themselves if they are attacked; they are, on the contrary, creatures among whose instinctual endowments is to be reckoned a powerful share of aggressiveness. As a result, their neighbor is for them…someone who tempts them to satisfy their aggressiveness on him, to exploit his capacity for work without compensation, to use him sexually without his consent, to seize his possessions, to humiliate him, to cause him pain, to torture and to kill him. *Homo homini lupus*." Therefore, for Freud, "[i]f you look at jokes, they are either about somebody getting hurt, or they have sexual connotations." (A. Chislenko 2010)

And Thomas Hobbes, for another, made a comparable point when he argued that humans are "nasty, brutish and short" in the state of nature, with "a war of every man, against every man." (T. Magstadt 1999:474-5)

(b) On the Bright Sides

On the affirmative side of the debate, however, are those who argue for the existence of the bright sides of human nature.

For instance, Confucius and Mencius argued that "humans are essentially good and, with the teaching of the right rules and duties, can contribute to a more harmonious society." (P. Baofu 2004: Ch.3)

And Jean-Jacques Rousseau (1984) in *A Discourse on Inequality* is on the same side, when he "criticized Hobbes for asserting that since man in the 'state of nature…has no idea of goodness, he must be naturally wicked; that he is vicious because he does not know virtue.' On the contrary, Rousseau holds that 'uncorrupted morals' prevail in the 'state of nature' and he especially praised the admirable moderation of the Caribbeans in expressing the sexual urge despite the fact that they live in a hot climate, which 'always seems to inflame the passions.'" (WK 2010h)

Of course, this romantic view by Rousseau also famously led his critics to criticize him as unrealistically defending "the idea of the noble savage," although "[t]he expression, 'the noble savage' was first used in 1672 by British poet John Dryden in his play *The Conquest of Granada*." (WK 2010h; T. Ellinson 2001)

Above the Fray

This introduction of the opposing views about the debate on human nature in the context of joking and black comedy does not mean to favor one side over the other but to teach us the different opposing sides of the debate, such that the possibility and desirability of joking (from the perspective of the mind with joking, black comedy, and the debate about human nature as a case study here) are not to the extent that the respective defenders would like us to believe.

In addition, this introduction to joking, black comedy, and the debate about human nature can reveal to us the relevancy of the ontological principles in existential dialectics, and good examples include the absoluteness-relativeness principle, the predictability-unpredictability principle, the explicability-inexplicability principle, the preciseness-vagueness principle, the simpleness-complicatedness principle, the openness-hiddenness principle, the denseness-emptiness principle, the change-constancy principle, the slowness-quickness principle, the expansion-contraction principle, the theory-praxis principle, the convention-novelty principle, the evolution-transformation principle, the symmetry-asymmetry principle, the softness-hardness principle, the seriousness-playfulness principle, the regression-progression principle, and the same-difference principle.

For instance, in relation to the absoluteness-relativeness principle, if there is absoluteness (e.g., the absolute dependence of "obscene humor" on "shock and revulsion" to be humorous), there is relativeness (e.g., what is obscene in obscene humor is not so in black humor, which is "more subtle and does not necessarily have the explicit intention of offending people"). And the reverse direction also holds true.

In relation to the predictability-unpredictability principle, if there is predictabillity (e.g., the predictable tendency of black comedy to deal wth the topic of death), there is unpredictability (e.g., the more difficult task to predict exactly to what extent a particular black comedy will end up producing discomfort, laughter, or both in the audience). And the reverse direction also holds true.

In relation to the explicability-inexplicability principle, if there is explicability (e.g., the explanation by black comedians that black comedy is not the same as obscene humor, because "it is more subtle and does not necessarily have the explicit intention of offending people"), there is inexplicability (e.g., the lack of sufficient explanation by black comedians of why black comedy cannot offend sensitive people, even if "it is more subtle and does not necessarily have the explicit intention of offending people"). And the reverse direction also holds true.

In relation to the preciseness-vagueness principle, if there is preciseness (e.g., the precise identification of the topic of death as the favorite satire in black comedy), there is vagueness (e.g., the vagueness in the identification of the topic of "death," since it can refer to different things to different people, like "murder, suicide, mutilation, war, barbarism, drug abuse, terminal illness, domestic violence, insanity, nightmare, disease, racism, disability..., chauvinism, corruption, and crime"). And the reverse direction also holds true.

In relation to the simpleness-complicatedness principle, if there is simpleness (e.g., the relatively simple analysis of black comedy in terms of its history, themes, authors, media outlets, etc.), there is complicatedness (e.g., the relatively more complicated analysis of black comedy by questioning its claims and assumptions, like its offensiveness to some people, the debate about the dark sides of human nature, etc., as pointed out by the critics). And the reverse direction also holds true.

In relation to the openness-hiddenness principle, if there is openness (e.g., the open exploration, in black comedy, of making "light of serious and often taboo subject matters"), there is hiddenness (e.g., the hidden bias in black comedy, because of its appeal to the dark sides of human nature, like the numerous destructive and violent issues in relation to the topic of death). And the reverse direction also holds true.

In relation to the denseness-emptiness principle, if there is denseness (e.g., the relatively denser concentration of the works by Jonathan Swift to deal with black comedy), there is emptiness (e.g., the relatively less dense, or more empty, concentration of the works by Confucius to deal with black comedy). And the reverse direction also holds true.

In relation to the change-constancy principle, if there is change (e.g., the changing nature of the sub-genre of comedy and satire, from being known as "black humor" to "black comedy," for instance), there is constancy (e.g., the ever constancy of the sub-genre of comedy and satire to focus on the topic of death, regardless of whether it is known as "black humor" or "black comedy"). And the reverse direction also holds true.

In relation to the slowness-quickness principle, if there is slowness (e.g., the relatively slower speed for people to get offended by "black humor"), there is quickness (e.g., the relatively faster speed for people to get offended by "obscene humor"). And the reverse direction also holds true.

In relation to the expansion-contraction principle, if there is expansion (e.g., the relatively more developed ability of black comedians to make good use of the satire on the topic of death), there is contraction (e.g., the relatively less developed ability of black comedians to present a serious scientific or academic discourse on the topic of death). And the reverse direction also holds true.

In relation to the theory-praxis principle, if there is theory (e.g., the theoretical construction, by the Surrealist theoretician André Breton in 1935, of the sub-genre of comedy known as black humor based on "cynism and skepticism"), there is praxis (e.g., the practical application of black humor to popular films later on). And the reverse direction also holds true.

In relation to the convention-novelty principle, if there is convention (e.g.,. the conventional wisdom on "black humor" based on the work by André Breton in 1935), there is novelty (e.g., the alternative novel challenge to black humor, by the later use of "black comedy" or "dark comedy…as alternatives to Breton's term" later on). And the reverse direction also holds true.

In relation to the evolution-transformation principle, if there is evolution (e.g., the natural evolution of humans to be playful in the state of nature), there is transformation (e.g., the technical transformation of human ability to be playful by the invention of "black comedy" to provide "the satire on the topic of death"). And the reverse direction also holds true.

In relation to the symmetry-asymmetry principle, if there is symmetry (e.g., the co-existence of different labels for the sub-genre of comedy based on "cynism and skepticism"), there is asymmetry (e.g., the popular use of the term "black humor" originated by Breton in the 1930's—but the more acceptance of the term "black comedy" later on, as an alternative to Breton's term). And the reverse direction also holds true.

In relation to the softness-hardness principle, if there is softeness (e.g., the production of "laughter" in black comedy), there is hardness (e.g., the production of "discomfort" in black comedy). And the reverse direction also holds true.

In relation to the seriousness-playfulness principle, if there is seriousness (e.g., the "serious" side in black comedy, when it addresses "taboo subject matters"), there is playfulness (e.g., the "funny" side in black comedy, when it makes light of "taboo subject matters"). And the reverse direction also holds true.

In relation to the regression-progression principle, if there is regression (e.g., the "discomfort" produced in black comedy), there is progression (e.g., the "laughter" produced in black comedy). And the reverse direction also holds true.

And in relation to the same-difference principle, if there is similarity in outcome (e.g., the contribution to the molding and control of beliefs and behaviors, regardless of whether this be done by way of black comedy or by way of scientific discourse), there is difference in outcome (e.g., the contribution to the molding and control of beliefs and behaviors by way of black comedy for a more cynical and skeptical worldview—but the contribution to the molding and control of beliefs and behaviors by way of scientific discourse for a more rational worldview). And the reverse direction also holds true.

Joking and Nature

Joking, when examined from the perspective of nature, can cast some further light on its possibility and desirability, and this can be done by way of a refreshiing case study—namely, joking, IFF, and the controversy about evolution.

Joking, IFF, and the Controversy about Evolution

J. A. Hewitt (2010), for instance, proposed what he called "the theory of humor as IFF," so as to provide an evolutionary theory of humor by comparing it with what is learned from military studies, namely, in relation to "the IFF systems used on aircraft (IFF = Identification Friend or Foe)."

As a background infomation, one of the serious problems that Darwin has with evolutionary theory is that it does not explain the existence of humor, because humor does not seem to have any survival value in evolution, other than being a by-product for courtship in "sexual selection" (which is not the same as "natural selection").

As already discussed in *Sec. 1.3*, Geoffrey Miller (2001) "contends that, from an evolutionary perspective, humor would have had no survival value to early humans living in the savannas of Africa. He proposes that cultural aspects like humor evolved by sexual selection. He argues that humor emerged as an indicator of other traits that were of survival value, such as human intelligence." (WK 2010c)

In so doing, "[b]y switching from a survival-centred to a courtship-centred view of evolution, he [Miller] attempts to show how we can understand the mysteries of mind." (WK 2010d)

By contrast, Hewitt addressed the evolution of humor in a different light, by showing how the larger environment becomes the battleground where different groups differentiate insiders from outsiders for their survival, and humor is precisely a good IFF system for group selection.

Eight Essential Points in the Theory of Humor as IFF

The theory of humor as IFF can be summarized in eight essential points, as shown below: (J. Hewitt 2010)

- "That 'incongruities in an input sensory data flow [as often found in jokes] can be used to identify parts in that data flow that are 'relevant' to the individual animal that is the receiver for that data flow."
- "The ability to detect relevance [in jokes] is a fitness enhancing skill and most animals have developed the ability to detect input data that is incongruous with their existing understanding [as often found in jokes]. This ability is manifested by such phenomena as the visual movement detectors found in almost all species. The necessary features of an incongruity detector are discussed and summarized as the I/R (Interpretation/Representation) model of learning and humor."
- "That advanced animals, especially while young, have come to enjoy incongruities [in jokes]. This enjoyment of incongruity [in jokes] will cause the young animal to focus on aspects of its surroundings that it does not presently understand and so help it to learn about its environment. Hence, young mammals enjoy play."

- "In humans, cognitive incongruity detection [in jokes] has become linked to laughter so that children laugh while playing. Such laughter is a submissive gesture which aids in social learning by ensuring transmission of knowledge down a social hierarchy and helps to synchronize group learning."
- "The coding properties of the joke/laughter interchange are found to be analogous to those of the IFF systems used on aircraft (IFF = Identification Friend or Foe). Hence humor appears to be an IFF system for humans in which a joke corresponds with the interrogation role of the aircraft IFF while laughter corresponds to its transducer response."
- "In bioepistemic evolution, all evolving systems are bounded—that is, all evolving creatures or cultural groups are, in some way, separated from competing evolving systems. This IFF interpretation sees humor functioning as a social boundary forming mechanism; humor is preceived as interrogating the membership of social groups and, in so doing, setting boundaries around them."
- "Further evidence for the IFF role of humor in real human societies is presented from the distribution of joking relationships formed by adolescent males in patrilineal societies."
- "The IFF interpretation of humor is an essentially group selective interpretation and supports the argument that humans have evolved as a group selected species. This viewpoint, that humans are a group seelcted species, presently seems to be unfashionable."

Of course, Hewitt elaborated these eight points in his work, not just listing them.

Humor in the Environment of IFF

What is most striking in the theory of humor as IFF (Identification Friend or Foe) is to compare humor as an IFF system (which Hewitt learned from military studies), as shown in the following table created by Hewitt (2010), in his own words:

	IFF	*Humor*
"Interrogation Signal"	"Initial interrogation is coded to be readable only by friends"	"Jokes are 'got' only within a shared social knowledge set or language."

"Response Signal"	"Positive response is broadcast."	"Positive response is broadcast as the sound of laughter."
	"Positive response is automatic and identifies friend."	"Response is automatic, to the extent that laughter is involuntary, and identifies friend."
	"Negative response identifies non-friend."	"Negative response identifies out-group."
"Linkage to Weapons"	"IFF is linked to weapons systems."	"Humor has aggressive modes."
"Linkage to Communications"	"Planes identified as friend take a place in the communications network and share information."	"Individuals who share humor take a place in the group hierarchy, are informed and listened to."
"Unidentified Targets"	"Planes identified as foe are excluded from the network and may be attacked."	"Individuals who do not share humor are excluded from groups and may be mocked, sneered at or attacked."

Of course, Hewitt (2010) also identified some differences between humor and IFF. For example, in IFF, "positive response is coded"; whereas, in humor, "positive response is not coded."

Problems with the Theory of Humor as IFF

However, for the critics, the theory of humor as IFF is controversial enough. Consider, for illustration, six major criticisms below.

Firstly, the theory of humor as IFF is too restrictive, in defining too many conditions to be met for a joke to take place, especially when the theory does not explain what it is supposed to.

For instance, whenever Hewitt had problems using his theory to explain some joking relationships, he offered restrictive conditions for jokes to be met in the first place. A good example concerns his description of "the relationship between adolescent males and their uncles," in that, in his own words, "a paternal uncle is an elder in a young male's patrilineal descent line. The two are of disparate age and social status and are linked both genetically and socially. Thus, they are unlikely to becomes foes. Therefore humor, as an IFF, need not query a paternal uncle's friend or foe status and a joking relationship will not form." (J. Hewitt 2010) But is this really true about the relationship between a male and a paternal uncle in regard to humor?

Secondly, the theory of humor as IFF is too counterproductive (or self-destructive) if put in practice, because it indulges in the orientation of group-think by insiders against outsiders. A society of humor with IFF has little chance to survive for long, because individuals are constantly put in a box of "friends" or "foes," in a "black" or "white" dichotomy.

Thirdly, the theory of humor as IFF is too metamphorical from military studies, without proving much of anything in reality, since a metaphor is not the same as a representation of reality. By comparison, Darwin provided a systematic analysis of his biological version of evolution with such underlying mechanisms like variation, mutation, inheritance, adaptation, and selection—but Hewitt provided no systematic analysis of any comparable underlying mechanisms for his evolutionary theory of humor as IFF. Therefore, one cannot help but wonder if Hewitt gets carried away by his military metaphor into self-deceivingly believing that humor works like a battleground between "friends" and "foes."

Fourthly, the theory of humor as IFF is too exclusive, in treating those who share a joke as friends and those who do not as foes. Contrary to what Hewitt believed, humor is not so serious (adversarial) in real life. Those who do not laugh at our jokes can be our good friends, just as there are people who are not capable of joking can be wonderful folks to share time with. Conversely, those who joke a lot do not necessarily make good friends, as they cannot be taken seriously when you need them.

Fifthly, the theory of humor as IFF is too narrow, in looking at humor solely from the vantage point of its social role for group selection. There can be many different roles for humor to play, as shown by different theories about humor (as presented in this book).

And sixthly, the theory of humor as IFF is too one-dimensional, without adequately considering other factors from the perspectives of the mind, nature, society, and culture, for instance (other than the focus on humor as IFF that Hewitt was so obessed with). For instance, although Hewit did say something about Darwin's evolutionary theory or about the impact of society and culture on an individual's ability to understand humor, the theory of humor as IFF only pays a lip service to the perspectives (in a reductionistic way), since its focus is on IFF.

A Lesson to Learn From

However, this critique of humor as IFF in the context of the controversy about evolution does not mean to reject it totally but to open our eyes to different viewpoints about the evolution of humor, such that the possibility and desirability of joking (from the perspective of nature with joking, IFF, and the controversy about evolution as a case study here) are not to the extent that the respective defenders would like us to believe.

In addition, this introduction to joking, IFF, and the controversy about evolution can teach us something valuable about the ontological principles in existential dialectics, and good examples include the formalness-informalness principle, the absoluteness-relativeness principle, the predictability-unpredictability principle, the explicability-inexplicability principle, the finiteness-transfiniteness principle, the preciseness-vagueness principle, the simpleness-complicatedness principle, the openness-hiddenness principle, the denseness-emptiness principle, the change-constancy principle, the slowness-quickness principle, the expansion-contraction principle, the theory-praxis principle, the convention-novelty principle, the evolution-transformation principle, the symmetry-asymmetry principle, the softness-hardness principle, the seriousness-playfulness principle, the regression-progression principle, and the same-difference principle.

For instance, in relation to the formalness-informalness principle, if there is formalness (e.g., the formal logical requirement of soundness and completeness in a system of ideas, as in science), there is informalness (e.g., the non-formal features of incompleteness in the theory of humor as IFF, as it relies on a metaphor of the IFF system from military studies without sucessfully proving that humor is in fact what it says it is). And the reverse direction also holds true.

In relation to the absoluteness-relativeness principle, if there is absoluteness (e.g., the absolute view of Hewitt that humor can be treated as an IFF system), there is relativeness (e.g., what is true for Hewitt about humor as an IFF system is not necessarily so for the critics, who question it). And the reverse direction also holds true.

In relation to the predictability-unpredictability principle, if there is predictability (e.g., the predictable tendency of people like Hewitt to analyze humor from the standpoint of an IFF system), there is unpredictability (e.g., the more difficult task to predict exactly when a particular incongruity will be interpreted as a "friend" or a "foe," because the theory suffers from many problems as shown in the criticisms). And the reverse direction also holds true.

In relation to the explicability-inexplicability principle, if there is explicability (e.g., the explanation by Hewitt that the evolution of humor can be explained on the basis of an IFF system), there is inexplicability (e.g., the lack of convincing explanation by Hewitt of why the evolution of humor is like an IFF system, especially when the criticisms against the theory are taken into account). And the reverse direction also holds true.

In relation to the finiteness-transfiniteness principle, if there is finiteness (e.g., the finite number of the categories of species who enjoy incongruities in playing, for Hewitt), there is transfiniteness (e.g., the transfinite number of individuals in all species who have ever enjoyed incongruities in playing in history). And the reverse direction also holds true.

In relation to the preciseness-vagueness principle, if there is precisenss (e.g., the precise identification of four kinds of data by Hewitt, namely, "data from DNA," "data from sense organs," "data from social learning," and "data from ethical knowledge"), there is vagueness (e.g., the vagueness in the identification of the four kinds of data, since it is not clear why there should be only four kinds of data there ever be in history as claimed by Hewitt—not three, five, six, seven, and so on). And the reverse direction also holds true.

In relation to the simpleness-complicatedness principle, if there is simpleness (e.g., the relatively simple analysis of humor as IFF by Hewitt), there is complicatedness (e.g., the relatively more complicated analysis of the theory of human as IFF by questioning its claims and assumptions, as shown in the various criticisms). And the reverse direction also holds true.

In relation to the openness-hiddenness principle, if there is openness (e.g., the open exploration of the relaitonship between humor and IFF in the work by Hewitt), there is hiddenness (e.g., the hidden bias in Hewitt's work, because of his obsession with the metaphor of IFF from military studies and his exclusion of other perspectives). And the reverse direction also holds true.

In relation to the denseness-emptiness principle, if there is denseness (e.g., the relatively denser concentration of concerns with IFF in the analysis of humor by people like Hewitt), there is emptiness (e.g., the relatively less dense, or more empty, concentration of concerns with IFF in the analysis of humor by people like Freud). And the reverse direction also holds true.

In relation to the change-constancy principle, if there is change (e.g., the ever changing view of humor, like the theory of humor as IFF by Hewitt), there is constancy (e.g., the ever constant mystery of humor, as it continues to puzzle people about its existence). And the reverse direction also holds true.

In relation to the slowness-quickness principle, if there is slowness (e.g., the relatively lesser speed for individuals to become friends with a group if they do not understand the jokes in that group, in accordance to Hewitt), there is quickness (e.g., the relatively faster speed for individuals to become foes with a group if they do not understand the jokes in that group, in accordance to Hewitt). And the reverse direction also holds true.

In relation to the expansion-contraction principle, if there is expansion (e.g., the relatively more devleoped ability for people trained in analyzing humor as an IFF system to treat individuals as "friends" or "foes," on the basis of sharing jokes), there is contraction (e.g., the relatively less devleoped ability for people trained in analyzing humor as an IFF system to treat individuals as "friends" when they do not share their jokes). And the reverse direction also holds true.

In relation to the theory-praxis principle, if there is theory (e.g., the theoretical construction of IFF in military studies), there is praxis (e.g., the practical applicatoin of IFF to the study of humor by Hewitt). And the reverse direction also holds true.

In relation to the convention-novelty principle, if there is convention (e.g., the conventional wisdom about humor as lacking survival value in Darwin's evolutionary theory), there is novelty (e.g., the alternative novel challenge to Darwin's evolutionary theory by Hewitt, on the basis of his novel view about human as an IFF system in evolution). And the reverse direction also holds true.

In relation to the evolution-transformation principle, if there is evolution (e.g., the natural evolution of humans in the state of nature to be playful and humorous), there is transformation (e.g., the technical transformation of human ability to be playful by the invention of new theories to study humor, like the theory of humor as IFF). And the reverse direction also holds true.

In relation to the symmetry-asymmetry principle, if there is symmetry (e.g., both IFF and humor can have a positive response to signal, according to Hewitt), there is asymmetry (e.g., in IFF, "positive response is coded"—but in humor, "positive response is not coded," according to Hewitt). And the reverse direction also holds true.

In relation to the softness-hardness principle, if there is softness (e.g., the treatment of those as friends who understand jokes within a group), there is hardness (e.g., the treatment of those as foes who do not understand jokes within a group). And the reverse direction also holds true.

In relation to the seriousness-playfulness principle, if there is seriousness (e.g, the serious nature of group relationship, such that those who are not friends can be subject to attacks), there is playfulness (e.g., the playful nature of group relationship, such that they can be playful too, though with the intention to detect friends or foes). And the reverse direction also holds true.

In relation to the regression-progression principle, if there is regression (e.g., the regression made by the theory of humor as IFF, as shown in the numerous criticisms against it), there is progression (e.g., the progress made by the theory of humor as IFF to help us understand the evolution of humor in a different way). And the reverse direction also holds true.

And in relation to the same-difference principle, if there is similarity in outcome (e.g., the contribution to the molding and control of beliefs and behaviors, regardless of whether this be done by way of humor as IFF or by way of normal relationship without the fixation on humor as IFF), there is difference in outcome (e.g., the contribution to the molding and control of beliefs and behaviors by way of humor as IFF for a more exclusive social world—but the contribution to the molding and control of beliefs and behaviors by way of normal relationship without the fixation on humor as IFF for a more tolerant social world). And the reverse direction also holds true.

Joking and Society

Joking, when examined from the perspective of society, can illuminate its possibility and desirability in a contentious way, and this can be shown by way of two case studies, namely, (2.4.1) joking, and the politics of satire, and (2.4.2) joking, race humor, and the power equation—to be addressed in what follows, respectively.

Joking, and the Politics of Satire

The term "satire" is derived "from the Latin word *satur* and the subsequent phrase *lanx satura*. *Satur* meant 'full,' but the juxtaposition with *lanx* shifted the meaning to 'miscellany or medley': the expression *lanx satura* literally means 'a full dish of various kinds of fruits.'" (WK 2010i; T. Kharpertian 1990)

Later, "the word *satura* as used by Quintilian however…indicated a narrower genre than what would be later intended as *satire*; it denoted only works in strictly hexameter form, which were a distinctly Roman genre...although today the origin of satire is considered to be Aristophanes' *Old Comedy*. The first critic to use satire in the modern broader sense was Apuleio." (WK 2010i; T. Kharpertian 1990)

Nowadays, "[s]atire is primarily a literary genre or form, although in practice it can also be found in the graphic and performing arts. In satire, vices, follies, abuses, and shortcomings are held up to ridicule, ideally with the intent of shaming individuals, and society itself, into improvement. Although satire is usually meant to be funny, its greater purpose is constructive social criticism, using wit as a weapon." (WK 2010i; R. Elliott 2004)

What is most potent in satire is its "strong irony or sarcasm—'in satire, irony is militant'—but parody, burlesque, exaggeration, juxtaposition, comparison, analogy, and double entendre are all frequently used in satirical speech and writing. This 'militant' irony or sarcasm often professes to approve (or at least accept as natural) the very things the satirist wishes to attack." (WK 2010i)

In the end, satire has its double sides, in that "the most light-hearted satire always has a serious 'after-taste.' The Ig Nobel Prize satire on trivial scientific research describes this as 'first make people laugh, and then make them think'—a fair definition of satire itself." (WK 2010i)

Two Types of Satire

In the literature, satire can be classified into two types, namely, (a) Horatian or (b) Juvenalian, as summarized in *Table 2.3*.

(a) Horatian

The first type of satire is called "Horatian," so named "for the Roman satirist, Horace," and is used to "playfully criticize...some social vice through gentle, mild, and light-hearted humour. It directs wit, exaggeration, and self-deprecating humour toward what it identifies as folly, rather than evil." (WK 2010i)

Horatian satire has a "sympathetic tone...common in modern society. Examples of Horatian satire: Jonathan Swift's *Gulliver's Travels*, Daniel Defoe's *The True-Born Englishman*, Alexander Pope's *The Rape of the Lock*, C.S. Lewis' *The Screwtape Letters*, *The Onion*, Matt Groening's *The Simpsons* and the Ig Nobel Prizes." (WK 2010i)

(b) Juvenalian

By contrast, the second type of satire is called "Juvenal," so named "after the Roman satirist Juvenal," and "is more contemptuous and abrasive than the Horatian. Juvenalian satire addresses social evil through scorn, outrage, and savage ridicule. This form is often pessimistic, characterized by irony, sarcasm, moral indignation and personal invective, with less emphasis on humour." (WK 2010i)

Good examples of Juvenalian satire are "Joseph Hall's *Virgidemiarum*, Jonathan Swift's *A Modest Proposal*, Samuel Johnson's *London*, George Orwell's *Nineteen Eighty-Four* and *Animal Farm*, Bret Easton Ellis's *American Psycho*, Ray Bradbury's *Fahrenheit 451*, William Golding's *Lord of the Flies*, Aldous Huxley's *Brave New World*, Anthony Burgess' *A Clockwork Orange*, Joseph Heller's *Catch 22*, William Burroughs' *Naked Lunch*, Stephen Colbert's performance at the 2006 White House Correspondents Dinner, anarcho-punk band Crass, and the cartoon *South Park*." (WK 2010i)

Satire and Its Politics

Yet, regardless of the types of satire, there is a political dimension of satire, which is also known as "political satire" (and summarized in *Table 2.3*). (WK 2010j)

By nature, "[p]olitical satire is a significant part of satire that specializes in gaining entertainment from politics; it has also been used with subversive intent where political speech and dissent are forbidden by a regime, as a method of advancing political arguments where such arguments are expressly forbidden." (WK 2010j)

However, one should not confuse "political satire" with "political protest or political dissent," because political satire "does not necessarily carry an agenda nor seek to influence the political process. While occasionally it may, it more commonly aims simply to provide entertainment. By its very nature, it rarely offers a constructive view in itself; when it is used as part of protest or dissent, it tends to simply establish the error of matters rather than provide solutions." (WK 2010j)

Yet, political satire is useful in a different way, as it allows one to say things which may not be openly allowed in an intolerant political environment. For instance, "[d]ue to lack of political freedom of speech in many ancient civilizations, covert satire is more usual than overt satire in ancient literatures of political liberalism. Historically, the public opinion in the Athenian democracy was remarkably influenced by the political satire performed by the comic poets at the theatres. Watching or reading satire has since ancient time been considered one of the best ways to understand a culture and a society," especially in proportion to the degree of its political intolerance. (WK 2010j)

In modern times, like "the 20th century, satire moved from print to other forms of media (in cartoons as political cartoons with heavy caricature and exaggeration, and in political magazines) and the parallel exposure of political scandals to performances (including television shows). Examples include musicians such as Tom Lehrer, live performance groups like the Capitol Steps, and public television and live performer Mark Russell. Additional subgenres include such literary classics as *Gulliver's Travels* and *Animal Farm*, and more recently, internet *Ezine* and website sources such as *The Onion*, *the Humor Times*, ArnoldSpeaks.com and the Happening Happy Hippy Party. Some websites exist solely to poke fun at politicians...." (WK 2010j; J. Henderson 1993; P. Meineck 2000; E. Piscitelli 1993)

One good illustration of political satire in action concerns "Maurice Joly's 1864 pamphlet entitled *The Dialogue in Hell Between Machiavelli and Montesquieu* (*Dialogue aux Enfers entre Machiavel et Montesquieu*), which attacks the political ambitions of Napoleon III. It was first published in Brussels in 1864. The piece used the literary device of a dialogue between two diabolical plotters in Hell, the historical characters of Machiavelli and Montesquieu, to cover up a direct, and illegal, attack on Napoleon's rule. The noble baron Montesquieu made the case for liberalism; the Florentine political writer Machiavelli presented the case for cynical despotism. In this manner, Joly communicated the secret ways in which liberalism might spawn a despot like Napoleon III." (WK 2010j)

Satire Under Attack

However, the politics of satire has been subject to different criticisms over the ages. Consider, for illustration, a few main criticisms below, as summarized in *Table 2.3*.

Firstly, satire does not necessarily lessen political intolerance.

For instance, quite often in history, "people in power who perceive themselves as attacked attempt to censor it or prosecute its practitioners. In a very early instance of this, Aristophanes was persecuted by the demagogue Cleon. In 1599, the Archbishop of Canterbury John Whitgift and the Bishop of London George Abbot, whose offices had the function of licensing books for publication in England, issued a decree banning verse satire. The decree ordered the burning of certain volumes of satire by John Marston, Thomas Middleton, Joseph Hall, and others; it also required histories and plays to be specially approved by a member of the Queen's Privy Council, and it prohibited the future printing of satire in verse....Various scholars have argued that the target was obscenity, libel, or sedition." (WK 2010i)

Even in liberal democracy, those in power are not fond of political satire and have done what they can to suppress it. For instance, in contemporary Italy, "Prime Minister Silvio Berlusconi attacked RAI

Television's satirical series, *Raiot*, Daniele Luttazzi's *Satyricon*, Enzo Biagi, Michele Santoro's *Sciuscià*, even a special Blob series on Berlusconi himself, by arguing that they were vulgar and full of disrespect to the government. He claimed that he would sue the RAI for 21,000,000 Euros if the show went on. RAI stopped the show." (WK 2010i)

Secondly, satire does not necessarily have public support.

For instance, "[i]n 2001 the British television network Channel 4 aired a special edition of the spoof current affairs series Brass Eye, which was intended to mock and satirize the fascination of modern journalism with child molesters and paedophiles. The TV network received an enormous number of complaints from members of the public, who were outraged that the show would mock a subject considered by many to be too 'serious' to be the subject of humour." (WK 2010i)

Thirdly, satire is not necesssarily innocent (non-offensive) as its practitioners may claim, under the cover of being funny.

For instance, "in 2005, the Jyllands-Posten Muhammad cartoons controversy caused global protests by offended Muslims and violent attacks with many fatalities in the Near East. It was not the first case of Muslim protests against criticism in the form of satire, but the Western world was surprised by the hostility of the reaction: Any country's flag in which a newspaper chose to publish the parodies was being burnt in a Near East country, then embassies were attacked, killing 139 people in mainly four countries; politicians throughout Europe agreed that satire was an aspect of the freedom of speech, and therefore to be a protected means of dialogue. Iran threatened to start an International Holocaust Cartoon Competition, which was immediately responded to by Jews with an Israeli Anti-Semitic Cartoons Contest." (WK 2010i)

In Retrospect

However, this analysis of satire under attack does not imply that satire is of no use in society but to let us understand the opposing viewpoints, such that the possibility and desirability of joking (from the perspective of society with joking, and the politics of satire as a case study here) are not to the extent that the respective defenders would like us to believe.

More fundamentlally, this analysis of satire can show us something important about the ontological principles in existential dialectics, and good examples include the absoluteness-relativeness principle, the predictability-unpredictability principle, the explicability-inexplicability principle, the preciseness-vagueness principle, the simpleness-complicatedness principle, the openness-hiddenness principle, the denseness-emptiness principle, the change-constancy principle, the slowness-quickness principle, the expansion-contraction principle, the theory-praxis principle, the convention-novelty principle, the evolution-transformation principle, the symmetry-asymmetry principle, the softness-hardness principle, the seriousness-playfulness principle, the regression-progression principle, and the same-difference principle.

For instance, in relation to the absoluteness-relativeness principle, if there is absoluteness (e.g., the absolute view of the practitioners of satire that "satire is usually meant to be funny," not offensive), there is relativeness (e.g., what is funny for the practitioners of satire is not necessarily so for its victims, like those "offended Muslims" against "the Jyllands-Posten Muhammad cartoons" which "caused global protests…and violent attacks with many fatalities in the Near East"). And the reverse direction also holds true.

In relation to the the predictability-unpredictability principle, if there is predictability (e.g., the predictable tendency of those in power to dislike political satire against them), there is unpredictability (e.g., the more difficult task to predict exactly when or to what extent a given political suppression against satire is successful, as shown in the subsequent success by Prime Minister Silvio Berlusconi to stop RAI Television's satirical series, *Raiot*—but in the unsuccessful attempt by the Archbishop of Canterbury John Whitgift and the Bishop of London George Abbot in 1599 to ban verse satire, because "the ban was little enforced, even by the licensing authority itself"). (WK 2010i) And the reverse direction also holds true.

In relation to the explicability-inexplicability principle, if there is explicability (e.g., the explanation by the practitioners of satire that "satire" is "an aspect of the freedom of speech" and therefore should be tolerated), there is inexplicability (e.g., the lack of sufficient explanation by the practitioners of satire of why it should be tolerated, in the name of "freedom of speech," because it also produces consequences which offend some other groups or attack those in power, as shown in the sub-section on satire under attack). And the reverse direction also holds true.

In relation to the preciseness-vagueness principle, if there is preciseness (e.g., the appeal to "the freedom of speech" by the defenders of satire), there is vagueness (e.g., the vagueness in the term "freedom of speech" since it can mean different things to different people, as revealed by the clashes among different groups in the sub-section on satire under attack). And the reverse direction also holds true.

In relation to the simpleness-complicatedness principle, if there is simpleness (e.g., the relatively simple analysis of satire as being "meant to be funny," while "using wit as a weapon"), there is complicatedness (e.g., the relatively more complicated analysis of satire by challenging its claims and assumptions by the critics). And the reverse direction also holds true.

In relation to the openness-hiddenness principle, if there is openness (e.g., the open exploration of the possibility of "constructive social criticism" by using "wit as a weapon" in satire), there is hiddenness (e.g., the hidden bias in satire, in its unwillingness to accept "offensiveness" as part of its consequences, under the protection behind the slogan of "the freedom of speech"). And the reverse direction also holds true.

In relation to the denseness-emptiness principle, if there is denseness (e.g., the relatively denser concentration of Westerners in Europe who supported "the Jyllands-Posten Muhammad cartoons"), there is emptiness (e.g., the relatively less dense, or more empty, concentration of Mulsims in the Near East who supported "the Jyllands-Posten Muhammad cartoons"). And the reverse direction also holds true.

In relation to the change-constancy principle, if there is change (e.g., the ever changing works of satire which have been produced in history, like those by musicians such as Tom Lehrer, live performance groups like the Capitol Steps, and public television and live performer Mark Russell"), there is constancy (e.g., the ever constancy of satire as funny to some but offensive to others). And the reverse direction also holds true.

In relation to the slowness-quickness principle, if there is slowness (e.g., the relatively slower speed for those in authority to like political satire against them), there is quickness (e.g., the relatively quicker speed for those in the profession of satire to like political satire). And the reverse direction also holds true.

In relation to the expansion-contraction principle, if there is expansion (e.g., the relatively more developed ability of the practitioners of satire to use "wit as a weapon"), there is contraction (e.g., the relatively less developed ability of dictators like Hitler to use "wit as a weapon," instead of military force). And the reverse direction also holds true.

In relation to the theory-praxis principle, if there is theory (e.g., the theoretical construction of satire as a literary genre, as shown Aristophanes' *Old Comedy*), there is praxis (e.g., the practical application of satire to politics as in "political satire"). And the reverse direction also holds true.

In relation to the convention-novelty principle, if there is convention (e.g., the conventional wisdom about satire in the time of Quintilian to "indicate…a narrower genre…in strictly hexameter form, which were a distinctly Roman genre"), there is novelty (e.g., the alternative novel challenge to the conventional wisdom about Roman satire, by the later new genres of satire which are much broader in graphic and performing arts, can have different types which can be Horatian or Juvenalian, and so on). And the reverse direction also holds true.

In relation to the evolution-transformation principle, if there is evolution (e.g., the natural evolution of humans in the state of nature to be funny), there is transformation (e.g., the technical transformation of human ability to be funny by the invention of political satire with such literary techniques as "parody, burlesque, exaggeration, juxtaposition, comparison, analogy, and double entendre," for instance). And the reverse direction also holds true.

In relation to the symmetry-asymmetry principle, if there is symmetry (e.g., the co-existence of different types of satire in hisory), there is asymmetry (e.g., the popularity of Horatian satire among those who prefer "gentle, mild, and light-hearted humour"—but the acceptance of Juvenal satire among those who prefer "more contemptuous and abrasive" humor). And the reverse direction also holds true.

In relation to softness-hardness principle, if there is softness (e.g., the "gentle, mild, and light-hearted humour" in Horatian satire), there is hardness (e.g. , the "contemptuous and abrasive" humor in Juvenal satire). And the reverse direction also holds true.

In relation to the seriousness-playfulness principle, if there is seriousness (e.g., the serious "after-taste" in satire which "makes people think"), there is playfulness (e.g., the "funny" aspect of satire which makes people "laugh"). And the reverse direction also holds true.

In relation to the regression-progression principle, if there is regression (e.g., the regresson made by satire, as shown in the criticisms by the critics), there is progression (e.g., the progress made by satire, as shown in its "constructive social criticism, using wit as a weapon"). And the reverse direction also holds true.

And in relation to the same-difference principle, if there is similarity in outcome (e.g., the contribution to the molding and regulation of beliefs and values, regardless of whether this be done by way of satire or by way of political decrees), there is difference in outcome (e.g., the contribution to the molding and control of beliefs and values by way of satire for a more witty, subtle way of communication—but the contribution to the molding and control of beliefs and values by way of polticial decrees for a more authoritarian way of communication). And the reverse direction also holds true.

Joking, Race/Ethnic Humor, and the Power Equation

Another way to evaluate the possibility and desirability of joking from the perspective of society is about joking, race/ethnic humor, and the power equation.

The term "race humor" is also known as "ethnic joke," which refers to "a humorous remark relating to an ethnic, racial or cultural group, often referring to a stereotype of the group in question for its punchline." (WK 2010l)

It is true, even though "the definition of what constitute a race, ethnicity or a social group varies from one nation or society to the next, about who is considered a racial minority or ethnic group." (WK 2010l)

Historically, "[e]thnic jokes have been around since people first noticed they were different from one another, and ethnocentrism and a sense of ethnic identity appeared. Jokes feed upon difference and distinctions (not only ethnic, of course) and if one of the functions of ethnic jokes is to ridicule and depreciate these in-out groups, another function is to maintain and strengthen a sense of one's identity in some in-group." (WK 2010l)

Race/Ethnic Humor against Both the Powerful and the Weak

In any event, race humor can cut both ways, in that it has been used to make fun of both the weak and the strong, the dominated and the dominating, and the like—in society.

(a) Against the Weak

An excellent illustration of race humor to target the weak has to do with "Polish jokes" in the United States during the 1960's, for instance.

The reason is that, "sadly for Polish people there were powerful anti-Polish Bigots in Hollywood and the U.S. TV media who introduced hateful Polish jokes to the American public in the 1960's in the hope that the American people would eventually have the same anti-Polish prejudice that Hollywood and media elites had." (WK 2010l)

At that time, "Hollywood, NBC-TV & CBS-TV for example did not tell the American public that so called 'Polish jokes' aka subhuman intelligence jokes about Polish people, were hypocritically taken from Nazi propaganda despite the fact Hollywood and NBC-TV and CBS-TV claimed to be anti-Nazi....The tremendous power of TV and movie imagery was used to malign the image of Polish people as having inferior intelligence...." (WK 2010l)

But how the public perceives these jokes as offensive or not can vary from case to case, from era to era, and the like. For instance, nowadays, "African American or black jokes told by non-blacks in the USA are viewed as rude, immoral and socially unacceptable"—but black jokes were regarded as quite acceptable in the older days of slavery. (WK 2010l)

So, "ethnic jokes come and go with social change," in that, when a minority group rises to wealth and power, they can become more accepted. For instance, "Irish jokes have become far less common in the United Kingdom as the social status of Irish people has risen with increased wealth in Ireland, the consequent reduction in Irish itinerant labour, and the absorption of Irish people into the community, and therefore the UK media was more tolerant of the Irish." (WK 2010l)

(b) Against the Powerful

But there is no guarantee either that, as a minority group rises to wealth and power, they will not be subject to race humor in the opposite direction.

For illustration, in some famous cases, "the ethnic jokes are addressed against those who are historically seen as the aggressors, like the multiple jokes published in Mexico about the Americans (also called gringos there). Similar jokes have also been published in Barcelona." (WK 2010l)

In the United States, there have been, for instance, "Jew jokes and Italian American jokes" (targeted against the Jews and Italian Americans). (WK 2010l)

However, "[a]s public awareness of racism has increased, racial and ethnic jokes have become increasingly socially unacceptable in recent years, and have become socially taboo to tell in public in many regions. This can however, depend on who is telling the joke. For example, it may be deemed offensive for a white person to make a joke about Asians, whereas it would be more acceptable for an Asian to make a similar joke about their own culture, or an Asian make a joke about white people can be variously funny or offending to some extent." (WK 2010l)

Some Proposed Explanations

It is one thing to describe race humor against both the weak and the powerful, but it is another to explain it.

For instance, one theory is that "ethnic humour helps us deal with hostility verbally instead of physically, but these slurs also reinforce our stereotypes and sometimes lead to calls for violence." (WK 2010l; A. Berger 1993)

Another theory is a bit more elaborated and is suggested by Christie Davies, who presented "the main arguments in his article "Ethnic Jokes, Moral Values and Social Boundaries" published in 1982. (WK 2010l)

Davies based his approach on "Victor Raskin's (1985) Semantic Script Theory of Humor (SSTH), or to be more precise, on the arguments connected with ethnic humor on binary oppositions. While Raskin merely describes the main binary oppositions providing examples mostly from the Jewish humor, Davies explores the situations where the scripts apply; for example, he has discovered that the most common opposition, stupid/clever, is applied under particular circumstances in the social reality of two ethnic groups concerned." (WK 2010l)

For Davies, "[l]inks have been established between the scripts of the jokes and social facts, such as, for example, modern society's hesitance in regarding people's primary actions such as working, eating and drinking, sexual life and warfare. Issues related to these actions are present in more or less all societies; the societies where these are absent also lack the corresponding jokes (e.g., jokes about alcohol are missing in Muslim and Jewish jokelore). The anecdote tradition of each individual culture are based on the presupposition that the joke centers on divergence from the norm and average." (WK 2010l; A. Berger 1993)

Then, Davies classified "ethnic jokes…around the three main themes of stupidity, canniness and sexual behavior," as shown below: (WK 2010l)

- "Stupidity"—This theme refers to "jokes in every country (or reasonably homogeneous cultural and linguistic domain)," which "have certain targets for stupidity jokes," in relation to "people who dwell on the edge of that nation or domain and who are perceived as culturally ambiguous by the dominant people of the center. In addition, they will likely be rustic people or immigrants in search of unskilled and low-prestige manual work. They are to a great extent similar to the joke-tellers themselves, share the same cultural background or even speak a similar or identical language." (WK 2010l)
- "Canniness"—This theme refers to "the counterpart of stupidity jokes…about canniness that usually depict unambiguous, well-integrated and economically successful group of people, either only locally known (e.g. the population of the Laihia (Laihela) village in Finland) or international (e.g. the Jews)." (WK 2010l)
- "Sexual Behavior"—This theme refers to "more culture-specific jokes about ludicrous behavior concerning…sexual behavior, etc. These jokes are based on the cultural background of the object of ridicule

> and the teller of the joke, and their mutual attitude towards the problems with the areas mentioned." (WK 2010l)

Surey, there can be other themes too; for instance, Davies also suggested the existence of other themes, which may include, at times, "militarism, alcohol consumption," and so on. (WK 2010l)

A Sober Reflection

But these explanations by the theories are not without criticisms. Consider, for illustration, a few of them below.

Firstly, a major criticism of the work by Davies is that it is not clear why there are only three main themes in ethnic jokes—not four, five, six, seven, and the like.

Secondly, another major criticism of the work by Davies is that it is question-begging to say that "the societies where [the themes in question] are absent also lack the corresponding jokes (e.g., jokes about alcohol are missing in Muslim and Jewish jokelore)." But, for the critics, one should ask deeper questions: Why should not the Muslims have jokes which make fun of others who drink, even if they themselves don't?

And thirdly, still another major criticism of the work by Davies is that he did not really offer any explanation of why different groups make jokes against each other in the first place? Is this because, as some other scholars had suggested, "ethnic humour helps us deal with hostility verbally instead of physically," or because of some other reasons? (WK 2010l; A. Berger 1993)

In any event, this critique of the work by Davies on ethnic jokes does not mean to dismiss the validity of his work completely or to learn nothing from the literature on ethnic jokes. Rather, the analysis here is to let us understand the opposing viewpoints, such that the possibility and desirability of joking (from the perspective of society with joking, race/ethnic humor, and the power equation as a case study here) are not to the extent that the respective defenders would like us to believe.

In addition, this analysis of ethnic jokes can show us something relevant about the ontological principles in existential dialectics, and good examples include the formalness-informalness principle, the absoluteness-relativeness principle, the partiality-totality principle, the predictability-unpredictability principle, the explicability-inexplicability principle, the preciseness-vagueness principle, the simpleness-complicatedness principle, the openness-hiddenness principle, the denseness-emptiness principle, the change-constancy principle, the slowness-quickness principle, the expansion-contraction principle, the theory-praxis principle, the convention-novelty principle, the evolution-transformation principle, the symmetry-asymmetry principle, the softness-hardness principle, the seriousness-playfulness principle, the regression-progression principle, and the same-difference principle.

For instance, in relation to the formalness-informalness principle, if there is formalness (e.g., the formal logical requirement of soundness and completeness in a system of ideas, as in a scientific work), there is informalness (e.g., the informal existence of some incompleteness and unsoundness in the theory of ethnic humor by Davies, because of the problems pointed out by the critics). And the reverse direction also holds true.

In relation to the absoluteness-relativeness principle, if there is absoluteness (e.g., the absolute view in Nazi propaganda about "subhuman intelligence jokes" targeting Polish people), there is relativeness (e.g., what is funny in Nazi propaganda about "subhuman intelligence jokes" targeting Polish people is not necessarily so for the Polish people themselves). And the reverse direction also holds true.

In relation to the partiality-totality principle, if there is partiality (e.g., the partial, limited info about the Polish people on which Hollywood and the U.S. TV media were originally based in the 1960's), there is totality (e.g,. the holistic view about the Polish people in terms of "ethnic jokes" by the American public, which simply does not add up, in light of the partial info on which Hollywood and the U.S. TV media were originally based, such that the whole is not the sum of its parts, because of the propaganda effect). And the reverse direction also holds true.

In relation to the predictability-unpredictability principle, if there is predictability (e.g., the predictable tendency of race/ethnic jokes to target both the weak and the strong in history), there is unpredictability (e.g., the more difficult task to predict when exactly the public will perceive particular ethnic jokes as offensive or not, because this can vary from case to case, from era to era, and the like, as illustrated by the evolution of the history about black jokes nowadays, as opposed to those in the older days of slavery). And the reverse direction also holds true.

In relation to the explicability-inexplicability principle, if there is explicability (e.g,. the explanation by some scholars that "ethnic humour helps us deal with hostility verbally instead of physically"), there is inexplicability (e.g., the lack of sufficient explanation by these scholars who argued that "ethnic humour helps us deal with hostility verbally instead of physically" but at the same time acknowledged that "these slurs also reinforce our stereotypes" and can "lead to calls for violence" instead, besides some other alternative theories as presented in this book). And the reverse direction also holds true.

In relation to the preciseness-vagueness principle, if there is preciseness (e.g., the precise identification by Davies of three main themes in ethnic jokes), there is vagueness (e.g., the vagueness in the identification of three main themes by Davies, as it is not clear why there are only three main themes in ethnic jokes—not four, five, six, seven, and the like). And the reverse direction also holds true.

In relation to the simpleness-complicatedness principle, if there is simpleness (e.g., the relatively simplistic analysis of ethnic jokes in terms of some main themes by Davies), there is complicatedness (e.g., the relatively more complicated account of the theory of ethnic jokes, by challenging its claims and assumptions, as shown in the criticisms). And the reverse direction also holds true.

In relation to the openness-hiddenness principle, if there is openness (e.g., the open exploration by Davies of the relationship between "the societies where [the themes in question] are absent" and the "lack [of] the corresponding jokes" in these societies, like "jokes about alcohol are missing in Muslim and Jewish jokelore"), there is hiddenness (e.g., the hidden bias in the work by Davies, because it is question-begging, since one can ask further: Why should not the Muslims have jokes which make fun of others who drink, even if they themselves don't?). And the reverse direction also holds true.

In relation to the denseness-emptiness principle, if there is denseness (e.g., the relatively denser concentration of concerns with the three main themes in ethnic jokes by people like Davies), there is emptiness (e.g., the relatively less dense, or more empty, concentration of concerns with the theme of social prohibition and sensory incongruity in ethnic jokes by people like Davies). And the reverse direction also holds true.

In relation to the change-constancy principle, if there is change (e.g., the ever new formation of ethnic jokes in society), there is constancy (e.g., the ever constant themes of "stupidity, canniness and sexual behavior" in ethnic jokes, no matter how much changes there are over time, for Davies). And the reverse direction also holds true.

In relation to the slowness-quickness principle, if there is slowness (e.g., the relatively slower speed for black Americans to get offended by black jokes if they are made by their own black people instead), there is quickness (e.g., the relatively faster speed for black Americans to get offended by black jokes if they are made by white people). And the reverse direction also holds true.

In relation to the expansion-contraction principle, if there is expansion (e.g., the relatively more developed ability of people like Davies to identifiy themes in ethnic jokes on the basis of "stupidity, canniness and sexual behavior"), there is contraction (e.g., the relatively less developed ability of people like Davies to understand ethnic jokes on the basis of an IFF system, as worked out by Hewitt in an earlier section). And the reverse direction also holds true.

In relation to the theory-praxis principle, if there is theory (e.g., the theoretical construction of ethnic jokes in history), there is praxis (e.g., the practical application of ethnic jokes to targeting Polish people in the 1960's by Hollywood and the U.S. TV media). And the reverse direction also holds true.

In relation to the convention-novelty principle, if there is convention (e.g., the conventional wisdom about using Irish jokes in the U.K. in the older days), there is novelty (e.g., the alternative novel challenge to the use of Irish jokes in the U.K. nowadays, because "the social status of Irish people has risen with increased wealth in Ireland, the consequent reduction in Irish itinerant labour, and the absorption of Irish people into the community, and therefore the UK media was more tolerant of the Irish"). And the reverse direction also holds true.

In relation to the evolution-transformation principle, if there is evolution (e.g., the natural evolution of humans to make fun of each other in the state of nature), there is transformation (e.g., the technical transformation of humans to make fun of each other by the invention of systematic propaganda campaigns, like the Nazi propaganda about "subhuman intelligence jokes" targeting Polish people). And the reverse direction also holds true.

In relation to the symmetry-asymmetry principle, if there is symmetry (e.g., the co-existence of different views about different ethnic groups in history), there is asymmetry (e.g., the negative view about Polish people in the U.S. during the 1960's—but the more tolerant environment for Polish people nowadays, "[a]s public awareness of racism has increased, racial and ethnic jokes have become increasingly socially unacceptable in recent years, and have become socially taboo to tell in public in many regions"). And the reverse direction also holds true.

In relation to the softness-hardness principle, if there is softness (e.g., the inclusion of an in-group), there is hardness (e.g., the exclusion of an out-group). And the reverse direction also holds true.

In relation to the seriousness-playfulness principle, if there is seriousness (e.g., the seriousness of an in-group to call "for violence" against an out-group), there is playfulness (e.g., the playfulness of an in-group to use ethnic jokes against an out-group, so as to "deal with hostility verbally instead of physically"). And the reverse direction also holds true.

In relation to the regression-progression principle, if there is regression (e.g., the regression made by the theory of ethnic jokes, as shown in the criticisms against it), there is progression (e.g., the progress made by the theory of ethnic jokes to help us understand the three main themes in ethnic jokes). And the reverse direction also holds true.

And in relation to the same-difference principle, if there is similarity in outcome (e.g., the contribution to the molding and regulation of beliefs and behaviors, regardless of whether this be done by way of ethnic jokes or by way of ethnic violence), there is difference in outcome (e.g., the contribution to the molding and control of beliefs and behaviors by way of ethnic jokes for a verbal resolution of hostility between groups—but the contribution to the molding and control of beliefs and behaviors by way of ethnic violence for a physical resolution of hostility between groups). And the reverse direction also holds true.

Joking and Culture

Joking, when explored from the perspective of culture, can reveal, in a different way, its possibility and desirability, and this can be shown by way of two case studies, namely, (2.5.1) joking, flatulence humor, and the culture of shifting blame, and (2.5.2) the techniques of joking, and the cultural factor—to be addressed hereafter, respectively.

Joking, Flatulence Humor, and the Culture of Shifting Blame

The term "flatulence humor" refers to "any type of joke, practical joke device, or other humor related to flatulence" (or to "the public passing of gas"). (WK 2010p)

The discussion of flatulence humor here is refreshing, because it tells us something about culture not often spoken of.

The Long History of Flatulence Humor

After all, flatulence humor has a long cultural history indeed. For instance "[t]wo important early texts are the 5th century BC plays *The Knights* and *The Clouds*, both by Aristophanes [2010 & 2010a], which contain numerous 'fart' jokes." (WK 2010p)

Another ancient example of flatulence humor is "*Apocolocyntosis* or *The Pumpkinification of Claudius*, a satire attributed to Seneca on the late

Roman emperor," as shown in the following joke: (WK 2010p; L. Seneca 1920)

> At once he bubbled up the ghost, and there was an end to that shadow of a life....The last words he was heard to speak in this world were these. When he had made a great noise with that end of him which talked easiest, he cried out, "Oh dear, oh dear! I think I have made a mess of myself."

Later, "[i]n the translated version of Penguin's *1001 Arabian Nights Tales*, a story entitled 'The Historic Fart' tells of a man that flees his country from the sheer embarrassment of farting at his wedding, only to return ten years later to discover that his fart had become so famous, that people used the anniversary of its occurrence to date other events. Upon learning this he exclaimed, 'Verily, my fart has become a date! I shall be remembered forever!'" (WK 2010p)

In early English literature, there is "*The Miller's Tale* by Geoffrey Chaucer which dates from the 14th century. The character Nicholas sticks his buttocks out of a window at night and humiliates his rival Absolom by farting in his face. But Absolom gets revenge by thrusting a red-hot plough blade between Nicholas's cheeks," as described in the following joke: (WK 2010p)

> "Sing, sweet bird, I kneen nat where thou art!"
> This Nicholas anon let fle a fart
> As greet as it had been a thonder-dent
> That with the strook he was almost yblent (blinded)
> And he was ready with iron hoot
> And Nicholas ammyd the ers he smoot.

Other flatulence jokes can be even more exaggerated; for instance, "François Rabelais' tales of *Gargantua and Pantagruel* are laden with acts of flatulence. In Chapter XXVII of the second book, the giant, Pantagruel, releases a fart that 'made the earth shake for twenty-nine miles around, and the foul air he blew out created more than fifty-three thousand tiny men, dwarves and creatures of weird shapes, and then he emitted a fat wet fart that turned into just as many tiny stooping women.'" (WK 2010p)

In America, a work by Mark Twain (1880) titled "1601," or, in its longer version, "1601: Conversation, as it was the Social Fireside, in the Time of the Tudors," there is this report by "a cupbearer at Court who's a Diarist": (WK 2010p)

> In ye heat of ye talk it befel yt one did breake wind, yielding an exceding mightie and distresfull stink, whereat all did laugh full sore.

In the 20th century, there was this "1940s a clandestine record called 'The Crepitation Contest'...produced, allegedly by Canadian Broadcast Corporation staff (narration by sportscaster Sidney S. Brown, who identifies himself in the closing seconds of the original unedited recording, and 'sound effects' by his producer, Jules Lipton). The recording is in the manner of a seemingly real radio broadcast of a live sporting event, complete with pre-game interviews of the contestants (the 'champion,' Lord Windismere and the challenger, Paul Boomer), detailed descriptions of all aspects of the competition as it unfolds, including the rules and traditions associated with the sport, play-by-play reporting, and crowd sounds reacting to the drama. The listener also hears a game official on the field as he announces scores attributed to the flatulence sounds emitted by each contestant in the competition." (WK 2010p)

The Culture of Shifting Blame

Funny as these fart jokes may sound, there is a culture of blame associated with the ritual of farting.

Fart jokes over time deal with "the sourcing of a fart" in an indirect way, which "involves a ritual of assignment that sometimes takes the form of a rhyming game. These are frequently used to discourage others from mentioning the fart. The trick is to pin the blame on someone else, often by means of deception, or using a back and forth rhyming game that includes phrases," as shown in the following examples in some fart jokes: (WK 2010p; A. Maddox 2006)

- "He/She who observed it served it."
- "He/She who detected it, ejected it."
- "Whoever rhymed it crimed it."
- "Whoever spoke last set off the blast."
- "Whoever smelt it, dealt it."
- "Whoever denied it supplied it."
- "The next person who speaks is the person who reeks."
- "The smeller's the feller."
- "He/She who inculpated promulgated."
- "The one who said the verse just made the atmosphere worse."
- "Whoever's poking fun is the smoking gun."
- "He/She who accuses blew the fuses."
- "Whoever said the rhyme did the crime."

- "He/She who refuted it, tooted it."
- "He/She who pointed the finger pulled the finger."
- "He/She who articulated it, particulated it."
- "He/She who deduced it produced it."
- "She who sniffed it biffed it."
- "The slanderer made the gland error."
- "He/She who eulogized it aerosolized it."

Other comparable rhyming phrases (related to fart jokes, albeit to some extent) are shown below: (WK 2010p)

- "A fox smells his own hole first."
- "Who cut the cheese?"
- "Barking spiders."
- "Who stepped on a frog?"
- "Mouse on a motorcycle."
- "The first chicken that cackles, laid the egg."
- "Somebody's baking brownies."
- "He/She who blew the whistle blew the flute."
- "Who sat on a duck?"

Surely, there can be other examples, but these ones here suffice for the illustration at hand.

The Redemption of a Scholarly Exercise

This introduction to flatulence humor and its culture of shifting blame is not meant to endorse farting in public as a polite act but to let us understand both its funny and disgusting sides, such that the possibility and desirability of joking (from the perspective of culture with joking, flatulence humor, and the culture of shifting blame as a case study here) are not to the extent that the respective defenders would like us to believe.

Besides, this introduction to flatulence humor and its culture of shifting blame can teach us a valuable insight about the ontological principles in existential dialectics, and good examples include the absoluteness-relativeness principle, the predictability-unpredictability principle, the explicability-inexplicability principle, the preciseness-vagueness principle, the simpleness-complicatedness principle, the openness-hiddenness principle, the denseness-emptiness principle, the change-constancy principle, the slowness-quickness principle, the expansion-contraction principle, the theory-praxis principle, the convention-novelty principle, the evolution-transformation principle, the symmetry-asymmetry principle, the seriousness-playfulness principle, the regression-progression principle, and the same-difference principle.

For instance, in relation to the absoluteness-relativeness principle, if there is absoluteness (e.g., the absolute view of those who does farting "to pin the blame on someone else, often by means of deception rhyming game" in fart jokes), there is relativeness (e.g., what is funny for those who does farting to make fart jokes which "pin the blame on someone else, often by means of deception rhyming game" is not necessarily so for the victims who consider farting as impolite and the shifting of blame as irresponsible). And the reverse direction also holds true.

In relation to the predictability-unpredictability principle, if there is predictability (e.g., the predictable tendency of those who make fart jokes to engage in shifting blame), there is unpredictabiltiy (e.g., the more difficult task to predict exactly which particular rhyming phrase the fart joker will use on a given occasion). And the reverse direction also holds true.

In relation to the explicability-inexplicability principle, if there is explicability (e.g., the explanation, by those making fart jokes, of the culture of shitting blame by the use of rhyming phrases), there is inexplicability (e.g., the lack of sufficient explanation, by those who make fart jokes, of why this culture of shifting blame is justified, other than being a joke, which is not sufficient, for the critics). And the reverse direction also holds true.

In relation to the preciseness-vagueness principle, if there is preciseness (e.g., the precise identification of the technique of rhyming in fart jokes), there is vaguenes (e.g., the vagueness in the identification of rhyming, since there can be so many different ways that the rhyming technique can be exploited, as shown in the examples aforecited). And the reverse direction also holds true.

In relation to the simpleness-complicatedness principle, if there is simpleness (e.g., the relatively simple analysis of fart jokes in terms of the long history and the culture of shifting blame), there is complicatedness (e.g., the relatively more complicated analysis of fart jokes by questioning the claims and assumptions, like the questioning of why it is justified for fart jokers to shift blame, without accepting it as impolite and irresponsible, for instance). And the reverse direction also holds true.

In relation to the openness-hiddenness principle, if there is openness (e.g., the open exploration of the link between doing fart and the fun of making fart jokes), there is hiddenness (e.g., the hidden bias in fart jokes, because of the culture of shifting blame to the victims). And the reverse direction also holds true.

In relation to the denseness-emptiness principle, if there is denseness (e.g., the relatively denser concentration of people doing farts in public in antiquity), there is emptiness (e.g., the relatively less dense, or more empty, concentration of people doing farts in public nowadays). And the reverse direction also holds true.

In relation to the change-constancy principle, if there is change (e.g., the ever new fart jokes to be made by people over time), there is constancy (e.g., the ever constancy of the tendency to shift blame in fart jokes). And the reverse direction also holds true.

In relation to the slowness-quickness principle, if there is slowness (e.g., the relatively slower readiness of modern presidents to play with fart jokes in public), there is quickness (e.g., the relatively quicker readiness of pre-modern emperors to play with fart jokes in public, as shown by the Roman Emperor Elagabulus who liked "to play practical [fart] jokes on his guests, employing whoopee cushions at dinner parties"). (WK 2010p; W. Ball 2001) And the reverse direction also holds true.

In relation to the expansion-contraction principle, if there is expansion (e.g., the relatively more developed ability of a fart joker to find tricks to shift the blame of farting to his victims), there is contraction (e.g., the relatively less developed ability of a fart joker to be morally responsible and to subsequently offer apology to his victim). And the reverse direction also holds true.

In relation to the theory-praxis principle, if there is theory (e.g., the theoretical construction of the rhyming phrases in fart jokes), there is praxis (e.g.,the practical application of fart jokes with their rhyming phrases to programs in modern "cinema and tv series," as shown in one scene of *Blazing Saddles*). (WK 2010p; J. Dawson 1999) And the reverse direction also holds true.

In relation to the convention-novelty principle, if there is convention (e.g., the conventional wisdom in antiquity which treated flatulence more as a call of nature than as a public embarassment), there is novelty (e.g., the alternative novel challenge to the conventional wisdom in antiquity about flatulence, by the contemporary cultural shift, which regards flatulence in public as rude or impolite). And the reverse direction also holds true.

In relation to the evolution-transformation principle, if there is evolution (e.g., the natural evolution of humans to fart in the state of nature), there is transformation (e.g., the technical transformation of human ability to fart in public, by the invention of social norms nowadays which regard flatulence in public as rude or impolite). And the reverse direction also holds true.

In relation to the symmetry-asymmetry principle, if there is symmetry (e.g., the co-existence of different viewpoints about farts in history), there is asymmetry (e.g., the more tolerance of farts in public in antiquity—but the less tolerance of farts in public nowadays). And the reverse direction also holds true.

In relation to the seriousness-playfulness principle, if there is seriousness (e.g., the serious part of fart jokes in its tendency to shift the blame of farting to someone else, so as "to discourage others from mentioning the fart"), there is playfulness (e.g., the playfulness of the fart jokes, to cause laughter). And the reverse direction also holds true.

In relation to the regression-progression principle, if there is regression (e.g., the regression made in fart jokes, as revealed in the problems associated with being rude, irresponsible, and the like), there is progression (e.g, the progress made in fart jokes, to deal with the nuissance of farting in a playful way, something like a call of nature). And the reverse direction also holds true.

And in relation to the same-difference principle, if there is similarity in outcome (e.g., the contribution to the molding and regulation of beliefs and behaviors, regardless of whether this be done by way of fart jokes or by way of social norms regulating farts), there is difference in outcome (e.g., the contribution to the molding and control of beliefs and behaviors by way of fart jokes for a more laid-back social lifeworld—but the contribution to the molding and control of beliefs and behaviors by way of social norms regulating farts for a more moralistic social lifeworld). And the reverse direction also holds true.

The Techniques of Joking, and the Cultural Factor

Another way to evaluate the possibility and desirability of joking from the perspective of culture has to do with the techniques of jokes and the cultural factor, as summarized in *Table 2.4*.

The Techniques of Jokes

Jokes are to be funny, so a good question to ask is, To what extent do they follow certain rules (or techniques), which can then be used by anyone to make jokes?

It turns out that humor follows certain rules (or techniques), up to a certain point, however—which can be compared with a related endeavor like creativity, which also follows certain rules (or techniques), again up to a certain point, however. In *The Future of Post-Human Creative Thinking*

(2009), I already went to great lengths to identify some techniques which one can use to be creative.

By the same logic, let me explore here some techniques of joking, which can be used to be funny too. Although what is appropriate for the techniques of creativity is not necessarily so for the techniques of joking (because what is creative is not necessarily funny), some techniques can be used for both (e.g., the techniques of reversal, stretching, and paradox, for example, as shown below).

With this caveat in mind—consider, for illustration, the following techniques of joking, which have been used by humorists over the ages.

(a) Precision

In this first technique of precision—"the comedian must choose the words in order to provide a vivid, in-focus image, and to avoid being generic as to confuse the audience, and provide no laughter. To properly arrange the words in the sentence is also crucial to get precision. An example by Woody Allen (from *Side Effects*, 'A Giant Step for Mankind' story)" is shown below: (WK 2010a)

> Grasping the mouse firmly by the tail, I snapped it like a small whip, and the morsel of cheese came loose.

Surely, there can be other examples, but this one above suffices for illustration.

(b) Economy

In this second technique of economy—"a joke is best when it expresses the maximum level of humour with a minimal number of words," and this is "today considered one of the key technical elements of a joke. An example from George Carlin [2010]" is shown below: (WK 2010a; JW 2010)

> I have as much authority as the Pope, I just don't have as many people who believe it.

In fact, "the familiarity of the pattern of 'brevity' has led to numerous examples of jokes where the very length is itself the pattern-breaking 'punchline.' Numerous examples from Monty Python exist, for instance, [in] the song 'I Like Traffic Lights.'" (WK 2010a)

(c) Rhythm (Timing)

In this third technique of rhythm (or timing)—"[t]he joke's content (meaning) is not what provokes the laugh; it just makes the salience of the joke and provokes a smile. What makes us laugh is the joke mechanism. Milton Berle demonstrated this with a classic theatre experiment in the 1950s: if during a series of jokes you insert phrases that are not jokes, but with the same rhythm, the audience laughs anyway. A classic is the ternary rhythm, with three beats: Introduction, premise, antithesis (with the antithesis being the punch line)." (WK 2010a)

(d) Disproportion (Stretching)

In this fourth technique of disproportion (also known as exaggeration or stretching)—the joke is to illustrate two things which are not in proportion, as shown in the classic example when "[a]n individual laughs because he recognises the child that is in himself. In clowns stumbling is a childish tempo. In the comic, the visual gags may be translated into a joke. For example in *Side Effects* ('By Destiny Denied' story) by Woody Allen," the technique of disproportion is used, as shown below:

> "My father used to wear loafers," she confessed. "Both on the same foot."

Again, there can be other examples, but this one above suffices for illustration.

(e) Danger

In this fifth technique of danger—a joke is made by overcoming any "censorship [which] prevents some 'dangerous ideas' from reaching the conscious mind, or helps us avoid saying everything that comes to mind." (WK 2010a) Sigmund Freud (1960) wrote about this danger of "censorship" in *Jokes and their Relation to the Unconscious.*

For instance, in "wit" (which is a form of intellectual humor), the task here is "circumvent…the censorship and bring…up those [dangerous] ideas. Different wit techniques allow one to express them in a funny way. The profound meaning behind a wit joke is 'I have dangerous ideas.' An example from Woody Allen" is shown below: (WK 2010a)

> I contemplated suicide again—this time by inhaling next to an insurance salesman.

The same can be said about the field of "irony." (WK 2010a) In fact, some scholars had suggested that "there are about 200 techniques (technically they are called tropes, a particular kind of figure of speech) that can be used to make jokes" like this. (WK 2010a; S. Attardo 1994)

(f) Void

In this sixth technique of void—the joke is to cancel or "erase...an emotion that should be felt about an event, making us insensitive to it, e.g.: 'yo momma' jokes....An example from Woody Allen" is shown below: (WK 2010a)

> Three times I've been mistaken for Robert Redford. Each time by a blind person.

So, "[t]he profound meaning of the void feeling of a humour joke" like this is "I'm a cynic," and "black humour and sarcasm belong to this field." (WK 2010a)

(g) Rhyme

In this seventh technique of rhyme—the joke is to make use of some correspondence of some words in sound. (WK 2010p)

For instance, as already discussed in the previous section on fart jokes, "[t]he trick is to pin the blame on someone else, often by means of deception, or using a back and forth rhyming game that includes phrases," as shown in the following examples: (WK 2010p)

- "He/She who observed it served it."
- "He/She who detected it, ejected it."
- "Whoever smelt it, dealt it."
- "Whoever denied it supplied it."
- "He/She who inculpated promulgated."
- "Whoever's poking fun is the smoking gun."
- "Whoever said the rhyme did the crime."
- "He/She who pointed the finger pulled the finger."
- "He/She who articulated it, particulated it."
- "He/She who deduced it produced it."
- "She who sniffed it biffed it."
- "He/She who eulogized it aerosolized it."

Once more, there can be other examples, as already showed in the previous section on fart jokes.

(h) Ambiguity

In this eighth technique of ambiguity (also known as "double entendre")—the joke consists of "a spoken phrase [which] is devised to be understood in either of two ways. Often the first meaning is straightforward, while the second meaning is less so: often risqué, inappropriate, or ironic." (WK 2010s)

For instance, in "the poem *Ozymandias* by Percy Shelley published in 1818," there is "an example of ironic double entendre. Looking upon the shattered ruins of a colossus, the traveler reads": (WK 2010s)

My name is Ozymandias, king of kings:
Look on my works, ye Mighty, and despair!

Here, "[t]he speaker believes that the king's sole intended meaning of 'despair' was that nobody could hope to equal his achievements, but the traveler seems to find another meaning—that the reader might 'despair' to find that all beings are mortal, that king and peasant alike inevitably share oblivion in the sands of time. This portrayal of an unintended double entendre exemplifies a case of the double entendre as the poet's figure of speech." (WK 2010s)

(i) Opposite Expectation (Reversal)

In this nineth technique of opposite expectations (by reversal)—the joke is to explore "the effect of opposite expectations," so that, as this is true in irony, the joke is to "convey a meaning exactly opposite from their literal meaning. In ironic situations (situational irony), actions often have an effect exactly opposite from what is intended." (WK 2010k & 2010t)

For instance, here is an example of a joke with opposite meaning or expectation: (WK 2010t)

Oh, that's beautiful.

Here, "when someone says 'Oh, that's beautiful'...; what they mean (probably conveyed by their tone) is they find 'that' quite ugly." (WK 2010t)

(k) Word-Order (Reversal)

In this tenth technique of word-order (by reversal)—the joke is to reverse the order of some words used, so as to give it a funny meaning.

For instance, English playwright William Shakespeare wrote the followiong witty joke: (WK 2010q)

Better a witty fool than a foolish wit.

Here, Shakespeare played with the order of the two words "wit" and "fool," such that they can be put like "witty fool" and "foolish wit," so as to "admonish…pretension." (WK 2010q; L. Salingar 1976)

Wit with word play like this kind of reversal often requires "conceptual thinking, as a kind of verbal display requiring attention, without intending to be laugh-aloud funny; in fact wit can be a thin disguise for more poignant feelings that are being versified." (WK 2010q)

(l) Paradox

In this eleventh technique of paradox (also known as incongruity or inconsistency)—the joke exploits a literary device for "an anomalous juxtaposition of incongruous ideas." (WK 2010u)

For instance, in the works of Oscar Wilde, there is the following joke with the use of paradox: (WK 2010u)

I can resist anything except temptation.

And G. K. Chesterton made use of the same literary technique with the statement like "spies do not look like spies." (WK 2010u)

The Cultural Factor

Surely, all these techniques of jokes are not meant to be exhaustive but solely illustrative.

Yet, there is also a cultural factor in understanding these techniques of jokes. Consider, for illustration, two major differences among cultures in terms of their receptiveness to humor (like the techniques of joking), as discussed below (and summarized in *Table 2.4*).

(a) Laid-Back Cultures

In *Sec. 4.2.3* of *Beyond Nature and Nurture* (2006), I already discussed "the case of the value system of the three H's," in which "humor" is "the last of the three H's," with the Sub-Saharan Africa as a case study.

The central point to remember here is that some cultures are more receptive to humor than others, and the Sub-Saharan Africa is a good example of a continent which is known for being joyful of joking and laughing.

For instance, "[t]he words of Fela, the great black African singer of the 1970s, spoke volumes of this indigenous value with these consoling words: 'We Nigerians look after each other. We suffer and we smile.' (J. Power 2003)" (P. Baofu 2006: 89-90)

In fact, "[t]his flavor of African humor…can be illustrated further in a 2006 South African film called 'Tsotsi,' which showed the 'humanizing portrait of a brutal young gang leader who is transformed when he unwittingly carjacks an automobile with a baby inside.' (S. Tomlinson 2006)" (P. Baofu 2006: 89-90)

And in "Teddy Mattera's 2004 comedy, 'Max and Mona' from South Africa, which 'follows a country boy's misadventures in the big city,' with its 'street language and earthy jokes.' (S. Tomlinson 2006)" (P. Baofu 2006: 89-90)

Not surprisingly, "a recent survey known as The World Values Survey, an inter-university study, ranked one of the poorest countries on Earth, Nigeria, a sub-Saharan African country, as 'the happiest people in the world,' in spite of their poverty and suffering. (J. Power 2003)" (P. Baofu 2006: 89-90)

By contrast, "[p]eople in Japan and the Western world are no more happy now than they were in the 1950s, despite a massive increase in income. In fact, extra money has little impact on people's happiness once a country has more than $15,000 (£8,000) per head." (BBC 2006; P. Baofu 2006: 89-90)

Even "W.E.B. Du Bois, in his travel to sub-Saharan Africa, once admiringly wrote about the preindustiral simplicity and merriness in the region: 'We are the supermen who sit idly by and laugh and look at civilization. We, who frankly want the bodies of our mates and conjure no blush to our bronze cheeks when we own it.' (F. Zakaria 1997)" (P. Baofu 2006: 89-90)

Unfortunately, this is also one of the reasons for "one of the origins of the derogatory stereotype by Europeans towards black Africans in their imperial encounter with the natives, namely, the so-called 'happy-go-lucky' disposition…." (P. Baofu 2006: 89-90)

(b) Authoritarian Cultures

But culture can have another impact on the use of humor, depending on its authoritarian tradition.

For instance, "Akinwande Oluwole 'Wole' Soyinka (born 13 July 1934) is a Nigerian writer, poet and playwright. He won the Nobel Prize in Literature in 1986." (WK 2010w)

As a writer, Soyinka is known for his use of humor (especially satire and parody to talk about "dangerous ideas") so as to criticize the political oppression in his country (like his critique of "Nigerian military dictators") and in Africa (like his critique of "the Mugabe regime in Zimbabwe"). (WK 2010a & 2010w)

For instance, during 1975-1984, "Soyinka...criticized the corruption in the government of democratically-elected President Shehu Shagari, and often found himself at odds with his military successor, Mohammadu Buhari. In 1984 a Nigerian court banned *The Man Died* and in 1985 the play *Requiem for a Futurologist* went into print in London." (WK 2001w)

Then, "[i]n July 1991 the BBC African Service transmits his radio play *A Scourge of Hyacinths*, and the next year (in June 1992) in Siena (Italy), his play *From Zia with Love* has its premiere. Both works are very bitter political parodies, based on events which took place in Nigeria in the 1980s." (WK 2010w)

Then, "[i]n November 1994 Soyinka fled from Nigeria through the border with Benin and then to the United States....His play *King Baabu*, premiered in Lagos in 2001, is a political satire on the theme of African dictatorship and the 'warped aspect of human nature that makes people think they have the right to dominate others and also inflict very agonising experiences on fellow humans.'" (WK 2010w; E. Ibagere 2005)

A Note of Caution

Lest misunderstanding easily occurs, it should be stressed that this intrdoduction to the cultural factor in regard to the techniques of joking does not mean to suggest that laid-back cultures are better overall, because they can enhance human happiness with the indulgence in joking and laughing. On the contrary, indeed, laid-back cultures are often not as efficient and competitive as non-laid-back ones in the global pecking order (like those in contemporary Western Europe, America, and Japan, for instance).

Nor should one erroneously assume that authoritarian cultures are always malevolent and non-authoritarian (democratic) ones are always benevolent. On the contrary, again, I also went to great lengths in *Beyond Democracy to Post-Democracy* (2004) to show the dark (malevolent) sides of democracy which have often been ignored in mainstream media. Then, in *The Rise of Authoritarian Liberal Democracy* (2007), I also vigorously explained that authoritarian and non-authoritarian (democratic) cultures have more in common than are often conventionally assumed, as shown in what I originally called "authoritarian liberal democracy," in that, as liberal democracy becomes more advanced, it can also become more authoritarian.

Rather, this intrdoduction to the cultural factor in regard to the techniques of joking is to show us the dark sides of joking (in its other, dubious relationships with laid-back and authoritarian cultures), such that the possibility and desirability of joking (from the perspective of culture with the techniques of joking and the cultural factor as a case study here) are not to the extent that the respective defenders would like us to believe.

In addition, this introduction to the techniques of joking and the cultural factor reveals something important about the ontological principles in existential dialectics, and good examples include the absoluteness-relativeness principle, the predictability-unpredictability principle, the explicability-inexplicability principle, the preciseness-vagueness principle, the simpleness-complicatedness principle, the openness-hiddenness principle, the denseness-emptiness principle, the change-constancy principle, the slowness-quickness principle, the expansion-contraction principle, the theory-praxis principle, the convention-novelty principle, the evolution-transformation principle, the symmetry-asymmetry principle, the seriousness-playfulness principle, the regression-progression principle, and the same-difference principle.

For instance, in relation to the absoluteness-relativeness principle, if there is absoluteness (e.g., the absolute orientation of satire and parody to criticize "Nigerian military dictators" by Soyinka), there is relativeness (e.g., what is funny for Soyinka in his satire and parody is not necessarily so for the "Nigerian military dictators" who condemned him, as "[i]n 1997 Soyinka was charged with treason by the government of General Sani Abacha"). (WK 2010w) And the reverse direction also holds true.

In relation to the predictability-unpredictability principle, if there is predictability (e.g., the predictable tendency of the cultrual factor in shaping the use of humor in a continent, as in black Africa), there is unpredictability (e.g., the more difficult task to predict exactly which cultural factor, be it laid-back culture or authoritarian culture, is more important in shaping the use of humor in a particular continent, to a particular extent, at a particular time, as in modern black Africa). And the reverse direction also holds true.

In relation to the explicability-inexplicability principle, if there is explicability (e.g., the explanation by people like Soyinka to use satire and parody for the critique of political oppression, because the ideas are "dangerous" for the regime in question), there is inexplicability (e.g., the lack of convincing explanation by people like Soyinka of why the use of satire and parody is effective and non-offensive to those in power). And the reverse direction also holds true.

In relation to the preciseness-vagueness principle, if there is preciseness (e.g., the precise identification of different techniques of joking in the literature), there is vagueness (e.g., the vagueness in the techniques themselves, since they can be interpreted and used in different ways by different users, as some scholars had even suggested that "there are about 200 techniques…that can be used to make jokes" with the use of "danger"). And the reverse direction also holds true.

In relation to the simpleness-complicatedness principle, if there is simpleness (e.g., the relatively simple analysis of the techniques of joking, so that people can use them to be funny), there is complicatedness (e.g., the relatively more complicated analysis of the techniques of joking, by analyzing their cultural contingency, so as to show us the dark sides of joking in its other, dubious relationships with laid-back and authoritarian cultures). And the reverse direction also holds true.

In relation to the openness-hiddenness principle, if there is openness (e.g., the open exploration of using satire and parody for political criticisms), there is hiddenness (e.g., the hidden bias in the use of satire and parody for political criticisms, because of the offensiveness towards those in power, as the other side of the same coin). And the reverse direction also holds true.

In relation to the denseness-emptiness principle, if there is denseness (e.g., the relatively denser concentration of people in a laid-back culture to indulge in joking and laughing), there is emptiness (e.g., the relatively less dense, or more empty, concentration of people in a highly efficient, competitive culture like modern Japan, to indulge in joking and laughing, again, relatively speaking). And the reverse direction also holds true.

In relation to the change-constancy principle, if there is change (e.g., the ever new ways to make jokes, as shown in the varieties of the techniques of joking over time), there is constancy (e.g., the ever constancy of the existence of different techniques of joking in humor). And the reverse direction also holds true.

In relation to the slowness-quickness principle, if there is slowness (e.g., the relatively slower readiness of people in authoritarian cultures to criticize their military dictators head-on, in a confrontional way), there is quickness (e.g., the relatively quicker readiness of people in authoritarian cultures to criticize their military dictators with the use of satire, parody, wit, and the like). And the reverse direction also holds true.

In relation to the expansion-contraction principle, if there is expansion (e.g., the relativley more developed ability of those in humor to make use of such techniques as "danger," "void," and "ambiguity," for instance), there is contraction (e.g., the relativley less developed ability of those in humor to make use of logical consistency, conventional wisdom, etc.). And the reverse direction also holds true.

In relation to the theory-praxis principle, if there is theory (e.g., the theoretical construction of such techniques of joking like "danger," and so on), there is praxis (e.g., the practical application of the technique of joking like "danger" in the fields of satire and parody to the critique of military dictactorship by Soyinka). And the reverse direction also holds true.

In relation to the convention-novelty principle, if there is convention (e.g., the conventional wisdom about military dictatorship in modern Nigeria), there is novelty (e.g., the alternative novel challenge to the conventional wisdom about military dictatorship in modern Nigeria, by the new daring thinking to condemn it and propose a more democratic one, as shown in the work of Soyinka). And the reverse direction also holds true.

In relation to the evolution-transformation principle, if there is evolution (e.g., the natural evolution of humans to be playful in the state of nature), there is transformation (e.g, the technical transformation of human playing with each other by the invention of the specific techniques of joking, as shown in the examples). And the reverse direction also holds true.

In relation to the symmetry-asymmetry principle, if there is symmetry (e.g., the co-existence of different techniques of joking over time), there is asymmetry (e.g., the more pervasive use of the technique of "danger" under the cover of satire, wit, and parody in authoritarian cultures—but the more pervasive use of direct critique in those non-authoritarian cultures which allow some degree of free speech). And the reverse direction also holds true.

In relation to the seriousness-playfulness principle, if there is seriousness (e.g., the serious nature of Soyinka's work to criticize political oppression in Nigeria), there is playfulness (e.g., the joyful, funny aspect of reading the satire, parody, and wit in Soyinka's work). And the reverse direction also holds true.

In relation to the regression-progression principle, if there is regression (e.g., the regression made by the techniques of joking, as shown by the dark sides of joking in its other, dubious relationships with laid-back and authoritarian cultures), there is progression (e.g., the progress made by the techniques of joking to criticize political oppression, for instance). And the reverse direction also holds true.

And in relation to the same-difference principle, if there is similarity in outcome (e.g., the contribution to the molding and regulation of beliefs and values, regardless of whether this be done by way of satire and parody or by way of direct political critique), there is difference in outcome (e.g., the contribution to the molding and control of beliefs and values by way of satire and parody for a more subtle, covert form of political culture—but the contribution to the molding and control of beliefs and values by way of direct political critique for a more confrontional form of poltical culture). And the reverse direction also holds true.

The Malignity of Joking

This comprehensive analysis of the possibility and desirability of joking, from the perspectives of the mind, nature, society, and culture, has the scholarly virtue to reveal the different ways in which joking is both possible and desirable, but not to the extent that the spokespersons from each side would like us to believe.

Joking thus has its benignity, just as it has its malignity too, as the other side of the same coin.

But this is only one part of a larger story, since there is the other side of the story, which is about laughing, the receiving end of humor. Since this chapter already deals with joking, the next chapter will therefore address the issue of laughing.

These dual analyses are important enough, because those on the side of joking often treat laughing merely as the receiving end of humor without really appreciating it from the side of laughing too.

With this in mind, let's now turn to Chapter Three for the study of laughing and its dual facets—for which we now turn to chapter three.

Table 2.1. Joking and Its Double Faces

- **Joking and the Mind**
  —Ex: joking, the mind, and the psychology of jokes
  —Ex: joking, black comedy, and the question about human nature

- **Joking and Nature**
  —Ex: joking, IFF, and the controversy about evolution

- **Joking and Society**
  —Ex: joking, and the politics of satire
  —Ex: joking, race/ethnic humor, and the power equation

- **Joking and Culture**
  —Ex: joking, flatulence humor, and the culture of shifting blame
  —Ex: the techniques of joking, and the cultural factor

Notes: The examples in the categories are solely illustrative (not exhaustive), and the comparison is relative (not absolute), nor are they necessarily mutually exclusive. And some can be easily re-classified elsewhere. As generalities, they allow exceptions.
Source: A summary of Ch.2 of *FPHH*

Table 2.2. Joking in Black Humor, and the Debate on Human Nature

- **On the Negative**
  —Ex: Sigmund Freud (1966), for instance, argued that "men are not gentle creatures who want to be loved, and who at the most can defend themselves if they are attacked; they are, on the contrary, creatures among whose instinctual endowments is to be reckoned a powerful share of aggressiveness. As a result, their neighbor is for them…someone who tempts them to satisfy their aggressiveness on him, to exploit his capacity for work without compensation, to use him sexually without his consent, to seize his possessions, to humiliate him, to cause him pain, to torture and to kill him. *Homo homini lupus*." Therefore, for Freud, "[i]f you look at jokes, they are either about somebody getting hurt, or they have sexual connotations." (A. Chislenko 2010)
  —Ex: Thomas Hobbes, for another, made a comparable point when he argued that humans are "nasty, brutish and short" in the state of nature, with "a war of every man, against every man." (T. Magstadt 1999:474-5)

- **On the Affirmative**
  –Ex: Confucius and Mencius argued that "humans are essentially good and, with the teaching of the right rules and duties, can contribute to a more harmonious society." (P. Baofu 2004: Ch.3)
  –Ex: Jean-Jacques Rousseau (1984) in *A Discourse on Inequality* is on the same side, when he "criticized Hobbes for asserting that since man in the 'state of nature…has no idea of goodness, he must be naturally wicked; that he is vicious because he does not know virtue.' On the contrary, Rousseau holds that 'uncorrupted morals' prevail in the 'state of nature' and he especially praised the admirable moderation of the Caribbeans in expressing the sexual urge despite the fact that they live in a hot climate, which 'always seems to inflame the passions.'" (WK 2010h)

Notes: The examples in the categories are solely illustrative (not exhaustive), and the comparison is relative (not absolute), nor are they necessarily mutually exclusive. And some can be easily re-classified elsewhere. As generalities, they allow exceptions.
Source: From *Sec. 2.2.2* of *FPHH.* See book for citations.

Table 2.3. Joking, and the Politics of Satire

- **Two Types of Satire**
  —Ex: Horatian
  —Ex: Juvenalian

- **Satire and Its Politics**
  —By nature, "[p]olitical satire is a significant part of satire that specializes in gaining entertainment from politics; it has also been used with subversive intent where political speech and dissent are forbidden by a regime, as a method of advancing political arguments where such arguments are expressly forbidden." (WK 2010j)
  —However, one should not confuse "political satire" with "political protest or political dissent," because political satire "does not necessarily carry an agenda nor seek to influence the political process. While occasionally it may, it more commonly aims simply to provide entertainment. By its very nature, it rarely offers a constructive view in itself; when it is used as part of protest or dissent, it tends to simply establish the error of matters rather than provide solutions." (WK 2010j)

- **Satire under Attack**
  —Firstly, satire does not necessarily lessen political intolerance.
  —Secondly, satire does not necessarily have public support.
  —Thirdly, satire is not necesssarily innocent (non-offensive) as its practitioners may claim, under the cover of being funny.

Notes: The examples in the categories are solely illustrative (not exhaustive), and the comparison is relative (not absolute), nor are they necessarily mutually exclusive. And some can be easily re-classified elsewhere. As generalities, they allow exceptions.
Source: From *Sec. 2.4.1* of *FPHH*. See book for more details and citations.

Table 2.4. The Techniques of Joking, Culture, and Rationality (Part I)

• **The Techniques of Joking**
—Ex: precision
—Ex: economy
—Ex: rhythm (timing)
—Ex: disproportion (stretching)
—Ex: danger
—Ex: void
—Ex: rhyme
—Ex: ambiguity
—Ex: opposite expectation (reversal)
—Ex: word-order (reversal)
—Ex: paradox (inconsistency)

• **The Cultural Factor**
—Ex: laid-back cultures
—Ex: authoritarian cultures

• **The Impact on Rationality**
—The essential techniques (like incongruity, paradox, ambiguity, disproportion, reversal, surprise, etc.) can challenge the conventional thinking about the nature of logic. In *The Future of Post-Human Mathematical Logic* (2008), I already went to great lengths to explain the need for alternative ways to understand logic, that is, "the contrastive theory of rationality," in that classical logics need to be transcended for a new "rationality of knowledge" at the meta-theoretical level—so as to include (or adjust for) heterogeneity, conflict, subjectivity, complexity, and so on.
—The role of humor precisely adds to this urgent need for a new "rationality of knowledge," because of the existence of the playful dimension of intelligent life, not just its serious one, with enormous implications for both humans and later, post-humans.

(continued on next page)

Table 2.4. The Techniques of Joking, Culture, and Rationality (Part II)

- **The Impact on Rationalty (*cont'd*)**
  —Yet, lest any misunderstanding occurs, this post-human rendition in regard to humor will bring neither utopia nor dystopia. In fact, in *The Future of Post-Human Creative Thinking* (2009), I already warned against the "ambivalent" legacy of different rationalities in practice (with both good and bad consequences), which results when theoretical constructs are used in practice for different applications to serve different human interests.
  —Three excellent categories of these rationalities in practice are "instrumental rationality" (e.g., for the sake of efficiency and effectiveness), "substantive rationality" (e.g., for the sake of God, the King, Motherland, or others), and "autonomous rationality" (e.g., for the sake of itself, the autonomy of creative endeavor).
  —In fact, I further analyzed the "ambivalent" legacy of these rationalities in practice in the context of technology in *The Future of Post-Human Engineering* (2009).
  —These three rationalities in practice to serve human interests can now be called the "rationalities of application" at the practical level, so as to be distinguished from the "rationalities of knowledge" at the meta-theoretical level.

Notes: The examples are solely illustrative (not exhaustive), and the comparison is relative (not absolute), nor are they necessarily mutually exclusive. And some can be easily re-classified elsewhere. As generalities, they allow exceptions.
Source: From *Sec. 2.5.1* and *Sec. 4. 20* of *FPHH.* See book for citations.

• PART THREE •

Laughing

CHAPTER 3
LAUGHING AND ITS DUAL FACETS

> One excellent test of the civilization of a country ...[is] the flourishing of the Comic idea and Comedy; and the test of true Comedy is that it shall awaken thoughtful laughter."
> —George Meredith (WK 2010k)

The Joy of Laughing

Humor has two sides, namely, joking (as its giving end) and laughing (as its receiving end)—as already analyzed in *Sec. 1.2*.

This relationship between joking and laughing is true, even though not all forms of laughing are related to joking at all, as some can result from being "tickled, or other stimuli" (like joy, playfulness, and so on), as already clarified in *Sec. 1.2*.

With this reminder in mind—any study of humor requires an inquiry of the nature of both joking and laughing, as one cannot be completely separated from the other.

Therefore, this book offers a dialectic treatment of joking and laughing in that, if joking has its benignity, it has its malignity too—just as, if laughing has its joy, it likewise has its sorrow.

The inquiry concernng laughing is the subject matter of this chapter (Chapter Three), whereas that of joking was already discussed in the prevoius chapter (Chapter Two).

Again, as was already warned in Chapter Two, this relationship between joking and laughing poses a scholarly challenge here, in that one cannot analyze laughing (or joking, for that matter) completely separately.

This then means that the issues concerning laughing in this chapter (Chapter Three) and joking in the previous chapter (Chapter Two) often overlap, as each issue on the former can be relevant to the latter too.

With this caveat in mind—a good way to examine laughing and its dual facets is by way of the evaluation of the extent to which it (laughing) is in fact both possible and desirabe.

This chapter thus takes the challenging task to provide a comprehensive analysis of laughing in the context of humor from the four perspectives of the mind, nature, society, and culture (in accordance to my sophisticated methodological holism, as explained in *Sec. 1.7*).

So, this chapter is organized in four main sections, in relation to (3.2) laughing and the mind, (3.3) laughing and nature, (3.4) laughing and society, and (3.5) laughing and culture—to be analyzed hereafter, in that order (and summarized in *Table 3.1*).

Laughing and the Mind

Laughing, when examined from the perspective of the mind, can teach us something interesting about its possibility and desirability, and this can be shown by way of two case studies, namely, (3.2.1) laughing, health, and the dark sides, and (3.2.2) laughing, therapy, and the debate in gelotology—to be addressed in what follows, in that order.

Laughing, Health, and the Dark Sides

Laughing, as already introduced in *Sec. 1.2*, refers to "an audible expression of happiness, or an inward feeling of joy. It may ensue from hearing a joke, being tickled, or other stimuli. It is in most cases a very pleasant sensation." (WK 2010b)

Laughing and the Brain

Laughter is by no means unique to humans, as it "is found among various animals....Scientists have noted the similarity in forms of laughter among various primates, which suggests that laughter derives from a common origin among primate species." (WK 2010b; BBC 2009)

In humans, however, laughing is more complicated, as it is "a part of human behavior regulated by the brain, helping humans clarify their intentions in social interaction and providing an emotional context to conversations." (WK 2010b)

Studies by neurophysiologists over the years showed that "laughter is linked with the activation of the ventromedial prefrontal cortex, that produces endorphins. Scientists have shown that parts of the limbic system are involved in laughter. This system is involved in emotions and helps us with functions necessary for human's survival. The structures in the limbic system that are involved in laughter: the hippocampus and the amygdala." (WK 2010b)

According to a report published in the December 7, 1984 issue of *Journal of the American Medical Association*, "the neurological causes of laughter" can be understood in what follows: (WK 2010b)

> Although there is no known "laugh center" in the brain, its neural mechanism has been the subject of much, albeit inconclusive, speculation. It is evident that its expression depends on neural paths arising in close association with the telencephalic and diencephalic centers concerned with respiration. Wilson considered the mechanism to be in the region of the mesial thalamus, hypothalamus, and subthalamus. Kelly and co-workers, in turn, postulated that the tegmentum near the periaqueductal grey contains the integrating mechanism for emotional expression. Thus, supranuclear pathways, including those from the limbic system that Papez hypothesised to mediate emotional expressions such as laughter, probably come into synaptic relation in the reticular core of the brain stem. So while purely emotional responses such as laughter are mediated by subcortical structures, especially the hypothalamus, and are stereotyped, the cerebral cortex can modulate or suppress them.

In addition, laughing also has a strong relationship with health.

Laughing and Health

In 2005, for instance, "[a] link between laughter and healthy function of blood vessels was first reported...by researchers at the University of Maryland Medical Center with the fact that laughter causes the dilatation of the inner lining of blood vessels, the endothelium, and increases blood flow." (WK 2010b; M. Miller 2006)

In the study, "Drs. Michael Miller (University of Maryland) and William Fry (Stanford), theorize that beta-endorphin like compounds released by the hypothalamus activate receptors on the endothelial surface to release nitric oxide, thereby resulting in dilation of vessels. Other cardioprotective properties of nitric oxide include reduction of inflammation and decreased platelet aggregation." (WK 2010b; C. Vlachopoulos 2009)

In 2010, Amber Angelle (2010) wrote in an artilce titled "Laugh Well, Live Well" in the October issue of *Discover* that "laughter boosts the immune system, lowers cholesterol and blood pressure, and reduces stress."

Nowadays, "[s]tudies show that people who laugh more often get sick less." (WK 2010k; G. Meredith 1897) And this confirms the old wisdom held by the ancient Greeks that humor is important to good health, as already described in *Sec. 1.2*.

Laughing and the Dark Sides

However, laughing also has its own dark sides. Consider, for illustration, the following three dark sides of laughing—to be summarized in *Table 3.2*.

(a) Stigmatization and Degradation

Laughing has its own dark side, namely, stigmatization and degradation, or "the 'sudden glory' that philosopher Thomas Hobbes saw as the heart of laughter that emerged, from a 'conception of some eminency in ourselves,'" as Jaak Pankseppa (2003) and Jeff Burgdorf once pointed out. (J. Gregory 1924)

For instance, "the children that prevail in play tend to laugh the most, suggesting that to some extent laughter may reflect a social dominance-seeking response, which may pave the way for laughter to stigmatize and degrade others through such behavior. All too often, especially in children, laughter tends to become a psychological tool for teasing and taunting—the establishment of exclusionary group identities that can set the stage for finding mirth in the misfortunes of others. These tendencies may arise rather naturally from the fact that within-group laughter promotes group solidarity, which can then be used to ostracize and exhibit scorn toward those outside the group." (J. Pankseppa 2003; N. Blurton 1992)

Similary, "[i]n adults, most laughter occurs in the midst of simple friendly social interactions while greeting and 'ribbing' each other rather than in response to explicit verbal jokes. The two are brought together in our institution of 'roasting' those we love and admire: The more dominant the targets of the roast, the more mirth there is to be had at their good-humored expense. Surely our appreciation of such subtle types of humor arises from fully matured comico-cognitive developments of the brain." (J. Pankseppa 2003)

(b) PLC

Laughing has another dark side, namely, the disorder called "pathological laughing and crying (PLC), also known as pseudobulbar affect (PBA)," which refers to "a syndrome in which patients experience relatively uncontrollable episodes of laughing or crying, or both." (WK 2010v)

PLC can be "provoked by nonsentimental or trivially-sentimental stimuli. These episodes are not manifestations of a mood disorder such as major depression or mania, where laughing and crying are expressed in tandem with feelings of happiness or sadness, nor do they represent ictal displays of affect. While there is general agreement that PLC is a disorder of affect, and not of mood, there are disagreements about both its core clinical features and whether PLC is the best diagnostic term for this condition." (WK 2010v; H. Wortzel 2008)

In any event, it is now known that "PLC is a frequent consequence of brain injury, seen in approximately 10-20% of stroke, 7-10% of multiple sclerosis, 20-50% of amyotrophic lateral sclerosis, 5-10% of traumatic brain injury patients, 6% of Parkinson's patients as well as about 5% of noncerebellar type multiple system atrophy (MSA), and 37% of patients with the cerebellar type of MSA. [A.] Tetano et al. [2004] found that the prevalence of PLC for the patients in their study (closed head injury) was 3.3% at the initial evaluation, 7.1% at 3 months, 6.1% at 6 months, and 1.7% at 12 months." (WK 2010v; H. Wortzel 2008; A.; J. Parvizi 2006)

In addition, "PLC has long been thought to result from loss of voluntary inhibition of a postulated centre for laughing and crying in the upper brainstem. More recent authors have suggested that the prefrontal cortex is involved or that lesions in the cerebro-ponto-cerebellar pathways influence cerebellar structures that adjust the expression of laughter and crying." (WK 2010v; S. Wilson 1924; S. McCullagh 1999; J. Parvizi 2001)

However, other aspects of PLC are still uncertain. For instance, "[t]he incidence of PLC in Alzheimer's is a matter of controversy, with a large variation of estimates between 10 and 74%." (WK 2010v; H. Wortzel 2008) In another case, "[s]tudies have reported an inconsistent pattern of association between PLC and major depression. Sometimes an association is found; other studies find none." (WK 2010v)

With this issue of uncertainty aside—PLC can be lessened by treatment under certain conditions. For instance, "[p]atients administered tricyclic antidepressants show significant improvements in PLC, with no effect on coexisting depression. Reports that patients show partial to full remission within a week of starting low doses of SSRI suggest that serotonergic systems are involved. By comparison, major depression does not respond to SSRIs before three to five weeks of treatment. AVP-923, a compound consisting of dextromethorphan and quinidine, has also shown significant therapeutic effect." (WK 2010v; R. Schiffer 1985; R. Robinson 1993; J. van Wattum 2001; B. Brooks 2004; H. Panitch 2006)

(c) Death from Laughter

Laughing has an additional dark side, namely, "death from laughter," which is postponed for analysis until *Sec. 3.5.2* on laughing, death, and the coverage in popular culture.

A Broader Perspective

Yet, this double take of laughing in relation to both health and the dark sides does not mean to trivialize laughing but to show us the opposing sides of the debate, such that the possibility and desirability of laughing (from the perspective of the mind with laughing, health, and the dark sides as a case study here) are not to the extent that the respective defenders would like us to believe.

More fundamentally, the analysis of laughing, health, and the dark sides can teach us something valuable about the ontological principles in existential dialectics, and good examples include the formalness-informalness principle, the absoluteness-relativeness principle, the predictability-unpredictability principle, the explicability-inexplicability principle, the preciseness-vagueness principle, the simpleness-complicatedness principle, the openness-hiddenness principle, the denseness-emptiness principle, the order-chaos principle, the slowness-quickness principle, the expansion-contraction principle, the theory-praxis principle, the convention-novelty principle, the evolution-transformation principle, the symmetry-asymmetry principle, the seriousness-playfulness principle, the regression-progression principle, and the same-difference principle.

For instance, in relation to the formalness-informalness principle, if there is formalness (e.g., the formal logical requirement of consistency and soundness in a system of ideas, like those in science), there is informalness (e.g., the nonformal existence of inconsistency and unsoundness, as shown in the research on the association "between PLC and major depression," as "[s]ometimes an association is found" but "other studies find none"). And the reverse direction also holds true.

In relation to the absoluteness-relativeness principle, if there is absoluteness (e.g., the absolute view by the ancient Greeks that laughing is important to good health), there is relativeness (e.g., what is true for the ancient Greeks that laughing is important to good health is not necessarily so for modern researchers on the dark sides of laughing). And the reverse direction also holds true.

In relation to the predictability-unpredictability principle, if there is predictability (e.g., the predictable tendency of PLC as "a frequent consequence of brain injury"), there is unpredictability (e.g., the more difficult task to predict exactly "[t]he incidence of PLC in Alzheimer's," which remains nowadays "a matter of controversy"). And the reverse direction also holds true.

In relation to the explicability-inexplicability principle, if there is explicability (e.g., the explanation by those like Angelle that laughing is important to good health, because "laughter boosts the immune system, lowers cholesterol and blood pressure, and reduces stress"), there is inexplicabiltiy (e.g., the lack of sufficient explanation, if looked only from the viewpoint of Angelle, of why laughing can be bad to the health of PLC patients and to those being stigmatized). And the reverse direction also holds true.

In relation to the preciseness-vagueness principle, if there is precisenss (e.g., the precise identification of the correlation between PLC and major depression), there is vagueness (e.g., the vagueness in the identification, since "studies have reported an inconsistent pattern of association between PLC and major depression"). And the reverse direction also holds true.

In relation to the simpleness-complicatedness principle, if there is simpleness (e.g., the relatively simple view by the ancient Greeks that laughing is important to good health), there is complicatedness (e.g., the relatively more complicated analysis of laughing by making some qualifications about its desirability, like the dark sides of laughing). And the reverse direction also holds true.

In relation to the openness-hiddenness principle, if there is openness (e.g., the open exploration of the positive relationship between laughing and health by the ancient Greeks), there is hiddenness (e.g., the hidden bias in the view about the importance of laughing to good health, because of its neglect of the dark sides of laughing). And the reverse direction also holds true.

In relation to the denseness-emptiness principle, if there is denseness (e.g., the relatively denser concentration of PLC patients to have brain injury), there is emptiness (e.g., the relativley less dense, or more empty, concentration of normal individuals without PLC to have brain injury). And the reverse direction also holds true.

In relation to the order-chaos principle, if there is order (e.g., the relatively orderly behavior of normal individuals when they laugh, when compared with those of PLC patients), there is chaos (e.g., the relatively chaotic behavior of PLC patients when they laugh, especially in regard to their "relatively uncontrollable episodes of laughing or crying, or both"). And the reverse direction also holds true.

In relation to the slowness-quickness principle, if there is slowness (e.g., the relatively slower speed of normal indivduals without PLC to laugh, when "provoked by nonsentimental or trivially-sentimental stimuli"), there is quickness (e.g., the relatively faster speed of PLC patients to laugh, when "provoked by nonsentimental or trivially-sentimental stimuli"). And the reverse direction also holds true.

In relation to the expansion-contraction principle, if there is expansion (e.g., the relatively more developed ability of normal individiuals to control their episodes of laughing or crying in daily life), there is contraction (e.g., the relatively less developed ability of normal individiuals to allow "relatively uncontrollable episodes of laughing or crying, or both" in daily life, even if for fun). And the reverse direction also holds true.

In relation to the theory-praxis principle, if there is theory (e.g., the theoretical construction of tricyclic antidepressants in chemistry), there is praxis (e.g., the practical application of tricyclic antidepressants in chemistry to the healing of PLC patients). And the reverse direction also holds true.

In relation to the convention-novelty principle, if there is convention (e.g.., the conventional wisdom about the importance of laughing to good health), there is novelty (e.g., the altenrative novel challenge to the conventional wisdom about the importantce of laughing to good health, by the sober view about the dark sides of laughing). And the reverse direction also holds true.

In relation to the evolution-transformation principle, if there is evolution (e.g., the natural evolution of humans to laugh in the state of nature), there is transformation (e.g., the technical transformation of human ability to laugh by the invention of drugs like tricyclic antidepressants to control "episodes of laughing or crying"). And the reverse direction also holds true.

In relation to the symmetry-asymmetry principle, if there is symmetry (e.g., the co-existence of different views about the importance of laughing to good health), there is asymmetry (e.g., the more popular view in ancient Greece that laughing is important to good health—but the more qualified view about laughing and health nowadays, because of the research on the dark sides of laughing). And the reverse direction also holds true.

In relation to the seriousness-playfulness principle, if there is seriousness (e.g., the serious side of laughing for good health), there is playfulness (e.g., the playful side of laughting for jokes). And the reverse direction also holds true.

In relation to the regression-progression principle, if there is regression (e.g., the regression made by laughing, as shown in the problems about the dark sides of laughing), there is progression (e.g., the progress made by laughing, as in the benefits for good health, under certain conditions). And the reverse direction also holds true.

And in relation to the same-difference principle, if there is similarity in outcome (e.g., the contribution to the molding and regulation of beliefs and behaviors, regardless of whether this be done by way of normal laughing or by way of excessive laughing), there is difference in outcome (e.g., the contribution to the molding and regulation of beliefs and behaviors by way of normal laughing for a more civilized lifeworld, with the proper etiquettes of laughing—but the contribution to the molding and regulation of beliefs and behaviors by way of excessive laughing, as in PLC individuals, for a more impulsive lifeworld, without the proper etiquettes of laughing). And the reverse direction also holds true.

Laughing, Therapy, and the Debate in Gelotology

There is another promise in the literature on laughing, besides its claim for good health (as discussed in the previous section), namely, that it is also good for therapy.

Thus, another way to evaluate the possibility and desirability of laughing from the perspective of the mind is to explore laughing, therapy, and this debate in gelotology—to be summarized in *Table 3.3*.

The term "gelotology" is related to this debate on laughing and therapy because it refers to "the study of laughter and its effects on the body, from a psychological and physiological perspective. Its proponents often advocate induction of laughter on therapeutic grounds....The word is from the Greek *gelos*, *geloto* meaning laugh, laughter, laughing." (WK 2010x; S. Cardoso 2010)

Laughing and Therapy

The issue of laughing in relation to therapy, according to a report by the *Journal of Psychosocial Nursing and Mental Health Services*, is "well documented" and an "ongoing research"; for instance, it "has led to new and beneficial therapies practiced by doctors, psychiatrists, and other mental health professionals using humor and laughter to help patients cope or treat a variety of physical and psychological issues." (WK 2010x; C. MacDonald 2004)

Altough "[t]The various therapies are not specific to health care professionals or clinicians...[s]ome of the therapies can be practiced individually or in a group setting to aid in a person's well-being. There seems to be something to the old saying 'laughter is the best medicine.' Or perhaps, as stated by Voltaire, 'The art of medicine consists of keeping the patient amused while nature heals the disease.'" (WK 2010x)

For illustration, hereafter are some of the most common therapies proposed over time: (WK 2010x)

- "Humor Therapy"—This type of therapy is "also known as therapeutic humor. Using humorous materials such as books, shows, movies, or stories to encourage spontaneous discussion of the patients' own humorous experiences. This can be provided individually or in a group setting. The process is facilitated by a clinician."

- "Laughter Therapy"—This type of therapy focuses on "[c]lients' laughter triggers," which "are identified...as people in their lives, things from childhood, situations, movies, jokes, comedians, etc. that make them laugh. Based on the information provided by the client, the clinician creates a personal humor profile to aid in the laughter therapy. In this one on one setting, the client is taught basic exercises that can be practiced. The intent of the exercises is to remind the importance of relationships and social support."

- "Laughter Meditation"—This type of therapy has "some similarities to traditional meditation. However, it is the laughter that focuses the person to concentrate on the moment. Through a three stage process of stretching, laughing and/or crying, and a period of meditative silence. In the first stage, the person places all energy into stretching every muscle without laughter. In the second stage, the person starts with a gradual smile, and then slowly begins to purposely belly laugh or cry, whichever occurs. In the final stage, the person abruptly stops laughing or crying, then with their eyes now closed they breathe without a sound and focus their concentration on the moment. The process is approximately a 15 minute exercise. This may be awkward for some people as the laughter is not necessarily spontaneous. This is generally practiced on an individual basis."

- "Laughter Yoga & Laughter Clubs"—This type of therapy is "somewhat similar to traditional yoga," because "laughter yoga is an exercise which incorporates breathing, yoga, and stretching techniques, along with laughter. The structured format includes several laughter exercises for a period of 30 to 45 minutes facilitated

> by a trained individual. Practicing it can be used as supplemental or preventative therapy. Laughter yoga can be performed in a group or a club. Therapeutic laughter clubs are extension of Laughter Yoga, but in a formalized club format. The need for humorous materials is not necessarily required. Laughter yoga is similar to yogic asana and the practice of Buddhist forced laughter."

Of course, there may be other types of therapy with the use of laughter too, but these examples here suffice for illustration at hand.

Main Problems with the Claim for Therapy

However, for the critics, the claim for therapy in gelotology is not what it may seem. For illustration, consider the following criticisms, as summarized in *Table 3.3*.

Firstly, one main criticism of using laughter for therapy is that it is often difficult in practice to find things that all participants find humorous.

For instance, in the case of humor therapy, it is well known that "[t]here can be a disadvantage to humor therapy in a group format, as it can be difficult to provide materials that all participants find humorous." (WK 2010x)

Secondly, another main criticism of using laughter for therapy is that it can be counterproductive, when some people are not sensitive enough to make a distinction between laughing "with" people and laughing "at" people.

For instance, in the case of humor therapy, this problem can all the more worsen, when a clinician in humor therapy is not "sensitive" enough to understand the distinction between "laughing 'with' clients rather than 'at' the clients. (WK 2010x)

Thirdly, still another main criticism of using laughter for therapy is that it is not quite natural (or "spontaneous") for some individuals to laugh in a "structured" format in these types of therapy.

For instance, this problem shows up in the case of laughter yoga, because "[s]ome participants may find it awkward as laughter is not necessarily spontaneous in the structured format." (WK 2010x)

Fourthly, one more main criticism of using laughter for therapy is that not everyone likes humor; in fact, some may find it "sick."

For instance, studies had shown that "[n]ot everyone will appreciate humor therapy. Some people may consider humor for the sick or injured as inappropriate or harmful. Therefore, it is important to know or sense when humor will be therapeutic and when it will be inappropriate. It should be used cautiously at first in situations in which the sensitivity of the person to whom it is directed is uncertain or unknown." (EC 2010a)

And fifthly, one last main criticism of using laughter for therapy is that there are negative side effects too.

For instance, one known "adverse side effect of humor therapy is that it can cause mental hurt, sadness, and alienation in persons who are not receptive to it, or if it is used insensitively." (EC 2010a)

And another adverse side effect of humor therapy is that there are the dark sides of laughter (as already discussed in the previous section), like "stigmatization," "ridicule," and "degradation."

Transcending the Debate

These criticisms against therapy in gelotology should not be mistakenly interperted as a total rejection of its benefits, because they are included so as to show us the opposing sides of the debate, such that the possibility and desirability of laughing (from the perspective of the mind with laughing, therapy, and the debate in gelotology as a case study here) are not to the extent that the respective defenders would like us to believe.

More importantly, the analysis of laughing, therapy, and the debate in gelotology can reveal something valuable about the ontological principles in existential dialectics, and good examples include the formalness-informalness principle, the absoluteness-relativeness principle, the predictability-unpredictability principle, the explicability-inexplicability principle, the preciseness-vagueness principle, the simpleness-complicatedness principle, the openness-hiddenness principle, the denseness-emptiness principle, the slowness-quickness principle, the expansion-contraction principle, the theory-praxis principle, the convention-novelty principle, the evolution-transformation principle, the symmetry-asymmetry principle, the softness-hardness principle, the seriousness-playfulness principle, the regression-progression principle, and the same-difference principle.

For instance, in relation to the formalness-informalness principle, if there is formalness (e.g., the formal logical requirement of soundness in a system of ideas, like those in gelotology), there is informalness (e.g., the non-formal existence of unsoundness about the claims and assumptions in regard to therapy in gelotology, as shown in the criticisms). And the reverse direction also holds true.

In relation to the absoluteness-relativeness principle, if there is absoluteness (e.g, the absolute view of the proponents in gelotology that laughter is good for therapy), there is relativeness (e.g., what is true for the proponents in gelotology that laughter is good for therapy is not necessarily so for the critics who question the claims and assumptions). And the reverse direction also holds true.

In relation to the predictability-unpredictability principle, if there is predictability (e.g., the predictable tendency of the practitioners in gelotology to use laughter for therapy), there is unpredictabiltiy (e.g., the more difficult task to predict exactly to what extent a group in a therapy session will respond to humor with laughter, or will respond "sponteanously," and so on, as the critics have questioned some of the claims). And the reverse direction also holds true.

In relation to the explicability-inexplicability principle, if there is explicabiltiy (e.g., the explanation by the practitioners of using laughter for therapy on the basis that laughter is good for health), there is inexplicability (e.g., the lack of sufficient explanation, if looked only within the worldview of the practitioners, of why laughter has its adverse side effects too). And the reverse direction also holds true.

In relation to the preciseness-vagueness principle, if there is preciseness (e.g., the precise identification of the four types of therapy by the practitioners in geolotolgy), there is vagueness (e.g., the vagueness in the identification, since it is not clear why there should be only four types, not five, six, seven, and so on). And the reverse direction also holds true.

In relation to the simpleness-complicatedness principle, if there is simpleness (e.g., the relatively simple analysis of gelotology on the basis of using laughter for therapy to improve health), there is complicatedness (e.g., the relatively more complicated analysis of using laughter for therapy by questioning its claims and assumptions, as shown in the criticisms by the critics). And the reverse direction also holds true.

In relation to the openness-hiddenness principle, if there is openness (e.g., the open exploration of the correlation between laughter and therapy in gelotology), there is hiddeness (e.g., the hiden bias in the field of study concerning laughter and therapy, because of its obsession with laughter without giving sufficient attention to the questionability of its claims and assumptions). And the reverse direction also holds true.

In relation to the denseness-emptiness principle, if there is denseness (e.g., the relatively denser concentration of people in gelotology to favor laughter for therapy to promote health), there is emptiness (e.g., the relatively less dense, or more emtpy, concentration of people who study the dark sides of laughter to advocate laughter for therapy to promote health, relatively speaking of course). And the reverse direction also holds true.

In relation to the slowness-quickness principle, if there is slowness (e.g., the relatively slower speed of individuals who "consider humor for the sick or injured as inappropriate or harmful" to engage in using laughter for therapy), there is quickness (e.g., the relatively quicker speed of the proponents in gelotology to engage in using laughter for therapy). And the reverse direction also holds true.

In relation to the expansion-contraction principle, if there is expansion (e.g., the relatively more developed ability of the proponents in gelotology to use laughter for therapy), there is contraction (e.g., the relatively less developed ability of those in gelotology to use psychoanalysis for therapy, like analyzing unconscious conflicts). And the reverse direction also holds true.

In relation to the theory-praxis principle, if there is theory (e.g., the theoretical construction of yoga), there is praxis (e.g., the practical application of yoga to therapy in gelotology). And the reverse direction also holds true.

In relation to the convention-novelty principle, if there is convention (e.g., the conventional wisdom in gelotology about laughter as good for health), there is novelty (e.g., the alternative novel challenge to the conventional wisdom in gelotology, by the critics who pointed out that there are adverse side effects in using laughter for therapy, as "it can cause mental hurt, sadness, and alienation in persons who are not receptive to it, or if it is used insensitively"). And the reverse direction also holds true.

In relation to the evolution-transformation principle, if there is evolution (e.g., the natural evolution of humans to laugh in the state of nature), there is transformation (e.g., the technical transformation of human ability to laugh by the invention of gelotology for using it in the domain of therapy, with different systematic therapeutic techniques). And the reverse direction also holds true.

In relation to the symmetry-asymmetry principle, if there is symmetry (e.g., the co-existence of different techniques for therapy in history over time), there is asymmetry (e.g., the use of humor for good health in ancient Greece—but the increasing popularity of using meditation and yoga in gelotology for good health, in conjunction with laugher, at our time). And the reverse direction also holds true.

In relation to the softness-hardness principle, if there is softness (e.g., the soft side of encouraging laughter for therapy in gelotology), there is hardness (e.g., the hard side of producing "mental hurt, sadness, and alienation in persons who are not receptive to it" in gelotology, as the adverse side effects). And the reverse direction also holds true.

In relation to the seriousness-playfulness principle, if there is seriousness (e.g., the serious side of gelotology to promote good health), there is playfulness (e.g., the playful side of gelotology to encourage laughter). And the reverse direction also holds true.

In relation to the regression-progression principle, if there is regression (e.g., the regression made by the use of laughter for therapy, as shown in the problems pointed out by the critics), there is progression (e.g., the progress made by the use of laugher for therapy, as shown in the benefits pointed out by the proponents). And the reverse direction also holds true.

And in relation to the same-difference principle, if there is similarity in outcome (e.g., the contribution to the molding and regulation of beliefs and behaviors, regardless of whether this be done by way of therapy in gelotology or by way of traditional healing without therapy), there is difference in outcome (e.g., the contribution to the molding and regulation of beliefs and behaviors by way of therapy in gelotology for a different form of "power" over individuals in contemporary society, as shown in the work of Michel Foucault like *The Birth of the Clinic* about the "truth" in the history of medicine—but the contribution to the molding and regulation of beliefs and behaviors by way of traditional healing without therapy for an alternative form of "power" over individuals in the older days, with a different undrestanding of the "truth" in the history of medicine). (WK 2010y & 2010z) And the reverse direction also holds true.

Laughing and Nature

Laughing, when examined from the perspective of nature, can reveal to us in a fascinating way its possibility and desirability, and this can be done by way of two case studies, namely, (3.3.1) laughing, animals, and the contentious comparison, and (3.3.2) laughing, animals, and the evolutionary claim—to be addressed below, in that order.

Laughing, Animals, and the Contentious Comparison

A fascinating study about laughter concerns to what extent it also exists in animals in the state of nature—to be summarized in *Table 3.4*.

Consider, for illustration, three well-known cases of laughter in non-humans, namely, (a) non-human primates, (b) rats, and (c) dogs, as described below, in that order.

Laughter in Non-Human Primates

In the case of non-human primates (like Chimpanzees, gorillas, bonobos and orangutans)—there are studies about "laughter-like vocalizations in response to physical contact, such as wrestling, play chasing, or tickling." (WK 2010aa)

There are a few indications used for the comparison between human primates and non-human ones.

Firstly, one indication concerns sound frequency and facial expressions. For instance, in one study analyzing and recording "sounds made by human babies and bonobos (also known as pygmy chimpanzees) when tickled," some researchers "found that although the bonobo's laugh was a higher frequency, the laugh followed the same spectrographic pattern of human babies," together with "similar facial expressions." (WK 2010aa)

Marina Davila-Ross of the University of Portsmouth, the lead author of the study, "made more than 800 recordings of the tickle-induced laughter of the apes and infants. Many of the characteristics of the actual frequencies in the recordings—such as the central and peak frequencies, and the variability of the frequencies within each laugh—were similar across all the subjects." (BBC 2009)

Secondly, another indication concerns the ticklish areas of the body. For instance, researchers also found that "[h]umans and chimpanzees share similar ticklish areas of the body such as the armpits and belly. The enjoyment of tickling in chimpanzees does not diminish with age." (WK2010aa)

Thirdly, still another indication concerns "voice stability" (which is about "the role that the voice plays in the sound of a laugh"). (BBC 2009)

For instance, as Davila-Ross explained, "[w]hen humans laugh, they voice stable sounds: that means the vocal folds are moving in a very regular synchronised way….We found these acoustic properties also in bonobos." (BBC 2009)

Therefore, "[b]ecause the sounds of the most closely related apes matched most closely in the analysis of the laughter, the researchers believe the work is proof of laughter's shared evolutionary origin, followed by adaptation to its form in the species we see today." (BBC 2009)

Laughter in Rats

In the case of rats—there are studies which also showed some similarities between humans and rats in laughing.

There are also a few indications used for the comparison between humans and rats.

Firstly, one indication is that "rats emit long, high frequency, ultrasonic, socially induced vocalization during rough and tumble play and when tickled. The vocalization is described as distinct 'chirping.'" (WK 2010aa)

In fact, "[c]hirping by rats is also reported in additional studies by Brian Knutson of the National Institutes of Health. Rats chirp when wrestling one another, before receiving morphine, or when mating. The sound has been interpreted as an expectation of something rewarding." (WK 2010aa; SN 2001)

And secondly, another indication is that, "like humans, rats have 'tickle skin.' These are certain areas of the body that generate more laughter response than others. The laughter is associated with positive emotional feelings and social bonding occurs with the human tickler, resulting in the rats becoming conditioned to seek the tickling. Additional responses to the tickling were those that laughed the most also played the most, and those that laughed the most preferred to spend more time with other laughing rats. This suggests a social preference to other rats exhibiting similar responses." (WK 2010aa)

Laughter in Dogs

And in the case of dogs—there are studies which showed that laughter can reduce stress in them.

For instance, it is now known that "[a] dog laugh sounds similar to a normal pant. By analyzing the pant using a sonograph, this pant varies with bursts of frequencies, resulting in a laugh. When this recorded dog-laugh vocalization is played to dogs in a shelter setting, it can initiate play, promote pro-social behavior, and decrease stress levels." (WK 2010aa)

In one study by Patricia Simonet (2005), Donna Versteeg, and Dan Storie, for instance, "120 subject dogs in a mid-size county animal shelter were observed. Dogs ranging from 4 months to 10 years of age were compared with and without exposure to a dog-laugh recording. The stress behaviors measured included panting, growling, salivating, pacing, barking, cowering, lunging, play-bows, sitting, orienting and lying down. The study resulted in positive findings when exposed to the dog laughing: significantly reduced stress behaviors, increased tail wagging and the display of a play-face when playing was initiated, and the increase of pro-social behavior such as approaching and lip licking were more frequent. This research suggests exposure to dog-laugh vocalizations can calm the dogs and possibly increase shelter adoptions." (WK 2010aa)

Main Problems in the Comparison

However, one should not get carried away with this comparison between human and non-human types of laughter without understanding its limits. Consider, for illustration, some problems in the comparison below (as summarized in *Table 3.4*).

Firstly, one main problem in the comparison between human and non-human laughters is that it is not clear if the animals really express joy.

For instance, "[c]himpanzee laughter is not readily recognizable to humans as such, because it is generated by alternating inhalations and exhalations that sound more like breathing and panting. It sounds similar to screeching....It is hard to tell...whether or not the chimpanzee is expressing joy. There are instances in which non-human primates have been reported to have expressed joy." (WK 2010aa)

Secondly, another main problem in the comparison between human and non-human laughters is that non-human laughter (like "chirping" in rats) cannot be heard by humans. So, to study laughter like this requires some special equipments and human interpretations.

Thirdly, still another main problem in the comparison between human and non-human laughters is that, in the case of rats, "as the rats age, there does appear to be a decline in the tendency to laugh and respond to tickle skin." (WK 2010aa) The same is not true for humans.

Fourthly, still one additional main problem in the comparison between human and non-human laughters is that laughter in animals does not suggest humor in animals.

For instance, in the case of rats, "the research was unable to prove rats have a sense of humor," although "it did indicate that they can laugh and express joy." (WK 2010aa; J. Pankseppa 2003)

And fifthly, still another additional main problem in the comparison between human and non-human laughters is that laughter in animals does not necessarily suggest comparable laugher in humans.

For instance, in the case of dogs, the research only reported "dog laugh sounds," which do not really show to what extent they are comparable to human ones.

Likewise, in the case of rats, the researchers for the study, Jaak Pankseppa (2003) and Jeff Burgdorf, even cautioned us with this conclusion, in that, "if we find a brain chemical that provokes rodent chirping, we will be most interested to see if it promotes human mirth,...but no comparable data is yet available at the human level."

It is thus no wonder that Robert Provine (1999) critically pointed out that "[o]ther animals produce vocalizations during play, but they are so different that it's difficult to equate them with laughter. Rats, for example, produce high-pitch vocalizations during play and when tickled. But it's very different in sound from human laughter."

Maneuvering between the Two Sides

Yet, these criticisms in regard to the contentious comparison between human and non-human laughters are not to mean that there is no laughter in animals at all but are to show us the opposing sides of the debate, such that the possibility and desirability of laughing (from the perspective of nature with laughing, animals, and the contentious comparison as a case study here) are not to the extent that the respective defenders would like us to believe.

More fundamentally, the analysis of laughing, animals, and the contentious comparison can teach us something relevant about the ontological principles in existential dialectics, and good examples include the formalness-informalness principle, the predictability-unpredictability principle, the explicability-inexplicability principle, the preciseness-vagueness principle, the simpleness-complicatedness principle, the openness-hiddenness principle, the denseness-emptiness principle, the slowness-quickness principle, the expansion-contraction principle, the theory-praxis principle, the convention-novelty principle, the evolution-transformation principle, the symmetry-asymmetry principle, the softness-hardness principle, the seriousness-playfulness principle, the regression-progression principle, and the same-difference principle.

For instance, in relation to the formalness-informalness principle, if there is formalness (e.g., the formal logical requirement of completeness in a system of ideas, like the research on laughter in animals), there is informalness (e.g., the non-formal existence of inconpleteness in the research on laugher in rats, as shown by "the research [which] was unable to prove rats have a sense of humor," although "it did indicate that they can laugh and express joy"). And the reverse direction also holds true.

In relation to the predictability-unpredictability principle, if there is predictability (e.g, the predictable tendency of non-human primates like chimpanzees and others to make "laughter-like vocalizations in response to physical contact, such as wrestling, play chasing, or tickling"), there is unpredictibility (e.g., the more difficult task to predict exactly when a particular "laughter-like vocalization" is really an expression of joy, because "[i]t is hard to tell…whether or not the chimpanzee is expressing joy"). And the reverse direction also holds true.

In relation to the explicability-inexplicability principle, if there is explanation (e.g., the explanation by the researchers in the study on rats, that, "as the rats age, there does appear to be a decline in the tendency to laugh and respond to tickle skin"), there is inexplicability (e.g., the lack of sufficient explanation, by the researchers in the study on rats, of why this decline occurs in rats, but not so in other primates, as shown in the study by Davila-Ross that "[t]he enjoyment of tickling in chimpanzees does not diminish with age"). And the reverse direction also holds true.

In relation to the preciseness-vagueness principle, if there is preciseness (e.g., the precise identification of sound frequency, facial expressions, and voice stability in the comparison between human and non-humans in regard to laughter), there is vagueness (e.g., the vagueness in the identification, since it is not clear to what extent the comparison is made, if measured in terms of "grades, degrees or spectrum," for instance). And the reverse direction also holds true.

In relation to the simpleness-complicatedness principle, if there is simpleness (e.g., the relatively simple analysis of the comparison between human and non-human laughters in the studies), there is complicatedness (e.g., the relatively more complicated analysis of the comparison between human and non-human laughters in the studies, as shown in the criticisms). And the reverse direction also holds true.

In relation to the openness-hiddenness principle, if there is openness (e.g., the open exploration of the similarities between human and non-human laughters), there is hiddenness (e.g., the hidden bias in the studies on laughter in animals, because of the assumption on comparability with human laughter, in spite of the problems as pointed out by the critics). And the reverse direction also holds true.

In relation to the denseness-emptiness principle, if there is denseness (e.g., the relatively denser concentration of non-human primates to have "laughter-like vocalizations"), there is emptiness (e.g., the relatively less dense, or more empty, concentration of worms to have "laughter-like vocalizations"). And the reverse direction also holds true.

In relation to the slowness-quickness principle, if there is slowness (e.g., the relatively slower readiness of rats to laugh and respond to tickled skin, as they age), there is quickness (e.g., the relatively quicker readiness of rats to laugh and respond to tickle skind, when they are still young). And the reverse direction also holds true.

In relation to the expansion-contraction principle, if there is expansion (e.g., the relatively more developed ability of dogs in the experiment to reduce stress, when exposed "to a dog-laugh recording"), there is contraction (e.g., the relatively less developed ability of dogs in the experiment to fight with other dogs instead, when exposed "to a dog-laugh recording"). And the reverse direction also holds true.

In relation to the theory-praxis principle, if there is theory (e.g., the theoretical construction of recording technology), there is praxis (e.g., the practical application of recording technology to the study of laughter in dogs by by Patricia Simonet and others). And the reverse direction also holds true.

In relation to the convention-novelty principle, if there is convention (e.g., the conventional wisdom about the study of laughter in apes "in terms of play faces and vocalisations"), there is novelty (e.g., the alternative novel challenge to this conventional wisdom about the study of laughter in apes "in terms of play faces and vocalisations," by way of the new idea of working "on tickle-induced laughter" instead, as shown in the team work led by Davila-Ross). And the reverse direction also holds true.

In relation to the evolution-transformation principle, if there is evolution (e.g., the natural evolution of dogs to laugh in the state of nature), there is transformation (e.g., the technical transformation of dogs to laugh, by the invention of the "dog-laugh recording" in the experiment, such that dogs can reduce stress with exposure to it). And the reverse direction also holds true.

In relation to the symmetry-asymmetry principle, if there is symmetry (e.g., both rats and chimpanzees can laugh and respond to tickle skin), there is asymmetry (eg., "as the rats age, there does appear to be a decline in the tendency to laugh and respond to tickle skin"—but "[t]he enjoyment of tickling in chimpanzees does not diminish with age"). And the reverse direction also holds true.

In relation to the softness-hardness principle, if there is softness (e.g., dogs can play with each other more, when exposed to dog laughing), there is hardness (e.g., dogs can fight with each other more, with exposed to dog fighting). And the reverse direction also holds true.

In relation to the seriousness-playfulness principle, if there is seriousness (e.g., the serious business of stress reduction in the experiment on dog laughing), there is playfulness (e.g., the playful side of the dog-laughing recording in the experiment for dogs to play with each other). And the reverse direction also holds true.

In relation to the regression-progression principle, if there is regression (e.g., the regression made by the studies on laughter in animals, as shown in the criticisms pointed out by the critics), there is progression (e.g., the progress made by the studies on laughter in animals to help us understand better the similarities between human and non-human laughters). And the reverse direction also holds true.

And in relation to the same-difference principle, if there is similarity in outcome (e.g., the contribution to the molding and regulation of beliefs and behaviors, regardless of whether this be done by way of the understanding of laughter in animals or by way of the understanding of fighting in animals), there is difference in outcome (e.g., the contribution to the molding and regulation of beliefs and behaviors by way of the understanding of laughing in animals for a more playful expierence with animals—but the contribution to the molding and regulation of beliefs and behaviors by way of the understanding of fighting in animals for a more careful encounter with animals). And the reverse direction also holds true.

Laughing, Animals, and the Evolutionary Claim

The study of laughing, animals, and the contentious comparison in the previous section also raises the deeper question: Why do we laugh in the history of evolution in the first place?

Robert Provine (1999) tried to answer this question, so he and "several undergraduate research assistants went to local malls and city sidewalks and recorded what happened just before people laughed. Over a 10-year period,...[they] studied over 2,000 cases of naturally occurring laughter."

They "found that most laughter does not follow jokes. People laugh after a variety of statements such as 'Hey John, where ya been?' 'Here comes Mary,' 'How did you do on the test?' and 'Do you have a rubber band?'. These certainly aren't jokes." (R. Provine 1999)

In the process, Provine (1999) offered his evolutionary perspective of laugher (which can be traced back to "the panting behavior of our ancient primate ancestors"), and his evolutionary perspective can be summarized into two essential claims, as shown below (and summarized in *Table 3.5*).

The First Claim: The Unconscious Nature of Laughing

The first claim in Provine's evolutionary perspective of laughter is that it is unconscious.

For Provine (1999), "[l]aughter is part of the universal human vocabulary. All members of the human species understand it. Unlike English or French or Swahili, we don't have to learn to speak it. We're born with the capacity to laugh."

This innate capacity has an unconscious basis, in that "it occurs unconsciously. You don't decide to do it. While we can consciously inhibit it, we don't consciously produce laughter. That's why it's very hard to laugh on command or to fake laughter. (Don't take my word for it: Ask a friend to laugh on the spot.)" (R. Provine 1999)

Thus, "[l]aughter provides powerful, uncensored insights into our unconscious. It simply bubbles up from within us in certain situations....[W]e do know that laughter is triggered by many sensations and thoughts, and that it activates many parts of the body. When we laugh, we alter our facial expressions and make sounds. During exuberant laughter, the muscles of the arms, legs and trunk are involved. Laughter also requires modification in our pattern of breathing." (R. Provine 1999)

In addition, for Provine (1999), "[w]e...know that laughter is a message that we send to other people. We know this because we rarely laugh when we are alone (we laugh to ourselves even less than we talk to ourselves). Laughter is social and contagious."

This social nature of laughter can be shown by the well-known case that "[t]he first laughter appears at about 3.5 to 4 months of age, long before we're able to speak. Laughter, like crying, is a way for a preverbal infant to interact with the mother and other caregivers." (R. Provine 1999)

The Second Claim: The Evolutionary Nature of Laughing

And the second claim in Provine's evolutionary perspective of laughter is that "laugher evolved from the panting behavior of our ancient primate ancestors." (R. Provine 1999)

For Provine (1999), "if we tickle chimps or gorillas, they don't laugh 'ha ha ha' but exhibit a panting sound. That's the sound of ape laughter. And it's the root of human laughter."

In apes, laughter is produced "in conditions in which human laughter is produced, like tickle, rough and tumble play, and chasing games. When we laugh, we're often communicating playful intent. So laughter has a bonding function within individuals in a group. It's often positive, but it can be negative too. There's a difference between 'laughing with' and 'laughing at.' People who laugh at others may be trying to force them to conform or casting them out of the group." (R. Provine 1999)

Although "[n]o one has actually counted how much people of different ages laugh, but young children probably laugh the most. At ages 5 and 6, we tend to see the most exuberant laughs. Adults laugh less than children, probably because they play less. And laughter is associated with play." (R. Provine 1999)

A Response from the Critics

Provine's evolutionary perspective of laughter is not without problems, however. Consider, for illustration, some criticisms below—to be summarized in *Table 3.5*.

Firstly, one major problem with Provine's evolutionary perspective is that, in the case of the first claim, "[v]ery little is known about the specific brain mechanisms responsible for laughter," as Provine (1999) himself acknowledged.

So, for the critics, one cannot be so sure about the unconscious nature of laughter in the specific way that Provine himself advocated. Freud, for instance, offered his alternative view about laughter in the context of the unconscious but he focused on the desires about sexuality and aggression instead.

Secondly, another major problem with Provine's evolutionary perspective is that, in the case of the second claim, it is not clear to what extent the differences between human and non-human laughters can really set them apart into different evolutionary lines altogether instead.

For instance, Provine (1999) is aware of this problem when he acknowledge that "[o]ther animals produce vocalizations during play, but they are so different that it's difficult to equate them with laughter. Rats, for example, produce high-pitch vocalizations during play and when tickled. But it's very different in sound from human laughter."

Precisely here, there are some dissenters who offered the alternative explanation, "which would be that it [laughter] evolved separately and independently in each group." (BBC 2009)

Other critics offered a different viewpoint instead, in that laughter, especially in the context of humor, is "a gift from God"). (WK 2010)

Thirdly, still another major problem with Provine's evolutionary perspective is that it does not really answer the difficult question of why there is humor at all (as humor also produces laughter).

Provine (1999) is aware of this distinction when he himself said that "[c]ontrary to folk wisdom, most laughter is not about humor." But then, why does humor exist in the first place, since it also produces laughter? Does it have a survival value in evolution?

And fourthly, still one more major problem with Provine's evolutionary perspective is that it does not answer some other related but important questions, like "the brain mechanisms of laughter," the mystery about "tickling" itself, and the like.

In fact, Provine (1999) seems to be aware of this problem, when he confessed that "[w]ork now underway will tell us more about the brain mechanisms of laughter, how laughter has evolved and why we're so susceptible to tickling — one of the most enigmatic of human behaviors."

Looking Beyond

These criticisms of Provine's evolutionary perspective of laughter are not to dismiss it outright but to show us the opposing sides of the debate, such that the possibility and desirability of laughing (from the perspective of nature with laughing, animals, and the evolutionary claim as a case study here) are not to the extent that the respective defenders would like us to believe.

Besides, the analysis of laughing, animals, and the evolutionary claim can teach us something important about the ontological principles in existential dialectics, and good examples include the absoluteness-relativeness principle, the predictability-unpredictability principle, the explicability-inexplicability principle, the finiteness-transfiniteness principle, the preciseness-vagueness principle, the simpleness-complicatedness principle, the openness-hiddenness principle, the denseness-emptiness principle, the slowness-quickness principle, the expansion-contraction principle, the theory-praxis principle, the convention-novelty principle, the evolution-transformation principle, the symmetry-asymmetry principle, the softness-hardness principle, the seriousness-playfulness principle, the regression-progression principle, and the same-difference principle.

For instance, in relation to the absoluteness-relativeness principle, if there is absoluteness (e.g., the absolute view by those like Provine that human and non-human laughters have a shared evolutionary origin), there is relativeness (e.g., what is true for people like Provine in regard to the shared evolutionary perspective of laughter is not necessarily so for some dissenters who offered the alternative explanation, "which would be that it [laughter] evolved separately and independently in each group," whereas other critics suggest that laughter, especially in the context of humor, is "a gift from God"). (WK 2010). And the reverse direction also holds true.

In relation to the predictability-unpredictability principle, if there is predictability (e.g., the predictable tendency of Provine to treat laughter as unconscious), there is unpredictabilty (e.g., the more difficult task to predict, if based solely on Provine's evolutionary perspective of laughter, if or to what extent the unconscious nature of a particular laughter has to do with "social bonding"—or, alternatively, with sexuality and aggression, as Freud would suggest instead). And the reverse direction also holds true.

In relation to the explicability-inexplicability principle, if there is explicability (e.g., the explanation by Provine that human and non-human laughters have a shared evolutionary origin), there is inexplicability (e.g., the lack of sufficient explanation, if viewed from Provine's perspective alone, of why there is humor at all, since it also produces laughter, but not all animals have humor). And the reverse direction also holds true.

In relation to the finiteness-transfiniteness principle, if there is finiteness (e.g.,. the finite number of the categories of species who have "laugh-like vocalizations"), there is transfiniteness (e.g., the transfinite number of individual animals, human or non-human, in history who have ever laughed). And the reverse direction also holds true.

In relation to the preciseness-vagueness principle, if there is preciseness (e.g., the precise identification of "ha ha ha" as a laughter which is uniquely human by Provine), there is vagueness (e.g., the vagueness in the identification of "ha ha ha" by Provine, because it is not clear to what exact degree, grade, or spectrum a human laughter differs from a non-human one). And the reverse direction also holds true.

In relation to the simpleness-complicatedness principle, if there is simpleness (e.g., the relatively simple view of laughter by Provine in regard to his two major claims), there is complicatedness (e.g., the relatively more complicated analysis of Provine's view of laughter, as shown in the criticisms which challenge its claims and assumptions). And the reverse direction also holds true.

In relation to the openness-hiddenness principle, if there is openness (e.g., the open exploration of the possibility of a shared evolutionary origin of both human and non-human laughters, as shown in the work by Provine), there is hiddenness (e.g., the hidden bias in Provine's work, because of his obsession with the shared evolutionary perspective that some other critical concerns, as shown in the criticisms against it, are sidelined). And the reverse direction also holds true.

In relation to the denseness-emptiness principle, if there is denseness (e.g., the relatively denser concentration of people who followed Freud's theory of the unconscious in the older days to treat laughter in the context of censored sexual and aggressive desires), there is emptiness (e.g., the relatively less dense, or more empty, concentration of believers nowadays who follow Provine's evolutionary perspective of laughter to treat laughter in the way that Freud did). And the reverse direction also holds true.

In relation to the slowness-quickness principle, if there is slowness (e.g., the relatively slower readiness of adults to laugh, when compared with children at ages 5 and 6, for instance), there is quickness (e.g., the relatively quicker readiness of children at ages 5 and 6 to laugh, because they play more at those ages than adults). And the reverse direction also holds true.

In relation to the expansion-contraction principle, if there is expansion (e.g., the relatively more developed ability of children at ages 5 and 6 to play and laugh), there is contraction (e.g., the relatively less developed ability of children at ages 5 and 6 to work as seriously as adults, who play less). And the reverse direction also holds true.

In relation to the theory-praxis principle, if there is theory (e.g., the theoretical construction of evolution by Darwin, for isntance), there is praxis (e.g., the practical application of evolutionary perspective to the field of laughter too, as shown by Provine's work, with his own modifications). And the reverse direction also holds true.

In relation to the convention-novelty principle, if there is convention (e.g., the conventional wisdom about laughter in the context of censored sexual and aggressive desires in the unconscious, as worked out by Freud), there is novelty (e.g., the alternative novel challenge to the conventional wisdom about laughter in the context of censored sexual and aggressive desires, by Provine's new idea for a different view of laughter in the context of the unconscious, but without the obsession on sexuality and aggression). And the reverse direction also holds true.

In relation to the evolution-transformation principle, if there is evolution (e.g., the natural evolution of humans to understand playing and laughing in the state of nature), there is transformation (e.g., the technical evolution of humans to understand playing and laughing by the invention of new ideas to understand them, like Provine's evolutionary perspective of laughter). And the reverse direction also holds true.

In relation to the symmetry-asymmetry principle, if there is symmetry (e.g., both humans and chimps can laugh), there is asymmetry (e.g., humans laugh "ha ha ha"—but chimps "exhibit a panting sound"). And the reverse direction also holds true.

In relation to the softness-hardness principle, if there is softness (e.g., the soft side of "laughing with" a group), there is hardness (e.g., the hard side of "laughing at" a group). And the reverse direction also holds true.

In relation to the seriousness-playfulness principle, if there is seriousness (e.g., the serious nature of laughing for social bonding, because, for Provine, "laughter has a bonding function within individuals in a group"), there is playfulness (e.g., the playful side of laughing for fun). And the reverse direction also holds true.

In relation to the regression-progression principle, if there is regression (e.g., the regression made by Provine's evolutoinary perspective of laughter, as shown in the criticisms against it), there is progression (e.g., the progress made by Provine's evolutionary perspective of laughter, to help us understand the shared evolutionary origin of human and non-human laughters). And the reverse direction also holds true.

And in relation to the same-difference principle, if there is similarity in outcome (e.g., the contribution to the molding and regulation of beliefs and values, regardless of whether this be done by way of the evolutionary perspective of laughter or by way of the creationist perspective of laughter), there is difference in outcome (e.g., the contribution to the molding and regulation of beliefs and values by way of the evolutionary perspective of laughter for a more secular lifeworld—but the contribution to the molding and regulation of beliefs and values by way of the creationist perspective of laughter for a more sacred lifeworld, as some believe that laughter, especially in the context of humor, is "a gift from God"). (WK 2010) And the reverse direction also holds true.

Laughing and Society

Laughing, when examined from the perspective of society, can illuminate some powerful features in relation to its possibility and desirability, and a good case study has to do with laughing and the dispute about social functions—to be addressed in what follows.

Laughing, and the Dispute about Social Functions

Different scholars in the literature on laughter often like to point out different social functions that laughter is to serve in society.

For illustration, consider the view by G. Christine (2010) on the different social functions of laugher, especially in the context of humor, as summarized in *Table 3.6*.

The Social Functions of Laughter

For Christine (2010), laughter in humor is social, in that "[h]umor has a strong social element. It is generally interactive. The person who is spotted laughing alone, or chuckling to him or herself, is suspected of being emotionally unstable."

There are different ways in which laughter can contribute to the social bonding of groups. Hereafter are some of the ways that Christine proposed.

Firstly, laughter can contribute to the formation of "corporate identity."

In other words, "[s]haring the humor of a particular group helps people integrate socially. Shared jokes, funny nicknames, and good-natured teasing on well-worn themes are an expression of corporate identity. Laughing at 'in' jokes, even if one does not fully understand them, is a way of saying, 'I'm one of you.'

Secondly, laughter can contribute to the maintenance of social hierarchy.

For instance, "[i]ndividuals show respect for the hierarchy of the group by responding positively to the clowning and jokes of the leadership. Groups often control their errant members by making fun of them. Those who choose to participate in the exchange of quips do it at the expense of those who are of lower status, or in a self-deprecating way." (G. Christine 2010)

Thirdly, laughter, especially in the context of humor, can test the limits of others.

For instance, "humor allows people to test the limits and reactions of others. If they get a negative response to a racist or sexist joke, for instance, they can laugh it off by saying they were just kidding. If someone makes a suggestion, and another person in the group says, 'That's so crazy it just might work!,' s/he will be able to back down without losing face if the Vice-President absolutely hates the idea." (G. Christine 2010)

Fourthly, laughter can let people be critical in a way which is more tolerated.

For instance, "[c]riticism is generally perceived as less caustic if it is delivered with a touch of humor. When an aspiring chess master loses a critical game, his buddy might say, 'Great strategy, dude. Now he'll be overconfident the next time.' When confronted with a lousy test result, a distressed father can pull his punches a bit by suggesting, 'What's this? Are you trying to make the top 70% of the class look good?' Compliments can also be toned down by using a back-handed or ironic approach. If a student scores 90% on a test, his classmates might jest, 'You missed two questions! How dumb is that?'" (G. Christine 2010)

Fifthly, laughter can defuse a tense situation.

For instance, "[i]n critical situations, a joke can defuse the tension. While waiting for the outcome of heart bypass surgery, a family member might say, 'I hope they haven't mislaid the jumper cables.' This could start a cascade of humorous suggestions about what is going on in the operating room. This might be grossly inappropriate under normal circumstances, but people who are emotionally close and tuned into each other can share their most threatening thoughts with each other by using a light touch." (G. Christine 2010)

Sixthly, laughter can be exploited to manipulate "the mood of groups." (G. Christine 2010)

For instance, "[w]hen rodeo bull riders are thrown off, they may be unable to get out of the way before the bull attacks them. A rodeo clown moves in to distract the bull, making his life-saving heroism seem like a joke. The audience is entertained and distracted from the danger." (G. Christine 2010)

Seventhly, laughter can be employed as a safety valve in a repressive political environement.

For instance, "[r]oyalty used to keep fools, comedians who would tell the truth in such a humorous way that they avoided being punished for treason. Political satire is often slanderous, but the comedians avoid law suits because, overtly, they are just kidding....Charlie Chaplin's impersonation of Hitler is an excellent example. How can someone so ridiculous be deadly?" (G. Christine 2010)

And eighthly, laughter can let people say things in public which they only want to say privately.

For instance, "[s]tand-up comics, especially when the audience is primed with alcohol, will get huge laughs for saying the things members of the audence are thinking secretly but are afraid to express. Many sitcoms use the same principle by including characters audiences love to hate. An ignorant, bigoted, self-centred jerk is not someone we care to identify with, but still, s/he's good for a laugh." (G. Christine)

Problems with the Claim of Social Functions

However, the claim of social functions in regard to laughter in humor is not without problems. Consider, for illustration, the following criticisms against the claim, as summarized in *Table 3.6.*

Firstly, one major criticism of Christine's functionalist argument about laughter in the context of humor is that, as Robert Merton (1968) once pointed out in his critique of functionalism in sociology (as originally proposed by Arthur R.Radcliffe-Brown and Bronislaw Malinwoski, for instance), social functons can be "undesirable," relative to different moral evaluations. (P. Baofu 2004: 69)

In the case of laughter, as Christine (2010) herself was cautious enough to mention it: "Humor can be dysfunctional when it is consistently used to avoid reality....Misused, it [laugher in humor] can damage self-esteem, light blazing fires of resentment, and create misunderstandings."

Secondly, another major criticism of Christine's functionalist argument about laughter in the context of humor is that, as Robert Merton (1968) also pointed out in his critique of functionalism in sociology, social functons "are not necessarily indispensable (since there can be 'functional alternatives,' 'functional equivalents or substitutes')." (P. Baofu 2004: 69)

In the case of laughter, there are alternative theories about laughter in the context of humor, as discussed in this chapter—and, for that matter, in Chapter One and Chapter Two.

And thirdly, still another major criticism of Christine's functionalist argument about laughter in the context of humor is that, as Robert Merton (1968) also pointed out in his critique of functionalism in sociology, social functons do not necessarily exist, because "there exist 'nonfunctions' which are consequences…left over from previous historical epochs but no longer relevant to a current system. (G. Ritzer 2003:93-4)" (P. Baofu 2004: 69)

In the case of laughter, there are some scholars like Darwin in evolutionary theory who argue that laughter in humor does not seem to have any survival value in evolution (that is, no evolutionary function), other than being a by-product for courtship in "sexual selection" (which is not the same as "natural selection"), as already discussed in *Sec. 1.3* and *Sec. 2.3*).

A Bigger Picture

These criticisms of Christine's argument about the social functions of laughter in humor are not to reject it totally but to show us the opposing sides of the debate, such that the possibility and desirability of laughing (from the perspective of society with laughing and the dispute about social functions as a case study here) are not to the extent that the respective defenders would like us to believe.

More importantly, the analysis of laughing and the dispute about social functions can reveal to us something relevant about the ontological principles in existential dialectics, and good examples include the absoluteness-relativeness principle, the predictability-unpredictability principle, the explicability-inexplicability principle, the preciseness-vagueness principle, the simpleness-complicatedness principle, the openness-hiddenness principle, the denseness-emptiness principle, the slowness-quickness principle, the expansion-contraction principle, the theory-praxis principle, the convention-novelty principle, the evolution-transformation principle, the symmetry-asymmetry principle, the softness-hardness principle, the seriousness-playfulness principle, the regression-progression principle, and the same-difference principle.

For instance, in relation to the absoluteness-relativeness principle, if there is absoluteness (e.g., the absolute view in Christine's claim about social functions), there is relativeness (e.g., what is true for Christine about the social functions of laughter is not necessarily so for others like Darwin who argue that laughter in humor does not seem to have any survival value in evolution, that is, no evolutionary function, other than being a by-product for courtship in "sexual selection"). And the reverse direction also holds true.

In relation to the predictability-unpredictability principle, if there is predictability (e.g., the predictable tendency of people like Christine to point out the social functions that laugher can serve), there is unpredictability (e.g,. the more difficult task to predict exactly which particular laugher will end up being functional, since it can be dysfunctional and non-functional too, for the critics). And the reverse direction also holds true.

In relation to the explicability-inexplicability principle, if there is explicability (e.g., the explanation by Christine that laughter exists because of its social functions), there is inexplicability (e.g., the lack of sufficient explanation by Christine of why laughter is necessarily functional in society, since for the critics, it can be dysfunctional or even non-functional, more often than we think). And the reverse direction also holds true.

In relation to the preciseness-vagueness principle, if there is preciseness (e.g., the precise identification of the eight different ways that laughter in humor can be functional by Christine), there is vagueness (e.g, the vagueness in the identification of the eight social functions of laughter by Christine, since it is not clear why there are only eight different ways that laughter in humor is functional, instead of four, five, six, nine, ten, eleven, twelve, and so on). And the reverse direction also holds true.

In relation to the simpleness-complicatedness principle, if there is simpleness (e.g., the relatively simple analysis of the social functions of laughter in humor by Christine), there is complicatedness (e.g., the relatively more complicated analysis of the social functions of laughter in humor, by challenging its claims and assumptions, as shown in the criticisms). And the reverse direction also holds true.

In relation to the openness-hiddenness principle, if there is openness (e.g., the open exploration of the relationship between social functions and laughter in humor by Christine), there is hiddenness (e.g,, the hidden bias in Christian's functonal account of laugther in humor, as shown in the problems about functionalism as pointed out by Merton, which remain relevant in the context of laughter). And the reverse direction also holds true.

In relation to the denseness-emptiness principle, if there is denseness (e.g., the relatively denser concentration of the use of laughter in the specific form of humor known as political satire as a safety valve in a repressive political environement), there is emptiness (e.g., the relatively less dense, or more empty, concentration of the use of laughter in the specific form of humor known as political satire as a safety valve in a free political environement, where dissent is tolerated). And the reverse direction also holds true.

In relation to the slowness-quickness principle, if there is slowness (e.g., the relatively slower readiness of a group to control a member by making fun of him if the member in question is not "errant"), there is quickness (e.g., the relatively quicker readiness of a group to control a member by making fun of him if the member in question is very "errant"). And the reverse direction also holds true.

In relation to the expansion-contraction principle, if there is expansion (e.g., the relatively more developed ability of a stand-up comic to joke so as to say "the things members of the audence are thinking secretly but are afraid to express"), there is contraction (e.g., the relatively less developed ability of a stand-up comic to lecture seriously, without the use of humor, about "the things members of the audence are thinking secretly but are afraid to express"). And the reverse direction also holds true.

In relation to the theory-praxis principle, if there is theory (e.g., the theoretical construction of functionalism in sociology), there is praxis (e.g., the practical application of functionalism to the field of laughter in humor by Christine for a functional explanation). And the reverse direction also holds true.

In relation to the convention-novelty principle, if there is convention (e.g., the conventional wisdom in the Darwinian evolutionary theory that humor does not seem to have any survival value or has no evolutionary function other than a by-product of sexual selection for courtship), there is novelty (e.g,. the alternative novel view to challenge the conventional wisdom of the Darwinian evolutionary theory, by the modern social functionalist interpretation of laughter in humor). And the reverse direction also holds true.

In relation to the evolution-transformation principle, if there is evolution (e.g., the natural evolution of humans to understand laughter in the state of nature), there is transformation (e.g., the technical transformation of human ability to understand laughter by the invention of social functionalism to explain its social functions). And the reverse direction also holds true.

In relation to the symmetry-asymmetry principle, if there is symmetry (e.g., the co-existence of different views about laughter in humor over the ages), there is asymmetry (e.g., the popularity of the Darwinian view about laugther in humor among those in evolutionary biology, relatively speaking—but the relative preference for the social functionalist view about laughter in humor among those in sociology, relatively speaking). And the reverse direction also holds true.

In relation to the softness-hardness principle, if there is softness (e.g., the soft side of laughter in humor, like laughing "with" a group), there is hardness (e.g., the hard side of laughter in humor, like laughing "at"a group). And the reverse direction also holds true.

In relation to the seriousness-playfulness principle, if there is seriousness (e.g., the serious side of laughter in humor to form "corporate identity," for instance), there is playfulness (e.g., the playful side of laughter in humor to enjoy funny jokes). And the reverse direction also holds true.

In relation to the regression-progression principle, if there is regression (e.g., the regression made by Christine's view about the social functions of laughter, as shown in the criticisms against it), there is progression (e.g., the progress made by Christine's view about the social functions of laughter, so as to help us understand better its social functions). And the reverse direction also holds true.

And in relation to the same-difference principle, if there is similarity in outcome (e.g., the contribution to the molding and regulation of beliefs and values, regardless of whether this be done by way of a functionalist view of laughter or by way of a critical view of laughter), there is difference in outcome (e.g., the contribution to the molding and regulation of beliefs and values by way of a functionalist view of laughter for a more conservative view of society for social bonding—but the contribution to the molding and regulation of beliefs and values by way of a critical view of laughter for a more skeptical view of society for deconstruction). And the reverse direction also holds true.

Laughing and Culture

Laughing, when examined from the perspective of culture, can reveal its possibility and desirability in an exotic way, and this can be shown by way of two case studies, namely, (3.5.1) laughing, writers, and the role of intellectual culture, and (3.5.2) laughing, death, and the coverage in popular culture—to be addressed hereafter, respectively.

Laughing, Writers, and the Role of Intellectual Culture

The subject of laughter "has received attention in the written word for millennia. The use of humor and laughter in literary works has been studied and analyzed by many thinkers and writers, from the Ancient

Greek philosophers onward. Henri Bergson's *Laughter: An Essay on the Meaning of the Comic* (*Le Rire*, 1901) is a notable 20th-century contribution." (WK 2010bb)

Laughter for the Ancients

In antiquity, some well-known writers had written on laughter and humor. Consider a few examples below, for illustration, as summarized in *Table 3.7*.

(a) Herodotus

Herodotus, who "was born in Caria, Halicarnassus (modern day Bodrum, Turkey) and lived in the 5th century BC (c. 484 BC–c. 425 BC)," is considered by many in the West as "the 'Father of History,' since he was the first historian known to collect his materials systematically, test their accuracy to a certain extent and arrange them in a well-constructed and vivid narrative." (WK 2010cc; NOAD 2010)

In the subject matter of laughter and humor, it was Herodotus who distinguished laughter into three main types, as shown below: (WK 2010bb; D. Lateiner 1977)

- "Those who are innocent of wrong-doing, but ignorant of their own vulnerability."
- "Those who are mad."
- "Those who are over-confident."

For Donald Lateiner (1977), "Herodotus believes either that both nature (better, the gods' direction of it) and human nature coincide sufficiently, or that the latter is but an aspect or analogue of the former, so that to the recipient the outcome is suggested." (WK 2010bb)

Because of the popular beliefs in the gods at the time, Herodotus also had a fair share of using the spirits of the gods when "reporting laughter," as "it is not conicidental that in about eighty percent of the times when Herodotus speaks about Laughter it is followed by a retribution. 'Men whose laughter deserves report are marked, because laughter connotes scornful disdain, disdain feeling of superiority, and this feeling and the actions which stem from it attract the wrath of the gods.'" (WK 2010bb; D. Lateiner 1977)

(b) Aristotle

Aristotle (384 BC–322 BC) approached the subject matter of laughter and humor a bit differently. As already introduced in *Sec. 1.3*, Aristotle, together with Plato, advanced "the superiority theory," which explains that a person laughs about misfortunes of others, because these misfortunes assert the person's superiority on the background of shortcomings of others." (WK 2010c; M. Mulder 2002)

For instance, "for Aristotle, we laugh at inferior or ugly individuals, because we feel a joy at being superior to them. Socrates was reported by Plato as saying that the ridiculous was characterized by a display of self-ignorance." (WK 2010c)

Laughter for the Moderns

In modern times, different scholars had contributed to the analysis of laughter and humor, with some of them following in the footsteps of the ancient Greeks. Consider a few below, for illustration.

(a)Thomas Hobbes

Thomas Hobbes (1588–1679) in England was influenced by the superiority theory of laughter as propounded by the ancient Greeks like Aristotle and Plato, but in the process, as David Heyd (1982) claimed, he (Hobbes) modified it "in a much wider sense than the aesthetic and quasi-moral sense of Aristotle" for a more general theory of emotions instead. (WK 2010bb)

As Hobbes put it, "[t]he passion of laughter is nothing else but sudden glory arising from sudden conception of some eminency in ourselves, by comparison with the infirmity of others, or with our own formerly." (WK 2010bb)

(b) Nikolai Gogol

Nikolai Vasilievich Gogol (1809–1852) was known as "a Ukrainian-born Russian novelist, humourist, and dramatist." (WK 2010dd)

Unlike many other scholars, there is something personal in Gogol's work on laugther and humor, as R. Hallett (1971) thus observed: "There exists a clear dichotomy in Gogol both as a writer and as a person. He battled with himself being a tragicomic figure and his expectations of himself and 'he was haunted by the desire to do something nobler, something of benefit to the Russian people, and it was this desire which destroyed him as an artist and as a man.'" (WK 2010bb)

With this personal note in mind—"[e]lements of the comic characterize most of the fiction of Gogol, who wrote less purely serious literature than, for example, Chekhov. The laughter aroused by this fiction has been a prime factor in guaranteeing that it continues to be read more than a century after Gogol's death." (WK 2010bb; R. Hallett 1971)

In the end, "[t]hroughout his life, indeed, Gogol remained a comic writer in spite of himself....Like so many blessed with the gift of making others laugh, he was himself an extremely unhappy man whose comic vein was both an escape from, and a consequence of a profound melancholia." (WK 2010bb; R. Hallett 1971)

And "Gogol's faulty judgment of his talent as a writer is evident almost from the beginning of his literary career he had first conceived of himself as a Romantic poet." (WK 2010bb; R. Hallett 1971)

(c) Friedrich Nietzsche

Friedrich Nietzsche (1844-1900) in Germany is known for his "fondness for metaphor, irony and aphorism" in his works on "religion, morality, contemporary culture, philosophy and science." (WK 2010ee)

For Nietzsche, there are "two different purposes for the use of laughter," namely, the positive and negative senses. (WK 2010bb)

On the one hand, in the positive sense, "man uses the comical as a therapy against the restraining jacket of logic, morality and reason. He needs from time to time a harmless demotion from reason and hardship and in this sense laughter has a positive character for Nietzsche." (WK 2010bb)

On the other hand, in the negative sense, "[l]aughter can…have a negative connotation when it is used for the expression of social conflict. This is expressed, for instance, in *The Gay Science*: 'Laughter—Laughter means to be schadenfroh, but with clear conscience." (WK 2010bb)

But there is also a personal note about Nietzsche's work on laughter here, in that he did not incorporate the playfulness of laughter into his works as much as his view on laughter would have us believe, as Tarmo Kunnas in 1982 wrote: "Possibly Nietzsche's works would have had a totally different effect, if the playful, ironical and joking in his writings would have been factored in better." (WK 2010bb)

(d) Henri Bergson

Henri Bergson (1859–1941) in France argued that "immediate experience and intuition are more significant than rationalism and science for understanding reality." (WK 2010ff)

In the process, he wrote his well-known 1911 work titled *Laughter: An Essay on the Meaning of the Comic*, in which he "tried to determine the laws of the comic and to understand the fundamental causes of comic situations." (WK 2010bb) There are three main points to be summarized here.

Firstly, for Bergson, laughter is a collective activity which has a social and moral role to get rid of the vices.

In other words, "[h]is method…dealt with laughter in relation to human life, collective imagination and art, to have a better knowledge of society. One of the theories of the essay is that laughter, as a collective activity, has a social and moral role, it forces people to eliminate their vices. It is a factor of uniformity of behaviours, it condemns ludicrous and eccentric behaviours." (WK 2010bb)

Secondly, for Bergson, laughter is caused by the inflexibility and rigidness in life.

For instance, Bergson argued that "there is a central cause all comic situations are derived from: mechanism applied to life. The fundamental source of comic is the presence of inflexibility and rigidness in life. Indeed, for Bergson the essence of life is movement, elasticity and flexibility, and every comic situation is due the presence of rigidness and inelasticity in life. Hence, for Bergson the source of the comic is not ugliness [like the view by Plato, Aristotle, and Hobbes] but rigidness. All the examples taken by Bergson (a man falling in the street, cartoons, imitation, the automatic application of conventions and rules, absent-mindedness, repetitive gestures of a speaker, the resemblance between two faces...) are comic situations because they give the impression that life is subject to rigidity, automatism and mechanism." (WK 2010bb)

And thirdly, for Bergson, comic situations are not laughable because they reflect the inflexibility and rigidness in life, so they require a detached approach, so as to focus on, and resist, this inflexibility and rigidness in life.

For Bergson, "most comic situations are not laughable because they are part of collective habits. Thus he defined laughter as an intellectual activity that requires an immediate approach to a comic situation, totally detached from any form of emotion or sensibility. A situation is laughable when the attention and the imagination are focused on the resistance and rigidity of of the body. Thus somebody is laughable every time (s)he gives the impression of being a thing or a machine." (WK 2010bb)

The Untold Aspects of Literary Works

But the role of literary works to analyze laughter in history is not without its own problems. Consider, for illustration, a few criticisms below, as summarized in *Table 3.7*.

Firstly, one major criticism against the validity of literary works is thatt it is not clear if their typologies about laughter are really accurate.

For instance, it is not clear why Herodotus should distinguish laughter into three main types—instead of four, five, six, seven, and so on.

By the same logic, it is also not clear why laughter should be distinguished into the positve and negative senses that Nietzsche would like us to believe—instead of three, four, five, and so on.

Secondly, another major criticism against the validity of literary works is that their analysis can be ideological too.

For instance, Herodotus often analyzed laughter and humor with the appeal to the spirits of "the gods" which were popular at the time in Greek culture.

And in the case of Bergson, what constitutes "vices," "rigidity in life," and so on, before they can even be resisted or eliminated (in accordance to his theory), is already so value-laden that it is hard to have everyone to agree upon them.

Thirdly, still another major criticism against the validity of literary works is that their analyses can be driven by personal conflicts.

For instance, in the case of Gogol, as R. Hallett (1971) reminded us, "[t]hroughout his life, indeed, Gogol remained a comic writer in spite of himself....Like so many blessed with the gift of making others laugh, he was himself an extremely unhappy man whose comic vein was both an escape from, and a consequence of a profound melancholia." (WK 2010bb)

And fourthly, an additional major criticism against the validity of literary works is that the scholars who propound their views on laughter and humor do not necessarily practice what they advocate.

For instance, in the case of Nietzsche, the observation by Tarmo Kunnas in 1982 is worth repeating: "Possibly Nietzsche's works would have had a totally different effect, if the playful, ironical and joking in his writings would have been factored in better." (WK 2010bb)

A Didactic Act

These criticisms of the writers in intellectual culture to analyze laugher and humor are not meant, needless to say, to dismiss their works outrgiht but to show us the opposing sides of the debate, such that the possibility and desirability of laughing (from the perspective of culture with laughing, writers, and the role of intellectual culture as a case study here) are not to the extent that the respective defenders would like us to believe.

In addition, the analysis of laughing and the role of literary works in intellectual works can teach us something valuable about the ontological principles in existential dialectics, and good examples include the formalness-informalness principle, the absoluteness-relativeness principle, the predictability-unpredictability principle, the explicability-inexplicability principle, the preciseness-vagueness principle, the simpleness-complicatedness principle, the openness-hiddenness principle, the denseness-emptiness principle, the change-constancy principle, the slowness-quickness principle, the expansion-contraction principle, the convention-novelty principle, the evolution-transformation principle, the symmetry-asymmetry principle, the softness-hardness principle, the seriousness-playfulness principle, the regression-progression principle, and the same-difference principle. And the reverse direction also holds true.

For instance, in relation to the formalness-informalness principle, if there is formalness (e.g., the formal logical requirement of soundness and completeness in a system of ideas, as in the theories about laughter and humor), there is informalness (e.g., the non-formal existence of incompleteness, as shown in the appeal to "the gods" in Herodotus in his analysis of laughter). And the reverse direction also holds true.

In relation to the absoluteness-relativeness principle, if there is absoluteness (e.g., the absolute, obsessive interest by Gogol in the comic, as driven by his "profound melancholia"), there is relativeness (e.g., what drives Gogal into his obsessed interest in the comic for personal reason is not necessarily so for Bergson, who is more interested in the laws of the comic in the context of the rigidness in life). And the reverse direction also holds true.

In relation to the predictability-unpredictability principle, if there is predictability (e.g.,the predictable tendency of different writers on the subject of laughter to propound different views), there is unpredictability (e.g., the more difficult task to predict exactly which particular view by which particular writer will be influential at a particular historical time). And the reverse direction also holds true.

In relation to the explicability-inexplicability principle, if there is explicability (e.g., the explanation by Aristotle that "a person laughs about misfortunes of others, because these misfortunes assert the person's superiority on the background of shortcomings of others"), there is inexplicabilty (e.g., the lack of sufficient explanation by Aristotle of why this feeling of superiority must necessarily exist, because, for the critics like Nietzsche, "man uses the comical as a therapy against the restraining jacket of logic, morality and reason"). And the reverse direction also holds true.

In relation to the preciseness-vagueness principle, if there is preciseness (e.g., the precise identification of three types of laughter by Herodotus), there is vagueness (e.g., the vagueness in the identification by Herodotus, since it is not clear why laughter should have only three main types—instead of four, five, six, seven, and so on). And the reverse direction also holds true.

In relation to the simpleness-complicatedness principle, if there is simpleness (e.g., the relatively simple analysis of laughter from the narrow perpective of each writer), there is complicatedness (e.g., the relatively more complicated analysis of laughter, by questioning the claims and assumptions of the works by these writers, as shown in the criticisms). And the reverse direction also holds true.

In relation to the openness-hiddenness principle, if there is openness (e.g., the open exploration of the relationship between laughter and the vices/rigidness in life by Bergson), there is hiddenness (e.g., the hidden bias in Bergson's work, because what constitutes "vices," "rigidity in life," and so on, before they can even be resisted or eliminated, in accordance to his theory, is already so value-laden that it is hard to have everyone to agree upon them). And the reverse direction also holds true.

In relation to the denseness-emptiness principle, if there is denseness (e.g., the relatively denser concentration of believers in the superiority theory of laughter by writers in the older days, like the followers of Aristotle, Plato, Hobbes, etc.), there is emptiness (e.g., the relatively less dense, or more empty, concentration of believers in the superiority theory of laughter nowadays, like the followers of Bergson, Nietzsche, and so on). And the reverse direction also holds true.

In relation to the change-constancy principle, if there is change (e.g., the ever changing views by writers on laughter in literary works), there is constancy (e.g., the ever constancy of the topic of laughter in literary works).

In relation to the slowness-quickness principle, if there is slowness (e.g., the relatively slower readiness of someone who rigidly follows a life based on reason and logic to engage in laughter and humor a lot), there is quickness (e.g., the relatively quicker readiness of someone who is against the rigidness in life to engage in laughter and humor as an escape or a resistance). And the reverse direction also holds true.

In relation to the expansion-contraction principle, if there is expansion (e.g., the relatively more developed ability of someone who resists the rigidness in life to engage in laughter and humor), there is contraction (e.g., the relatively less developed ability of someone who resists the rigidness in life to indulge in a life based on logic and reason). And the reverse direction also holds true.

In relation to the convention-novelty principle, if there is convention (e.g., the conventional wisdom in ancient Greek, as propounded by Plato and Aristotle, that laugher is caused by a feeling of superiority over the ugliness of others), there is novelty (e.g., the alternative challenge by

Bergson to this Greek view, in that laughter is caused by the rigidness in life, not ugliness in others). And the reverse direction also holds true.

In relation to to the evolution-transformation principle, if there is evolution (e.g,. the natural evolution of humans to laugh and joke in the state of nature), there is transformation (e.g, the technical transformation of human tendency to laugh and joke by the invention of a different approach to laughter by Bergson that requires a detachment from emoton or sensibility, so as to focus on, and resist, the inflexibility and rigidness in life). And the reverse direction also holds true.

In relation to the symmetry-asymmetry principle, if there is symmetry (e.g., the co-existence of different views about laughter in history), there is asymmetry (e.g., the popularity of the superiority theory of laughter in the older days, especially among those in the intellectual circles of Plato, Aristotle, and Hobbes—but the emergence of alternative popular views nowadays, like those by Bergson, Nietzsche, and others). And the reverse direction also holds true.

In relation to the softness-hardness principle, if there is softness (e.g., the soft side of laughter, in relation to its "harmless demotion from reason and hardship," for Nietzsche), there is hardness (e.g.,the hard side of laughter, in relation to its use for "social conflict," for Nietzsche). And the reverse direction also holds true.

In relation to the seriousness-playfulness principle, if there is seriousness (e.g., the serious business of laughter, in that an individual can use it to resist the rigidness in life, for Bergson), there is playfulness (e.g., the playful side of laugther, in that an individual can use it to laugh in the comic situations). And the reverse direction also holds true.

In relation to the regression-progression principle, if there is regression (e.g., the regression made by the different writings on laughter, as shown in the criticisms against them), there is progression (e.g., the progress made by the different writings on laughter, so as to give us different views about the nature of laughter). And the reverse direction also holds true.

And in relation to the same-difference principle, if there is similarity in outcome (e.g., the contribution to the molding and control of beliefs and behaviors, regardless of whether this be done by way of logic and reason or by way of laughter and humor), there is difference in outcome (e.g., the contribution to the molding and regulation of beliefs and behaviors by way of logic and reason for a more rationalist rigid lifeform, relatively speaking, as Nietzsche pointed out—but the contribution to the molding and regulation of beliefs and behaviors by way of laughter and humor for a more socially/morally uniform lifeform, relatively speakiing, as argued by Bergson). And the reverse direction also holds true.

Laughing, Death, and the Coverage in Popular Culture

Another way to evaluate the possibility and desirability of laughing from the perspective of culture has to do with laughing in the context of death as covered in popular culture.

In other words, does laughing have another dark side too—besides those already discussed in *Sec. 3.2.1*?

Death from Laughter in Popular Culture

In popular culture, one fascinating topic which often props up concerns "death from laughter," as a way to tell us something about another dark side of laughter in an entertaining way.

For illustration, consider the following examples of death from laughter in popular culture: (WK 2010gg)

- "In the film *Mary Poppins*, the director of the bank at which George Banks works died of laughter."
- "In the Monty Python sketch 'The Funniest Joke In The World,' a joke is discovered (but never revealed to the viewer, other than a gibberish pseudo-translation into German) that causes people to die from laughter."
- "In the film *Who Framed Roger Rabbit*, aside from The Dip (turpentine/acetone/benzene), too much laughter is one of the few things that can kill a cartoon character. The most notable victims are the Toon Patrol weasels."
- "In Tex Avery's *Symphony in Slang*, the hipster's cause of death is laughter."
- "In the *Batman* comics, his archenemy The Joker's main weapon is 'Joker venom,' a drug that causes death from uncontrollable laughter."
- "In the film *Ice Age: Dawn of the Dinosaurs*, while searching for Sid, Manny, Diego, Crash, Eddie and Ellie cross the Chasm of Death, at the bottom of which are skeletons of dinosaurs who died laughing due to the mix of helium and nitrous oxide in the chasm."
- "The post-punk band *Killing Joke*'s name is a direct reference to the concept of the fatal hilarity of Monty Python's 'Funniest Joke In The World.'.
- "In the *AdventureQuest* online games by Artix Entertainment, a skeleton called Chuckles is said to have told a joke so funny that he

died of laughter, and even continued to laugh (as an undead) after he died."

- "In *Gregor and the Curse of the Warmbloods*, in a subterranean orchard called the Vineyard of Eyes, a certain carnivorous plant emits a gas that causes euphoria and laughter, rendering the victims defenseless to attacks by the plant."
- "In an episode of *1000 Ways to Die*, one man suffers cardiac arrest after laughing uncontrollably for 36 hours."
- "In the animated television series *South Park*, on the episode *Scott Tenorman Must Die*, Kenny McCormick died of laughter after seeing Cartman being humiliated."
- "In an episode of *The Grim Adventures of Billy & Mandy*, 'Billy & Mandy's Jacked-Up Halloween,' several pumpkins brought to life by Jack O'Lantern with Grim's scythe laughed so much that they exploded and their souls rose to a dimensional portal to the underworld."
- "In an episode of *Garfield and Friends*, 'No Laughing Matter,' aliens from the planet of Clarion come to Earth for Earth's humour because it is a devastating weapon that will disintegrate any of their kind. Eventually, Roy slips on a banana causing the aliens to laugh and disintegrate."
- "In a *Ben 10* episode, 'Last Laugh,' Zombozo feeds on everyone's laughter while they watch his acts. Victims keep laughing until they die."

Then, of course, an important question to ask here is, How much is there any truth about "death from laughter" as covered in popular culture like this? In other words, is this "fiction" or "reality"?

Fiction or Reality?

The phenomenon of "death from laughter" has historical and scientific evidences to support it. But the problem here is that it is not clear how much the way that it is portrayed in popular culture is really accurate, from the historical and scientific standpoints.

Consider a few instances from science and history hereafter, for illustration.

(a) From Science

From the standpoint of science, scientists found that "[d]eath may result from several pathologies that deviate from benign laughter." (WK 2010gg)

For instance, "[i]nfarction of the pons and medulla oblongata in the brain may cause pathological laughter." (WK 2010gg; F. Gondim 2001)

In some other cases, "[l]aughter can cause atonia and collapse ('gelastic syncope'), which in turn can cause trauma." (WK 2010gg; A. Reiss 2008; K. Nishida 2008; A. Totah 2002; R. Lo 2007)

In still some other cases, "[g]elastic seizures can be due to focal lesions to the hypothalamus. Depending upon the size of the lesion, the emotional lability may be a sign of an acute condition, and not itself the cause of the fatality." (WK 2010gg; G. Famularo 2007)

(b) From History

From the standpoint of history, there are likewises cases about death from laughter, as shown below. (WK 2010gg)

- "In the third century B.C., the Greek stoic philosopher Chrysippus died of laughter after giving his donkey wine, then seeing it attempt to feed on figs." (WK 2010gg; Peter Bowler 2002)
- "King Martin of Aragon died from a combination of indigestion and uncontrollable laughter in 1410." (WK 2010gg)
- "Pietro Aretino, who died in 1556, 'is said to have died of suffocation from laughing too much.'" (WK 2010gg; G. Waterfield 1966)
- "In 1599, the Burmese king Nanda Bayin laughed to death when informed, by a visiting Italian merchant, that Venice was a free state without a king." (WK 2010gg; B. Schott 2003)
- "In 1660, the Scottish aristocrat, polymath and first translator of Rabelais into English Thomas Urquhart, is said to have died laughing upon hearing that Charles II had taken the throne." (WK 2010gg; H. Brown1968)
- "On 24 March 1975, Alex Mitchell, a 50-year-old bricklayer from King's Lynn, England, died laughing while watching the 'Kung Fu Kapers' episode of The Goodies, featuring a kilt-clad Scotsman battling a vicious black pudding with his bagpipes. After twenty-five minutes of continuous laughter, Mitchell finally slumped on the sofa and died from heart failure. His widow later sent *The Goodies* a letter thanking them for making Mitchell's final moments of life so pleasant." (WK 2010gg; B. Mikkelson 2009; R. Ross 2000; T. Staveacre 1987)
- "In 1989, a Danish audiologist, Ole Bentzen, died laughing while watching *A Fish Called Wanda*. His heart was estimated to have beaten at between 250 and 500 beats per minute, before he succumbed to cardiac arrest." (WK 2010gg; CG 2009)

- "In 2003, Damnoen Saen-um, a Thai ice cream salesman, is reported to have died while laughing in his sleep at the age of 52. His wife was unable to wake him, and he stopped breathing after two minutes of continuous laughter. He is believed to have died of either heart failure or asphyxiation." (WK 2010gg; B. Mikkelson 2009)

Of course, there can be other cases, both scientific and historical, other than the ones presented above, so the listing is only illustrative, not exhaustive.

Beyond Fiction and Reality

The presentation of these illustrative historical and scientific evidences about "death from laughter" is not to prove the validity of the coverage in popular culture but shows us some evidences about the phenomenon as covered in popular culture but without telling us to what extent exactly death from laughter is accurate in the numerous ways that it has so often been portrayed in popular culture.

In other words, how much the coverage of death from laughter in popular culture is fictional or real remains unanswered. But the scholarly virtue of the presentation here is to show us the opposing sides of the debate, such that the possibility and desirability of laughing (from the perspective of culture with laughing, death, and the coverage in popular culture as a case study here) are not to the extent that the respective defenders would like us to believe.

Furthermore, the analysis of laughing, death, and the coverage in popular culture can teach us something valuable about the ontological principles in existential dialectics, and good examples include the absoluteness-relativeness principle, the predictability-unpredictability principle, the explicability-inexplicability principle, the preciseness-vagueness principle, the simpleness-complicatedness principle, the openness-hiddenness principle, the denseness-emptiness principle, the change-constancy principle, the slowness-quickness principle, the expansion-contraction principle, the theory-praxis principle, the convention-novelty principle, the evolution-transformation principle, the symmetry-asymmetry principle, the softness-hardness principle, the seriousness-playfulness principle, the regression-progression principle, and the same-difference principle. And the reverse direction also holds true.

For instance, in relation to the absoluteness-relativeness principle, if there is absoluteness (e.g., the absolute view within the novel of *Gregor and the Curse of the Warmbloods*, in which "a certain carnivorous plant emits a gas that causes euphoria and laughter, rendering the victims defenseless to attacks by the plant"), there is relativeness (e.g., what is true in the novel about the carnivorous plant that causes death from laughter is not necessarily so in science which explains death from laughter in a different way). And the reverse direction also holds true.

In relation to the predictability-unpredictability principle, if there is predictability (e.g., the predictable tendency of films and novels in popular culture to talk about death from laughter in entertaining ways), there is unpredictability (e.g., the more difficult task to predict exactly which particular death from laughter in a given film or novel will become true in real life in a particular historical era later). And the reverse direction also holds true.

In relation to the explicability-inexplicability principle, if there is explicability (e.g., the explanation by the author in the *AdventureQuest* online games that "a skeleton called Chuckles is said to have told a joke so funny that he died of laughter, and even continued to laugh…as an undead…after he died"), there is inexplicability (e.g., the lack of sufficient explanation by the author in the *AdventureQuest* online games of why Chuckles could die of laughter and yet continue to laugh as an undead after he already died). And the reverse direction also holds true.

In relation to the preciseness-vagueness principle, if there is precision (e.g., the precise identification of the heart of Ole Bentzen which had beaten between 250 and 500 beats per minute before he died of laughter in 1989), there is vagueness (e.g., the vagueness in the identification, since it is not clear at which particular rate that his heart was beating right before he died). And the reverse direction also holds true.

In relation to the simpleness-complicatedness principle, if there is simpleness (e.g., the relatively simple analysis of death from laughter in popular culture), there is complicatedness (e.g., the relatively more complicated analysis of death from laughter by questioning its claims and assumptions by the critics, like those in science, who offered different accounts of death from laughter in real life). And the reverse direction also holds true.

In relation to the openness-hiddenness principle, if there is openness (e.g., the open exploration of the relationship between death and laughter in different ways, as portrayed in popular culture), there is hiddenness (e.g., the hidden bias in popular culture about its portrayal of death from laughter, because of its entertaining motivation, not for scientific discovery). And the reverse direction also holds true.

In relation to the denseness-emptiness principle, if there is denseness (e.g.., the relatively denser concentration of deaths from laughter in an entertaining way as portrayed in popular culture, like films and novels), there is emptiness (e.g., the relatively less dense, or more empty, concentration of deaths from laughter in an entertaining way in real life, when examined by scientists instead). And the reverse direction also holds true.

In relation to the change-constancy principle, if there is change (e.g., the ever changing ways in which death by laughter is portrayed in popular culture), there is constancy (e.g., the ever constancy of the entertaining value in the topic of death from laughter in popular culture).

In relation to the slowness-quickness principle, if there is slowness (e.g., the heart tends to beat at a relatively slower rate, if no laughter occurs), there is quickness (e.g., the heart tends to beat at a relatively faster rate, if laughter occurs). And the reverse direction also holds true.

In relation to the expansion-contraction principle, if there is expansion (e.g.., the relatively more developed ability of film producers and writers to deal with death from laughter in a highly amusing, entertaining way), there is contraction (e.g., the relatively less developed ability of film producers and writers to deal with death from laughter in a highly vigorous, scientific way). And the reverse direction also holds true.

In relation to the theory-praxis principle, if there is theory (e.g., the theoretical construction about the brain in pathophysiology), there is praxis (e.g., the practical application of pathophysiology to the study of death from laughter). And the reverse direction also holds true.

In relation to the convention-novelty principle, if there is convention (e.g,. the conventional wisdom about death from laughter from the scientific standpoint of pathophysiology), there is novelty (e.g., the alternative novel challenge to the scientific account of death from laughter, by way of the entertaining accounts of death from laughter in films and novels). And the reverse direction also holds true.

In relation to the evolution-transformation principle, if there is evolution (e.g., the natural evolution of humans to encounter death from laughter in real life), there is transformation (e.g., the technical transformation of human ability to encounter death from laughter by the invention of films and novels, so that humans can encounter them in a way different from real life). And the reverse direction also holds true.

In relation to the symmetry-asymmetry principle, if there is symmetry (e.g., the co-existence of different ways to talk about death from laughter in history), there is asymmetry (e.g., the fashionable way to deal with death from laughter in an entertaining way as portrayed in popular culture—but the accepted way to deal with death from laughter in a vigorous or robust way as explored in science). And the reverse direction also holds true.

In relation to the softness-hardness principle, if there is softness (e.g., the soft side of laughter, like having fun), there is hardness (e.g., the hard side of laughter, like dying from so much fun in laughing). And the reverse direction also holds true.

In relation to the seriousness-playfulness principle, if there is seriousness (e.g., the serious business of popular culture to entertain, even when addressing the issue of death from laughter), there is playfulness (e.g., the playful nature of popular culture to portray death from laughter in a funny way). And the reverse direction also holds true.

In relation to the regression-progression principle, if there is regression (e.g., the regression made by popular culture in addressing death from laughter often in an unrealistic, non-scientific way), there is progression (e.g., the progress made by popular culture to entertain people even when addressing the difficult issue of death from laughter). And the reverse direction also holds true.

And in relation to the same-difference principle, if there is similarity in outcome (e.g., the contribution to the molding and regulation of beliefs and values, regardless of whether this be done by way of popular culture or by way of real science), there is difference in outcome (e.g., the contribution to the molding and regulation of beliefs and values by way of popular culture for a more entertaining lifeworld—but the contribution to the molding and regulation of beliefs and values by way of real science for a more serious lifeworld). And the reverse direction also holds true.

The Sorrow of Laughing

This comprehensive analysis of the possibility and desirability of laughing from the perspectives of the mind, nature, society, and culture is serious enough to show us the different ways in which laughing is both possible and desirable, but not to the extent that the spokespersons from each side would like us to believe.

Laughing thus has its sorrow, just as it has its joy too, as the other side of the same mirror.

But this is only one part of a larger story, since there is the other side of the story, which concerns joking, the opposite of laughing. While this chapter deals with laughing, the previous chapter (Chapter Two) already addressed the issue of joking.

The analysis in this chapter should not be dismissed as redundant, because those on the side of joking often downgrade laughing merely as the receiving end of humor without really appreciating it from the vantage point of laughing too. And the reverse also holds true.

Now that we have reached the end of this long intellectual journey, what then can be concluded about the future of humor, in the context of both joking and laughing?

This is the issue, for which we now turn to the concluding chapter, that is, Chapter Four on the future of humor.

Table 3.1. Laughing and Its Dual Facets

- **Laughing and the Mind**
  - —Ex: laughing, health, and the dark sides
  - —Ex: laughing, therapy, and the debate in gelotology

- **Laughing and Nature**
  - —Ex: laughing, animals, and the contentious comparison
  - —Ex: laughing, animals, and the evolutionary claim

- **Laughing and Society**
  - —Ex: laughing, and the dispute about social functions

- **Laughing and Culture**
  - —Ex: laughing, writers, and the role of intellectual culture
  - —Ex: laughing, death, and the coverage in popular culture

Notes: The examples in the categories are solely illustrative (not exhaustive), and the comparison is relative (not absolute), nor are they necessarily mutually exclusive. And some can be easily re-classified elsewhere. As generalities, they allow exceptions.
Source: A summary of Ch.3 of *FPHH*

Table 3.2. Laughing, Health, and the Dark Sides

- **Laughing and Health**
  —Ex: in 2005, for instance, "[a] link between laughter and healthy function of blood vessels was first reported…by researchers at the University of Maryland Medical Center with the fact that laughter causes the dilatation of the inner lining of blood vessels, the endothelium, and increases blood flow." (WK 2010b; M. Miller 2006)

- **Laughing and the Dark Sides**
  —Ex: stigmatization and degradation
  —Ex: pathological laughing and crying (PLC)
  —Ex: death from laughter (in *Sec. 3.5.2*)

Notes: The examples in the categories are solely illustrative (not exhaustive), and the comparison is relative (not absolute), nor are they necessarily mutually exclusive. And some can be easily re-classified elsewhere. As generalities, they allow exceptions.
Source: From *Sec. 3.2.1* of *FPHH.* See book for citations.

Table 3.3. Laughing, Therapy, and the Debate in Gelotology

- **Laughing and Therapy**
  - —Ex: humor therapy
  - —Ex: laughter therapy
  - —Ex: laughter meditation
  - —Ex: laughter yoga and laughter clubs

- **Main Problems with the Claim for Therpay**
  - —Firstly, one main criticism of using laughter for therapy is that it is often difficult in practice to find things that all participants find humorous.
  - —Secondly, another main criticism of using laughter for therapy is that it can be counterproductive, when some people are not sensitive enough to make a distinction between laughing "with" people and laughing "at" people.
  - —Thirdly, still another main criticism of using laughter for therapy is that it is not quite natural (or "spontaneous") for some individuals to laugh in a "structured" format in these types of therapy.
  - —Fourthly, one more main criticism of using laughter for therapy is that not everyone likes humor; in fact, some may find it "sick."
  - —And fifthly, one last main criticism of using laughter for therapy is that there are negative side effects too.

Notes: The examples in the categories are solely illustrative (not exhaustive), and the comparison is relative (not absolute), nor are they necessarily mutually exclusive. And some can be easily re-classified elsewhere. As generalities, they allow exceptions.
Source: From *Sec. 3.2.2* of *FPHH*. See book for more details and citations.

Table 3.4. Laughing, Animals, and the Contentious Comparison

- **Laughing and Animals**
  —Ex: laughter in non-human primates
  —Ex: laughter in rats
  —Ex: laughter in dogs

- **Main Problems in the Comparison**
  —Firstly, one main problem in the comparison between human and non-human laughters is that it is not clear if the animals really express joy.
  —Secondly, another main problem in the comparison between human and non-human laughters is that non-human laughter (like "chirping" in rats) cannot be heard by humans. So, to study laughter like this requires some special equipments and human interpretations.
  —Thirdly, still another main problem in the comparison between human and non-human laughters is that, in the case of rats, "as the rats age, there does appear to be a decline in the tendency to laugh and respond to tickle skin." (WK 2010aa) But this is not true for humans.
  —Fourthly, still one additional main problem in the comparison between human and non-human laughters is that laughter in animals does not suggest humor in animals.
  —And fifthly, still another additional main problem in the comparison between human and non-human laughters is that laughter in animals does not necessarily suggest comparable laugher in humans.

Notes: The examples are solely illustrative (not exhaustive), and the comparison is relative (not absolute), nor are they necessarily mutually exclusive. And some can be easily re-classified elsewhere. As generalities, they allow exceptions.
Source: From *Sec. 3.3.1* of *FPHH*. See book for citations.

Table 3.5. Laughing, Animals, and the Evolutionary Claim

- **Two Claims**
  —The first claim in Provine's evolutionary perspective of laughter is that it is unconscious.
  —The second claim in Provine's evolutionary perspective of laughter is that "laugher evolved from the panting behavior of our ancient primate ancestors." (R. Provine 1999)

- **A Response from the Critics**
  —Firstly, one major problem with Provine's evolutionary perspective is that, in the case of the first claim, "[v]ery little is known about the specific brain mechanisms responsible for laughter," as Provine (1999) himself acknowledged.
  —Secondly, another major problem with Provine's evolutionary perspective is that, in the case of the second claim, it is not clear to what extent the differences between human and non-human laughters can really set them apart into different evolutionary lines altogether instead.
  —Thirdly, still another major problem with Provine's evolutionary perspective is that it does not really answer the difficult question of why there is humor at all (as it also produces laughter).
  —And fourthly, still one more major problem with Provine's evolutionary perspective is that it does not answer some other related but important questions, like "the brain mechanisms of laughter," the mystery about "tickling" itself, and the like.

Notes: The examples are solely illustrative (not exhaustive), and the comparison is relative (not absolute), nor are they necessarily mutually exclusive. And some can be easily re-classified elsewhere. As generalities, they allow exceptions.
Source: From *Sec. 3.3.2* of *FPHH.* See book for citations.

Table 3.6. Laughing, and the Dispute about Social Functions (Part I)

- **The Social Functions of Laughter**
  - —Firstly, laughter can contribute to the formation of "corporate identity."
  - —Secondly, laughter can contribute to the maintenance of social hierarchy.
  - —Thirdly, laughter, especially in the context of humor, can test the limits of others.
  - —Fourthly, laughter can let people be critical in a way which is more tolerated.
  - —Fifthly, laughter can defuse a tense situation.
  - —Sixthly, laughter can be exploited to manipulate "the mood of groups." (G. Christine 2010)
  - —Seventhly, laughter can be employed as a safety valve in a repressive political environement.
  - —And eighthly, laughter can let people say things in public which they only want to say privately.

- **Problems with the Claim of Social Functions**
  - —Firstly, one major criticism of Christine's functionalist argument about laughter in the context of humor is that, as Robert Merton (1968) once pointed out in his critique of functionalism in sociology (as originally proposed by Arthur R.Radcliffe-Brown and Bronislaw Malinwoski, for instance), social functons can be "undesirable," relative to different moral evaluations. (P. Baofu 2004: 69) In the case of laughter, as Christine (2010) herself was cautious enough to mention it: "Humor can be dysfunctional when it is consistently used to avoid reality….Misused, it [laugher in humor] can damage self-esteem, light blazing fires of resentment, and create misunderstandings."

(continued on next page)

Table 3.6. Laughing, and the Dispute about Social Functions (Part II)

- **Problems with the Claim of Social Functions** ***(cont'd)***
  —Secondly, another major criticism of Christine's functionalist argument about laughter in the context of humor is that, as Robert Merton (1968) also pointed out in his critique of functionalism in sociology, social functons "are not nccessarily indispensable (since there can be 'functional alternatives,' 'functional equivalents or substitutes')." (P. Baofu 2004: 69) In the case of laughter, there are alternative theories about laughter in the context of humor, as discussed in this chapter—and, for that matter, in Chapter One and Chapter Two.
  —And thirdly, still another major criticism of Christine's functionalist argument about laughter in the context of humor is that, as Robert Merton (1968) also pointed out in his critique of functionalism in sociology, social functons do not necessarily exist, because "there exist 'nonfunctions' which are consequences...left over from previous historical epochs but no longer relevant to a current system. (G. Ritzer 2003:93-4)" (P. Baofu 2004: 69) In the case of laughter, there are some scholars like Darwin in evolutionary theory who argue that laughter in humor does not seem to have any survival value in evolution (that is, no evolutionary function), other than being a by-product for courtship in "sexual selection" (which is not the same as "natural selection"), as already discussed in *Sec. 1.3* and *Sec. 2.3*).

Notes: The examples are solely illustrative (not exhaustive), and the comparison is relative (not absolute), nor are they necessarily mutually exclusive. And some can be easily re-classified elsewhere. As generalities, they allow exceptions.
Source: From *Sec. 3.4.1* of *FPHH*. See book for citations.

Table 3.7. Laughing, Writers, and the Role of Intellectual Culture

• **Writers on Laughter**
—Ex: Herodotus
—Ex: Aristotle
—Ex: homas Hobbes
—Ex: Nikolai Gogol
—Ex: Friedrich Nietzsche
—Ex: Henri Bergson

• **The Untold Aspects of Literary Works**
—Firstly, one major criticism against the validity of literary works is thatt it is not clear if their typologies about laughter are really accurate. For instance, Why should Herodotus distinguish laughter into three main types—instead of four, five, six, seven, and so on?
—Secondly, another major criticism against the validity of literary works is that their analysis can be ideological. For instance, Herodotus often analyzed laughter and humor with the appeal to the spirits of "the gods" which were popular in Greek antiquity.
—Thirdly, still another major criticism against the validity of literary works is that their analyses can be driven by personal conflicts. For instance, in the case of Gogol, as R. Hallett (1971) reminded us, "[t]hroughout his life, indeed, Gogol remained a comic writer in spite of himself....Like so many blessed with the gift of making others laugh, he was himself an extremely unhappy man whose comic vein was both an escape from, and a consequence of a profound melancholia." (WK 2010bb)
—And fourthly, an additional major criticism against the validity of literary works is that the scholars who propound their views on laughter do not necessarily practice what they advocate. For instance, in the case of Nietzsche, Tarmo Kunnas in 1982 apty wrote: "Possibly Nietzsche's works would have had a totally different effect, if the playful, ironical and joking in his writings would have been factored in better." (WK 2010bb)

Notes: The examples are solely illustrative (not exhaustive), and the comparison is relative (not absolute), nor are they necessarily mutually exclusive. And some can be easily re-classified elsewhere. As generalities, they allow exceptions.
Source: From *Sec. 3.5.1* of *FPHH*. See book for citations.

• PART FOUR •

Conclusion

CHAPTER 4
CONCLUSION—THE FUTURE OF HUMOR

> Imagination was given to man to compensate him for what he is not; a sense of humor to console him for what he is.
> —Sir Francis Bacon (WK 2010)

Beyond Joking and Laughing

The analyses of joking (in Chapter Two) and laughing (in Chapter Three) have the scholarly value to show the extent of their possibility and desirability in humor.

These analyses are important enough, in light of the opposing views on the nature of humor (as already described in *Sec. 1.1*). Contrary to the two opposing views (and other ones as already discussed in the book), joking (on the giving end of humor) and laughing (on the receiving end of humor) are neither possible nor desirable to the extent that their respective ideologues would like us to believe.

Surely, one should not misconstrue this critique of the conventional wisdom about the nature of humor as a suggestion that humor is a joyless endeavor, or that some fields of study (related to humor) like evolutionary biology, psychology, sociology, or even culture studies are to be disregarded. Needless to say, neither of these extreme views is reasonable either.

On the contrary, this book provides an alternative (better) way to understand the future of humor, especially in the dialectic context of joking and laughing—while learning from different approaches in the literature but without favoring any one of them (nor integrating them, since they are not necessarily compatible with each other).

Thus, this book offers a new theory (that is, *the metamorphic theory of humor*) to go beyond the existing approaches in the literature on humor in a novel way.

Already indicated in *Sec. 1.4*, the word "metamorphic" is derived from "metamorphism" in geology, which is defined, in a formal definition, as "a change in the constitution of rock." (MWD 2010)

In the current context of humor, I use the word "metamorphic" for the title of my argument, because it provides an unconventional way to understand humor to account for its endless changes over different historical eras, and my metamorphic theory of humor has four distinctive features to remember.

Firstly, my theory makes good use of all theoretical approaches in the literature on humor, be they about the mental argument, the natural argument, the societal argument, or the cultural argument—especially from the most comprehensive combined perspectives of the mind, nature, society, and culture (as will be clear in Chapter Two and Chapter Three).

Secondly, just like many other theories of mine in my previous books, my theory here does not heavily favor any specific theory over others in the literature, nor trying to integrate them (as they are not necessarily compatible with each other).

Thirdly, my theory treats the issue of humor in the distinctive dialectic context of joking and laughing, such that one is not to be reduced as part of the analysis of the other—even though laughing can exist outside humor (like the situations when one is tickled, playful, and so on).

And fourthly, it contains eighteen major theses, namely, (a) the first thesis: the absoluteness-relativeness principle, (b) the second thesis: the predictability-unpredictability principle, (c) the third thesis: the explicability-inexplicability principle, (d) the fourth thesis: the preciseness-vagueness principle, (e) the fifth thesis: the simpleness-complicatedness principle, (f) the sixth thesis: the openness-hiddenness principle, (g) the seventh thesis: the denseness-emptiness principle, (h) the eighth thesis: the slowness-quickness principle, (i) the nineth thesis: the expansion-contraction principle, (j) the tenth thesis: the theory-praxis principle, (k) the eleventh thesis: the convention-novelty principle, (l) the twelveth thesis: the evolution-transformation principle, (m) the thirteenth thesis: the symmetry-asymmetry principle, (n) the fourteenth thesis: the softness-hardness principle, (o) the fifteenth thesis: the seriousness-playfulness principle, (p) the sixteenth thesis: the regression-progression principle, (q) the seventeenth thesis: the sameness-difference principle, and (r) the eighteenth thesis: the post-human rendition—to be elaborated in the rest of the book, with a summary in the concluding chapter.

Of course, as this is something that I often emphasized in my previous books, other principles (besides the 17 as cited above) are also relevant, but these 17 are the most relevant in the current case study (in terms of the number of citations of each principle in the book).

Even then, in some cases, the difference between any two given principles, for instance, in terms of the number of citations in a book, is rather small, so the reason in those cases is more aesthetic (than otherwise), because it looks nicer to list only 17 theses for 17 principles (than 22 theses for all of the 22 principles) in the Table of Contents.

This is true, even if different studies of the same kind can yield different views about the degree of relevance for each principle, depending on the specific nature of a research in question, needless to say. So, if a different author analyzes the same subject matter in a different way, the relevance of the principles will be different.

With this clarification in mind—the seminal project here, if successful, is to fundamentally change the way that we think about humor, from the combined perspectives of the mind, nature, society, and culture, with enormous implications for the human future and what I originally called its "post-human" fate.

In the Category of Method

Firstly, in regard to the formalness-informalness principle (on the formal requirements of logical systems), if there is formalness (e.g., the formal requirement of consistency in a system of ideas, like rational thought in science, in *Sec. 2.2.1*; the formal logical requirement of soundness and completeness in a system of ideas, as in science, in *Sec. 2.3.1*; the formal logical requirement of soundness and completeness in a system of ideas, as in a scientific work, in *Sec. 2.4.2*; the formal logical requirement of consistency and soundness in a system of ideas, like those in science, in *Sec. 3.2.1*; the formal logical requirement of soundness in a system of ideas, like those in gelotology, in *Sec. 3.2.2*; the formal logical requirement of completeness in a system of ideas, like the research on laughter in animals, in *Sec. 3.3.1*; and the formal logical requirement of soundness and completeness in a system of ideas, as in the theories about laughter and humor, in *Sec. 3.5.1*), there is informalenss too (e.g., the non-formal allowance of non-rational thought in humor, as shown by Arthur Koestler's work, in *Sec. 2.2.1*; ., the non-formal features of incompleteness in the theory of humor as IFF, as it relies on a metaphor of the IFF system from military studies without sucessfully proving that humor is in fact what it says it is, in *Sec. 2.3.1*; the informal existence of some incompleteness and unsoundness in the theory of ethnic humor by Davies, because of the problems pointed out by the critics, in *Sec. 2.4.2*; the nonformal existence of inconsistency and unsoundness, as shown in the research on the association "between PLC and major depression," as "[s]ometimes an association is found" but "other studies find none," in *Sec. 3.2.1*; the non-formal existence of unsoundness about the claims and assumptions in regard to therapy in gelotology, as shown in the criticisms, in *Sec. 3.2.2*; the non-formal existence of inconpleteness in the research on laugher in rats, as shown by "the research [which] was unable to prove rats have a sense of humor," although "it did indicate that they can laugh and express joy," in *Sec. 3.3.1*; and the non-formal existence of incompleteness, as shown in the appeal to "the gods" in Herodotus in his analysis of laughter, in *Sec. 3.5.1*). And the reverse direction also holds true.

And secondly, in regard to the partiality-totality principle (on the relationships between parts and whole), if there is partial analysis (e.g., the partial, limited info about the Polish people on which Hollywood and the U.S. TV media were originally based in the 1960's, in *Sec. 2.4.2*), there is also holistic analysis (e.g., the holistic view about the Polish people in terms of "ethnic jokes" by the American public, which simply does not add up, in light of the partial info on which Hollywood and the U.S. TV media were originally based, such that the whole is not the sum of its parts, because of the propaganda effect, in *Sec. 2.4.2*). And the reverse direction also holds true.

In the Category of Structure

Firstly, in regard to the finiteness-transfiniteness principle (on the nature of numbers), if there is finiteness (e.g., the finite number of the categories of species who enjoy incongruities in playing, for Hewitt, in *Sec. 2.3.1*; and the finite number of the categories of species who have "laugh-like vocalizations," in *Sec. 3.3.2*), there is also transfiniteness (e.g., the transfinite number of individuals in all species who have ever enjoyed incongruities in playing in history, in *Sec. 2.3.1*; and the transfinite number of individual animals, human or non-human, in history who have ever laughed, in *Sec. 3.3.2*). And the reverse direction also holds true.

In the Category of Process

Firstly, in regard to the change-constancy principle (on the alteration of things), if there is change (e.g., the ever new links to disrupt the familiar connections in the brain, when successful jokes are made, according to de Bono, in *Sec. 2.2.1*; the changing nature of the sub-genre of comedy and satire, from being known as "black humor" to "black comedy," for instance, in *Sec. 2.2.2*; the ever changing view of humor, like the theory of humor as IFF by Hewitt, in *Sec. 2.3.1*; the ever changing works of satire which have been produced in history, like those by musicians such as Tom Lehrer, live performance groups like the Capitol Steps, and public television and live performer Mark Russell," in *Sec. 2.4.1*; the ever new formation of ethnic jokes in society, in *Sec. 2.4.2*; the ever new fart jokes to be made by people over time, in *Sec. 2.5.1*; the ever new ways to make jokes, as shown in the varieties of the techniques of joking over time, in *Sec. 2.5.2*; the ever changing views by writers on laughter in literary works, in *Sec. 3.5.1*; and the ever changing ways in which death by laughter is portrayed in popular culture, in *Sec. 3.5.2*), there is constancy too (e.g., the ever constant nature of the mind as "a pattern-matching machine," even when new jokes are made over time, in *Sec. 2.2.1*; the ever constancy of the sub-genre of comedy and satire to focus on the topic of death, regardless of whether it is known as "black humor" or "black comedy," in *Sec. 2.2.2*; the ever constant mystery of humor, as it continues to puzzle people about its existence, in *Sec. 2.3.1*; the ever constancy of satire as funny to some but offensive to others, in *Sec. 2.4.1*; the ever constant themes of "stupidity, canniness and sexual behavior" in ethnic jokes, no matter how much changes there are over time, for Davies, in *Sec. 2.4.2*; the ever constancy of the tendency to shift blame in fart jokes, in *Sec. 2.5.1*; the ever constancy of the existence of different techniques of joking in humor, in *Sec. 2.5.2*; the ever constancy of the topic of laughter in literary works, in *Sec. 3.5.1*; and the ever constancy of the entertaining value in the topic of death from laughter in popular culture, in *Sec. 3.5.2*). And the reverse direction also holds true.

And secondly, in relation to the order-chaos principle (on the pattern of things), if there is order (e.g., the relatively orderly behavior of normal individuals when they laugh, when compared with those of PLC patients, in *Sec. 3.2.1*), there is chaos too (e.g., the relatively chaotic behavior of PLC patients when they laugh, especially in regard to their "relatively uncontrollable episodes of laughing or crying, or both," in *Sec. 3.2.1*). And the reverse direction also holds true.

1st Thesis: The Absoluteness-Relativeness Principle

The first thesis refers to the absoluteness-relativeness principle (on the multiplicity of things) in the category of "method" in existential dialectics, which was first proposed in *FPHK*, in that there is the multiplicity of things in reality, be they about entities, qualities (or properties), and relationships. If there is something absolute, there is likewise something relative. And there is no absoluteness without relativeness—and vice versa.

Both absoluteness and relativeness here are also relevant to different modalities often cited in the literature on ontology, such as possibility (e.g., something "can" happen) and its opposite (e.g., impossibility), probability (e.g., something "will" happen) and its opposite (e.g., improbability), and necessity (e.g., something "should" happen) and its opposite (e.g., contingency).

For instance, on the one hand, there are absolute viewpoints (e.g., the absolute view by Freud that jokes "let…in forbidden thoughts and feelings which society suppresses into the conscious mind," in *Sec. 2.2.1*; the absolute dependence of "obscene humor" on "shock and revulsion" to be humorous, in *Sec. 2.2.2*; the absolute view of Hewitt that humor can be treated as an IFF system, in *Sec. 2.3.1*; the absolute view of the practitioners of satire that "satire is usually meant to be funny," not offensive, in *Sec. 2.4.1*; the absolute view in Nazi propaganda about "subhuman intelligence jokes" targeting Polish people, in *Sec. 2.4.2*; the absolute view of those who does farting "to pin the blame on someone else, often by means of deception rhyming game" in fart jokes, in *Sec. 2.5.1*; the absolute orientation of satire and parody to criticize "Nigerian military dictators" by Soyinka, in *Sec. 2.5.2*; the absolute view by the ancient Greeks that laughing is important to good health, in *Sec. 3.2.1*; the absolute view of the proponents in gelotology that laughter is good for therapy, in *Sec. 3.2.2*; the absolute view by those like Provine that human and non-human laughters have a shared evolutionary origin, in *Sec. 3.3.2*; the absolute view in Christine's claim about social functions, in *Sec. 3.4.1*; the absolute, obsessive interest by Gogol in the comic, as driven by his "profound melancholia," in *Sec.* 3.5.1; and the absolute view within the novel of *Gregor and the Curse of the Warmbloods*, in which "a certain carnivorous plant emits a gas that causes euphoria and laughter, rendering the victims defenseless to attacks by the plant," in *Sec. 3.5.2*).

On the other hand, there are likewise relative counterparts (e.g., what is true for Freud in regard to social prohibitions in jokes is not so for Chislenko, who argued that "people are ready to openly express more aggression, sexuality, and disagreement with authorities," in *Sec. 2.2.1*; what is obscene in obscene humor is not so in black humor, which is "more subtle and does not necessarily have the explicit intention of offending people," in *Sec. 2.2.2*; what is true for Hewitt about humor as an IFF system is not necessarily so for the critics, who question it, in *Sec.*

2.3.1; what is funny for the practitioners of satire is not necessarily so for its victims, like those "offended Muslims" against "the Jyllands-Posten Muhammad cartoons" which "caused global protests...and violent attacks with many fatalities in the Near East," in *Sec. 2.4.1*; what is funny in Nazi propaganda about "subhuman intelligence jokes" targeting Polish people is not necessarily so for the Polish people themselves, in *Sec. 2.4.2*; what is funny for those who does farting to make fart jokes which "pin the blame on someone else, often by means of deception rhyming game" is not necessarily so for the victims who consider farting as impolite and the shifting of blame as irresponsible, in *Sec. 2.5.1*; what is funny for Soyinka in his satire and parody is not necessarily so for the "Nigerian military dictators" who condemned him, as "[i]n 1997 Soyinka was charged with treason by the government of General Sani Abacha," in *Sec. 2.5.2*; what is true for the ancient Greeks that laughing is important to good health is not necessarily so for modern researchers on the dark sides of laughing, in *Sec. 3.2.1*; what is true for the proponents in gelotology that laughter is good for therapy is not necessarily so for the critics who question the claims and assumptions, in *Sec. 3.2.2*; what is true for people like Provine in regard to the shared evolutionary perspective of laughter is not necessarily so for some dissenters who offered the alternative explanation, "which would be that it [laughter] evolved separately and independently in each group," whereas other critics suggest that laughter, especially in the context of humor, is "a gift from God," in *Sec. 3.3.2*; what is true for Christine about the social functions of laughter is not necessarily so for others like Darwin who argue that laughter in humor does not seem to have any survival value in evolution, that is, no evolutionary function, other than being a by-product for courtship in "sexual selection," in *Sec. 3.4.1*; what drives Gogal into his obsessed interest in the comic for personal reason is not necessarily so for Bergson, who is more interested in the laws of the comic in the context of the rigidness in life, in *Sec. 3.5.*1; and what is true in the novel about the carnivorous plant that causes death from laughter is not necessarily so in science which explains death from laughter in a different way, in *Sec. 3.5.2*).

And the reverse direction also holds true.

However, it should be stressed (as this is something that I regularly did in my previous books, *almost verbatim*) that there are different shades of gray (or different degrees of truth) in the two opposites, and the classification is not necessarily mutually exclusive either. In fact, even when some combinations of the two occur, they only end up sharing the same dialectic relationship, but in a different degree.

Also, there are some other relationships (as a kind of family resemblance) which have something in common with the principle, but they are not exactly the same but only more or less comparable, which varies from case to case.

Good examples of family resemblance in relation to the principle are uniformity-diversity, internalness-externalness, immanence-transcendence, and so forth.

2nd Thesis: The Predictability-Unpredictability Principle

The second thesis is called the predictability-unpredictability principle (on the occurrence of events) in the category of "method" in existential dialectics (which was first proposed in *FC* and, later, other books of mine), in that both predictability and unpredictability have a major role to play in the occurrence of things, so that neither determinism nor indeterminism wins the centuries-old fight. There is no predictability without unpredictability—and vice versa.

There are events which are predictable, just as there are those which are not. Or what is regarded as unpredictable at one point in time may turn out to be predictable later, and, conversely, what is deemed as predictable may turn out to not be so predictable. Even in predictability, outcomes are subject to uncertainty, the degree of which varies from case to case.

For instance, on the one hand, there is predictability (e.g., the predictable tendency, by those who accept de Bono's view about humor, to show a joke as "an alternative unexpected new link…in the brain via a different route than expected" from a conventional "familiar connection," in *Sec. 2.2.1*; the predictable tendency of black comedy to deal wth the topic of death, in *Sec. 2.2.2*; the predictable tendency of people like Hewitt to analyze humor from the standpoint of an IFF system, in *Sec. 2.3.1*; the predictable tendency of those in power to dislike political satire against them, in *Sec. 2.4.1*; the predictable tendency of race/ethnic jokes to target both the weak and the strong in history, in *Sec. 2.4.2*; the predictable tendency of those who make fart jokes to engage in shifting blame, in *Sec. 2.5.1*; the predictable tendency of the cultrual factor in shaping the use of humor in a continent, as in black Africa, in *Sec. 2.5.2*; the predictable tendency of PLC as "a frequent consequence of brain injury," in *Sec. 3.2.1*, the predictable tendency of the practitioners in gelotology to use laughter for therapy, in *Sec. 3.2.2*; the predictable tendency of non-human primates like chimpanzees and others to make "laughter-like vocalizations in response to physical contact, such as wrestling, play chasing, or tickling," in *Sec. 3.3.1*; the predictable tendency of Provine to treat laughter as unconscious, in *Sec. 3.3.2*; the predictable tendency of people like Christine to point out the social functions that laugher can serve, in *Sec. 3.4.1*; the predictable tendency of different writers on the subject of laughter to propound different views, in *Sec. 3.5.1*; and the predictable tendency of films and novels in popular culture to talk about death from laughter in entertaining ways, in *Sec .3.5.2*).

On the other hand, there is unpredictability (e.g., the more difficult task to predict exactly when a given "new link" will necessarily produce a laughter, since not all forms of creativity in new links are humorous, in *Sec. 2.2.1*; the more difficult task to predict exactly to what extent a particular black comedy will end up producing discomfort, laughter, or both in the audience, in *Sec. 2.2.2*; the more difficult task to predict exactly when a particular incongruity will be interpreted as a "friend" or a "foe," because the theory suffers from many problems as shown in the criticisms, in *Sec. 2.3.1*; the more difficult task to predict exactly when or to what extent a given political suppression against satire is successful, as shown in the subsequent success by Prime Minister Silvio Berlusconi to stop RAI Television's satirical series, *Raiot*—but in the unsuccessful attempt by the Archbishop of Canterbury John Whitgift and the Bishop of London George Abbot in 1599 to ban verse satire, because "the ban was little enforced, even by the licensing authority itself," in *Sec. 2.4.1*; the more difficult task to predict when exactly the public will perceive particular ethnic jokes as offensive or not, because this can vary from case to case, from era to era, and the like, as illustrated by the evolution of the history about black jokes nowadays, as opposed to those in the older days of slavery, in *Sec. 2.4.2*; the more difficult task to predict exactly which particular rhyming phrase the fart joker will use on a given occasion, in *Sec. 2.5.1*; the more difficult task to predict exactly which cultural factor, be it laid-back culture or authoritarian culture, is more important in shaping the use of humor in a particular continent, to a particular extent, at a particular time, as in modern black Africa, in *Sec. 2.5.2*; the more difficult task to predict exactly "[t]he incidence of PLC in Alzheimer's," which remains nowadays "a matter of controversy," in *Sec. 3.2.1*; the more difficult task to predict exactly to what extent a group in a therapy session will respond to humor with laughter, or will respond "sponteanously," and so on, as the critics have questioned some of the claims, in *Sec. 3.2.2*; the more difficult task to predict exactly when a particular "laughter-like vocalization" is really an expression of joy, because "[i]t is hard to tell...whether or not the chimpanzee is expressing joy," in *Sec. 3.3.1*; the more difficult task to predict, if based solely on Provine's evolutionary perspective of laughter, if or to what extent the unconscious nature of a particular laughter has to do with "social bonding"—or, alternatively, with sexuality and aggression, as Freud would suggest instead, in *Sec. 3.3.2*; the more difficult task to predict exactly which particular laugher will end up being functional, since it can be dysfunctional and non-functional too, for the critics, in *Sec. 3.4.1*; the more difficult task to predict exactly which particular view by which particular writer will be influential at a particular historical time, in *Sec. 3.5.1*; and the more difficult task to predict exactly which particular death from laughter in a given film or novel will become true in real life in a particular historical era later, in *Sec. 3.5.2*).

And the reverse direction also holds true.

Again, it should be stressed, however, that there are different shades of gray (or different degrees of truth) in the two opposites, and the classification is not necessarily mutually exclusive either. In fact, even when some combinations of the two occur, they only end up sharing the same dialectic relationship, but in a different degree.

Also, there are some other relationships (as a kind of family resemblance) which have something in common with the principle, but they are not exactly the same but only more or less comparable, which varies from case to case.

Good examples of family resemblance in relation to the principle are sureness-arbitrariness, and so forth.

3rd Thesis: The Explicability-Inexplicability Principle

The third thesis is called the explicability-inexplicability principle (on the underlying mechanisms of things) in the category of "method" in existential dialectics (which was proposed in *FPHU* and other books of mine), in that both explicability and inexplicability are part of the understanding of things. There is no explicability without inexplicability—and vice versa.

This principle tells us the dual nature of the research dilemma, in that, if reality can be explained in some ways, it also has its other ways which are not quite explainable, at a given point in time.

For instance, on the one hand, there is explicability (e.g., the explanation by Kant that a joke "arises if a tense expectation [in a joke] is transformed into nothing," in *Sec. 2.2.1*; the explanation by black comedians that black comedy is not the same as obscene humor, because "it is more subtle and does not necessarily have the explicit intention of offending people," in *Sec. 2.2.2*; the explanation by Hewitt that the evolution of humor can be explained on the basis of an IFF system, in *Sec. 2.3.1*; the explanation by the practitioners of satire that "satire" is "an aspect of the freedom of speech" and therefore should be tolerated, in *Sec. 2.4.1*; the explanation by some scholars that "ethnic humour helps us deal with hostility verbally instead of physically," in *Sec. 2.4.2*; the explanation, by those making fart jokes, of the culture of shitting blame by the use of rhyming phrases, in *Sec. 2.5.1*; the explanation by people like Soyinka to use satire and parody for the critique of political oppression, because the ideas are "dangerous" for the regime in question, in *Sec. 2.5.2*; the explanation by those like Angelle that laughing is important to good health, because "laughter boosts the immune system, lowers cholesterol and blood pressure, and reduces stress," in *Sec. 3.2.1*; the explanation by the practitioners of using laughter for therapy on the basis that laughter is good for health, in *Sec. 3.2.2*; the explanation by the researchers in the study on rats, that, "as the rats age, there does appear to be a decline in the tendency to laugh and respond to tickle skin," in *Sec. 3.3.1*; the explanation by Provine that human and non-human laughters have a shared evolutionary origin, in Sec. 3.3.2; the explanation by Christine that laughter exists because of its social functions, in *Sec. 3.4.1*; the explanation by Aristotle that "a person laughs about misfortunes of others, because these misfortunes assert the person's superiority on the background of shortcomings of others," in *Sec. 3.5.1*; and the explanation by the author in the *AdventureQuest* online games that "a skeleton called Chuckles is said to have told a joke so funny that he died of laughter, and even continued to laugh…as an undead…after he died," in *Sec. 3.5.2*).

On the other hand, there is inexplicability (e.g., the lack of sufficient explanation by Kant of why many jokes do not have anything to do with transforming a tense expectation into nothing, as already shown in the opposing views in Ch.1 and others in the rest of the book, in *Sec. 2.2.1*; the lack of sufficient explanation by black comedians of why black comedy cannot offend sensitive people, even if "it is more subtle and does not necessarily have the explicit intention of offending people," in *Sec. 2.2.2*; the lack of convincing explanation by Hewitt of why the evolution of humor is like an IFF system, especially when the criticisms against the theory are taken into account, in *Sec. 2.3.1*; the lack of sufficient explanation by the practitioners of satire of why it should be tolerated, in the name of "freedom of speech," because it also produces consequences which offend some other groups or attack those in power, as shown in the sub-section on satire under attack, in *Sec. 2.4.1*; the lack of sufficient explanation by these scholars who argued that "ethnic humour helps us deal with hostility verbally instead of physically" but at the same time acknowledged that "these slurs also reinforce our stereotypes" and can "lead to calls for violence" instead, besides some other alternative theories as presented in this book, in *Sec. 2.4.2*; the lack of sufficient explanation, by those who make fart jokes, of why this culture of shifting blame is justified, other than being a joke, which is not sufficient, for the critics, in *Sec. 2.5.1*; the lack of convincing explanation by people like Soyinka of why the use of satire and parody is effective and non-offensive to those in power, in *Sec. 2.5.2*; the lack of sufficient explanation, if looked only from the viewpoint of Angelle, of why laughing can be bad to the health of PLC patients and to those being stigmatized, in *Sec. 3.2.1*; the lack of sufficient explanation, if looked only within the worldview of the practitioners, of why laughter has its adverse side effects too, in *Sec. 3.2.2*; the lack of sufficient explanation, by the researchers in the study on rats, of why this decline occurs in rats, but not so in other primates, as shown in the study by Davila-Ross that "[t]he enjoyment of tickling in chimpanzees does not diminish with age," in *Sec. 3.3.1*; the lack of sufficient explanation, if viewed from Provine's perspective alone, of why there is humor at all, since it also produces laughter, but not all animals have humor, in *Sec. 3.3.2*; the lack of sufficient explanation by Christine of why laughter is necessarily functional in society, since for the critics, it can be dysfunctional or even non-functional, more often than we think, in *Sec. 3.4.1*; the lack of sufficient explanation by Aristotle of why this feeling of superiority must necessarily exist, because, for the critics like Nietzsche, "man uses the comical as a therapy against the restraining jacket of logic, morality and reason," in *Sec. 3.5.1*; and the lack of sufficient explanation by the author in the *AdventureQuest* online games of why Chuckles could die of laughter and yet continue to laugh as an undead after he already died, in *Sec. 3.5.2*).

And the reverse direction also holds true.

Once more, it should be stressed, however, that there are different shades of gray (or different degrees of truth) in the two opposites, and the classification is not necessarily mutually exclusive either. In fact, even when some combinations of the two occur, they only end up sharing the same dialectic relationship, but in a different degree.

Also, there are some other relationships (as a kind of family resemblance) which have something in common with the principle, but they are not exactly the same but only more or less comparable, which varies from case to case.

Good examples of family resemblance in relation to the principle are underlyingness-regularness, causation-regularity, causation-correlation and so forth.

4th Thesis: The Preciseness-Vagueness Principle

The fourth thesis is called the preciseness-vagueness principle (on the refinement of things) in the category of "structure" in existential dialectics (which was first out worked out in *FIA*), in that both preciseness and vagueness are important, not that one is better than the other, but that both are used, in different degrees of preference, in accordance to the contextual application from the perspectives of nature, the mind, culture, and society. There is no preciseness without vagueness—and vice versa.

For instance, on the one hand, there is preciseness (e.g., the precise identification of humor in terms of three different forms by Freud, in *Sec. 2.2.1*; the precise identification of the topic of death as the favorite satire in black comedy, in *Sec. 2.2.2*; the precise identification of four kinds of data by Hewitt, namely, "data from DNA," "data from sense organs," "data from social learning," and "data from ethical knowledge," in *Sec. 2.3.1*; the appeal to "the freedom of speech" by the defenders of satire, in *Sec. 2.4.1*; the precise identification by Davies of three main themes in ethnic jokes, in *Sec. 2.4.2*; the precise identification of the technique of rhyming in fart jokes, in *Sec. 2.5.1*; the precise identification of different techniques of joking in the literature, in *Sec. 2.5.2*; the precise identification of the correlation between PLC and major depression, in *Sec. 3.2.1*; the precise identification of the four types of therapy by the practitioners in geolotolgy, in *Sec. 3.2.2*; the precise identification of sound frequency, facial expressions, and voice stability in the comparison between human and non-humans in regard to laughter, in *Sec. 3.3.1*; the precise identification of "ha ha ha" as a laughter which is uniquely human by Provine, in *Sec. 3.3.2*; the precise identification of the eight different ways that laughter in humor can be functional by Christine, in *Sec .3.4.1*; the precise identification of three types of laughter by Herodotus, in *Sec. 3.5.1*; and the precise identification of the heart of Ole Bentzen which had beaten between 250 and 500 beats per minute before he died of laughter in 1989, in *Sec. 3.5.2*).

On the other hand, there is vagueness (e.g., the vagueness in the three forms of humor as identified by Freud, as the critics pointed out that they are "artificial and not very clear," and for Altman, "these three different types of humor are divided more in a semantically way than in a functional one," in *Sec. 2.2.1*; the vagueness in the identification of the topic of "death," since it can refer to different things to different people, like "murder, suicide, mutilation, war, barbarism, drug abuse, terminal illness, domestic violence, insanity, nightmare, disease, racism, disability..., chauvinism, corruption, and crime," in *Sec. 2.2.2*; the vagueness in the identification of the four kinds of data, since it is not clear why there should be only four kinds of data there ever be in history as claimed by Hewitt—not three, five, six, seven, and so on, in *Sec. 2.3.1*; the vagueness in the term "freedom of speech" since it can mean different things to different people, as revealed by the clashes among different groups in the sub-section on satire under attack, in *Sec. 2.4.1*; the vagueness in the identification of three main themes by Davies, as it is not clear why there are only three main themes in ethnic jokes—not four, five, six, seven, and the like, in *Sec. 2.4.2*; the vagueness in the identification of rhyming, since there can be so many different ways that the rhyming technique can be exploited, as shown in the examples aforecited, in *Sec. 2.5.1*; the vagueness in the techniques themselves, since they can be interpreted and used in different ways by different users, as some scholars had even suggested that "there are about 200 techniques...that can be used to make jokes" with the use of "danger," in *Sec. 2.5.2*; the vagueness in the identification, since "studies have reported an inconsistent pattern of association between PLC and major depression," in *Sec. 3.2.1*; the vagueness in the identification, since it is not clear why there should be only four types, not five, six, seven, and so on, in *Sec. 3.2.2*; the vagueness in the identification, since it is not clear to what extent the comparison is made, if measured in terms of "grades, degrees or spectrum," for instance, in *Sec. 3.3.1*; the vagueness in the identification of "ha ha ha" by Provine, because it is not clear to what exact degree, grade, or spectrum a human laughter differs from a non-human one, in *Sec. 3.3.2*; the vagueness in the identification of the eight social functions of laughter by Christine, since it is not clear why there are only eight different ways that laughter in humor is functional, instead of four, five, six, nine, ten, eleven, twelve, and so on, in *Sec. 3.4.1*; the vagueness in the identification by Herodotus, since it is not clear why laughter should have only three main types—instead of four, five, six, seven, and so on, in *Sec. 3.5.1*; and the vagueness in the identification, since it is not clear at which particular rate that his heart was beating right before he died, in *Sec. 3.5.2*).

And the reverse direction also holds true.

Once more, it should be stressed, however, that there are different shades of gray (or different degrees of truth) in the two opposites, and the classification is not necessarily mutually exclusive either. In fact, even when some combinations of the two occur, they only end up sharing the same dialectic relationship, but in a different degree.

Also, there are some other relationships (as a kind of family resemblance) which have something in common with the principle, but they are not exactly the same but only more or less comparable, which varies from case to case.

Good examples of family resemblance in relation to the principle are clarity-ambiguity, directness-indirectness, quantitativeness-qualitativeness, specificity-obscurity, thickness-thinness, describability-nondescribability, specificity-generality, concretness-abstractness, and the like.

5th Thesis: The Simpleness-Complicatedness Principle

The fifth thesis refers to the simpleness-complicatedness principle (on the interconnection among things) in the category of "structure" in existential dialectics (which was first out worked out in *FIA*), in that both simpleness and complicatedness are vital, without favoring one over the other, and each is utilized, depending on the basis of the perspectives of nature, the mind, culture, and society. There is no simpleness without complicatedness—and vice versa.

For instance, on the one hand, there is simple analysis (e.g., the relatively simple analysis of jokes in the context of the psychology of jokes, in *Sec. 2.2.1*; the relatively simple analysis of black comedy in terms of its history, themes, authors, media outlets, etc., in *Sec. 2.2.2*; the relatively simple analysis of humor as IFF by Hewitt, in *Sec. 2.3.1*; the relatively simple analysis of satire as being "meant to be funny," while "using wit as a weapon," in *Sec. 2.4.1*; the relatively simplistic analysis of ethnic jokes in terms of some main themes by Davies, in *Sec. 2.4.2*; the relatively simple analysis of fart jokes in terms of the long history and the culture of shifting blame, in *Sec. 2.5.1*; the relatively simple analysis of the techniques of joking, so that people can use them to be funny, in *Sec. 2.5.2*; the relatively simple view by the ancient Greeks that laughing is important to good health, in *Sec. 3.2.1*; the relatively simple analysis of gelotology on the basis of using laughter for therapy to improve health, in *Sec. 3.2.2*; the relatively simple analysis of the comparison between human and non-human laughters in the studies, in *Sec. 3.3.1*; the relatively simple view of laughter by Provine in regard to his two major claims, in *Sec. 3.3.2*; the relatively simple analysis of the social functions of laughter in humor by Christine, in *Sec. 3.4.1*; the relatively simple analysis of laughter from the narrow perpective of each writer, in *Sec. 3.5.1*; and the relatively simple analysis of death from laughter in popular culture, in *Sec. 3.5.2*).

On the other hand, there is also complicated counterpart (e.g., the relatively more complicated analysis of jokes in the context of the psychology of jokes, by challenging the claims and assumptions, as shown in the criticisms by the critics, in *Sec. 2.2.1*; the relatively more complicated analysis of black comedy by questioning its claims and assumptions, like its offensiveness to some people, the debate about the dark sides of human nature, etc., as pointed out by the critics, in *Sec. 2.2.2*; the relatively more complicated analysis of the theory of human as IFF by questioning its claims and assumptions, as shown in the various criticisms, in *Sec. 2.3.1*; the relatively more complicated analysis of satire by challenging its claims and assumptions by the critics, in *Sec. 2.4.1*; the relatively more complicated account of the theory of ethnic jokes, by challenging its claims and assumptions, as shown in the criticisms, in *Sec. 2.4.2*; the relatively more complicated analysis of fart jokes by questioning the claims and assumptions, like the questioning of why it is justified for fart jokers to shift blame, without accepting it as impolite and irresponsible, for instance, in *Sec .2.5.1*; the relatively more complicated analysis of the techniques of joking, by analyzing their cultural contingency, so as to show us the dark sides of joking in its other, dubious relationships with laid-back and authoritarian cultures, in *Sec. 2.5.2*; the relatively more complicated analysis of laughing by making some qualifications about its desirability, like the dark sides of laughing, in *Sec. 3.2.1*; the relatively more complicated analysis of using laughter for therapy by questioning its claims and assumptions, as shown in the criticisms by the critics, in *Sec. 3.2.2*; the relatively more complicated analysis of the comparison between human and non-human laughters in the studies, as shown in the criticisms, in *Sec. 3.3.1*; the relatively more complicated analysis of Provine's view of laughter, as shown in the criticisms which challenge its claims and assumptions, in *Sec. 3.3.2*; the relatively more complicated analysis of the social functions of laughter in humor, by challenging its claims and assumptions, as shown in the criticisms, in *Sec. 3.4.1*; the relatively more complicated analysis of laughter, by questioning the claims and assumptions of the works by these writers, as shown in the criticisms, in *Sec. 3.5.1*; and the relatively more complicated analysis of death from laughter by questioning its claims and assumptions by the critics, like those in science, who offered different accounts of death from laughter in real life, in *Sec. 3.5.2*).

And the reverse direction also holds true.

Again, it should be stressed, however, that there are different shades of gray (or different degrees of truth) in the two opposites, and the classification is not necessarily mutually exclusive either. In fact, even when some combinations of the two occur, they only end up sharing the same dialectic relationship, but in a different degree.

Also, there are some other relationships (as a kind of family resemblance) which have something in common with the principle, but they are not exactly the same but only more or less comparable, which varies from case to case.

Good examples of family resemblance in relation to the principle are inflexibility-flexibility, standardization-specialization, imperfectness-perfectness, superficiality-depth, shallowness-deepness, economicalness-elaboratedness, plainness-circumspection, onesidedness-multisidedness, and the like.

6th Thesis: The Openness-Hiddenness Principle

The sixth thesis refers to the openness-hiddenenss principle (on the detection of things) in the category of "structure" in existential dialectics (which was already worked out in my previous books, especially in *FPHU*), in that reality has its hidden face, just as it is open to outside view in some other ways. There is no openness without hiddenness—and vice versa.

For instance, on the one hand, there is openness (e.g., the open exploration of the relationships "between the unconscious and the conscious thoughts" in jokes by Freud, in *Sec .2.2.1*; the open exploration, in black comedy, of making "light of serious and often taboo subject matters," in *Sec. 2.2.2*; the open exploration of the relaitonship between humor and IFF in the work by Hewitt, in *Sec. 2.3.1*; the open exploration of the possibility of "constructive social criticism" by using "wit as a weapon" in satire, in *Sec. 2.4.1*; the open exploration by Davies of the relationship between "the societies where [the themes in question] are absent" and the "lack [of] the corresponding jokes" in these societies, like "jokes about alcohol are missing in Muslim and Jewish jokelore," in *Sec. 2.4.2*; the open exploration of the link between doing fart and the fun of making fart jokes, in *Sec. 2.5.1*; the open exploration of using satire and parody for political criticisms, in *Sec. 2.5.2*; the open exploration of the positive relationship between laughing and health by the ancient Greeks, in *Sec. 3.2.1*; the open exploration of the correlation between laughter and therapy in gelotology, in *Sec. 3.2.2*; the open exploration of the similarities between human and non-human laughters, in *Sec. 3.3.1*; the open exploration of the possibility of a shared evolutionary origin of both human and non-human laughters, as shown in the work by Provine, in *Sec. 3.3.2*; the open exploration of the relationship between social functions and laughter in humor by Christine, in *Sec. 3.4.1*; the open exploration of the relationship between laughter and the vices/rigidness in life by Bergson, in *Sec. 3.5.1*; and the open exploration of the relationship between death and laughter in different ways, as portrayed in popular culture, in *Sec. 3.5.2*).

On the other hand, there is also hiddenness (e.g., the hidden bias in Freud's psychoanalysis of jokes, in focusing too much on sexuality and aggression, as pointed out by Chislenko, in *Sec. 2.2.1*; the hidden bias in black comedy, because of its appeal to the dark sides of human nature, like the numerous destructive and violent issues in relation to the topic of death, in *Sec. 2.2.2*; the hidden bias in Hewitt's work, because of his obsession with the metaphor of IFF from military studies and his exclusion of other perspectives, in *Sec. 2.3.1*; the hidden bias in satire, in its unwillingness to accept "offensiveness" as part of its consequences, under the protection behind the slogan of "the freedom of speech," in *Sec. 2.4.1*; the hidden bias in the work by Davies, because it is question-begging, since one can ask further: Why should not the Muslims have jokes which make fun of others who drink, even if they themselves don't?, in *Sec. 2.4.2*; the hidden bias in fart jokes, because of the culture of shifting blame to the victims, in *Sec. 2.5.1*; the hidden bias in the use of satire and parody for political criticisms, because of the offensiveness towards those in power, as the other side of the same coin, in *Sec. 2.5.2*; the hidden bias in the view about the importance of laughing to good health, because of its neglect of the dark sides of laughing, in *Sec. 3.2.1*; the hiden bias in the field of study concerning laughter and therapy, because of its obsession with laughter without giving sufficient attention to the questionability of its claims and assumptions, in *Sec. 3.2.2*; the hidden bias in the studies on laughter in animals, because of the assumption on comparability with human laughter, in spite of the problems as pointed out by the critics, in *Sec. 3.3.1*; the hidden bias in Provine's work, because of his obsession with the shared evolutionary perspective that some other critical concerns, as shown in the criticisms against it, are sidelined, in *Sec. 3.3.2*; the hidden bias in Christian's functonal account of laugther in humor, as shown in the problems about functionalism as pointed out by Merton, which remain relevant in the context of laughter, in *Sec. 3.4.1*; the hidden bias in Bergson's work, because what constitutes "vices," "rigidity in life," and so on, before they can even be resisted or eliminated, in accordance to his theory, is already so value-laden that it is hard to have everyone to agree upon them, in *Sec. 3.5.1*; and the hidden bias in popular culture about its portrayal of death from laughter, because of its entertaining motivation, not for scientific discovery, in *Sec. 3.5.2*).

And the reverse direction also holds true.

Again, it should be stressed, however, that there are different shades of gray (or different degrees of truth) in the two opposites, and the classification is not necessarily mutually exclusive either. In fact, even when some combinations of the two occur, they only end up sharing the same dialectic relationship, but in a different degree.

Also, there are some other relationships (as a kind of family resemblance) which have something in common with the principle, but they are not exactly the same but only more or less comparable, which varies from case to case.

Good examples of family resemblance in relation to the principle are overtness-covertness, publicness-privateness, openness-closedness, transparency-secrecy, openness-biasedness, and so on.

7th Thesis: The Denseness-Emptiness Principle

The seventh thesis concerns the denseness-emptiness principle (on the distribution of entities in space) in the category of "structure" in existential dialectics, which is first proposed in *FPHUP*, in that both density and void are needed, in relation to the mind, nature, culture, and society, albeit in different ways. There is no denseness without emptiness—and vice versa.

Lest any misunderstanding occurs, the term "void" is used here only as an approximation of emptiness (depending on the degree of the lack of density), since, in physics, it is well known that "empty" space is not really empty all the way, because it can be full of energy (e.g., random quantum fluctuations at the sub-atomic level, and, for that matter, dark energy in the universe) and matter (e.g., different versions of sub-atomic particles, and, for that matter, dark matter in the universe). (F. Wilczek 2008)

For instance, on the one hand, there is denseness (e.g., the relatively denser concentration of individuals who accept the Freudian interpretation of jokes to focus on sexuality and aggression, in *Sec. 2.2.1*; the relatively denser concentration of the works by Jonathan Swift to deal with black comedy, in *Sec. 2.2.2*; the relatively denser concentration of concerns with IFF in the analysis of humor by people like Hewitt, in *Sec. 2.3.1*; the relatively denser concentration of Westerners in Europe who supported "the Jyllands-Posten Muhammad cartoons," in *Sec. 2.4.1*; the relatively denser concentration of concerns with the three main themes in ethnic jokes by people like Davies, in *Sec. 2.4.2*; the relatively denser concentration of people doing farts in public in antiquity, in *Sec. 2.5.1*; the relatively denser concentration of people in a laid-back culture to indulge in joking and laughing, in *Sec. 2.5.2*; the relatively denser concentration of PLC patients to have brain injury, in *Sec. 3.2.1*; the relatively denser concentration of people in gelotology to favor laughter for therapy to promote health, in *Sec. 3.2.2*; the relatively denser concentration of non-human primates to have "laughter-like vocalizations," in *Sec. 3.3.1*; the relatively denser concentration of people who followed Freud's theory of the unconscious in the older days to treat laughter in the context of censored sexual and aggressive desires, in *Sec. 3.3.2*; the relatively denser concentration of the use of laughter in the specific form of humor known as political satire as a safety valve in a repressive political environement, in *Sec. 3.4.1*; the relatively denser concentration of believers in the superiority theory of laughter by writers in the older days, like the followers of Aristotle, Plato, Hobbes, etc., in *Sec. 3.5.1*; and the relatively denser concentration of deaths from laughter in an entertaining way as portrayed in popular culture, like films and novels, in *Sec. 3.5.2*).

On the other hand, there is emptiness (e.g., the relatively less dense, or more empty, concentration of individuals who accept the critique of Freud by Chislenko to focus on sexuality and aggression in their interpretation of jokes, in *Sec. 2.2.1*; the relatively less dense, or more empty, concentration of the works by Confucius to deal with black comedy, in *Sec. 2.2.2*; the relatively less dense, or more empty, concentration of concerns with IFF in the analysis of humor by people like Freud, in *Sec. 2.3.1*; the relatively less dense, or more empty, concentration of Mulsims in the Near East who supported "the Jyllands-Posten Muhammad cartoons," in *Sec. 2.4.1*; the relatively less dense, or more empty, concentration of concerns with the theme of social prohibition and sensory incongruity in ethnic jokes by people like Davies, in *Sec. 2.4.2*; the relatively less dense, or more empty, concentration of people doing farts in public nowadays, in *Sec. 2.5.1*; the relatively less dense, or more empty, concentration of people in a highly efficient, competitive culture like modern Japan, to indulge in joking and laughing, again, relatively speaking, in *Sec. 2.5.2*; the relativley less dense, or more empty, concentration of normal individuals without PLC to have brain injury, in *Sec. 3.2.1*; the relatively less dense, or more emtpy, concentration of people who study the dark sides of laughter to advocate laughter for therapy to promote health, relatively speaking of course, in *Sec. 3.2.2*; the relatively less dense, or more empty, concentration of worms to have "laughter-like vocalizations," in *Sec. 3.3.1*; the relatively less dense, or more empty, concentration of believers nowadays who follow Provine's evolutionary perspective of laughter to treat laughter in the way that Freud did, in *Sec. 3.3.2*; the relatively less dense, or more empty, concentration of the use of laughter in the specific form of humor known as political satire as a safety valve in a free political environement, where dissent is tolerated, in *Sec. 3.4.1*; the relatively less dense, or more empty, concentration of believers in the superiority theory of laughter nowadays, like the followers of Bergson, Nietzsche, and so on, in *Sec. 3.5.1*; and the relatively less dense, or more empty, concentration of deaths from laughter in an entertaining way in real life, when examined by scientists instead, in *Sec. 3.5.2*).

And the reverse direction also holds true.

Again, it should be stressed, however, that there are different shades of gray (or different degrees of truth) in the two opposites, and the classification is not necessarily mutually exclusive either. In fact, even when some combinations of the two occur, they only end up sharing the same dialectic relationship, but in a different degree.

Also, there are some other relationships (as a kind of family resemblance) which have something in common with the principle, but they are not exactly the same but only more or less comparable, which varies from case to case.

Good examples of family resemblance in relation to the principle are fullness-voidness, nearness-farness, concentration-dispersion, and the like.

8th Thesis: The Slowness-Quickness Principle

The eighth thesis concerns the slowness-quickness principle (on the speed of change) in the category of "process" in existential dialectics (which was first worked out in *FIA*), in that both slowness and quickness co-exist, with their own internal tension, to the extent that each fights for its own relevance with the other, in accordance to the perspectives of nature, the mind, culture, and society, without one being the victor and the other being the vanquished in the long haul. There is no slowness without quickness—and vice versa.

For instance, on the one hand, there is slowness (e.g., the relatively slower speed for a very humorous person to follow rational thoughts in his daily life, in *Sec. 2.2.1*; the relatively slower speed for people to get offended by "black humor," in *Sec. 2.2.2*; the relatively lesser speed for individuals to become friends with a group if they do not understand the jokes in that group, in accordance to Hewitt, in *Sec. 2.3.1*; the relatively slower speed for those in authority to like political satire against them, in

Sec. 2.4.1; the relatively slower speed for black Americans to get offended by black jokes if they are made by their own black people instead, in *Sec. 2.4.2*; the relatively slower readiness of modern presidents to play with fart jokes in public, in *Sec. 2.5.1*; the relatively slower readiness of people in authoritarian cultures to criticize their military dictators head-on, in a confrontional way, in *Sec .2.5.2*; the relatively slower speed of normal indivduals without PLC to laugh, when "provoked by nonsentimental or trivially-sentimental stimuli," in *Sec. 3.2.1*; the relatively slower speed of individuals who "consider humor for the sick or injured as inappropriate or harmful" to engage in using laughter for therapy, in *Sec. 3.2.2*; the relatively slower readiness of rats to laugh and respond to tickled skin, as they age, in *Sec. 3.3.1*; the relatively slower readiness of adults to laugh, when compared with children at ages 5 and 6, for instance, in *Sec. 3.3.2*; the relatively slower readiness of a group to control a member by making fun of him if the member in question is not "errant," in *Sec. 3.4.1*; the relatively slower readiness of someone who rigidly follows a life based on reason and logic to engage in laughter and humor a lot, in *Sec. 3.5.1*; and the heart tends to beat at a relatively slower rate, if no laughter occurs, in *Sec. 3.5.2*).

On the other hand, there is quickness (e.g., the relatively quicker speed for a very humorous person to abandon rational thoughts for creative imagination in his daily life, in *Sec. 2.2.1*; the relatively faster speed for people to get offended by "obscene humor," in *Sec. 2.2.2*; the relatively faster speed for individuals to become foes with a group if they do not understand the jokes in that group, in accordance to Hewitt, in *Sec. 2.3.1*; the relatively quicker speed for those in the profession of satire to like political satire, in *Sec. 2.4.1*; the relatively faster speed for black Americans to get offended by black jokes if they are made by white people, in *Sec. 2.4.2*; the relatively quicker readiness of pre-modern emperors to play with fart jokes in public, as shown by the Roman Emperor Elagabulus who liked "to play practical [fart] jokes on his guests, employing whoopee cushions at dinner parties," in *Sec. 2.5.1*; the relatively quicker readiness of people in authoritarian cultures to criticize their military dictators with the use of satire, parody, wit, and the like, in *Sec. 2.5.2*; the relatively faster speed of PLC patients to laugh, when "provoked by nonsentimental or trivially-sentimental stimuli," in *Sec. 3.2.1*; the relatively quicker speed of the proponents in gelotology to engage in using laughter for therapy, in *Sec. 3.2.2*; the relatively quicker readiness of rats to laugh and respond to tickled skin, when they are still young, in *Sec. 3.3.1*; the relatively quicker readiness of children at ages 5 and 6 to laugh, because they play more at those ages than adults, in *Sec.*

3.3.2; the relatively quicker readiness of a group to control a member by making fun of him if the member in question is very "errant," in *Sec. 3.4.1*; the relatively quicker readiness of someone who is against the rigidness in life to engage in laughter and humor as an escape or a resistance, in *Sec. 3.5.1*; and the heart tends to beat at a relatively faster rate, if laughter occurs, in *Sec. 3.5.2*).

And the reverse direction also holds true.

Again, it should be stressed, however, that there are different shades of gray (or different degrees of truth) in the two opposites, and the classification is not necessarily mutually exclusive either. In fact, even when some combinations of the two occur, they only end up sharing the same dialectic relationship, but in a different degree.

Also, there are some other relationships (as a kind of family resemblance) which have something in common with the principle, but they are not exactly the same but only more or less comparable, which varies from case to case.

Good examples of family resemblance in relation to the principle are inconvenience-convenience, passiveness-activenessness, gradualness-abruptness, deceleration-acceleration, and the like.

9th Thesis: The Expansion-Contraction Principle

The nineth thesis is called the expansion-contraction principle in the category of "process" in existential dialectics, in that entities in the world can both expand in some ways and contract in other ones, as part of their nature. There is no expansion without contraction—and vice versa.

This principle, although not so explicitly called, was already used in my previous works on different topics (e.g., the theory of floating consciousness in *FCD* and *FPHC*, the union of the unions in *BWT*, and the cyclical progression of system fragmentation and integration in *FCD*).

For instance, on the one hand, there is expansion (e.g., the relatively more developed ability of a person who likes to joke a lot to make good use of creative imagination, in *Sec. 2.2.1*; the relatively more developed ability of black comedians to make good use of the satire on the topic of death, in *Sec. 2.2.2*; the relatively more devleoped ability for people trained in analyzing humor as an IFF system to treat individuals as "friends" or "foes," on the basis of sharing jokes, in *Sec. 2.3.1*; the relatively more developed ability of the practitioners of satire to use "wit as a weapon," in *Sec. 2.4.1*; the relatively more developed ability of people like Davies to identifiy themes in ethnic jokes on the basis of "stupidity, canniness and sexual behavior," in *Sec. 2.4.2*; the relatively more developed ability of a fart joker to find tricks to shift the blame of farting to his victims, in *Sec. 2.5.1*; the relativley more developed ability of those in humor to make use of such techniques as "danger," "void," and "ambiguity," for instance, in *Sec. 2.5.2*; the relatively more developed ability of normal individiuals to control their episodes of laughing or crying in daily life, in *Sec. 3.2.1*; the relatively more developed ability of the proponents in gelotology to use laughter for therapy, in *Sec. 3.2.2*; the relatively more developed ability of dogs in the experiment to reduce stress, when exposed "to a dog-laugh recording," in *Sec. 3.3.1*; the relatively more developed ability of children at ages 5 and 6 to play and laugh, in *Sec. 3.3.2*; the relatively more developed ability of a stand-up comic to joke so as to say "the things members of the audence are thinking secretly but are afraid to express," in *Sec. 3.4.1*; the relatively more developed ability of someone who resists the rigidness in life to engage in laughter and humor, in *Sec. 3.5.1*; and the relatively more developed ability of film producers and writers to deal with death from laughter in a highly amusing, entertaining way, in *Sec. 3.5.2)*.

On the other hand, there is contraction (e.g., the relatively less developed ability of a person who likes to joke a lot to make good use of rational thoughts in science, in *Sec. 2.2.1*; the relatively less developed ability of black comedians to present a serious scientific or academic discourse on the topic of death, in *Sec. 2.2.2*; the relatively less devleoped ability for people trained in analyzing humor as an IFF system to treat individuals as "friends" when they do not share their jokes, in *Sec. 2.3.1*; the relatively less developed ability of dictators like Hitler to use "wit as a weapon," instead of military force, in *Sec. 2.4.1*; the relatively less developed ability of people like Davies to understand ethnic jokes on the basis of an IFF system, as worked out by Hewitt in an earlier section, in *Sec. 2.4.2*; the relatively less developed ability of a fart joker to be morally responsible and to subsequently offer apology to his victim, in *Sec. 2.5.1*; the relativley less developed ability of those in humor to make use of logical consistency, conventional wisdom, etc., in *Sec. 2.5.2*; the relatively less developed ability of normal individiuals to allow "relatively uncontrollable episodes of laughing or crying, or both" in daily life, even if for fun, in *Sec. 3.2.1*; the relatively less developed ability of those in gelotology to use psychoanalysis for therapy, like analyzing unconscious conflicts, in *Sec. 3.2.2*; the relatively less developed ability of dogs in the experiment to fight with other dogs instead, when exposed "to a dog-laugh recording," in *Sec. 3.3.1*; the relatively less developed ability of children at ages 5 and 6 to work as seriously as adults, who play less, in *Sec. 3.2.2*; the relatively less developed ability of a stand-up comic to lecture seriously, without the use of humor, about "the things members of the audence are thinking secretly but are afraid to express," in *Sec. 3.4.1*; the relatively less developed ability of someone who resists the rigidness in life to indulge in a life based on logic and reason, in *Sec. 3.5.1*; and the relatively less developed ability of film producers and writers to deal with death from laughter in a highly vigorous, scientific way, in *Sec. 3.5.2*).

And the reverse direction also holds true.

Again, it should be stressed, however, that there are different shades of gray (or different degrees of truth) in the two opposites, and the classification is not necessarily mutually exclusive either. In fact, even when some combinations of the two occur, they only end up sharing the same dialectic relationship, but in a different degree.

Also, there are some other relationships (as a kind of family resemblance) which have something in common with the principle, but they are not exactly the same but only more or less comparable, which varies from case to case.

Good examples of family resemblance in relation to the principle are conquest-autarky, rise-fall (or up-down), spread-shrink, extendingness-shorteningness, and so forth.

10th Thesis: The Theory-Praxis Principle

The tenth thesis is the theory-praxis principle (on the duality of knowledge) in the category of "agency" in existential dialectics (which was first worked out in *FPHE*), in that, if there is theoretical construction, there is likewise its practical application, both technical and normative. There is no theory without praxis—and vice versa.

For instance, on the one hand, there is theory (e.g., the theoretical construction, by the Surrealist theoretician André Breton in 1935, of the sub-genre of comedy known as black humor based on "cynism and skepticism," in *Sec. 2.2.2*; the theoretical construction of IFF in military studies, in *Sec. 2.3.1*; the theoretical construction of satire as a literary genre, as shown Aristophanes' *Old Comedy*, in *Sec. 2.4.1*; the theoretical construction of ethnic jokes in history, in *Sec. 2.4.2*; the theoretical construction of the rhyming phrases in fart jokes, in *Sec. 2.5.1*; the theoretical construction of such techniques of joking like "danger," and so on, in *Sec. 2.5.2*; the theoretical construction of tricyclic antidepressants in chemistry, in *Sec. 3.2.1*; the theoretical construction of yoga, in *Sec. 3.2.2*; the theoretical construction of recording technology, in *Sec. 3.3.1*; the theoretical construction of evolution by Darwin, for isntance, in *Sec. 3.3.2*; the theoretical construction of functionalism in sociology, in *Sec. 3.4.1*;

and the theoretical construction about the brain in pathophysiology, in *Sec. 3.5.2*).

On the other hand, there is praxis (e.g., the practical application of black humor to popular films later on, in *Sec .2.2.2*; the practical applicatoin of IFF to the study of humor by Hewitt, in *Sec. 2.3.1*; the practical application of satire to politics as in "political satire," in *Sec. 2.4.1*; the practical application of ethnic jokes to targeting Polish people in the 1960's by Hollywood and the U.S. TV media, in *Sec. 2.4.2*; the practical application of fart jokes with their rhyming phrases to programs in modern "cinema and tv series," as shown in one scene of *Blazing Saddles*, in *Sec. 2.5.1*; the practical application of the technique of joking like "danger" in the fields of satire and parody to the critique of military dictactorship by Soyinka, in *Sec. 2.5.2*; the practical application of tricyclic antidepressants in chemistry to the healing of PLC patients, in *Sec. 3.2.1*; the practical application of yoga to therapy in gelotology, in *Sec. 3.2.2*; the practical application of recording technology to the study of laughter in dogs by by Patricia Simonet and others, in *Sec. 3.3.1*; the practical application of evolutionary perspective to the field of laughter too, as shown by Provine's work, with his own modifications, in *Sec. 3.3.2*; the practical application of functionalism to the field of laughter in humor by Christine for a functional explanation, in *Sec. 3.4.1*; and the practical application of pathophysiology to the study of death from laughter, in Sec. 3.5.2).

And the reverse direction also holds true.

Again, it should be stressed, however, that there are different shades of gray (or different degrees of truth) in the two opposites, and the classification is not necessarily mutually exclusive either. In fact, even when some combinations of the two occur, they only end up sharing the same dialectic relationship, but in a different degree.

Also, there are some other relationships (as a kind of family resemblance) which have something in common with the principle, but they are not exactly the same but only more or less comparable, which varies from case to case.

Good examples of family resemblance in relation to the principle are discovery-application, knowledge-action, invention-innovation, and so forth.

11th Thesis: The Convention-Novelty Principle

The eleventh thesis is the convention-novelty principle (on the nature of creative thinking) in the category of "agency" in existential dialectics (which was first worked out in *FPHCT*), in that, if there is conventional wisdom, there is likewise novel challenge, to the extent that both convergent and divergent thinking are part of life. There is no convention without novelty—and vice versa.

As srummarized from *FPHCT* (almost verbatim here), there are (a) "creative techniques" and (b) "creative traits," which, when satisfied—in relation to the larger context of the mind, nature, society, and culture—can be used to enhance creative works.

In addition, creative thinking has its own possibilities and limits (in relation to invention), just as it has its own promises and pitfalls (in relation to innovation)— as already analyzed in *FPHCT*).

In the end, creative thinking has its own desirability and dark sides (as also already analyzed in *FPHCT*).

With these clarifications in mind—there are good empirical examples for the convention-novelty princple.

For instance, on the one hand, there is convention (e.g., the conventional way of expressing things, as shown in the "familiar connections" in the brain, as shown in the work on jokes by de Bono, in *Sec. 2.2.1*; the conventional wisdom on "black humor" based on the work by André Breton in 1935, in *Sec. 2.2.2*; the conventional wisdom about humor as lacking survival value in Darwin's evolutionary theory, in *Sec. 2.3.1*; the conventional wisdom about satire in the time of Quintilian to "indicate…a narrower genre…in strictly hexameter form, which were a distinctly Roman genre," in *Sec. 2.4.1*; the conventional wisdom about using Irish jokes in the U.K. in the older days, in *Sec. 2.4.2*; the conventional wisdom in antiquity which treated flatulence more as a call of nature than as a public embarassment, in *Sec. 2.5.1*; the conventional wisdom about military dictatorship in modern Nigeria, in *Sec. 2.5.2*; the conventional wisdom about the importance of laughing to good health, in *Sec. 3.2.1*; the conventional wisdom in gelotology about laughter as good for health, in *Sec. 3.2.2*; the conventional wisdom about the study of laughter in apes "in terms of play faces and vocalisations," in *Sec. 3.3.1*; the conventional wisdom about laughter in the context of censored sexual and aggressive desires in the unconscious, as worked out by Freud, in *Sec. 3.3.2*; the conventional wisdom in the Darwinian evolutionary theory that humor does not seem to have any survival value or has no evolutionary function other than a by-product of sexual selection for courtship, in *Sec. 3.4.1*; the conventional wisdom in ancient Greek, as propounded by Plato and Aristotle, that laugher is caused by a feeling of superiority over the ugliness of others, in *Sec. 3.5.1*; and the conventional wisdom about death from laughter from the scientific standpoint of pathophysiology, in *Sec. 3.5.2*).

On the other hand, there is novelty (e.g., the alternatively novel challenge to the "familiar connections" by way of "alternative unexpected new links" in jokes, in *Sec. 2.2.1*; the alternative novel challenge to black humor, by the later use of "black comedy" or "dark comedy...as alternatives to Breton's term" later on, in *Sec. 2.2.2*; the alternative novel challenge to Darwin's evolutionary theory by Hewitt, on the basis of his novel view about human as an IFF system in evolution, in *Sec. 2.3.1*; the alternative novel challenge to the conventional wisdom about Roman satire, by the later new genres of satire which are much broader in graphic and performing arts, can have different types which can be Horatian or Juvenalian, and so on, in *Sec. 2.4.1*; the alternative novel challenge to the use of Irish jokes in the U.K. nowadays, because "the social status of Irish people has risen with increased wealth in Ireland, the consequent reduction in Irish itinerant labour, and the absorption of Irish people into the community, and therefore the UK media was more tolerant of the Irish," in *Sec. 2.4.2*; the alternative novel challenge to the conventional wisdom in antiquity about flatulence, by the contemporary cultural shift, which regards flatulence in public as rude or impolite, in *Sec. 2.5.1*; the alternative novel challenge to the conventional wisdom about military dictatorship in modern Nigeria, by the new daring thinking to condemn it and propose a more democratic one, as shown in the work of Soyinka, in *Sec. 2.5.2*; the altenrative novel challenge to the conventional wisdom about the importantce of laughing to good health, by the sober view about the dark sides of laughing, in *Sec. 3.2.1*; the alternative novel challenge to the conventional wisdom in gelotology, by the critics who pointed out that there are adverse side effects in using laughter for therapy, as "it can cause mental hurt, sadness, and alienation in persons who are not receptive to it, or if it is used insensitively," in *Sec. 3.2.2*; the alternative novel challenge to this conventional wisdom about the study of laughter in apes "in terms of play faces and vocalisations," by way of the new idea of working "on tickle-induced laughter" instead, as shown in the team work led by Davila-Ross, in *Sec. 3.3.1*; the alternative novel challenge to the conventional wisdom about laughter in the context of censored sexual and aggressive desires, by Provine's new idea for a different view of laughter in the context of the unconscious, but without the obsession on sexuality and aggression, in *Sec. 3.3.2*; the alternative novel view to challenge the conventional wisdom of the Darwinian evolutionary theory, by the modern social functionalist interpretation of laughter in humor, in *Sec. 3.4.1*; the alternative challenge by Bergson to this Greek view, in that laughter is caused by the rigidness in life, not ugliness in others, in *Sec. 3.5.1*; and the alternative novel challenge to the scientific account of death from laughter, by way of the entertaining accounts of death from laughter in films and novels, in *Sec. 3.5.2*).

And the reverse direction also holds true.

Again, it should be stressed, however, that there are different shades of gray (or different degrees of truth) in the two opposites, and the classification is not necessarily mutually exclusive either. In fact, even when some combinations of the two occur, they only end up sharing the same dialectic relationship, but in a different degree.

Also, there are some other relationships (as a kind of family resemblance) which have something in common with the principle, but they are not exactly the same but only more or less comparable, which varies from case to case.

Good examples of family resemblance in relation to the principle are convergence-divergence (or convergent thinking vs. divergent thinking), normalness-nonnormalness, conformity-nonconformity, and so on.

12th Thesis: The Evolution-Transformation Principle

The twelveth thesis refers to the evolution-transformation principle (on the multiple kinds of agency). in the category of "agency" in existential dialectics (which was first worked out in *FAE* and then in other books of mine).

This principle—and the symmetry-asymmetry principle, for instance—are both about agency. More precisely, the word "agency," in a formal definition, refers to "a person or thing through which power is exerted or an end is achieved." (MWD 2007) It therefore does not have to necessarily involve an intelligent lifeform.

Because of this dual meaning in agency, the evolution-transformation principle is more concerned with *the kind of agency*, that is, both about the *evolution* in the state of nature (e.g., an object of natural beauty) and the *transformation* in the world of intelligent lifeforms (e.g., a work of art). There is no evolution without transformation—and vice versa.

In classical Darwinian evolutionary theory (as more detailedly analyzed in *BNN*), evolution is "blind." But in the human world, change often takes place because of the conscious intervention of humans in transforming society and culture, just to cite two instances.

And the transformative part of the principle precisely refers to the other dimension in the dual meaning of agency, in giving technology (as invented by intelligent lifeforms like humans and, soon, post-humans) a major role to play in the change of the world, which is something that I extensively analyzed in *FHC* in the context of the technophilic lifeworld, espeically though not exclusively since modern times.

For instance, on the one hand, there is evolution (e.g., the natural evolution of humans to be playful in the state of nature, in *Sec. 2.2.1*; the natural evolution of humans to be playful in the state of nature, in *Sec. 2.2.2*; the natural evolution of humans in the state of nature to be playful and humorous, in *Sec. 2.3.1*; the natural evolution of humans in the state of nature to be funny, in *Sec. 2.4.1*; the natural evolution of humans to make fun of each other in the state of nature, in *Sec. 2.4.2*; the natural evolution of humans to fart in the state of nature, in *Sec. 2.5.1*; the natural evolution of humans to be playful in the state of nature, in *Sec. 2.5.2*; the natural evolution of humans to laugh in the state of nature, in *Sec. 3.2.1*; the natural evolution of humans to laugh in the state of nature, in *Sec. 3.2.2*; the natural evolution of dogs to laugh in the state of nature, in *Sec. 3.3.1*; the natural evolution of humans to understand playing and laughing in the state of nature, in *Sec. 3.3.2*; the natural evolution of humans to understand laughter in the state of nature, in *Sec. 3.4.1*; the natural evolution of humans to laugh and joke in the state of nature, in *Sec. 3.5.1*; and the natural evolution of humans to encounter death from laughter in real life, in Sec. 3.5.2).

On the other hand, there is transformation (e.g., the technical transformation of human ability to be playful with the invention of language to make elaborated jokes, as shown in the example by Kant, in *Sec. 2.2.1*; the technical transformation of human ability to be playful by the invention of "black comedy" to provide "the satire on the topic of death," in *Sec. 2.2.2*; the technical transformation of human ability to be playful by the invention of new theories to study humor, like the theory of humor as IFF, in *Sec. 2.3.1*; the technical transformation of human ability to be funny by the invention of political satire with such literary techniques as "parody, burlesque, exaggeration, juxtaposition, comparison, analogy, and double entendre," for instance, in *Sec. 2.4.1*; the technical transformation of humans to make fun of each other by the invention of systematic propaganda campaigns, like the Nazi propaganda about "subhuman intelligence jokes" targeting Polish people, in *Sec. 2.4.2*; the technical transformation of human ability to fart in public, by the invention of social norms nowadays which regard flatulence in public as rude or impolite, in *Sec. 2.5.1*; the technical transformation of human playing with each other by the invention of the specific techniques of joking, as shown in the examples, in *Sec. 2.5.2*; the technical transformation of human ability to laugh by the invention of drugs like tricyclic antidepressants to control "episodes of laughing or crying," in *Sec. 3.2.1*; the technical transformation of human ability to laugh by the invention of gelotology for using it in the domain of therapy, with different systematic therapeutic techniques, in *Sec. 3.2.2*; the technical transformation of dogs to laugh, by the invention of the "dog-laugh recording" in the experiment, such that dogs can reduce stress with exposure to it, in *Sec. 3.3.1*; the technical evolution of humans to understand playing and laughing by the invention of new ideas to understand them, like Provine's evolutionary perspective of laughter, in *Sec. 3.3.2*; the technical transformation of human ability to understand laughter by the invention of social functionalism to explain its social functions, in *Sec. 3.4.1*; the technical transformation of human tendency to laugh and joke by the invention of a different approach to laughter by Bergson that requires a detachment from emoton or sensibility, so as to focus on, and resist, the inflexibility and rigidness in life, in *Sec. 3.5.1*; and the technical transformation of human ability to encounter death from laughter by the invention of films and novels, so that humans can encounter them in a way different from real life, in *Sec. 3.5.2*).

And the reverse direction also holds true.

Again, it should be stressed, however, that there are different shades of gray (or different degrees of truth) in the two opposites, and the classification is not necessarily mutually exclusive either. In fact, even when some combinations of the two occur, they only end up sharing the same dialectic relationship, but in a different degree.

Also, there are some other relationships (as a kind of family resemblance) which have something in common with the principle, but they are not exactly the same but only more or less comparable, which varies from case to case.

Good examples of family resemblance in relation to the principle are inorganicness-volition, naturalness-technologicalness, naturalness-nonnaturalness, nonwillingness-willingness, and so on.

13th Thesis: The Symmetry-Asymmetry Principle

The thirteenth thesis is labeled as the symmetry-asymmetry principle (on the relationships among existents) in the category of "agency" in existential dialectics (which was also already worked out in my previous books), in that there is no asymmetry without symmetry—and vice versa.

For instance, the Same can be symmetric and asymmetric towards the Others. But in case of asymmetry (as analyzed in *BDPD*), oppression and self-oppression can occur. So, when the Same is asymmetric towards the Others, the Same can also be relatively asymmetric towards itself in self-oppression, just as the Others can be likewise towards themselves. The subsequent oppressiveness is dualistic, as much by the Same against the Others and itself, as by the Others against the Same and themselves. Both oppression and self-oppression can be achieved by way of downgrading differences between the Same and the Others and of accentuating them.

This is true, even though not all forms of asymmetry have to be about oppression and self-oppression.

In addition, from Chapter Three of *FPHG*, symmetry is not perfect, to be understood in an approximate sense under many life circumstances. With this clarification in mind, hereafter are some empirical examples.

For instance, on the one hand, there is symmetry (e.g., the co-existence of different views about jokes in history, in *Sec. 2.2.1*; the co-existence of different labels for the sub-genre of comedy based on "cynism and skepticism," in *Sec. 2.2.2*; both IFF and humor can have a positive response to signal, according to Hewitt, in *Sec. 2.3.1*; the co-existence of different types of satire in hisory, in *Sec. 2.4.1*; the co-existence of different views about different ethnic groups in history, in *Sec. 2.4.2*; the co-existence of different viewpoints about farts in history, in *Sec. 2.5.1*; the co-existence of different techniques of joking over time, in *Sec. 2.5.2*; the co-existence of different views about the importance of laughing to good health, in *Sec. 3.2.1*; the co-existence of different techniques for therapy in history over time, in *Sec. 3.2.2*; both rats and chimpanzees can laugh and respond to tickle skin, in *Sec. 3.3.1*; both humans and chimps can laugh, in *Sec. 3.3.2*; the co-existence of different views about laughter in humor over the ages, in *Sec. 3.4.1*; the co-existence of different views about laughter in history, in *Sec. 3.5.1*; and the co-existence of different ways to talk about death from laughter in history, in *Sec. 3.5.2*).

On the other hand, there is also asymmetry (e.g., the popularity of the superiority theory about jokes in ancient Greece—but the acceptance of the theory of social prohibitions about jokes in modern times, especially among those in psychoanalysis, in *Sec. 2.2.1*; the popular use of the term "black humor" originated by Breton in the 1930's—but the more acceptance of the term "black comedy" later on, as an alternative to Breton's term, in *Sec. 2.2.2*; in IFF, "positive response is coded"—but in humor, "positive response is not coded," according to Hewitt, in *Sec. 2.3.1*; the popularity of Horatian satire among those who prefer "gentle, mild, and light-hearted humour"—but the acceptance of Juvenal satire among those who prefer "more contemptuous and abrasive" humor, in *Sec. 2.4.1*; the negative view about Polish people in the U.S. during the 1960's—but the more tolerant environment for Polish people nowadays, "[a]s public awareness of racism has increased, racial and ethnic jokes have become increasingly socially unacceptable in recent years, and have become socially taboo to tell in public in many regions," in *Sec. 2.4.2*; ., the more tolerance of farts in public in antiquity—but the less tolerance of farts in public nowadays, in *Sec. 2.5.1*; the more pervasive use of the technique of "danger" under the cover of satire, wit, and parody in authoritarian cultures—but the more pervasive use of direct critique in those non-authoritarian cultures which allow some degree of free speech, in *Sec. 2.5.2*; the more popular view in ancient Greece that laughing is important to good health—but the more qualified view about laughing and health nowadays, because of the research on the dark sides of laughing, in *Sec. 3.2.1*; the use of humor for good health in ancient Greece—but the increasing popularity of using meditation and yoga in gelotology for good health, in conjunction with laugher, at our time, in *Sec. 3.2.2*; "as the rats age, there does appear to be a decline in the tendency to laugh and respond to tickle skin"—but "[t]he enjoyment of tickling in chimpanzees does not diminish with age," in *Sec. 3.3.1*; humans laugh "ha ha ha"—but chimps "exhibit a panting sound," in *Sec. 3.3.2*; the popularity of the Darwinian view about laugther in humor among those in evolutionary biology, relatively speaking—but the relative preference for the social functionalist view about laughter in humor among those in sociology, relatively speaking, in *Sec. 3.4.1*; popularity of the superiority theory of laughter in the older days, especially among those in the intellectual circles of Plato, Aristotle, and Hobbes—but the emergence of alternative popular views nowadays, like those by Bergson, Nietzsche, and others, in *Sec. 3.5.1*; and the fashionable way to deal with death from laughter in an entertaining way as portrayed in popular culture—but the accepted way to deal with death from laughter in a vigorous or robust way as explored in science, in *Sec. 3.5.2*).

And the reverse direction also holds true.

Again, for the last time, it should be stressed, however, that there are different shades of gray (or different degrees of truth) in the two opposites, and the classification is not necessarily mutually exclusive either. In fact, even when some combinations of the two occur, they only end up sharing the same dialectic relationship, but in a different degree.

Also, there are some other relationships (as a kind of family resemblance) which have something in common with the principle, but they are not exactly the same but only more or less comparable, which varies from case to case.

Good examples of family resemblance in relation to the principle are strength-weakness, potence-impotence, balance-extremity, reflexiveness-unreflexiveness, equality-inequality, harmoniousness-unharrmoniousness, and something like that.

14th Thesis: The Softness-Hardness Principle

The fourteenth thesis refers to the softness-hardness principle (on the force of change) in the category of "agency" in existential dialectics (which was first worked out in *ALD*), in that any change by an agent, be it organic (like humans) or non-organic (like natural objects), can occur in a forceful (aggressive) or gentle (pacific) way, which can come in all shapes and sizes, of course. There is no softness without hardness—and vice versa.

For instance, on the one hand, there is softness (e.g., "a benevolent superego allows a light and comforting type of humor," in *Sec. 2.2.1*; the production of "laughter" in black comedy, in *Sec. 2.2.2*; the treatment of those as friends who understand jokes within a group, in *Sec. 2.3.1*; the "gentle, mild, and light-hearted humour" in Horatian satire, in *Sec. 2.4.1*; the inclusion of an in-group, in *Sec. 2.4.2*; the soft side of encouraging laughter for therapy in gelotology, in *Sec. 3.2.2*; dogs can play with each other more, when exposed to dog laughing, in *Sec. 3.3.1*; the soft side of "laughing with" a group, in *Sec. 3.3.2*; the soft side of laughter in humor, like laughing "with" a group, in *Sec. 3.4.1*; the soft side of laughter, in relation to its "harmless demotion from reason and hardship," for Nietzsche, in *Sec. 3.5.1*; and the soft side of laughter, like having fun, in *Sec. 3.5.2*).

On the other hand, there is hardness (e.g., "a very harsh superego suppresses humor all together," in *Sec. 2.2.1*; the production of "discomfort" in black comedy, in *Sec. 2.2.2*; the treatment of those as foes who do not understand jokes within a group, in *Sec. 2.3.1*; the "contemptuous and abrasive" humor in Juvenal satire, in *Sec. 2.4.1*; the exclusion of an out-group, in *Sec. 2.4.2*; the hard side of producing "mental hurt, sadness, and alienation in persons who are not receptive to it" in gelotology, as the adverse side effects, in *Sec. 3.2.2*; dogs can fight with each other more, with exposed to dog fighting, in *Sec. 3.3.1*; the hard side of "laughing at" a group, in *Sec. 3.3.2*; the hard side of laughter in humor, like laughing "at"a group, in *Sec. 3.4.1*; the hard side of laughter, in relation to its use for "social conflict," for Nietzsche, in *Sec. 3.5.1*; and the hard side of laughter, like dying from so much fun in laughing, in *Sec. 3.5.2*).

And the reverse direction also holds true.

Again, it should be stressed, however, that there are different shades of gray (or different degrees of truth) in the two opposites, and the classification is not necessarily mutually exclusive either. In fact, even when some combinations of the two occur, they only end up sharing the same dialectic relationship, but in a different degree.

Also, there are some other relationships (as a kind of family resemblance) which have something in common with the principle, but they are not exactly the same but only more or less comparable, which varies from case to case.

Good examples of family resemblance in relation to the principle are peacefulness-violence, cooperation-competition, pacificity-aggression, dovishness-hawkishness, reward-punishment, peace-war, and the like.

15th Thesis: The Seriousness-Playfulness Principle

The fifteenth thesis refers to the seriousness-playfulness principle (on the extent of seriousness) in the category of "agency" in existential dialectics (which is first worked out in *FPHH*), in that, if there is seriousness, there is also playfulness, especially for any agent with some kind of intelligence life, be it about humans, animals, or, later, post-humans. There is no seriousness without playfulness—and vice versa.

Lest any misunderstanding occurs, the word "playfulness" here should not be confused with other terms like "laughter," "smile," "joke," "tickleness," and "laugh-like vocalization" (in some animals), for instance.

Being playful can come in all shapes and sizes and therefore is not necessarily tied up with any of these terms, alhough it can result from any of them, or a combination of them, or something else altogether.

This principle, together with some other principles (especially though not exclusively, like the formalness-informalness principle), have important implications for what constitutes rationality, be it about "rationality of application" at the practical level or "rationality of knowledge" at the meta-theoretical level (as summarized in *Sec. 4.20* of *FPHH*).

For instance, on the one hand, there is seriousness (e.g., the serious business of rational thoughts in science, in *Sec. 2.2.1*; the "serious" side in black comedy, when it addresses "taboo subject matters," in *Sec. 2.2.2*; the serious nature of group relationship, such that those who are not friends can be subject to attacks, in *Sec. 2.3.1*; the serious "after-taste" in satire which "makes people think," in *Sec. 2.4.1*; the seriousness of an in-group to call "for violence" against an out-group, in *Sec. 2.4.2*; the serious part of fart jokes in its tendency to shift the blame of farting to someone else, so as "to discourage others from mentioning the fart," in *Sec. 2.5.1*; the serious nature of Soyinka's work to criticize political oppression in Nigeria, in *Sec. 2.5.2*; the serious side of laughing for good health, in *Sec. 3.2.1*; the serious side of gelotology to promote good health, in *Sec. 3.2.2*; the serious business of stress reduction in the experiment on dog laughing, in *Sec. 3.3.1*; the serious nature of laughing for social bonding, because, for Provine, "laughter has a bonding function within individuals in a group," in *Sec. 3.3.2*; the serious side of laughter in humor to form "corporate identity," for instance, in *Sec. 3.4.1*; the serious business of laughter, in that an individual can use it to resist the rigidness in life, for Bergson, in *Sec. 3.5.1*; and the serious business of popular culture to entertain, even when addressing the issue of death from laughter, in *Sec. 3.5.2*).

On the other hand, there is playfulness (e.g., the playful nature of creative imagnation in humor, in *Sec. 2.2.1*; the "funny" side in black comedy, when it makes light of "taboo subject matters," in *Sec. 2.2.2*; the playful nature of group relationship, such that they can be playful too, though with the intention to detect friends or foes, in *Sec. 2.3.1*; the "funny" aspect of satire which makes people "laugh," in *Sec. 2.4.1*; the playfulness of an in-group to use ethnic jokes against an out-group, so as to "deal with hostility verbally instead of physically," in *Sec. 2.4.2*; the playfulness of the fart jokes, to cause laughter, in *Sec. 2.5.1*; the joyful, funny aspect of reading the satire, parody, and wit in Soyinka's work, in *Sec. 2.5.2*; the playful side of laughting for jokes, in *Sec. 3.2.1*; the playful side of gelotology to encourage laughter, in *Sec. 3.2.2*; the playful side of the dog-laughing recording in the experiment for dogs to play with each other, in *Sec. 3.3.1*; the playful side of laughing for fun, in *Sec. 3.3.2*; the playful side of laughter in humor to enjoy funny jokes, in *Sec. 3.4.1*; the playful side of laugther, in that an individual can use it to laugh in the comic situations, in *Sec. 3.5.1*; and the playful nature of popular culture to portray death from laughter in a funny way, in *Sec. 3.5.2*).

And the reverse direction also holds true.

Again, it should be stressed, however, that there are different shades of gray (or different degrees of truth) in the two opposites, and the classification is not necessarily mutually exclusive either. In fact, even when some combinations of the two occur, they only end up sharing the same dialectic relationship, but in a different degree.

Also, there are some other relationships (as a kind of family resemblance) which have something in common with the principle, but they are not exactly the same but only more or less comparable, which varies from case to case.

Good examples of family resemblance in relation to the principle are seriousness-jokingness, seriousness-humorousness, seriousness-wittiness, seriousness-nonseriousness, and so forth.

16th Thesis: The Regression-Progression Principle

The sixteenth thesis is called the regression-progression princple (on the direction of history) in the category of "outcome" in existential dialectics (which was also already worked out in my previous books), in that neither the cyclical nor the linear views are adequate for explaining many phenomena at all levels. There is no regression without progression—and vice versa.

History progresses to more advanced forms, but with a regressive touch. Examples include no freedom without unfreedom, no equality without inequality, and no civilization without barbarity. This is not an inevitable law, but merely a highly likely empirical trend.

For instance, on the one hand, there is regression (e.g., the regression made by the Freudian interpretation of jokes in fixating its understanding on sexuality and aggression, in *Sec. 2.2.1*; the "discomfort" produced in black comedy, in *Sec. 2.2.2*; the regression made by the theory of humor as IFF, as shown in the numerous criticisms against it, in *Sec. 2.3.1*; the regresson made by satire, as shown in the criticisms by the critics, in *Sec. 2.4.1*; the regression made by the theory of ethnic jokes, as shown in the criticisms against it, in *Sec. 2.4.2*; the regression made in fart jokes, as revealed in the problems associated with being rude, irresponsible, and the like, in *Sec. 2.5.1*; the regression made by the techniques of joking, as shown by the dark sides of joking in its other, dubious relationships with laid-back and authoritarian cultures, in *Sec. 2.5.2*; the regression made by laughing, as shown in the problems about the dark sides of laughing, in *Sec. 3.2.1*; the regression made by the use of laughter for therapy, as shown in the problems pointed out by the critics, in *Sec. 3.2.2*; the regression made by the studies on laughter in animals, as shown in the criticisms pointed out by the critics, in *Sec. 3.3.1*; the regression made by Provine's evolutoinary perspective of laughter, as shown in the criticisms against it, in *Sec. 3.3.2*; the regression made by Christine's view about the social functions of laughter, as shown in the criticisms against it, in *Sec. 3.4.1*; the regression made by the different writings on laughter, as shown in the criticisms against them, in *Sec. 3.5.1*; and the regression made by popular culture in addressing death from laughter often in an unrealistic, non-scientific way, in *Sec. 3.5.2*).

On the other hand, there is progress (e.g., the progress made by the Freudian interpretation of jokes in showing the interactions "between the unconscious and the conscious thoughts" in jokes, in *Sec. 2.2.1*; the "laughter" produced in black comedy, in *Sec. 2.2.2*; the progress made by the theory of humor as IFF to help us understand the evolution of humor in a different way, in *Sec. 2.3.1*; the progress made by satire, as shown in its "constructive social criticism, using wit as a weapon," in *Sec. 2.4.1*; the progress made by the theory of ethnic jokes to help us understand the three main themes in ethnic jokes, in *Sec. 2.4.2*; the progress made in fart jokes, to deal with the nuissance of farting in a playful way, something like a call of nature, in *Sec. 2.5.1*; the progress made by the techniques of joking to criticize political oppression, for instance, in *Sec. 2.5.2*; the progress made by laughing, as in the benefits for good health, under certain conditions, in *Sec. 3.2.1*; the progress made by the use of laugher for therapy, as shown in the benefits pointed out by the proponents, in *Sec. 3.2.2*; the progress made by the studies on laughter in animals to help us understand better the similarities between human and non-human laughters, in *Sec. 3.3.1*; the progress made by Provine's evolutionary perspective of laughter, to help us understand the shared evolutionary origin of human and non-human laughters, in *Sec. 3.3.2*; the progress made by Christine's view about the social functions of laughter, so as to help us understand better its social functions, in *Sec. 3.4.1*; the progress made by the different writings on laughter, so as to give us different views about the nature of laughter, in *Sec. 3.5.1*; and the progress made by popular culture to entertain people even when addressing the difficult issue of death from laughter, in *Sec. 3.5.2*).

And the reverse direction also holds true.

Again, it should be stressed, however, that there are different shades of gray (or different degrees of truth) in the two opposites, and the classification is not necessarily mutually exclusive either. In fact, even when some combinations of the two occur, they only end up sharing the same dialectic relationship, but in a different degree.

Also, there are some other relationships (as a kind of family resemblance) which have something in common with the principle, but they are not exactly the same but only more or less comparable, which varies from case to case.

Good examples of family resemblance in relation to the principle are undesirability-desirability, risk-opportunity, badness-goodness, cost-benefit, and so on.

17th Thesis: The Same-Difference Principle

The seventeenth thesis refers to the same-difference principle (on the metamorphosis of change) in the category of "outcome" in existential dialectics (which was worked out in *ALD* and other books of mine), in that an entity, as it evolves over time, can be both different from and similar to its opposing alternatives and does not have to be solely more different from them over time. There is no similarity without difference—and vice versa.

Opposites are not absolute in a black-or-white fashion; so, an entity can become relatively more similar to (or more different from) its opposite over time.

This is further constrained by another principle, that is, the symmetry-asymmetry principle about the relationships among existents under the category about agency in existential dialectics, in that if there is symmetry (equality) between two entities, there is likewise asymmetry (inequality) emerging in a different way.

For instance, on the one hand, there is similarity in outcome (e.g., the contribution to the molding and regulation of values and behaviors, regardless of whether this be done by way of humor or by way of rational thought, in *Sec. 2.2.1*; the contribution to the molding and control of beliefs and behaviors, regardless of whether this be done by way of black comedy or by way of scientific discourse, in *Sec. 2.2.2*; the contribution to the molding and control of beliefs and behaviors, regardless of whether this be done by way of humor as IFF or by way of normal relationship without the fixation on humor as IFF, in *Sec. 2.3.1*; the contribution to the molding and regulation of beliefs and values, regardless of whether this be done by way of satire or by way of political decrees, in *Sec. 2.4.1*; the contribution to the molding and regulation of beliefs and behaviors, regardless of whether this be done by way of ethnic jokes or by way of ethnic violence, in *Sec. 2.4.2*; the contribution to the molding and regulation of beliefs and behaviors, regardless of whether this be done by way of fart jokes or by way of social norms regulating farts, in *Sec. 2.5.1*; the contribution to the molding and regulation of beliefs and values, regardless of whether this be done by way of satire and parody or by way of direct political critique, in *Sec. 2.5.2*; the contribution to the molding and regulation of beliefs and behaviors, regardless of whether this be done by way of normal laughing or by way of excessive laughing, in *Sec. 3.2.1*; the contribution to the molding and regulation of beliefs and behaviors, regardless of whether this be done by way of therapy in gelotology or by way of traditional healing without therapy, in *Sec. 3.2.2*; the contribution to the molding and regulation of beliefs and behaviors, regardless of whether this be done by way of the understanding of laughter in animals or by way of the understanding of fighting in animals, in *Sec. 3.3.1*; the contribution to the molding and regulation of beliefs and values, regardless of whether this be done by way of the evolutionary perspective of laughter or by way of the creationist perspective of laughter, in *Sec. 3.3.2*; the contribution to the molding and regulation of beliefs and values, regardless of whether this be done by way of a functionalist view of laughter or by way of a critical view of laughter, in *Sec. 3.4.1*; the contribution to the molding and control of beliefs and behaviors, regardless of whether this be done by way of logic and reason or by way of laughter and humor, in *Sec. 3.5.1*; and the contribution to the molding and regulation of beliefs and values, regardless of whether this be done by way of popular culture or by way of real science, in *Sec. 3.5.2*).

On the other hand, there is difference in outcome (e.g., the contribution to the molding and regulation of values and behaviors by way of rational thought for a more scientific-technical lifeworld—but the contribution to the molding and regulation of values and behaviors by way of humor for a more happy-go-lucky lifeworld, in *Sec. 2.2.1*; the contribution to the molding and control of beliefs and behaviors by way of black comedy for a more cynical and skeptical worldview—but the contribution to the molding and control of beliefs and behaviors by way of scientific discourse for a more rational worldview, in *Sec. 2.2.2*; the contribution to the molding and control of beliefs and behaviors by way of humor as IFF for a more exclusive social world—but the contribution to the molding and control of beliefs and behaviors by way of normal relationship without the fixation on humor as IFF for a more tolerant social world, in *Sec. 2.3.1*; the contribution to the molding and control of beliefs and values by way of satire for a more witty, subtle way of communication—but the contribution to the molding and control of beliefs and values by way of polticial decrees for a more authoritarian way of communication, in *Sec. 2.4.1*; the contribution to the molding and control of beliefs and behaviors by way of ethnic jokes for a verbal resolution of hostility between groups—but the contribution to the molding and control of beliefs and behaviors by way of ethnic violence for a physical resolution of hostility between groups, in *Sec. 2.4.2*; the contribution to the molding and control of beliefs and behaviors by way of fart jokes for a more laid-back social lifeworld—but the contribution to the molding and control of beliefs and behaviors by way of social norms regulating farts for a more moralistic social lifeworld, in *Sec. 2.5.1*; the contribution to the molding and control of beliefs and values by way of satire and parody for a more subtle, covert form of political culture—but the contribution to the molding and control of beliefs and values by way of direct political critique for a more confrontional form of poltical culture, in *Sec. 2.5.2*; the contribution to the molding and regulation of beliefs and behaviors by way of normal laughing for a more civilized lifeworld, with the proper etiquettes of laughing—but the contribution to the molding and regulation of beliefs and behaviors by way of excessive laughing, as in PLC individuals, for a more impulsive lifeworld, without the proper etiquettes of laughing, in *Sec. 3.2.1*; the contribution to the molding and regulation of beliefs and behaviors by way of therapy in gelotology for a different form of "power" over individuals in contemporary society, as shown in the work of Michel Foucault like *The Birth of the Clinic* about the "truth" in the history of medicine—but the contribution to the molding and regulation of beliefs and behaviors by way of traditional healing without therapy for an alternative form of "power" over individuals in the older days, with a different undrestanding of the "truth" in the history of medicine, in *Sec. 3.2.2*; the contribution to the molding and regulation of beliefs and behaviors by way of the understanding of laughing in animals for a more playful expierence with animals—but the contribution to the molding and regulation of beliefs and behaviors by way of the understanding of fighting in animals for a more careful encounter with animals, in *Sec. 3.3.1*; the contribution to the molding and regulation of beliefs and values by way of the evolutionary perspective of laughter for a more secular lifeworld—but the contribution to the molding and regulation of beliefs and values by way of the creationist perspective of laughter for a more sacred lifeworld, as some believe that laughter, especially in the context of humor, is "a gift from God," in *Sec. 3.3.2*; the contribution to the molding and regulation of beliefs and values by way of a functionalist view of laughter for a more conservative view of society for social bonding—but the contribution to the molding and regulation of beliefs and values by way of a critical view of laughter for a more skeptical view of society for deconstruction, in *Sec. 3.4.1*; the contribution to the molding and regulation of beliefs and behaviors by way of logic and reason for a more rationalist rigid lifeform, relatively speaking, as Nietzsche pointed out—but the contribution to the molding and regulation of beliefs and behaviors by way of laughter and humor for a more socially/morally uniform lifeform, relatively speakiing, as argued by Bergson, in *Sec. 3.5.1*;

and the contribution to the molding and regulation of beliefs and values by way of popular culture for a more entertaining lifeworld—but the contribution to the molding and regulation of beliefs and values by way of real science for a more serious lifeworld, in *Sec. 3.5.2*).

And the reverse direction also holds true.

Again, it should be stressed, however, that there are different shades of gray (or different degrees of truth) in the two opposites, and the classification is not necessarily mutually exclusive either. In fact, even when some combinations of the two occur, they only end up sharing the same dialectic relationship, but in a different degree.

Also, there are some other relationships (as a kind of family resemblance) which have something in common with the principle, but they are not exactly the same but only more or less comparable, which varies from case to case.

Good examples of family resemblance in relation to the principle are homogeneity-heterogeneity, we-they, and so forth.

18th Thesis: The Post-Human Rendition

And the eighteenth thesis is about the role of "post-humans," which I originally proposed in my previous books, starting with the first book titled *The Future of Human Civilization* in 2000 and all others afterwards.

As already pointed out in *Sec. 1.6*, I need to emphasize, as this is something that I used to repeat (*almost verbatim*) from my previous books, two clarifications here about the term "post-human" as a neologism in my works.

Firstly, the word "post-human" here should *not* be confused with another term which looks similar but has a totally different meaning in the literature of postmodernism, namely, "post-humanism"—which constitutes a critique of "humanism" as tradionally understood (especially, though not exclusively, in relation to the idea of progress in science and reason in the Enlightenment project). (WK 2008)

My works reject the project of "postmodernism" and propose the future world of what I orignally called "after-postmodernity" in *FHC* and *FCD*, for instance.

And secondly, the word "post-human" here should also *not* be confused with a similar term which is used to champion the ideology of technology for the future co-existence between humans and cyborgs in "trans-humanism." (WK 2008a)

Instead, my term "post-human" in relation to "posthuman-ism" also rejects "transhumanism" (especially, though not exclusively, in relation to the promises of technology) and refers to something else altogether, that is, the future extinction of humans and its post-human successors in deep space and beyond unto multiverses.

My critique of "transhumanism" was more extensively elabroated in *Sec. 2.4.1* of *BEPE*.

With these two clarifications in mind (as summarized in *Table 1.31*)—the post-human rendition in humor can be addressed in relation to five main directions, based on the metamorphic theory of humor as analysed in this book (together with my visions as already worked out in my previous books).

Firstly, the post-human rendition in humor will learn from the metamorphic theory of humor in relation to the dialectic context of joking and laughing—especially in the larger dialectic context of no joking without laughing (and vice versa), in the context of humor.

Secondly, the post-human rendition in humor will learn from the metamorphic theory of humor in relation to the four perspectives of the mind, nature, society, and culture.

Thirdly, the post-human rendition in humor will learn from the metamorphic theory of humor in relation to the non-privilege of any specific theory over others in the literature and the non-integration of them all (as they are not necessarily compatible with each other).

Fourthly, the post-human rendition in humor will have to confront the new challenges as posed by the long-term civilizational development of intelligent life in the distant future, both here on this planet Earth and elsewhere in deep space until multiverses.

As this is something that I regularly pointed out in my previous books for background information (and summarize here, *almost verbatim*), I already worked out, in my numerous books, what these new challenges will be and provide different original visions to meet them—especially, in regard to the future evolutions of the mind (e.g., "the contrarian personality," "the hyper-martial body," "the hyper-sexual body," "floating consciousness," "hyper-spatial consciousness," "thinking machines," "unfolding unconsciousness," "thinking robots," "genetically altered superior beings," "cyborgs," and others), of nature (e.g., "resettlement geology," "post-cosmology," "the alteration of space-time," "the creation of new matter-energy," "selective geometry," and the like), of society (e.g., "heterodox education," "multifaceted war and peace," "virtual organizations," different versions of "post-capitalism" and "post-democracy," the movement of "cyclical progression" at both structural and systemic levels, "ambivalent technology," and so forth), and of culture (e.g., "post-human mind games," "comparative-substitutive religion," "post-ethics," "post-civilization," "transformative aesthetic experience," "contrastive mathematical-logic," and the whatnot) in history (e.g., the age of "after-postmodernity"), in the context of my approaches in relation to methodology (e.g., "sophisticated methodologial holism," "critical-dialectic formal science," etc,) and ontology (e.g., "existential dialectics," "contrastive rationality").

Of course, the examples (as listed above) are not exhaustive but illustrative, since my numerous books have worked out many other visions (as already roughly summarized in *Sec.1.6* and *Sec. 1.7*). Many, though not all, of my visions on the mind, nature, society, culture, history, methodology, and ontology (as cited above) are summarized in the tables as shown in Chapter One and Chapter Four (especially in *Table 4.43* about my original theories on numerous topics).

And finally, or fifthly, the post-human rendition in humor will learn from the metamorphic theory of humor in regard to the need to go beyond joking and laughing (as further elaborated in the next section).

Towards the Post-Human Rendition

This "post-human" rendition in humor to transcend both joking and laughing can be understood in terms of four great future transformations of humor, as explained below (and summarized in *Table 1.2*).

Four Great Future Transformations of Humor

The four great future transformations of humor can be explained hereafter, with the caveat, however, that the classification in terms of the number four is solely aesthetic and utilitarian (illustrative), as there is no objective basis that it must be classified in term of the number four.

The First Great Future Transformation of Humor

The first great future transformation of humor in the post-human era concerns what I originally call *virtual humor*.

Virtual humor has to do with the use of computers to generate jokes in the future, especially when computers will be developed to the point of artificial intelligence unto what I had already extensively discussed as the "post-human" future (in my numerous books—38 of them so far).

This is not as far-stretched as one might think, because, already in our time, there is research on "computational humor," which refers to "a branch of computational linguistics and artificial intelligence which uses computers in humor research. It is not to be confused with computer humor (i.e., jokes about computers, programmers, users, and computing). It is a relatively new area, with the first dedicated conference organized in 1996. Nevertheless, the first 'computer model of a sense of humor' was suggested by Suslov as early as 1992." (WK 2010hh; J. Hulstijn 1996; I. Suslov 1992)

For instance, the research on computational humor showed how "to generate jokes basing on the rules that underlie classification. Simple prototypes for computer pun generation were reported in the early 1990s, based on a natural language generator program, VINCI. Graeme Ritchie and Kim Binsted in their 1994 research paper described a computer program, JAPE, designed to generate question-answer-type puns from a general, i.e., non-humorous, lexicon. (The program name is an acronym for 'Joke Analysis and Production Engine'.) Some examples produced by JAPE are" shown below: (WK 2010hh; G. Lessard 1992; K. Binsted 1994)

Q: "What is the difference between leaves and a car?"
A: "One you brush and rake, the other you rush and brake."
Q: "What do you call a strange market?"
A: "A bizarre bazaar."

These puns may not be much now, but the point here is that this is only a beginning, because, "since then the approach has been improved, and the latest report, dated 2007, describes the STANDUP joke generator, implemented in Java programming language." (WK 2010hh; G. Ritchie 2007)

This vision of "virtual humor" of mine can be compared with other visions of mine in different contexts, like "virtual education" (as already discussed in *FPHEDU*), "virtual experience" in chess (as already discussed in *FPHCESS*) and "virtual memory" (or "virtual recall") in terms of uploading info into the brain for sexual fantasy (as already discussed in *The Future of Post-Human Sexuality* or *FPPHS*) and for general purposes (as already discussed in *The Future of Human Civilization* or *FHC*).

In the current context, virtual humor will further transform humor at the virtual level that the human world has never known.

The Second Great Future Transformation of Humor

The second great future transformation of humor in the post-human era concerns what I originally call *novel humor*.

In *Sec. 1.2* (and the rest of the book), I already showed the creation of different subjects, styles, and forms of humor over time in history, be they about "satire," "professional humor," "mathematical joke," "ethnic joke," "black humor," "religious joke," "self-deprecating humor," "dirty joke," "surrealist joke," "wit," "anti-joke," "non-sequitur joke," "question/answer joke," "parody," "burlesque," "farce," "flatulence humor," "double-act joke," "shagy dog joke,"and so on.

In the post-human era, the post-humans will no doubt create new subjects, styles, and forms of humor which will better suite their tastes and the environments that they encoutner in deep space and beyond unto multiverse—in a way that the human world has never known.

The Third Great Future Transformation of Humor

The third great future transformation of humor in the post-human era concerns what I originally call *holistic humor*.

For instance, just as there are "holistic education" (as already discussed in *FPHEDU*), "holistic knowledge" (as already discussed in *The Future of Post-Human Knowledge* or *FPHK*, and other books of mine) and "holistic methodology" (as already discussed in many books of mine like *FCD, FPHC, BCPC, FC, FPHK*, etc.)—there is likewise "holistic humor," in that humor will be constructed more and more in a broader scope and with a greater depth, in accordance to the future evolutions of the mind in relation to perception, conception, imagination, intuition, emotions, and behaviors, for example.

More specifically, my visions of the future evolutions of the mind (including the brain and the body) are especially relevant, especially in relation to "unfolding unconsciousness" (as already discussed in *FPHU*), "floating consciousness" (as already discussed in *FCD* and *FPHC*), "hyper-spatial consciousness" (as already discussed in *FPHG* and *FPHC*), "multilogical learning" (as already discussed in *FPHL*), "comprehensive creating thinking" (as already discussed in *FPHCT*), "hyper-martial body" (as already discussed in *FPHMA*), "hyper-sexual body" (as already discussed in *FPHS*), "transformative aesthetic experience" (as already discussed in *FAE*), "beyond normality and abnormality" (as already discussed in *FPHP*), "beyond morality and immorality" (as already discussed in *BEPE*), and the like.

In the post-human era, the post-human mind will evolve to a different advanced stage of complexity both in scope and depth, such that humor will be transformed in a different dimension of scope and depth that the human world has never known.

The Fourth Great Future Transformation of Humor

And the fourth great future transformation of humor in the post-human era concerns what I originally call *spiritual humor.*

For instance, in *The Future of Capitalism and Democracy* (2002), I already went to great lengths to show why and how there will be more spiritual transformations to come, especially in relation to the two value ideals of (i) transcending freedom in floating existence and (ii) transcending equality in the rivalry of cosmic hegemony.

Even then, as this is something I often stressed in many of my previous books, almost verbatim, that these two value ideals constitute only a form of transcendent state of higher spiritual concerns, with other more ideals to come in the distant future, especially when considered in conjunction with other future transformations of the mind, nature, society, and culture (as already addressed in my other books on numerous topics).

Some good examples of my other visions of the spiritual transformations to come include "spiritual education" (as already discussed in *FPHEDU*), "contrarian personality" (as already discussed in *FPHP*), "post-civlization" (as already discussed in *BCIV*), "post-ethics" (as already discussed in *BEPE*), "beyond aggression and pacificity" (as already discussed in *FPHWP*), "post-human religion" (as already discussed in *FPHR*), "post-human law" (as already discussed in *FPHLAW*), and so on.

Thus, in the post-huamn era, the post-humans will further transform humor in a spiritual direction in a way that the human world has never known.

Enormous Implications

These future great transformations of humor have enormous implications for some of the most unresolved mysteries which have puzzled some of the finest minds in human history—Does humor have a survival value in evolution (or alternatively, does it merely serve as its by-product)? What is the future of humor in a world which has been dominated by the serious scientific mode of thinking since modern times? And….?

Questions like this will yield new answers in post-human humor in the context of going beyond joking and laughing—such that their possibility and desirability are not to the extent that the respective defenders would like us to believe.

In addition, the post-humans will also give humor a different role to play, in that its essential techniques (like incongruity, paradox, ambiguity, disproportion, reversal, surprise, etc.) can challenge the conventional thinking about the nature of logic.

In *The Future of Post-Human Mathematical Logic* (2008), I already went to great lengths to explain the need for alternative ways to understand logic, that is, "the contrastive theory of rationality," in that classical logics need to be transcended for a new "rationality of knowledge" at the meta-theoretical level—so as to include (or adjust for) heterogeneity, conflict, subjectivity, complexity, and so on. For this reason, *the formalness-informalness principle* was proposed in that book.

The role of humor precisely adds to this urgent need for a new "rationality of knowledge," because of the existence of the playful dimension of intelligent life, not just its serious one. It is for this reason that a new principle of existential dialectics is added in this book, namely, *the seriousness-playfulness principle.*

Yet, lest any misunderstanding occurs, two clarifications are needed here.

Firstly, one should keep in mind that seriousness (in the seriousness-playfulness principle) does not necessarily imply formalness (in the formalness-informalness principle), because one can be serious in working for formalness or informalness. Similarly, one should remember that playfulness does not necessarily imply informalness, because one can be playful, which can lead towards either formalness or informalness, depending on how it is done.

In other words, the two principles are not equivalent, although they both have implications for the nature of rationality.

And secondly, this post-human rendition in regard to humor will bring neither utopia nor dystopia. In fact, in *The Future of Post-Human Creative Thinking* (2009), I already warned against the "ambivalent" legacy of different rationalities in practice (with both good and bad consequences), which results when theoretical constructs are used in practice for different applications to serve different human interests.

Three excellent categories of these rationalities in practice are "instrumental rationality" (e.g., for the sake of efficiency and effectiveness), "substantive rationality" (e.g., for the sake of God, the King, Motherland, or others), and "autonomous rationality" (e.g., for the sake of itself, the autonomy of creative endeavor).

In fact, I further analyzed the "ambivalent" legacy of these rationalities in practice in the context of technology in *The Future of Post-Human Engineering* (2009).

These three rationalities in practice to serve human interests can now be called the "rationalities of application" at the practical level, so as to be distinguished from the "rationalities of knowledge" at the meta-theoretical level.

As a caveat, however, it is also not up to us to judge whether or not, or to what extent, the post-human future of humor will be for better and for worse, because it will be decided by the values and beliefs of future post-humans in a way that the entire history of our human world hitherto existing has never known.

At the very least, we can take this bold visionary step for a new way to understand rationality, so as to contribute to the future of humor and its post-human fate.

Table 4.1. Sophisticated Methodological Holism (Part I)

• "My methodological holism implies the partiality-totality principle in the ontology of existential dialectics (see the table on the partiality-totality principle for summary), which is against the varieties of (a) reductionism and (b) reverse-reductionism, in relation to (i) concept, (ii) theory, (iii) methodology, and (iv) ontology." (*FC*)

• "[M]y methodological holism here is not opposed to methodological individualism but includes it (and, for that matter, other methodologies too)…." (*FPHC*) For this reason (and others too, as summarized hereafter), my version of methodological holism is sophisticated—not vulgar as sometimes used by inapt scholars using the same term. (*FC*)

• "[M]y methodological holism does not democratically presume that all levels are equally valid, as all levels are not created equal. In other words, in relation to issue X, level A may be more relevant than level B, but in relation to Y, level B can be more relevant than level A instead." (*FPHC*) One excellent example of this vulgar democratic presumption is what I called in *BNN* "the compromise fallacy." (*FC*)

• My methodological holism does not presume that a lower level of analysis is more important than a higher level, solely because the former serves as the foundation for the latter—and vice versa, for that matter. One excellent example of this reductionistic presumption is what I called in *FPHST* "the foundation fallacy." (*FPHST*, *FC*)

(continued on next page)

Table 4.1. Sophisticated Methodological Holism (Part II)

• "[M]y methodological holism does not make any a-priori postulation that there must be a definite (and, for that matter, indefinite) number of levels" in any analysis. (*FPHC*) Nor does it dogmatically require that there must be a certain combination of levels of analysis in a given inquiry. (*FC*)

• "[M]ethodological holism, in my usage, does not assume that all levels…can necessarily be integrated, since methodological holism is not aimed to search for the holy grail of 'an integral theory…' (as is the case for Wilber). In other words, it allows that sometimes some levels may experience irreducible gaps between them, to be understood, at best, as empirical correlations, not as causal relations…." (*FPHC*)

• "[D]ifferent levels may overlap and even interact with each other in a given context (but sometimes may not), and the fact that I even proposed different ways of re-classifying the levels (whenever needed) in *FDC* reinforces this point….The dual danger here is either forcefully making different levels interact when they are just different (or, metaphorically speaking, apples and oranges) or inappropriately ignoring their interactions when some situations instead require them." (*FPHC*)

• "[T]o understand different levels from their own (unique) perspectives (as required by my methodological holism) is not the same as trying to reduce them to a preferred level in the process of learning from other levels. This second kind of multidisciplinary work is not genuine and does no justice to the unique complexities and merits inherent at each level." (*FPHC*)

(continued on next page)

Table 4.1. Sophisticated Methodological Holism (Part III)

• "[My] methodological holism walks a fine line between the artificial classification (separation) of levels and the simultaneous incorporation of them, if only for the sake of human scholarly endeavor. It should be reminded that nature does not impose upon itself the academic classification of the levels of analysis as humans have. The enterprise of classification is therefore anthropocentric." (*FPHC*)

• "[M]y methodological holism advocates neither epistemic subjectivism nor epistemic non-subjectivism (e.g., realism, idealism, and historicism), neither epistemic relativism (e.g., subjectivism, historicism) nor epistemic absolutism (e.g., realism, positivism), neither epistemic reductionism nor epistemic emergencism, and neither epistemic objectivism (e.g., realism, idealism) nor epistemic historicism….Neither does methodological holism, in my usage, accept the false meta-conceptual dichotomy between nominalism and realism….These false dichotomies…are to be transcended. In other words, methodological holism does not fully accept epistemic realism, positivism (a form of epistemic idealism), historicism, subjectivism, and reductionism in epistemology and philosophy of science but learns from the strengths and weaknesses of all of the opposing approaches without siding with any of them…." (*FPHC*)

• "Sophisticated methodological holism is subject to the constraints as imposed by the syntax of existential dialectics (e.g., the partiality-totality principle and the predictability-unpredictability principle). Even in predictability, outcomes are subject to uncertainty, the degree of which varies from case to case." (*FC*)

(continued on next page)

Table 4.1. Sophisticated Methodological Holism (Part IV)

• "Sophisticated methodological holism—when applied, especially though not exclusively, as illustrated in my numerous works—can enrich the understanding of reality in some distinctive ways. Here are three examples (as revealed in each of my books)." (*FPHCT*; *FPHL*)

—"Firstly, it provides a comprehensive analysis of a subject matter, from which much can be learned about reality," "both in relation to the perspectives of the mind, nature, society, and culture and also in relation to a new classification of the subject matter."

—"Secondly, it suggests some visions of the future in relation to the subject matter in question."

—"And thirdly, it proposes some insights on meta-theory (e.g., methodology and ontology) in general—with the clear understanding, however, of the dilemma of specific vs. general ontology (as shown in the table on the syntax of existential dialectics in the context of the dilemma of ontology). For this very reason, all of these ways are important, without reducing one into the analysis of another."

• "In the end, my meta-theory (both sophisticated methodological holism and existential dialectics) serves as a foundation to unify all domains of knowledge into *an unified theory of everything* (by way of some ontological principles and the comprehensive perspectives of the mind, nature, society, and culture). This is so, without commiting the sins of reductionism and reverse-reductionism (as often seen in many holistic approaches, with the fad of sysems approach—be it about systems theory, chaos theory, complexity theory, or else—as a most recent notorious example, which I debunked in *The Future of Complexity* and also in *The Future of Post-Human Formal Science*). My distinctive approach makes good use of different schools of thought without favoring any of them nor trying to integrate them (as they are not necessarily compatible with each other), so as to adjust for subjectivity, diversity, conflict, and complexity, for example. In this sense, the word "unified" does not have to mean integrative approach, in a narrow sense, nor systems approach, in a broad one, both of which I reject while learning from them." (*FPHFS*; *FPHS*)

Sources: A summary of *Sec.1.2* in *FPHC*—and also from *BNN*, *FPHST*, *ALD*, *FC*, *FPHCT*, and the rest of all other books of mine. See the books for more detail.

Table 4.2. On Reductionism and Reverse-Reductionism (Part I)

- **The Partiality-Totality Principle**
  —The partiality-totality principle in the ontology of existential dialectics targets against the varieties of reductionism and reverse-reductionism (as already worked out in my previous books).

- **Against the Varieties of Reductionism**
  —*Conceptual Reductionism*
  - Some illustrative instances involve myriad dualities like mind vs. body, self vs. world, democracy vs. non-democracy, and the like (as already addressed in *FHC*, *FPHC*, and *BDPD*, for instance).

  —*Theoretical Reductionism*
  - A fascinating case study concerns what I originally called "the foundation fallacy" in *FPHST*, in any attempt to naively understand space-time from the physical perspective as the foundation and, consequently, to dangerously dismiss other perspectives.
  - In *FAE*, I elaborated further these versions of reductionism in the literature on aesthetics (e.g., form vs. content, representation vs. expression, critics vs. artists, and externalism vs. internalism).
  - In *FIA*, I revealed other forms of reductionism in the literature on information architecture (e.g., the constructivist argument).
  - In *FPHU*, I showed the persistent legacy of reductionism, this time, in the literature on anomalous experience (e.g., the obsession with physics, chemistry, and biology for explaining anomalous experience).
  - In *FPHE*, I examined another case of reductionism in action, in the context of engineering (e.g., technical constraints vs. normative constraints).
  - In *FPHMM*, I elaborated one more version of reductionism, in relation to the three domains of communication (e.g., the competing views on sending, connecting, and receiving).
  - In *FPHCT*, I explored another version of reductionism, in relation to invention and innovation (e.g., the bio-psychological argument vs. the socio-cultural arguments).

(continued on next page)

Table 4.2. On Reductionism and Reverse-Reductionism (Part II)

- **Against the Varieties of Reductionism *(cont'd)***
  —*Theoretical Reductionism (cont'd)*
  - In *FPHG*, I identify another version of reductionism, in relation to infinity, symmetry, and dimensionality (e.g., the Euclidean argument vs. the non-Euclidean arguments).
  - In *FPHUP*, I analyzed another version of reductionism, in relation to density and void (e.g., the engineering argument and the ecology argument).
  - In *FPHL*, I examined another version of reductionism, in relation to structure and context (e.g., the structuralist argument and the contextualist argument).
  - In *PFHO*, I explored another version of reductionism, in relation to communcation, decision-making, and leadership (e.g., the rational-system argument vs. the natural-system argument).
  - In *PFHMA*, I revealed another version of reductionism, in relation to the martial body and spirit (e.g., the spiritual argument vs. the materialist argument vs. the defensive argument).
  - In *PFHS*, I analyzed another version of reductionism, in relation to the sexual body and spirit (e.g., the naturalist argument vs. the constructivist argument).
  - In *PFHLAW*, I examined another version of reductionism, in relation to law (e.g., the necessity argument vs. the contengency argument).
  - In *FPHWP*, I showed another version of reductionism, in relation to war and peace (e.g., the aggressivist argument vs. the pacifist argument).
  - In *BEPE*, I analyzed another version of reductionism, in relation to morality and immorality (e.g., the objectivist argument vs. the non-objectivist argument vs. the skeptical argument).
  - In *BCOS*, I examined another version of reductionism, in relation to the contested beginnings and speculative ends of the universe (e.g., the scientific argument vs. the religious argument vs. the esoteric argument vs. the metaphysical argument).
  - In *FPHP*, I show another version of reductionism, in relation to normality and abnormality (e.g., the natural argument vs. the social argument vs. the cultural argument vs. the mental argument).

(continued on next page)

Table 4.2. On Reductionism and Reverse-Reductionism (Part III)

- **Against the Varieties of Reductionism *(cont'd)***
  —*Theoretical Reductionism (cont'd)*
  - In *FPHGEOL*, I scrutinized another version of reductionism, in relation to statics and dynamics (e.g., the catastrophe argument vs. the uniformity argument vs. the revision argument).
  - In *FPHCHESS*, I showed another version of reductionism, in relation to tactics and strategy (e.g., the natural argument vs. the social argument vs. the cultural argument vs. the mental argument).
  - In *FPHR*, I revealed another version of reductionism, in relation to secularness and sacredness (e.g., the critical argument vs. the skeptical argument vs. the theist argument).
  - In *FPHEDU*, I examined another version of reductionism, in relation to teaching and learning (e.g., the teacher-centered argument vs. the student-centered argument vs. the balanced argument).
  - And in *FPHH*, I explore another version of reductionism, in relation to joking and laughing (e.g., the natural argument vs. the social argument vs. the cultural argument vs. the mental argument).

  —*Methodological Reductionism*
  - A good instance concerns the debate between different versions of qualitative and quantitative methods (as already analyzed in *FC* and also *FHC*). In *FPHML*, I examined similar reductionism, this time, in the literature on mathematical logic (e.g., the obsession with consistency, soundness, and completeness). And in *FPHFS*, I also explored the problems of reductionism in the context of formal science (e.g., the analytical argument).

  —*Ontological Reductionism*
  - An excellent example is the debate between emergentism and reductionism in complexity theory and also in psychology (as elaborated in *FPHC*, in the context of Being and Becoming).

(continued on next page)

Table 4.2. On Reductionism and Reverse-Reductionism (Part IV)

- **Against the Varieties of Reverse-Reductionism**
  —*Conceptual Reverse-Reductionism*
  - Any concept of "art" (e.g., fine art, cave art, outsider art, junk art) is deemed acceptable in postmodernism (as already addressed in Ch.4 of *FHC*).

  —*Theoretical Reverse-Reductionism*
  - There are numerous art and literary theories co-exist. Take the case of literary studies, as there are now Literary Structuralism, Marxist Literary Criticism, New Criticism, Phenomenology, Hermeneutics, Language-Game Literary Criticism, Feminist Literary Criticism, Reception Theory, Reader Response Criticism, Poststructuralism, Semiotics, Pyschoanalytic Literary Criticism, just to cite some well-known ones, with no one being said to be better than any others (as detailedly analyzed in Ch.4 of *FHC*). (S. Raman 1997) In *BNN*, I even introduced "the compromise fallacy" as another good illustration of theoretical reverse-reductionism, in misleadingly treating both genetic and environmental approaches as equally valid.

  —*Methodological Reverse-Reductionism*
  - There is the "anything-goes" mentality in postmodernism (e.g., doing art without praxis, doing art with praxis, and doing art by sublation), as analyzed in Ch.4 of *FHC*. And in *FPHFS*, I also exposed the problems of reverse-reductionism in the context of formal science in relation to systems theory.

  —*Ontological Reverse-Reductionism*
  - There are likewise no privileged ontology, and the door is open for anything in postmodernism (e.g., the equal status of the ontology of Being vs. that of Becoming, as already addressed in Ch.4 of *FHC*—and also in *FPHC)*. In *FAE*, I also introduced another version of reverse-reductionism, that is, "the pluralist fallacy," in the context of understanding aesthetic experience, for instance—although this fallacy has been committed not exclusively in relation to the ontological level (but also at the conceptual, theoretical, and methodological ones).

Sources: From my previous books.

Table 4.3. The Concepton of Existential Dialectics (Part I)

- **Sets and Elements**
  - —Sets
    - Ex: the Same
    - Ex: the Others
  - —Elements
    - Ex: whites in 20th century America (in the set of "the Same")
    - Ex: Iraq during the U.S. invasion in 2003 (in the set of "the Others")

- **Relations, Operations, Functions**
  - —Relations (e.g., "belongs," "equals to," "is greater than")
    - Ex: symmetric interactions within the Same (or the Others)
    - Ex: asymmetric interactions between the Same and the Others
  - —Operations (e.g., "and," "or," "not," "if…then")
    - Ex: if the Same oppresses the Others, it will also oppress itself.
    - Ex: the Same is not the Others.
  - —Functions (e.g., goals)
    - Ex: the Same is hegemonic in relation to the Others.

- **Truth Values**
  - —"1" if True (in Symbolic Logic)
    - Ex: the proposition that imperial Japan was hegemonic to China during WWII
  - —"0" if False (in Symbolic Logic)
    - Ex: the proposition that Grenada invaded France in 2003
  - —"1" & "0" if Both True and False (in Dialectic Logic)
    - Ex: the proposition that the rabbit-duck picture refers to a duck
  - —"~1" & "~0" if Neither True Nor False (or N/A, in Dialectic Logic)
    - Ex: the proposition that God really exists

(continued on next page)

Table 4.3. The Conception of Existential Dialectics (Part II)

- **Axioms, Postulates, Theorems, Principles**
  - —Axioms
    - Ex: the reflexive axiom—"any quantity is equal to itself"
  - —Postulates
    - Ex: the SSS postulate—"if the three sides of a triangle are congruent to their corresponding parts, then the triangles are congruent"
  - —Theorems (and Principles) in Existential Dialectics
    - <u>In Relation to Method</u>
      - –#1: The formalness-informalness principle
      - –#2: The absoluteness-relativeness principle
      - –#3: The partiality-totality principle
      - –#4: The predictability-unpredictability principle
      - –#5: The explicability-inexplicability principle
    - <u>In Relation to Structure</u>
      - –#6: The finiteness-transfiniteness principle
      - –#7: The preciseness-vagueness principle
      - –#8: The simpleness-complicatedness principle
      - –#9: The openness-hiddenness principle
      - –#10: The denseness-emptiness principle
    - <u>In Relation to Process</u>
      - –#11: The change-constancy principle
      - –#12: The order-chaos principle
      - –#13: The slowness-quickness principle
      - –#14: The expansion-contraction principle
    - <u>In Relation to Agency</u>
      - –#15: The theory-praxis principle
      - –#16: The convention-novelty principle
      - –#17: The evolution-transformation principle
      - –#18: The symmetry-asymmetry principle
      - –#19: The softness-hardness principle
      - –#20: The seriousness-playfulness principle
    - <u>In Relation to Outcome</u>
      - –#21: The regression-progression principle
      - –#22: The same-difference principle

(continued on next page)

Table 4.3. The Conception of Existential Dialectics (Part III)

Notes: The categories and examples in each are solely illustrative (not exhaustive). The comparison is also relative (not absolute), nor are they mutually exclusive. As generalities, they allow exceptions.
Sources: Starting from Ch.6 of *BCPC* and also from other books of mine

Table 4.4. The Syntax of Existential Dialectics I: The Principles (Part I)

- **In Relation to Method**

—*The Formalness-Informalness Principle*
(On the Formal Requirements of Logical Systems)

- The formal requirements of a logical system (e.g., consistency, soundness, and completeness) have both usefulness and non-usefulness, to the extent that, if there are formal systems requiring them, there are alternative ones which do not. Thus, it does *not* exclude classical logics but simply goes beyond both classical and non-classical logics, while learning something from each. There is no formalness without informalness—and vice versa.
- For instance, existential dialectics can make use of both classical logics under certain conditions (e.g., especially, though not exclusively, when they are clear-cut, etc.) and non-classical logics under alternative conditions (especially, though not exclusively, when they are "unknown," "irrelevant," "ambiguous," "possible," with "different degrees of truth," empirically inconsistent in a desirable way, etc.). (WK 2008u)
- Family resemblance: e.g., logicalness-nonlogicalness, rationality-nonrationality, etc.
- Sources: From *FPHML*. See also my later books.

—*The Explicability-Inexplicability Principle*
(On the Underlying Mechanisms of Things)

- Both explicability and inexplicability are part of the understanding of things. There is no explicability without inexplicability—and vice versa.
- This principle tells us the duality of the research dilemma, in that, if reality can be explained in some ways, it also has its other ways which are not quite explainable, at a given point in time.
- Family resemblance: e.g., underlyingness-regularness, causation-regularness, causation-correlation, etc.
- Sources: Especially from *FPHU*—and also *FPHC*. See also my later books.

(continued on next page)

Table 4.4. The Syntax of Existential Dialectics I: The Principles (Part II)

- **In Relation to Method** ***(cont'd)***

—*The Predictability-Unpredictability Principle*
(On the Occurrence of Events)

- Both predictability and unpredictability have a major role to play in the occurrence of things, so that neither determinism nor indeterminism wins the centuries-old fight. There is no predictability without unpredictability—and vice versa.
- There are events which are predictable, just as there are those which are not. Or what is regarded as unpredictable at one point in time may turn out to be predictable later, and, conversely, what is deemed as predictable may turn out to not be so predictable. Even in predictability, outcomes are subject to uncertainty, the degree of which varies from case to case.
- Family resemblance: e.g., sureness-arbitrariness, etc.
- Sources: Especially from *FC*. See also my later books.

—*The Partiality-Totality Principle*
(On the Relationships between Whole and Parts)

- The whole is not the sum of the parts. There is no partiality without totality—and vice versa.
- Any inquiry about a phenomenon in the work is to guard against the varieties of (a) reductionism and (b) reverse-reductionism.
- Reductionism and reverse-reductionism can be (i) conceptual, (ii) theoretical, (iii) methodological, and (iv) ontological.
- Family resemblance: e.g., individualisticness-holisticness, partness-wholeness, analysis-synthesis, etc.
- Sources: Especially from *FC*. See also my later books.

(continued on next page)

Table 4.4. The Syntax of Existential Dialectics I: The Principles (Part III)

- **In Relation to Method** ***(cont'd)***

  —*The Absoluteness-Relativeness Principle*
  (On the Multiplicity of Things)

  - There is the multiplicity of things in reality, be they about entities, qualities (or properties), and relationships, such that what is acceptable from one standpoint may not be so from another. For instance, if there is something absolute, there is likewise something relative. There is no absoluteness without relativeness—and vice versa.
  - Both absoluteness and relativeness here are also relevant to different modalities often cited in the literature on ontology, such as possibility (e.g., something "can" happen) and its opposite (e.g., impossibility), probability (e.g., something "will" happen) and its opposite (e.g., improbability), and necessity (e.g., something "should" happen) and its opposite (e.g., contingency).
  - Family resemblance: e.g., uniformity-diversity, internalness-externalness, immanence-transcendence, etc.
  - Sources: From *FPHK*. See also my later books.

(continued on next page)

Table 4.4. The Syntax of Existential Dialectics I: The Principles (Part IV)

- **In Relation to Structure**
  —*The Finiteness-Transfiniteness Principle*
  (On the Nature of Numbers)
  - If there are finite things, there are likewise transfinite ones. There is no finiteness without transfiniteness—and vice versa.
  - To avoid confusion, my usage of the word "transfinite" here differs radically from the one used by Cantor (and other mathematicians) for "relative" infinity—and is more limited, in light of the problems confronting any attempt to understand the idea of infinity, be it by intuition, imagination, and conception (as detailedly analyzed in *Sec. 2.2.3* of *FPHG*).
  - Instead, by "transfinity," I allow numbers which can be many times larger—or smaller, for that matter—than the finite things that we encounter in daily life, but they do not have to be related to the idea of infinity at all (which may not exist).
  - Of course, there may be some *borderline* cases, in which it is not clear whether the number in question is transfinite (in my usage) or simply a mathematical convenience. A good example of a borderline case is the Planck unit of length for "the smallest space possibly measured in nature," which is "less than billionths of trillionths of trillionths of an inch" (or something like 1.6×10^{-35} meters).
  - That said—my usage of "transfinity" can also resolve (or better, dissolve) an age-old problem in philosophy known as "Zeno's paradoxes" (as already explained in *Sec. 2.2.3* of *FPHG*).
  - Family resemblance: e.g., boundedness-quasiunboundedness, smallness-largeness, microness-macroness, etc.
  - Source: From *FPHG*. See also my later books.

(continued on next page)

Table 4.4. The Syntax of Existential Dialectics I: The Principles (Part V)

- **In Relation to Structure** ***(cont'd)***

  —*The Simpleness-Complicatedness Principle*
  (On the Interconnection among Things)

  - Both simpleness and complicatedness are vital, without favoring one over the other, in that each is utilized, depending on the basis of the perspectives of nature, the mind, culture, and society. And even when a combination of them is preferred, the dilemma is only shifted to a combinational degree of concern. There is no simpleness without complicatedness—and vice versa.
  - In relation to taxonomy, simpleness has its heuristic usefulness, just as complicatedness has its realistic representation, for instance. And in relation to network, simpleness has its economical attractiveness, just as complicatedness has its practical reliability, for instance.
  - Family resemblance: e.g., inflexibility-flexibility, standardization-specialization, imperfectness-perfectness, superficiality-depth, shallowness-deepness, economicalness-elaboratedness, plainness-circumspection, onesidedness-multisidedness, etc.
  - Sources: Especially from *FIA*. See also my later books.

  —*The Denseness-Emptiness Principle*
  (On the Distribution of Entities in Space)

  - Both density and void are needed, in relation to the mind, nature, culture, and society, albeit in different ways. There is no denseness without emptiness—and vice versa.
  - For clarity, the term "void" is used here only as an approximation of emptiness (depending on the degree of the lack of density), since, in physics, it is well known that "empty" space is not really empty all the way, because it can be full of energy (e.g., random quantum fluctuations at the sub-atomic level, and, for that matter, dark energy in the universe) and matter (e.g., different versions of sub-atomic particles, and, for that matter, dark matter in the universe).
  - Family resemblance: e.g., fullness-voidness, nearness-farness, concentration-dispersion, etc.
  - Sources: First worked out in *FPHUP*. See also my later books.

(continued on next page)

Table 4.4. The Syntax of Existential Dialectics I: The Principles (Part VI)

- **In Relation to Structure** ***(cont'd)***

  —*The Preciseness-Vagueness Principle*
  (On the Refinement of Things)

  - Both preciseness and vagueness are important, not that one is better than the other, but that both are used, in different degrees of preference, in accordance to the contextual application from the perspectives of nature, the mind, culture, and society. Even when both are used in a combination, the dilemma is shifted instead to one of combinational concern. There is no preciseness without vagueness—and vice versa.
  - In relation to taxonomy, preciseness has its taxonomic clarity, just as vagueness has its classificatory flexibility, for instance. And in relation to network, vagueness has its explorative liberty, just as preciseness has its conceptual definitiveness, for instance.
  - Family resemblance: e.g., clarity-ambiguity, directness-indirectness, quantitativeness-qualitativeness, describability-nondescribability, specificity-obscurity, specificity-generality, thickness-thinness, concretness-abstractness, etc.
  - Sources: Especially from *FIA*. See also my later books.

(continued on next page)

Table 4.4. The Syntax of Existential Dialectics I: The Principles (Part VII)

- **In Relation to Structure** ***(cont'd)***
  —The Openness-Hiddenness Principle
  (On the Detection of Things)
  - Reality has its hidden face, just as it is open to outside view in some other ways. There is no openness without hiddenness—and vice versa.
  - For instance, in the context of anomalous experience, certain aspects of reality can be open for examination (e.g., the experiment with SPECT images, the transmission of telepathemic bit, and the use of metonymies and metaphors). Other aspects, however, remain hidden, and examples include the elusive deeper nature of spiritual reality in the intangible realm, the undetectability of different branched universes, the underlying mechanisms of signals traveling between different folds of physical space-time, and the dependence on language and the bias for science and logic).
  - Family resemblance: e.g., overtness-covertness, publicness-privateness, openness-closedness, transparency-secrecy, openness-biasedness, etc.
  - Sources: Especially from *FPHU*. See also my later books.

- **In Relation to Process**
  —The Change-Constancy Principle
  (On the Alteration of Things)
  - Change occurs over time, although constancy is also allowed. There is no change without constancy—and vice versa.
  - Asymmetry undergoes changes over time, so does symmetry.
  - Old players fade away, and new ones emerges, with ever new causes and ever new forms.
  - Family resemblance: e.g., dynamicness-staticness, instability-stability, etc.
  - Sources: First named in *BCPC*. Especially from *FHC*, *FCD*, and *FPHC*. See also other books of mine (from that point on).

(continued on next page)

Table 4.4. The Syntax of Existential Dialectics I: The Principles (Part VIII)

- **In Relation to Process *(cont'd)***
  —*The Expansion-Contraction Principle*
  (On the Growth of Things)
  - Entities in the world can both expand in some ways and contract in other ones, as part of their nature. There is no expansion without contraction—and vice versa.
  - For instance, in the context of anomalous experience, one of its most fascinating expressions is none other than the analysis of different causes of the slow but steady expansion (and, furthermore, if put in a different way, unfolding) of unconsciousness.
  - Family resemblance: e.g., conquest-autarky, rise-fall (or up-down), spread-shrink, extendingness-shorteningness, etc.
  - Sources: Especially from *FPHU*. See also my later books.

  —*The Slowness-Quickness Principle*
  (On the Speed of Change)
  - Both slowness and quickness co-exist, with their own internal tension, to the extent that each fights for its own relevance with the other, in accordance to the perspectives of nature, the mind, culture, and society, without one being the victor and the other being the vanquished in the long haul. Even when both are chosen in other cases, this dilemma is only transferred into something else with a combinational character. There is no slowness without quickness—and vice versa.
  - In relation to taxonomy, quickness has its efficient usability, just as slowness has its aesthetic appeal, for instance. And in relation to network, quickness has its adventurous readiness, just as slowness has its risk-adverse convenience, for instance.
  - Family resemblance: e.g., inconvenience-convenience, passiveness-activenessness, gradualness-abruptness, deceleration-acceleration, etc.
  - Sources: Especially from *FIA*. See also my later books.

(continued on next page)

Table 4.4. The Syntax of Existential Dialectics I: The Principles (Part IX)

- **In Relation to Process *(cont'd)***

  —*The Order-Chaos Principle*

  (On the Pattern of Things)

  - Both order and chaos are vital in the process of change in the world. The preference for order is biased, since it does not give sufficient attention to the vital role of chaos in the transformation of the world (without somehow reducing it for the understanding of order). There is no order without chaos—and vice versa.
  - The scientific search for order in the world is often a hidden bias in its ontological obsession with order, since chaos is often treated as the "bad" guy, with order as the "good" guy (for the end goal of science).
  - Neither order nor chaos is the final end of the world, and one is not to be treated as the means for the other in the transformation of things. Both are fundamental in their recurrent dialectical interactions with each other over time, without reducing one for the other.
  - Family resemblance: e.g., lawfulness-disorder, order-disorder, etc.
  - Sources: Especially from *FC*. See also my later books.

- **In Relation to Agency**

  —*The Softness-Hardness Principle*

  (On the Force of Change)

  - This has to do with *the force of change* under the category about agency in existential dialectics, in that any change by an agent, be it organic (like humans) or non-organic (like natural objects), can occur in a forceful (aggressive) or gentle (pacific) way, which can come in all shapes and sizes, of course. There is no softness without hardness—and vice versa.
  - Family resemblance: e.g., peacefulness-violence, cooperation-competition, dovishness-hawkishness, reward-punishment, peace-war, pacificity-aggression, etc.
  - Sources: Especially from *ALD*. See also my later books.

(continued on next page)

Table 4.4. The Syntax of Existential Dialectics I: The Principles (Part X)

- **In Relation to Agency *(cont'd)***
  —*The Symmetry-Asymmetry Principle*
  (On the Relationships among Existents)
  - There is no symmetry without asymmetry—and vice versa.
  - For instance, the Same can be symmetric and asymmetric towards the Others. But in case of asymmetry, oppression and self-oppression can occur. So, when the Same is asymmetric towards the Others, the Same can also be relatively asymmetric towards itself in self-oppression, just as the Others can be likewise towards themselves.
  - The subsequent oppressiveness is dualistic, as much by the Same against the Others and itself, as by the Others against the Same and themselves.
  - Both oppression and self-oppression can be achieved by way of downgrading differences between the Same and the Others and of accentuating them.
  - This is true, even though not all forms of asymmetry have to be about oppression and self-oppression.
  - In addition, from Chapter Three of *FPHG*, symmetry is not perfect, to be understood in an approximate sense under many life circumstances.
  - Family resemblance: e.g., strength-weakness, balance-extremity, harmoniousness-unharrmoniousness, reflexiveness-unreflexiveness, equality-inequality, potence-impotence, etc.
  - Sources: From all my books, starting with *FHC*. First named in *BCPC*. See, for instance, *FCD* for more details on the Same and the Others.

(*continued on next page*)

Table 4.4. The Syntax of Existential Dialectics I: The Principles (Part XI)

• **In Relation to Agency** ***(cont'd)***

—*The Theory-Praxis Principle*
(On the Duality of Knowledge))

• This has to do with the duality of knowledge in existential dialectics, in that, if there is theoretical construction, there is likewise its practical application, both technical and normative. There is no theory without praxis—and vice versa.
• Family resemblance: e.g., discovery-application, knowledge-action, invention-innovation, etc.
• Source: Especially from *FPHE*. See also my later books.

—*The Evolution-Transformation Principle*
(On the Multiple Kinds of Agency)

• This principle (and the symmetry-asymmetry principle) are both about *the agency of change*. The word "agency," in a formal definition, refers to "a person or thing through which power is exerted or an end is achieved." (MWD 2007b) It therefore does not have to necessarily involve an intelligent lifeform.
• Because of this dual meaning in agency, the evolution-transformation principle is more concerned with *the multiple kinds of agency*, that is, both about the *evolution* in the state of nature (e.g., an object of natural beauty) and the *transformation* in the world of intelligent lifeforms (e.g., a work of art, an air-conditioner, etc.). There is no evolution without transformation—and vice versa.
• And the transformative part of the principle precisely refers to the other dimension in the dual meaning of agency, in giving technology a major role to play in the change of the world, which is something that I extensively analyzed in *FHC* in the context of the technophilic lifeworld, espeically though not exclusively since modern times.
• Family resemblance: e.g., nonwillingness-willingness, naturalness-technologicalness, naturalness-nonnaturalness, inorganicness-volition, inorganicness-motivation, etc.
• Sources: Especially from *FAE*. See also other books of mine.

(*continued on next page*)

Table 4.4. The Syntax of Existential Dialectics I: The Principles (Part XII)

- **In Relation to Agency *(cont'd)***
  —*The Convention-Novelty Principle*
  (On the Nature of Creative Thinking)
  - If there is conventional wisdom, there is likewise novel challenge, to the extent that both convergent and divergent thinking are part of life. There is no convention without novelty—and vice versa.
  - In addition, in this context of the convention-novelty principle, there are, in the absence of better words, what I want to call (a) *creative techniques* and (b) *creative traits*, which, when satisfied—in relation to the larger context of the mind, nature, society, and culture—can be used to enhance creative works. The list of creative techniques and traits (as summarized in *Table 4.1* of *FPHCT*) are not exhaustive, of course, but the examples here constitute a great beginning of understanding the structure of creative thinking.
  - Yet, lest the reader gets carried away by the euphoria about creative thinking in our time, it should be reminded that creative thinking has its own possibilities and limits (as shown in *Table 2.1* of *FPHCT* on invention), just as it has its own promises and pitfalls (as shown in *Table 3.1* of *FPHCT* on innovation). In the end, it should also be stressed that creative thinking has its own desirability and dark sides (as shown in *Table 4.2* of *FPHCT*).
  - This has important daily implications for an average individual, and the word "average" here allows different degrees of variation from one individual to another in a population, at any given point in history.
  - Family resemblance: e.g., normalness-nonnormalness, conformity-nonconformity, convergence-divergence, etc.
  - Sources: First from *FPHCT*. See also my later books.

(*continued on next page*)

Table 4.4. The Syntax of Existential Dialectics I: The Principles (Part XIII)

- **In Relation to Agency** ***(cont'd)***
  - *—The Seriousness-Playfulness Principle*
    (On the Extent of Seriousness)
    - If there is seriousness, there is also playfulness, especially for any agent with some kind of intelligence life, be it about humans, animals, or, later, post-humans. There is no seriousness without playfulness—and vice versa.
    - Lest any misunderstanding occurs, the word "playfulness" here should not be confused with other terms like "laughter," "smile," "joke," "tickleness," and "laugh-like vocalization" (in some animals), for instance.
    - Being playful can come in all shapes and sizes and therefore is not necessarily tied up with any of these terms, alhough it can result from any of them, or a combination of them, or something else altogether.
    - This principle, together with some other principles (especially though not exclusively, like the formalness-informalness principle), have important implications for what constitutes rationality, be it about "rationality of application" at the practical level or "rationality of knowledge" at the meta-theoretical level (as summarized in *Sec. 4.20* of *FPHH*).
    - Family resemblance: e.g., seriousness-jokingness, seriousness-humorousness, seriousness-wittiness, seriousness-nonseriousness, etc.
    - Sources: First from *FPHH*. See also my later books.

(*continued on next page*)

Table 4.4. The Syntax of Existential Dialectics I: The Principles (Part XIV)

- **In Relation to Outcome**
  —*The Regression-Progression Principle*
  (On the Direction of History)
  - Neither the cyclical nor the linear views are adequate for explaining many phenomena at all levels. There is regression without progression—and vice versa.
  - History progresses to more advanced forms, but with a regressive touch. Examples include no freedom without unfreedom, no equality without inequality, and no civilization without barbarity.
  - This is not an inevitable law, but merely a highly likely empirical trend.
  - Family resemblance: e.g., cost-benefit, undesirability-desirability, badness-goodness, risk-opportunity, etc.
  - Sources: From all my books, starting with *FHC*. First named in *BCPC*.

  —*The Same-Difference Principle*
  (On the Metamorphosis of Change)
  - An entity, as it evolves over time, can be both different from and similar to its opposing alternatives and does not have to be solely more different from them over time. There is no similarity without difference—and vice versa.
  - Opposites are not absolute in a black-or-white fashion; so, an entity can become relatively more similar to (or more different from) its opposite over time.
  - Family resemblance: e.g., homogeneity-heterogeneity, we-they, etc.
  - Sources: Especially from ALD. See also my later books.

Notes: The features in each principle are solely illustrative (not exhaustive). The comparison is also relative (not absolute), nor are they mutually exclusive. As generalities, they allow exceptions.

Table 4.5. The Syntax of Existential Dialectics II: The Principles as Short Cuts (Part I)

• The principles should be treated with caution, lest misunderstanding occurs, since they do not constitute rigid dualities (or dichotomies).

• The reason is that each pair in an ontological principle consists of two opposites, which are, however, merely short cuts both for multiple variations and degrees, as well as for different interactions with multiple other entities unlike them. In this light, each pair can end up having hundred (or even thousand, if not more) different versions, which interact with hundred (or even thousand, if not more) other entities. There are two clarifications here.

• Firstly, this conception of shortcuts is not mutually exclusive nor absolute, in that the opposites can come in all shapes and sizes, with different degrees. For instance, by analogy, just as there are different degrees of the two colors "white" and "black"—there are likewise different degrees of the opposites in each ontological pair, to the extent that there can be multiple entities (not only two) interacting with each other in each pair.

• And secondly, this conception of shortcuts do not ignore other possible entities in interacting with the two opposites (with their different versions) in each pair. For instance, by analogy, there are not only the two colors "white" and "black" as opposites, since there are other colors too besides them like "yellow," "green," "purple," or else. The same logic can be applied to each ontological pair, in that they also interact with other entities, not with only two of them (with their different versions).

• Therefore, with these two clarifications in mind—each pair in an ontological principle serves only as an abbreviation for something more complicated and, therefore, although it contains two opposites, it should not be confused as a duality (dualism).

(continued on next page)

Table 4.5. The Syntax of Existential Dialectics II: The Principles as Short Cuts (Part II)

• Existential dialectics rejects any dualism (or dichotomy) as too rigid and instead allows the multiplicity of entities, to the extent that between the two opposites in each pair exist many other alternatives to choose from. They are named in that short form for aesthetic elegance, instead of listing all possible entities between the two opposites in the title.

• To be dialectic is to go beyond any rigid dichotomy and transcend into something different altogether in the long haul. One may be tempted to call the dialectic logic here with a different name like existential "multilectics" (instead of "dialectics"), but this naming is incorrect (or even misleading), for the two reasons aforestated.

• After all, each ontological pair come in all shapes and sizes (with different degrees) and do not exist by themselves but also interact with other entities unlike them. The virtue of revealing an ontological pair is to show how they relate within themselves (in multiple versions) and also interact with others unlike them (also in multiple versions).

• This will be clear in the table on "the dialectic constraints imposed by the principles."

Source: From Ch.1 of *FPHK*

Table 4.6. The Syntax of Existential Dialectics III: The Principles as Family Resemblances

• Each ontological principle is generic, with some other comparable ontological pairs to be put in the same family (like a *family resemblance*). Ludwig Wittgenstein (1953) once suggested the idea of "family resemblance" in explaining different games classified under the same family called *games*.

• Why should, for instance, playing football and chess as playing "games," when it is well understood that football is not the same as chess? The answer is that, although each game is different and has different rules, many of them (though not all) share, more or less, some commonalites (e.g., scoring as necessary for winning).

• And this is so, even though some games share more than some others in any given selection of critieria, and no two games are exactly identical. So, his point here is that there is no essential core which is common to all games, and the best that one can look for is some characteristics which are common to many (but not all) games. (A. Biletzki 2006)

• By the same logic—in the previous section on selection criteria, the flexibility-inflexibility pair can be put in the family resemblance of the simpleness-complicatedness principle, although the two pairs are not exactly identical. Likewise, the directness-indirectness pair can be put in the family resemblance of the preciseness-vagueness principle, although, again, the two pairs are not exactly identical.

• In this sense, which specific pair in a family should be used to designate the name of the family can be at times a bit arbitrary, but with good reason.

• For illustration, in the context of method, the partiality-totality principle can take the different form like individualisticness-holisticness, just as the explicability-inexplicability principle can take the different form like underlyingness-regularness—although each two pairs are not exactly identical and have slightly different meanings and usages. A more comprehensive listing of this family resemblance for all other principles is shown in the table on the syntax of existential dialectics.

Source: From Ch.1 of *FPHK*

Table 4.7. The Syntax of Existential Dialectics IV: The Dialectic Constraints Imposed by the Principles (Part I)

- **Co-Existent and Asymmetric**
  - —The principles, as they constitute the syntax of existential dialectics, are dialectic in character, such that, when they are applied, they impose dialectic constraints on how reality is to be understood. Consider, say, the symmetry-asymmetry principle as an illustration here, in order to summarize two main characters of the dialectic constraints in question.
  - —Firstly, to be dialectic here is to go beyond the narrow dichotomies (and, for that matter, any rigid multi-dimensional classificatory scheme), be they about "self" vs. "world," "freedom" vs. "unfreedom," "barbarity" vs. "civilization," "individuality" vs. "communality," and so on.
  - —One way to do so (to go beyond) is to consider them all in terms of co-existence (without favoring one over the rest). For instance, my theory of "post-civilization" (to be summarized later in the section on the pragmatics of existential dialectics) is to go beyond barbarity and civilization in terms of understanding barbarity and civilization as being co-existent. And the same logic can be said in relation to my theories of "post-democracy," "post-capitalsm," and others (also to be introduced later in the section on the pragmatics of existential dialectics), in regard to freedom vs. unfreedom, equality vs. inequality, communality vs. individuality, spirituality vs. materiality, and so on.
  - —But to consider them all (in the dichotomies—and, for that matter, in any rigid multi-dimensional classifactory schme) as co-existent is not the same as to imply that the opposites in any classificatory scheme are all equal, since, in accordance to the symmetry-asymmetry principle (as an illustration here), if they are equal in terms of being considered as co-existent, they are asymmetric in terms of being unequal in dialectic interaction (e.g., X can be more dominant than Y in case A, or Y is more dominant than X in case B).

(continued on next page)

Table 4.7. The Syntax of Existential Dialectics IV: The Dialectic Constraints Imposed by the Principles (Part II)

—For this reason, there are different versions of "post-democracy" and "post-capitalism" in my theories. As an illustration, in version I of the theory of post-democracy, freedom is more dominant than equality, whereas in version II of the theory of post-democracy, equality is more so than freedom.

—But this "X more than Y" has to be understood in the context of dialectic logic (not in conventional logic), in that both "X" and "Y" are important in post-democracy (in the context of dialectic logic), but in an asymmetry way. By contrast, in conventional logic, it often favors one over the other—be it in regard to privileging freedom over equality in Fascism, favoring freedom relatively more than equality in Liberal Democracy, or favoring equality relatively more than freedom in Socialist Democracy. In the latter two cases (about Liberal Democracy and Socialist Democracy), the difference between dialectic logic and conventional logic can be one in degree, not in kind—in this sense, albeit not in other senses.

—The same logic can be said about the relatonships between individuality and communality, between spirituality and materiality, and between formal legalism and informal legalism in the different versions of my theory of post-capitalism.

• **Transcendent**

—Secondly, to be dialectic is to go beyond the narrow dichotomies (and, for that matter, any rigid multi-dimensional classificatory scheme) in another way, this time, in a transcendent way, that is, in exploring other possibilities or even other issues not considered within the narrow confines of narrow dichotomies (and, for that matter, any rigid multi-dimensional classificatory scheme).

(continued on next page)

Table 4.7. The Syntax of Existential Dialectics IV: The Dialectic Constraints Imposed by the Principles (Part III)

—As an analogy, to go beyond the narrow color dichotomy of "black" and "white" is not just to choose both "black" and "white" (as in the first meaning) but also to explore other color options (e.g., "green," "purple," "blue," etc.—and, alternatively, "shade," "line," "curve," etc.). By the same logic, to go beyond "democracy" is to transcend democracy (as in version III of the theory of "post-democracy") and to explore other possibilties of lifeforms (e.g., floating consciousness, hyper-spatial consciousness, etc., to live beyond the narrow obsession with freedom and equality).

—This dialectic character of the principles in existential dialectics has important implications for the pragmatics of existential dialectics (as will be clear shortly, in the section on the pragmatics of existential dialectics).

Notes: The examples here are solely illustrative (not exhaustive). The comparison is also relative (not absolute), nor are they mutually exclusive. As generalities, they allow exceptions.
Sources: First explicitly stated in *ALD*. Also from all other books of mine.

Table 4.8. The Syntax of Existential Dialectics V: Further Clarifications (Part I)

• **Pioneering**

—Firstly, the total number of ontological principles is unknown, to be discovered later, as our knowledge of the world becomes more advanced.

—Consequently, the principles as introduced in my books are not exhaustive, with new ones being added, whenever more of them are discovered in later research.

—At least, future generations can pick up where I leave off and continue the discovery.

—In this sense, my work should be treated as a pioneering effort for the development of a systematic, comprehensive analysis of a new general ontology for the future of knowledge.

• **Flexible**

—Secondly, the principles are not rigidly classified, as they can be reclassified in a different way.

—For instance, the preciseness-vagueness principle is classified under the category of "structure" but can be reclassified under the category of "method," although in so doing, it has a different meaning in the context of method.

—The same logic applies to the same-difference principle under the category of "outcome," which can be reclassified under the category of "structure," although in so doing, once more, it has a different meaning in the context of structure.

• **Mutually Constraining**

—Thirdly, the principles are to be understood together, not that each prinicple is to be analyzed independently of others. After all, the principles are mutually constraining, in that they work together as a whole.

(continued on next page)

Table 4.8. The Syntax of Existential Dialectics V: Further Clarifications (Part II)

- **Selectively Useful**
  —Fourthly, the principles are relevant to all subject matters, but some principles are more useful to some subject matters than others—as implied in the symmetry-asymmetry principle. This is true, even if different studies of the same kind can yield different views about the degree of relevance for each ontological principle, depending on the specific nature of a research in question, needless to say.

- **Anti-Reductionistic**
  —And fifthly, the principles constitute only two levels of analysis, this time, at the ontological and methodological levels—while other levels of analysis (from the perspectives of the mind, nature, society, and culture) are also needed, in order to understand reality in its totality (as explained in the section on "sophisticated methodological holism," so as to avoid the dual dangers of reductionism and reverse-reductionism).

Notes: The examples here are solely illustrative (not exhaustive). The comparison is also relative (not absolute), nor are they mutually exclusive. As generalities, they allow exceptions.
Sources: From my previous books like *FHC*, *FCD*, *FPHC*, *BDPD*, *BCPC*, *BNN*, *FC*, *FAE*, and so on.

Table 4.9. The Syntax of Existential Dialectics VI: The Dilemma of Specific vs. General Ontology (Part I)

• Ontology is often more complicated and imposes some seemingly insurmountable difficulties concerning what constitutes a kind of ontology which can be valid enough to be accepted by the wider intellectual community in question. An excellent example concerns what I want to call *the dilemma of ontology* in relation to the relationship between "specific ontology" and "general ontology." (M. Bunge 1999; R. Corazzon 2007)

• On the one hand, "general ontology," as Mario Bunge (1999) put it, "studies all existents." But, on the other hand, "special ontology studies one genus of thing or process—physical, chemical, biological, social, etc." (M. Bunge 1999; R. Corazzon 2007)

• Consequently, the relationship between the former and the latter is that, as an illustration, "whereas general ontology studies the concepts of space, time, and event, the ontology of the social investigates such general sociological concepts as those of social system, social structure, and social change." (M. Bunge 1999; R. Corazzon 2007)

• With this formal definition in mind, the relationship between the two forms of ontology only poses *the dilemma of ontology*, in that general ontology is possible to the extent that its general contructs must be broad enough to serve as the "lowest common denominator" for all disciplines, but this character of the lowest common denominator is not only hard to find but also its usefulness is limited. (WK 2008b)

• But specific ontology fares no better either, in that its specific constructs primarily serve a specific discipline in question, although other disciplines can appropriate them for their own purposes, but in a different context (especially, though not exclusively, when used as a metaphor from one field to another). For instance, the Kantian category of understanding under the heading of "quantity" constitutes a type of specific ontology, which is specific to the discipline of mathematics, although other disciplines can make use of the categories in their own context.

(continued on next page)

Table 4.9. The Syntax of Existential Dialectics VI: The Dilemma of Specific vs. General Ontology (Part II)

• A solution lies in my proposal of "sophisticated methodological holism," which requires all levels of analysis in any subject matter. See the tables on sophisticated methodological holism, and on reductionism and reverse-reductionism, for more details.

Source: From *Sec. 1.4* of *FPHK*

Table 4.10. The Syntax of Existential Dialectics VII: Types of Inappropriate Family Resemblances

- **Inadequate Family Resemblances**
  —Ex: consistency-inconsistency: the formalness-informalenss principle
  —Ex: cognition-noncognition: the formalness-informalness principle

- **Compound Family Resemblances**
  —Ex: reality-nonreality: the formalness-informalness principles, the absoluteness-relativeness principle
  —Ex: normality-abnormality: the symmetry-asymmetry principle, the density-emptiness principle, the convention-novelty principle, the same-difference principle
  —Ex: structure-context: the simpleness-complicatedness principle, the theory-praxis principle
  —Ex: freedom-unfreedom: the symmetry-asymmetry principle, the expansion-contraction principle
  —Ex: morality-immorality: the denseness-emptiness principle, the symmetry-asymmetry, the same-difference principle
  —Ex: particularness-universalness: the preciseness-vagueness principle, the simpleness-complicatedness principle
  —Ex: pureness-mixedness: the absoluteness-relativeness principle, the simpleness-complicatedness principle, the same-difference principle
  —Ex: shortsightedness-foresightedness: the partiality-totality principle, the simpleness-complicatedness principle
  —Ex: shorttermness-longtermness: the partiality-totality principle, the simpleness-complicatedness principle, the slowness-quickness principle

Notes: The examples here are solely illustrative (not exhaustive). The comparison is also relative (not absolute), nor are they mutually exclusive. As generalities, they allow exceptions.
Source: First summarized in *BEPE* (and updated in later books)

Table 4.11. The Semantics of Existential Dialectics

- **Abstract Structure vs. Specific Meanings**
  —The syntax of existential dialectics so understood in terms of ontological principles only gives us the structure of ontology in the world, in an abstract (general) sense. These principles by themselves do not tell us the specific meanings in a given context.
  —In order to grasp the specific meanings of the principles in a given context, it is necessary to study the semantics of existential dialectics. And the analysis of the ontological principles as family resemblances in the section on syntax is only a starting point (and thus overlaps a bit with the semantics of existential dialectics here).
  —With this caveat in mind, the reason that I have often gone in great lengths in my previous books on different subjects is to explain the specific meanings of the principles when applied in different contexts.

- **Specific Meanings in Specific Fields**
  —For instance, in *FPHST*, I used the first three principles (i.e., the change-constancy principle, the regression-progression principle, and the symmetry-asymmetry principle) to propose "the perspectival theory of space-time," for a better way to understand space and time—especially, though not exclusively, in relation to future post-human history (as summarized in *Table 3.6*, *Table 3.7*, *Table 3.8*, and *Table 3.9*). In so doing, I had to introduce concepts and theories specific to the field of physics and other related fields (e.g., "absolute space" and "absolute time" in "classical mechanics" and "relative space-time" in "the theory of relativity").
  —In *BNN*, I also exploited the three principles to propose the "transcendent" approach to the study of genes and memes as a new way to understand the interaction between nature and nurture. In so doing, I had to explore concepts and theories in the world of evolutionary theory (e.g., "mutation," "variation," "adaptation," "selection," and "inheritance" in Darwinian evolutionary theory) and neural biology (e.g., "chromosome," "gene," "DNA," "RNA," "protein," "neuron," "neural network," and "behavior").

Notes: The categories and examples in each are solely illustrative (not exhaustive). The comparison is also relative (not absolute), nor are they mutually exclusive. As generalities, they allow exceptions.
Sources: First explicitly stated in *ALD*. Also from all other books of mine.

Table 4.12. The Pragmatics of Existential Dialectics (Part I)

- **The Two-Way Street Connecting Theory and Meta-Theory**
  - —The pragmatics of existential dialectics is not a one-way street (that is, using the ontological principles for theoretical insights in praxis) but a two-way one, that is, (a) from meta-theory to theory, and (b) from theory to meta-theory.
  - —(a) On one side of the street, the ontological principles can inspire some theoretical insights in praxis, that is, in relation to some specific fields.
  - —(b) On the other (opposing) side of the street, however, the study of a subject matter in the specific fields in turn reveals some more hitherto unknown ontological principles to be discovered and identified. For this reason, three new principles were added in *FC*, one in *FAE*, and two in *ALD*, on top of the original three in *BCPC*—after some research on the specific subject matters.

- **Direct and Indirect Applications**
  - —*Direct*
    - The logic of existential dialectics can shed some theoretical insights on diverse phenomena in the world, and good instances are the pertinent use of the principles of existential dialectics for the theoretical insights on the freedom/unfreedom dialectics, the equality/inequality dialectics, and the wealth/poverty dialectics in my previous works.
    - My latest books like *FPHST* and *BNN* also use the principles to reveal some theoretical insights on the perspectives of space and time (as in *FPHST*) and of nature and nurture (as in *BNN*).
  - —*Indirect*
    - The theoretical insights can further be used to reveal other phenomena directly from them (viz., the theoretical insights) and therefore indirectly from the principles themselves. A good instance is the use of the theoretical insights on the freedom/unfreedom and equality/inequality dialectics for the understanding of the civilization/barbarity dialectics.

(continued on next page)

Table 4.12. The Pragmatics of Existential Dialectics (Part II)

- **Direct and Indirect Applications (*cont'd*)**
  - Even in indirect applications, however, a phenomenon under study can still be directly related back to the principles themselves. In the example as cited above, the civilization/barbarity dialectics can be directly related to the principles of existential dialectics without the intermediate role of the freedom/unfreedom and equality/inequality dialectics.

- **Multiple Levels of Application**

  —The theoretical insights can be applied to different levels of analysis, even though in a given example, it may refer to one level only. For instance, in the example concerning the freedom/unfreedom dialectics, it can be used at the structural level (e.g., in relation to the theory of cyclical progression of hegemony), but it can be exploited as well for other levels (e.g., the theory of post-capitalism at the institutional level).

Notes: The categories and examples in each are solely illustrative (not exhaustive). The comparison is also relative (not absolute), nor are they mutually exclusive. As generalities, they allow exceptions.
Sources: From Ch.6 of *BCPC*. See also other books of mine.

Table 4.13. The Freedom-Unfreedom Dialectics (Part I)

• **On Having**

—*In Relation to the Technological*

(1) if freer from submission to Nature, then less free from ecological degradation (Deep and Social Ecology), even if in a hi-tech form

(2) if freer from technological inconvenience / backwardness, then less free from technological control and the loss of privacy

(3) if freer from technological (material) backwardness, then less free from the abusive (barbaric) maltreatment of the primitive Others

—*In Relation to the Everyday*

(1) if freer from abject poverty, then less free from artificial needs/discontents (Frankfurt School)

(2) if freer from sensual suppression, then less free from violent sublimation (Freud)

(3) if freer from the snobbishness of high culture, then less free from the shabbiness (leveling-off effect) of mass culture (Tocqueville)

(4) if freer from the inefficiency of traditional "compassionate economy," then less free from the bondage of a "ruthless [competitive] economy" (Keynes)

(5) if freer from anarchy in the state of nature (system fragmentation), then less free from government regulations and controls in system integration

---

(continued on next page)

Table 4.13. The Freedom-Unfreedom Dialectics (Part II)

• **On Belonging**

—*In Relation to the Good and the Just*

(1) if freer from disciplinary society, then less free from society of control (Foucault)

(2) if freer from the tyranny of one or a few, then less free from the tyranny of the majority (or sometimes, minority veto)

(3) if freer from elitist decision making, then less free from political gridlock/cleavage

(4) if freer from arbitrary (discretionary) administration, then less free from bureaucratic irrationality (Weber) and legal trickery (loopholes)

• **On Being**

—*In Relation to the True*

(1) if freer from unscientific dogmas, then less free from instrumental abyss (nihilism). Or conversely, if freer from meaninglessness, then less free from dogmas.

(2) if freer from the bondage of partiality/partisanship (e.g., prejudice, discrimination), then less free from the danger of impartiality and neutrality (e.g., opportunism, unrealisticness, lack of compassion, inaction)

(3) if freer from making generalizations, then less free from being unable to understand much of anything

—*In Relation to the Holy*

(1) if freer from collective conscience, then less free from social loneliness

(2) if freer from religious absoluteness, then less free from spiritual emptiness

—*In Relation to the Beautiful/Sublime*

(1) if freer from artistic non-autonomy, then less free from aesthetic disillusion (deconstruction)

(continued on next page)

Table 4.13. The Freedom-Unfreedom Dialectics (Part III)

Notes: The examples in each category are solely illustrative (not exhaustive), and the comparison is relative (not absolute), nor are they necessarily mutually exclusive. And some can be easily re-classified elsewhere. As generalities, they allow exceptions.
Sources: A reconstruction from Ch.10 of *FCD*, based on *FHC*

Table 4.14. The Equality-Inequality Dialectics (Part I)

• **On Having**

—*In Relation to the Technological*

(1) if more equal in treating Nature with spiritual unity, then less equal in suppressing the dominant drive to transcend it altogether

—*In Relation to the Everyday*

(1) if more equal in building social plurality, then less equal in leveling-off effects (e.g., the subsequent relative intolerance of high/intellectual ethos in mass culture industry)

(2) if more equal in socioeconomic distribution beyond a certain point, then less equal in efficiency (e.g. resentment, the erosion of work ethics)

(3) if more equal in urging an affirmative action program, then less equal in creating victim mentality (in oneself), stigma (from others), reverse discrimination (against the once privileged), and mediocracy (against the more able)

• **On Belonging**

—*In Relation to the Good and the Just*

(1) if more equal in banning monarchic/oligarchic exclusion, then less equal in producing "the tyranny of the majority" or of "minority veto"

(2) if more equal in encouraging participatory decision making, then less equal in inducing political divisiveness (gridlock/cleavage in power blocs) and organizational oligarchy

(3) if more equal in institutionalizing a decentralized bureaucracy, then less equal in falling into more territorial/turf politics (intrigues)

(continued on next page)

Table 4.14. The Equality-Inequality Dialectics (Part II)

- **On Being**
  - —In Relation to the Beautiful / Sublime
    - (1) if more equal in accepting diverse styles ("anything goes" mentality), then less equal in artistic good quality (in leveling-off effects against the best)
  - —In Relation to the True
    - (1) if more equal in tolerating multiple viewpoints (no matter how extreme), then less equal in epistemic standards
  - —In Relation to the Holy
    - (1) if more equal in celebrating any cults and sects (no matter how questionable), then less equal in spiritual depth and authenticity

Notes: The examples in each category are solely illustrative (not exhaustive), and the comparison is relative (not absolute), nor are they mutually exclusive. And some can be easily reclassified elsewhere. As generalities, they allow exceptions.
Sources: A reconstruction from Ch.10 of *FCD*, based on *FHC*

Table 4.15. The Duality of Oppression in Existential Dialectics: Oppression and Self-Oppression (Part I)

- **From the Same to the Others and Itself**
  - —The Oppression by the Same against the Others
    - *By way of downgrading differences*
      - –Ex: on judiciary caprice for corporate crimes (*Sec.2.2.1.2.1*)
      - –Ex: on the deceptive politics of liberation (*Sec.3.5*)
      - –Ex: on the humanitarian mystique (*Sec.4.4*)
      - –Ex: on the fad of emotional intelligence (*Sec.5.3*)
    - *By way of accentuating differences*
      - –Ex: on the legal sophistry of self-defense (*Sec.2.3*)
      - –Ex: on the legal semantics of proportionality (*Sec.2.4*)
      - –Ex: on the tricky politics of external threat (*Sec.3.4*)
      - –Ex: on the appeal of the Far Right for democracy (*Sec.5.4*)
      - –Ex: on the democratic axis of evil (*Sec.5.5*)
      - –Ex: on the democratic way of brutality and revenge (*Sec.5.6*)
      - –Ex: on democratic autocracy (*Sec.6.4*)
  - —The Oppression by the Same against Itself
    - *By way of downgrading differences*
      - –Ex: on the politics of fear (*Sec.2.2*)
      - –Ex: on the trickery of compassionate conservatism (*Sec.3.2*)
      - –Ex: on the deceptive politics of patriotism (*Sec.3.3*)
    - *By way of accentuating differences*
      - –Ex: on the caprice of due process on domestic suspects (*Sec.2.2*)
      - –Ex: on the false security/freedom dilemma (*Sec.6.5.2*)

(continued on next page)

Table 4.15. The Duality of Oppression in Existential Dialectics: Oppression and Self-Oppression (Part II)

- **From the Others to the Same and Themselves**
  —The Oppression by the Others against the Same
  - *By way of downgrading differences*
    –Ex: on judiciary caprice in the reverse direction (*Sec.2.2.1.2.2*)
    –Ex: on equal pay (*Sec.6.2.1.1*)
    –Ex: on equal representation (*Sec.6.2.1.2*)
    –Ex: on affirmative action program (*Sec.6.3.1.1*)
    –Ex: on same-sex marriage (*Sec.6.3.1.2*)
  - *By way of accentuating differences*
    –Ex: on sexual harassment (*Sec.6.2.2.1*)
    –Ex: on physical violence (*Sec.6.2.2.2*)
    –Ex: on sexual exploitation (*Sec.6.2.2.3*)

  —The Oppression by the Others against Themselves
  - *By way of downgrading differences*
    –Ex: on the reverse-class mystique (*Sec.4.2*)
    –Ex: on the reverse-black mystique (*Sec.4.3*)
    –Ex: on self-discrimination by downgrading (*Sec.6.3.2.2*)
  - *By way of accentuating differences*
    –Ex: on self-discrimination by accentuating (*Sec.6.3.2.1*)

Notes: The examples are solely illustrative (not exhaustive), nor are they mutually exclusive. As generalities, they allow exceptions. Also, both forms of oppression co-exist in all of the examples, so the listing of them are only meant in a relative, not absolute, sense.
Source: A summary of the sections (as cited) in Chs.2-6 of *BDPD*. See text for more info and references.

Table 4.16. The Structure of Existential Dialectics I: The Freedom/Unfreedom and Equality/Inequality Dialectics

---

• Each freedom and equality produces its own unfreedom and inequality, regardless of whether the pair occurs in political society (with the nation-state), in civil society (with some autonomy from the state), or elsewhere (e.g., in the private sphere of individual homes)—and regardless of whether freedom and equality are understood as "negative" or "positive."

• Oppression is dualistic, as much by the Same against the Others and itself, as by the Others against the Same and themselves.

• Both forms of oppression and self-oppression can be achieved by way of downgrading differences (between the Same and the Others) and of accentuating them.

• The relationships are relatively asymmetric between the Same and the Others and relatively symmetric within them. This is true, even when the Same can be relatively asymmetric towards itself in self-oppression, just as the Others can be likewise towards themselves.

• Symmetry and asymmetry change over time, with ever new players, new causes, and new forms.

Notes: The examples in each category are solely illustrative (not exhaustive) nor necessarily mutually exclusive, and the comparison is relative (not absolute). As generalities, they allow exceptions. "Negative" freedom is freedom "from" (e.g., freedom from poverty), whereas "positive" freedom is freedom "to" (e.g., freedom to the state of enlightenment). "Negative" equality is "procedural" equality (e.g., equality of opportunity), while "positive" equality is "substantive" equality (e.g., equality of outcome). Existential dialectics impose constraints on freedom and equality in democracy, non-democracy, and post-democracy. There is no utopia, in the end; even should there be one, dystopia would exist within it.
Sources: From *Table 1.5* of *BDPD*—and also from *FHC*, *FCD*, and *FPHC*

Table 4.17. The Structure of Existential Dialectics II: The Wealth/Poverty Dialectics

• There is no wealth without poverty, just as there is no poverty without wealth.

• The wealth/poverty dialectics occurs in the realms of having, belonging, and being, in relation to the material, relational, and spiritual.

• The wealth/poverty dialectics also expresses itself at the multiple levels of analysis in accordance to methodological holism, be they about the micro-physical, the chemical, the biological, the psychological, the organizational, the institutional, the structural, the systemic, the cultural, and the cosmological.

• The wealth/poverty dialectics is a different manifestation of existential dialectics in general, subject to the principles in its logic of ontology—just as the freedom/unfreedom and equality/inequality dialectics are likewise.

• There is no economic utopia, in the end; even should there be one, dystopia would exist within it.

Notes: The main points here are solely illustrative (not exhaustive) nor necessarily mutually exclusive, and the comparison is relative (not absolute). As generalities, they allow exceptions.
Sources: From *BCPC*. See also *FCD* and *FHC*.

Table 4.18. The Structure of Existential Dialectics III: The Civilization/Barbarity Dialectics

---

• There is no civilization without barbarity.

• The civilization/barbarity dialectics applies in the four civilizing processes (e.g., the rationalizing process, the pacifying process, the stewardizing process, and the subliming process).

• The civilization/barbarity dialectics is another (different) manifestation of existential dialectics in general, subject to the principles in its logic of ontology—just as the freedom/unfreedom and equality/inequality dialectics and the wealth/poverty dialectics are likewise.

• There is no utopia, in the end; even should there be one, dystopia would exist within it.

Notes: The main points here are solely illustrative (not exhaustive) nor necessarily mutually exclusive, and the comparison is relative (not absolute). As generalities, they allow exceptions.
Sources: From *BCIV*. See also *FCD*, *FHC*, and *BDPD*.

Table 4.19. The Double Sides of Virtual Organizations (Part I)

- **Psychological**
  —Ex: virtual psychosis
  —Ex: impersonality and loneliness in quaternary social relations

- **Organizational**
  —Ex: the race for power and interests
  —Ex: the world of unequal successes
  —Ex: the bureaucratic life of its own
  —Ex: lesser accountability and transparency

- **Economic**
  —Ex: the economic divides
  —Ex: the erosive impact of commercialization

- **Political**
  —Ex: the anti-authoritarian myth
  —Ex: different power struggles among groups (e.g., Conservative, Reformist, Radical)

- **Structural**
  —Ex: different localities (e.g., climates, scenery)
  —Ex: divided domains (e.g., core, peripheral, sub-peripheral)
  —Ex: substitution effect of social capital

- **Systemic**
  —Ex: uneven advances in transportation and communications, and geographical migration

- **Cultural**
  —Ex: conflicting civilizational fabrics (e.g., Confucian, Islamic, Western)
  —Ex: the bias of the Liberal Democratic agenda
  —Ex: the addiction to moral fanaticism

(continued on next page)

Table 4.19. The Double Sides of Virtual Organizations (Part II)

Notes: These categories and examples are solely illustrative (not exhaustive), and some of the items can be reclassified somewhere else. Nor are they mutually exclusive. Since they are generalities, exceptions are expected.
Source: From Ch.7 of *FCD*

Table 4.20. Beyond the World of Titans, and the Remaking of the World Order

- **Hyper-Empires**
  - —Ex: The Chinese Union
  - —Ex: The Indian Union

- **Meso-Empires**
  - —Ex: The European Union
  - —Ex: The North American Union

- **Micro-Empires**
  - —Ex: The Latin American Union
  - —Ex: The Middle Eastern Union

- **The Rest of the World**
  - —<u>Odd Powers</u>
    - Ex: Japan
    - Ex: Russia
  - —<u>The Poor Club</u>
    - Ex: The African Union
  - —<u>Ambivalent Regions</u>
    - Ex: Southeast Asia
    - Ex: Oceania
    - Ex: South Asia
    - Ex: Central Asia
    - Ex: Southern/Eastern Europe
    - Ex: North Africa
    - Ex: Central America
    - Ex: Others (e.g., the Korean peninsula)

Source: A summary of Chs.2-5 (of *BWT*)

Table 4.21. The Origins of Authoritarian Liberal Democracy

- **The Geopower of Nature (Ch.4 of *ALD*)**
  —Ex: Power Character and Geographical Strategy
  —Ex: Living Space and Territorial Expansion
  —Ex: Strategic Heartland and Containment

- **The Biopsychology of the Mind (Ch.5 of *ALD*)**
  —Ex: The Bell Curve and Mass Intelligence
  —Ex: Group Analysis and Mass Knowledge
  —Ex: Groupthink and Elite (Mis)calculation

- **The Disciplinary Control of Society (Ch.6 of *ALD*)**
  —Ex: Social Organizations of Ruthlessness
  —Ex: Social Institutions of Greed
  —Ex: Social Structure of Exclusion
  —Ex: Social Systems of Violence

- **The Molding Force of Culture (Ch.7 of *ALD*)**
  —Ex: The Tradition of Conquest
  —Ex: The Rationalization of Unreason

Notes: The examples in each category are solely illustrative (not exhaustive), and they are also relative (not absolute), nor are they mutually exclusive. As generalities, they allow exceptions.
Source: A summary of Chs.4-7 of *ALD*

Table 4.22. The Theory of Post-Democracy I: The Priority of Freedom over Equality (Part I)

- **Differences**
  - *For the aggressive Lions (the strong Elitists)*
    - Setting up rank distinctions among unequals (e.g., between inferior humans and superior post-humans, or later among inferior post-humans and superior ones, relatively speaking)
    - Yearning for being not only distinguished from unequals, but also the first among equals (the best of the very best)
    - Soul-searching for a high spiritual culture (not the trashy one for the masses). Mass culture is a dirty joke for them.
  - *For the manipulative Foxes (the weak Counter-Elitists)*
    - Seeking a gentle hegemony by way of more communitarian concerns (for inferior humans and, later, inferior post-humans)
    - Being more sympathetic to less formal-legalistic institutions and values

- **Similarities**
  - *For both Lions and Foxes*
    - Exploring different spheres of non-human consciousness in the cosmos (something vastly superior than the human one)
    - Recognizing the democratic illusions (e.g., no freedom without unfreedom, no equality without inequality, or simply no justice without injustice, and vice versa)

(continued on next page)

Table 4.22. The Theory of Post-Democracy I: The Priority of Freedom over Equality (Part II)

Notes: The two callings and examples in each category are solely illustrative (not exhaustive), since there will be many different post-human value ideals in the distant future of post-human civilization. The comparison is also relative (not absolute) towards post-democracy, so this is not just a version of free-market democracy (nor Fascism/Nazism, as shown in the table later on democracy, non-democracy, and post-democracy). Nor are they mutually exclusive. As generalities, they allow exceptions. And the specific forms of post-human post-democratic ideals need to be further developed in future after-postmodern history, as they will be different from the ones we now know. The point here is to solely give an extremely rough picture of a small part of the world to come that we have never known.
Source: From Ch.10 of *FCD*. Refer to text for more info and references.

Table 4.23. The Theory of Post-Democracy II: The Priority of Equality over Freedom

- **Hybrid Versions of**
  —Ex: the Trans-Feminine Calling
  —Ex: the Trans-Sinitic Calling
  —Ex: the Trans-Islamic Calling
  —Ex: the Trans-Outerspace Calling

- **Qualifications**
  —These four versions of post-capitalist value ideals need not automatically be post-democratic, just as capitalism does not necessarily mean democracy. They are two different entities—though closely related.
  —But up to a certain threshold of elevating equality at the farther expense of freedom, the democratic ideals will be overcome and cease to exist.
  —The overcome will not be socialist or communist, but post-democratic with no freedom without unfreedom and no equality without inequality, subject to the constraints of existential dialectics.

Notes: The callings are solely illustrative (not exhaustive), since there will be many different post-human value ideals in the distant future of post-human lifeforms. The comparison is also relative (not absolute), nor are they mutually exclusive. As generalities, they allow exceptions. And the specific forms of post-human post-democratic ideals need to be further developed in future after-postmodern history, as they will be different from the ones we now know. The point here is to solely give an extremely rough picture of a small part of the world to come that we have never known.
Source: From Ch.10 of *FCD*. Refer to text for more info and references.

Table 4.24. The Theory of Post-Democracy III: The Transcendence of Freedom and Equality (Part I)

- **Transcending Freedom in Floating Existence**
  - —*Freedom*: seeking an ultimate elimination of the body. Being without the body. The aim is to transcend freedom in the end into a metaphysical state (i.e., beyond the physique).
  - —*Unfreedom*: yet facing difficult trade-offs. The sacrifice of bodily existence and its joyfulness. An eternal boredom in floating existence in dark deep space, though with alternative pleasures. There is no free lunch even in the state of transcending freedom.

- **Transcending Equality in the Rivalry of Cosmic Hegemony**
  - —*Inequality*: competing to outlast other lifeforms in floating existence, or just marginalizing them for one's hegemonic expansiveness in the rest of the cosmos (and even beyond). Universalism is only for the mediocre.
  - —*Equality*: accepting only those of one's rank as equal partners in the vast spacetime for cosmic supremacy. Even here, the aim is to transcend equality into a metaphysical state.

(continued on next page)

Table 4.24. The Theory of Post-Democracy III: The Transcendence of Freedom and Equality (Part II)

Notes: Do not confuse this transcendence of freedom and equality (as one version of post-democracy) with the naïve temptation to transcend the freedom/unfreedom and equality/inequality dialectics. Existential dialectics hold true for freedom and equality in all cultures and societies—past, present, or future (i.e., democracy, non-democracy, and post-democracy), regardless of whether freedom and equality are conventionally understood as "negative" or "positive."
Also, the two features and examples in each are solely illustrative (not exhaustive), since there will be many different post-human value ideals in the distant future of post-human lifeforms. The comparison is also relative (not absolute), nor are they mutually exclusive. As generalities, they allow exceptions. And the specific forms of post-human ideals even for these radically alien floating lifeforms (and others unknown to us) need to be further developed in future after-postmodern history, as they will likely be different from the ones herein illustrated. The point here is to solely give a very rough picture of a small part of the extremely alien world to come that we have never known.
Source: From Ch.10 of *FCD*. Refer to text for more info and references.

Table 4.25. Democracy, Non-Democracy, and Post-Democracy (Part I)

- **Democracy**
  - —*Theoretical Constructs*
    - •The pursuit of freedom and equality (in various degrees), regardless of whether freedom and equality can be understood as "negative" or "positive"
      - (1) more equality than freedom: The relative priority of the good over the right
      - (2) more freedom than equality: The relative priority of the right over the good
  - —*Types*
    - •Only (1): Different versions of communitarian moral universalism
    - •Only (2): Different versions of liberal moral universalism
    - •(1) or (2): Different versions of anarchic (non-nation-state) moral universalism
    - •(1) or (2): Different versions of postmodern moral localism

- **Non-Democracy**
  - —*Theoretical Constructs*
    - •The focus on (1') equality or (2') freedom, but not both, regardless of whether freedom and equality can be understood as "negative" or "positive"
  - —*Types*
    - •Only (1'): Different versions on the Far Left (e.g., Stalinism, Robespierrianism)
    - •Only (2'): Different versions on the Far Right (e.g., Nazism, absolute monarchism)

(continued on next page)

Table 4.25. Democracy, Non-Democracy, and Post-Democracy (Part II)

- **Post-Democracy**
  - *—Theoretical Constructs*
    - •The priority of (1'') equality over freedom, or (2'') freedom over equality, or (3'') the transcendence of freedom and equality, regardless of whether freedom and equality are "negative" or "positive." In degree, (1'') or (2'') is less than (1') or (2') but more than (1) or (2)—respectively.
    - •Like democracy and non-democracy, post-democracy is also subject to the freedom/unfreedom and equality/inequality dialectics (or existential dialectics in general). Unlike them, post-democracy acknowledges the constraints of existential dialectics and no longer value freedom and equality as sacred virtues. There is no utopia, in the end; even were there one, dystopia would exist within it.
  - *—Types*
    - •(1''): Different versions of trans-Sinitic value ideals
    - •(1''): Different versions of trans-feminine value ideals
    - •(1''): Different versions of trans-Islamic value ideals
    - •(1''): Different versions of trans-outerspace value ideals
    - •(2''): Different versions of post-human elitist value ideals
    - •(3''): Different versions of the value ideals of floating consciousness (etc.)

(continued on next page)

Table 4.25. Democracy, Non-Democracy, and Post-Democracy (Part III)

Notes: The examples are solely illustrative (not exhaustive), nor are they mutually exclusive. As generalities, they allow exceptions. "Negative" freedom is freedom "from" (e.g., freedom from poverty), whereas "positive" freedom is freedom "to" (e.g., freedom to the state of enlightenment). "Negative" equality is "procedural" equality (e.g., equality of opportunity), while "positive" equality is "substantive" equality (e.g., equality of outcome). Existential dialectics impose constraints on freedom and equality in democracy, non-democracy, and post-democracy, regardless of whether freedom and equality can be understood as "negative" or "positive" in conventional discourse. Therefore, do not confuse the transcendence of freedom and equality in (3'') with the naïve temptation to transcend existential dialectics. There is no utopia, in the end; even should there be one, it would not exist without dystopia embedded within it.
Sources: A summary, based on my previous works, especially Ch.5 of *FHC*, Chs.5-10 of *FCD*, Chs.2-4 of *FPHC*, and Chs.1 & 7 of *BDPD*. The reader should consult the books for more analysis, as this is only a summary here.

Table 4.26. Multiple Causes of the Emergence of Post-Democracy (Part I)

• **At the Micro-Physical Level**
—Ex: intelligent life without the human physical-chemical system
—Sources: Ch.7 of *FHC*; Chs.9-10 of *FCD*; Ch.1 of *FPHC*

• **At the Chemical Level**
—Ex: space radiation and toxins
—Sources: Ch.7 of *FHC*; Chs.9-10 of *FCD*

• **At the Bio-Psychological Level**
—Ex: exo-biological evolution in deep space
—Ex: genetic engineering of new beings
—Ex: limits of cognitive partiality
—Ex: illusions of emotional neutrality
—Ex: human biological inequality
—Ex: the rise of unfolding unconsciousness
—Sources: Ch.2 & Chs.9-10 of *FCD*; Ch.7 of *FHC*; Ch.4 of *BCPC*; *FPHU*

• **At the Institutional Level**
—Ex: the flawed logic of equality
—Ex: the conflicting nature of governance
—Sources: Ch. 5 of *FHC*; Chs. 6 & 10 of *FCD*; Ch. 3 of *FPHC*; Chs.2-5 of *BDPD*

• **At the Organizational Level**
—Ex: e-civic alienation
—Ex: the dark sides of formal-legalistic routines
—Sources: Ch.3 of *FHC*; Ch.7 of *FCD*; Ch.3 of *FPHC*

• **At the Structural Level**
—Ex: ever new forms of inequities, at home and abroad
—Ex: the emergence of China, women, and Islam as major actors
—Sources: Chs.5-6 of *FHC*; Chs.7, 9 & 10 of *FCD*; Chs.4-5 of *BDPD*

(continued on next page)

Table 4.26. Multiple Causes of the Emergence of Post-Democracy (Part II)

- **At the Cultural Level**
  —Ex: freedom/unfreedom dialectics
  —Ex: equality/inequality dialectics
  —Ex: system fragmentation and integration
  —Sources: Ch.5 of *FHC*; Chs. 3, 9 & 10 of *FCD*; Ch.4 of *FPHC*; Ch.1 of *BDPD*; Ch.4 of *BCPC*

- **At the Systemic Level**
  —Ex: space habitats (in zero-gravity) and colonization
  —Ex: ultra advanced future info systems
  —Ex: qualitative demography
  —Sources: Ch.7 of *FHC*; Chs.9 &10 of *FCD*

- **At the Cosmological Level**
  —Ex: the colonization of multiverses
  —Ex: the alteration of space-time and the creation of new matter-energy
  —Ex: the expansion of floating consciousness
  —Ex: the spread of hyper-spatial consciousness
  —Sources: Ch.7 of *FHC*; Chs.9 &10 of *FCD*; Ch.4 of *FPHC*; *FPHST*

Notes: The examples in each category are solely illustrative (not exhaustive), and some of the items can be reclassified somewhere else. Nor are they always mutually exclusive. Since they are generalities, exceptions are expected.
Sources: Especially from *FHC*, *FCD*, *FPHC*, *BCPC*, *BDPD*, *FPHST*, and *FPHU*. See also other books and my perspectives on civilizational holism.

Table 4.27. Some Clarifications about Post-Capitalism and Post-Democracy (Part I)

• The prefix "trans-" in the first category of post-capitalism (with its four versions) refers to something "going beyond" (not "uniting" or "combining"). Ex: *Sec.10.3.3* of *FCD*; *Sec.2.4* & *Sec.4.4* of *FPHC*; *Sec.7.2* of *BCPC*

• Such terms like "post-democracy," "post-capitalism," "post-human elitist," "trans-feminine calling," and the like as used in my works are more for our current intellectual convenience than to the liking of future humans and post-humans, who will surely invent more tasteful neologisms to call their own eras, entities, and everything else, for that matter. But the didactic point here is to use the terms to foretell what the future might be like, not that its eras and entities must be called so exactly and permanently.
Ex: *Sec.11.1* of *FCD*; *Sec.7.2* of *BCPC*

• The four versions in the first category of post-capitalist value ideals need not automatically be post-democratic, just as capitalism does not necessarily mean democracy. They are two different entities—though closely related. But up to a certain threshold of elevating equality at the farther expense of freedom, the democratic ideals will be overcome and cease to exist. The same is true for the post-human elitist calling in the second category of post-capitalism in relation to post-democracy, depending on the extent to which freedom is elevated at the expense of equality.
Ex: *Sec.10.4.3.3* of *FCD*; *Table 3.9* of *FPHC*; *Table 7.6* of *BDPD*

• The comparison in each of the three realms of existence in all forms of post-capitalism is not absolute, but relative. Examples include "communal" vs. "individualistic," and the like.
Ex: Notes in *Table 10.8*, *Table 10.9*, *Table 10.10*, & *Table 10.11* of *FCD*; Chs.2-4 of *FPHC*; *Sec.7.2* of *BCPC*

(continued on next page)

Table 4.27. Some Clarifications about Post-Capitalism and Post-Democracy (Part II)

• The emergence of post-capitalism (and post-democracy, for that matter) has multiple causes (to not be reduced to one or only a few).
Ex: Ch.10 of *FCD*, Chs.2-4 of *FPHC*; *Sec.1.3* & *Sec.7.2* of *BCPC* (or *Table 1.8* & *Table 7.11*)

• The specific forms of post-capitalism (and post-democracy, for that matter) need to be further developed in future after-postmodern history, as they will be different from the ones we now know. The point here is to solely give an extremely rough sketch of a world to come that we have never known.
Ex: *Sec.10.3.3* & *Sec.10.4.3.3* of *FCD*; *Table 10.14* & *Table 10.15* of *FCD*; *Sec.7.2* of *BCPC*

• All forms of post-capitalism are not part of a "teleological law," but of "historical trends" only. The same is also true for all forms of post-democracy.
Ex: *Sec.7.1* of *FHC*; *Sec.9.5.3.2* & *Sec.10.3.4.2* of *FCD*; *Sec.7.2* of *BCPC*

• Post-capitalism is not better than capitalism in an "absolute" sense but only fits in better, on the basis of the historical contingency of culture, society, nature, and the mind in some future eras. The same is true for post-democracy in relation to democracy. The term "better" is historically relative.
Ex: *Sec.10.3.3* of *FCD*; *Sec.1.7* of *BDPD*; *Sec.1.5* of *BCPC*

(continued on next page)

Table 4.27. Some Clarifications about Post-Capitalism and Post-Democracy (Part III)

• All forms of post-capitalism and post-democracy are subject to the constraints of existential dialectics. In the process, the dialectic direction is to go beyond the conventional "either-or" dichotomies (e.g., freedom vs. unfreedom, equality vs. inequality, freedom vs. equality, individuality vs. communality, spirituality vs. materiality, formal legalism vs. informal legalism, etc.). As is true in post-civilization, to go beyond the dichotomies is to acknowledge the co-existence of both in each dichotomy, although the degree of scaling one over the over varies from case to case (e.g., the theory of post-capitalism I, the theory of post-capitalism II, the theory of post-democracy I, the theory of post-democracy II, etc.)—but is not to be extreme in largely favoring one over the other, *on average* (all things considered). There is no utopia to be had in the end; even should there be one, dystopia would exist within it.
Ex: Ch.5 of *FHC*; *Sec.10.4.4.2* of *FCD*; *Sec.1.5* of *BDPD*; *Sec.1.3* of *BCPC*; *BCIV*

• All forms of post-capitalism, however different from each other though they are, share one common feature, in that they all inspire for a higher spiritual culture. The same is also true for post-democracy.
Ex: *Sec.10.3*, *Sec.10.4* & *Sec.10.5* of *FCD*; *Chs.2-4* of *FPHC*; *Sec.7.2* of *BCPC*

• All forms of post-capitalism try to avoid the excess in capitalist consumerism by favoring more basic than artificial needs in having, but the quality and quantity of these "basic" needs will be measured by future standards, not by our current ones. Standards are historically relative.
Ex: *Sec.10.3*, *Sec.10.4* & *Sec.10.5* of *FCD*; Ch.2 of *FPHC*; *Sec.7.2* of *BCPC*

(continued on next page)

Table 4.27. Some Clarifications about Post-Capitalism and Post-Democracy (Part IV)

• All forms of post-capitalism make use of a different degree of political authority with advanced info systems in future history and strives for higher spiritual cultures (especially in the post-human age), while acknowledging the constraints of existential dialectics and no longer valuing free market (as in capitalism) and economic control (as in non-capitalism) as sacred virtues.
Ex: *Sec.10.3.4.2*, *Sec.10.3*, *Sec.10.4* & *Sec.10.5* of *FCD*; Chs.2-4 of *FPHC*; *Sec.1.5* of *BDPD*; *Sec.7.2* of *BCPC*

Notes:: The main points here are solely illustrative (not exhaustive) nor necessarily mutually exclusive, and the comparison is relative (not absolute). As generalities, they allow exceptions. The sections as cited are only illustrative (not exhaustive).
Sources: From *FHC*, *FCD*, *FPHC*, and *BDPD*

Table 4.28. The Theory of Post-Capitalism I.1: By Group— Ex: Spiritual/Communal in the Trans-Feminine Calling

- **More Communal Than Individual**
  —*Sharing*: learning from others, as different ideas mutually enrich
  —*Cooperative*: encouraging a sense of shared leadership and teamwork

- **More Informal-Legalistic Than Formal-Legalistic**
  —*Specific*: listening more from the heart than from the head, to know a person as a concrete, not as an abstract, unit
  —*Affective*: thinking and acting with others on a more affective tone. Business can mix with an emotional touch.
  —*Ascriptive*: hiring (or firing) can be done on the basis of merit (or lack of it), but deep solidarity (sisterhood) is important too.
  —*Particularistic*: making decisions on the basis of cost-benefit analysis, but a given group relationship is vital

- **More Spiritual Than Secular**
  —*Long-Term Looking*: sharing for a long-term relationship (e.g., love, friendship), not just for a short-term gain
  —*Loving/Caring*: showing compassion for the sufferings of others, without quickly blaming and pre-judging
  —*Respectful*: showing acceptance about others' feelings (and thoughts)

Notes: The categories and examples are solely illustrative, since there can be different versions, and the comparison is relative (not absolute), nor are they mutually exclusive. As generalities, they allow exceptions. The specific forms of the trans-feminine version need to be further developed in future after-postmodern history, as they will be different from the ones we now know, since the prefix "trans-" here means going beyond or deconstructing the feminine values, while using them as the inspirational point at the beginning.
Source: From Ch.10 of *FCD*. Refer to text for more info and references.

Table 4.29. The Theory of Post-Capitalism I.2: By Nation-State— Ex: Spiritual/Communal in the Trans-Sinitic Calling

- **More Communal Than Individualistic**
  —*Centralized*: being more top-down in management
  —*Collective*: encouraging more group cooperation
  —*Social*: investing in trust and connection

- **More Informal-Legalistic Than Formal-Legalistic**
  —*Specific*: knowing more of those related or connected
  —*Affective*: behaving in a paternalistic, hierarchical way
  —*Ascriptive*: favoring family members and those related
  —*Particularistic*: building connection (guanxi) as imperative

- **More Spiritual Than Secular**
  —*Expansionist*: diffusing civilizational values (e.g., the superiority complex of civilizationalism)
  —*Holistic*: synthesizing things into a panoramic horizon
  —*Historical*: learning from the lessons of the ancient past
  —*Respectful*: deferential to elders and superiors

Notes: The categories and examples are solely illustrative, since there can be different versions, and the comparison is relative (not absolute), nor are they mutually exclusive. As generalities, they allow exceptions. The specific forms of the trans-Sinitic version need to be further developed in future after-postmodern history, as they will be different from the ones we now know, since the prefix "trans-" here means going beyond or deconstructing the Sinitic values, while using them as the inspirational point at the beginning.
Source: From Ch.10 of *FCD*. Refer to text for more info and references.

Table 4.30. The Theory of Post-Capitalism I.3: By Region— Ex: Spiritual/Communal in the Trans-Islamic Calling

- **More Communal Than Individualistic**
  —*Collective*: building the webs of relationships to bind individuals
  —*Sharing*: cultivating the established "wisdom" through common experience
  —*Cooperative*: stressing harmony, solidarity, and commonality

- **More Informal-Legalistic Than Formal-Legalistic**
  —*Specific*: making efforts to know well the participants (family and larger community) in matters of common concern
  —*Affective*: mixing work with language and ritual on explicit religious (Islamic) ideals, texts, stories, and examples
  —*Ascriptive*: privileging local history and custom on relationships among kinship groups
  —*Particularistic*: preferring an unbiased insider with ongoing connections to all parties

- **More Spiritual Than Secular**
  —*Historical*: learning from the lessons of the past as a source of stability and guidance
  —*Deferential*: showing respect for age, experience, status, and leadership in communal affairs
  —*Honorable*: emphasizing face, dignity, prestige, and fairness
  —*Compassionate*: giving mercy and charity ("Zahah") to others

Notes: The categories and examples are solely illustrative (not exhaustive), and the comparison is relative (not absolute), nor are they mutually exclusive. As generalities, they allow exceptions. The specific forms of the trans-Islamic version need to be further developed in future after-postmodern history, as they will be different from the ones we now know, since the prefix "trans-" here means going beyond or deconstructing the Islamic values, while using them as the inspirational point at the beginning.

Sources: From Ch.10 of *FCD*. Refer to text for more info and references, especially from the works by George Irani (2000) and C. Murphy (September 19, 2001).

Table 4.31. The Theory of Post-Capitalism I.4: By Universe— Ex: Spiritual/Communal in the Trans-Outerspace Calling

- **More Communal Than Individual**
  —*Cooperative*: requiring teamwork in small space habitats
  —*Sharing*: learning from, and enjoying being with, each other in a small group in outer space

- **More Informal-Legalistic Than Formal-Legalistic**
  —*Specific*: knowing more about each other to facilitate living and working together in space, both as fellow astronauts and space-mates
  —*Affective*: being friendly and social to each other as vital to working and living in small space quarters
  —*Ascriptive*: nurturing comaraderie among fellow astronauts as if they are family members over time
  —*Particularistic*: building work relationship with enduring memory in a space mission

- **More Spiritual Than Secular**
  —*Long-Term*: looking beyond selfish materialistic concerns in a precarious space environment with potential life or death
  —*Loving/Caring*: cultivating deep bondage for the success of a long term space mission
  —*Transcendent*: searching for life meaning in outer space

Notes: The calling and examples in each category are solely illustrative (not exhaustive), since there will be many different outer-space value ideals in the distant future of space colonization. The comparison is also relative (not absolute), nor are they mutually exclusive. As generalities, they allow exceptions. And the specific forms of trans-outer-space calling need to be further developed in future after-postmodern history, as they will be different from the ones we now know, since the prefix "trans-" here means going beyond or deconstructing the current outer-space values, while using them as the inspirational point at the beginning. The point here is to solely give an extremely rough picture of a small part of the world to come that we still do not know much about.
Source: From Ch.10 of *FCD*. Refer to text for more info and references.

Table 4.32. The Theory of Post-Capitalism II: Spiritual/Individualistic in the Post-Human Elitist Calling (Part I)

• **More Individualistic Than Communal**
—Setting up rank distinctions among unequals (e.g., between inferior humans and superior post-humans, or later among inferior post-humans and superior ones, relatively speaking)
—Yearning for being not only distinguished from unequals, but also the first among equals (the best of the very best)
—Recognizing the constraints of equality/inequality dialectics (or existential dialectics in general)

• **More Spiritual Than Secular**
—Soul-searching for a high spiritual culture (not the trashy one for the masses). Mass culture is a dirty joke for them.
—Exploring different spheres of non-human consciousness in the cosmos (something vastly superior than the human one)
—Recognizing the constraints of freedom/unfreedom dialectics (or existential dialectics in general)

• **Qualifications**
—Although post-human elitist post-democracy is comparable to post-human elitist post-capitalism in some respects, the former does not necessarily imply the latter (post-human elitist post-capitalism), just as democracy does not have to entail capitalism. They are two different (though related) entities.
—But up to a certain threshold of incorporating government intervention with advanced info systems in future civilizations for higher spiritual concerns at the expense of the free market and materialist pursuit, the capitalist ideal will be overcome.
—The overcome will not be Fascist or feudalistic, but post-capitalist, subject to the constraints of existential dialectics.

(continued on next page)

Table 4.32. The Theory of Post-Capitalism II: Spiritual/Individualistic in the Post-Human Elitist Calling (Part II)

Notes: The calling and examples in each category are solely illustrative (not exhaustive). The comparison is also relative (not absolute), nor are they mutually exclusive. As generalities, they allow exceptions. And the specific forms of post-human elitist post-capitalism need to be further developed in future after-postmodern history, as they will be different from the ones we now know, while using them as the inspirational point at the beginning. The point here is to solely give an extremely rough picture of a small part of the world to come that we still do not know much about.
Sources: From Ch.10 of *FCD* (and also *FPHC*, *BDPD*, and *BCPC*). Refer to the text for more info and references.

Table 4.33. Capitalism, Non-Capitalism, and Post-Capitalism (Part I)

- **Capitalism**
  - —*Theoretical Constructs*
    - •Allocation of scarce resources among alternative wants largely by free market for competition (whose characteristics in its ideal form include, for instance, no barrier to entry or exit, homogeneity, perfect information, a large number of buyers/sellers, and perfect factor mobility)
    - •More formal-legalistic than informal-legalistic, more individualistic than communal, and more material (secular) than spiritual
    - •Either (1) minimal government or (2) relatively active government
  - —*Types*
    - •Only (1): Different versions of market capitalism (e.g., the U.S.)
    - •Only (2): Different versions of welfare capitalism (e.g., Sweden)

- **Non-Capitalism**
  - —*Theoretical Constructs*
    - •Allocation of scarce resources among alternative wants mainly by political authority for policies (which can be regulative, redistributive, symbolic, and participatory)
    - •More informal-legalistic than formal-legalistic
    - •Either (1') more individualistic (for the elites), often (though not always) for material (secular) concerns, or (2') more communal (for the masses), often (though not always) for spiritual concerns
  - —*Types*
    - •Only (1'): Different versions on the Right (e.g., Fascist corporate-state economy for the glory of the new Rome, medieval lord-vassal-serf economy for the power of the feudalistic order)
    - •Only (2'): Different versions on the Left (e.g., Soviet command economy for the creation of the New Socialist Man)

(continued on next page)

Table 4.33. Capitalism, Non-Capitalism, and Post-Capitalism (Part II)

- **Post-Capitalism**
  - —*Theoretical Constructs*
    - •Allocation of scarce resources among alternative wants largely by political authority with advanced info systems in future civilizations, subject to existential dialectics. In degree of allocating by authority, post-capitalism is more than capitalism but less than non-capitalism.
    - •More spiritual than secular (material)
    - •Either (1'') more individualistic or (2'') more communal
    - •Like capitalism and non-capitalism, post-capitalism is also subject to the freedom/unfreedom and equality/inequality dialectics (or existential dialectics in general). There is no utopia, in the end; even were there one, dystopia would exist within it.
    - •Unlike capitalism and non-capitalism, post-capitalism makes use of a different degree of political authority with advanced info systems in future civilizations and strives for higher-spiritual cultures (especially in the post-human age), while acknowledging the constraints of existential dialectics and no longer valuing free market (as in capitalism) and economic control (as in non-capitalism) as sacred virtues.
  - —*Types*
    - •Only (1''): Different versions of post-human elitist value ideals
    - •Only (2''): Different versions of trans-Sinitic value ideals
    - •Only (2''): Different versions of trans-feminine value ideals
    - •Only (2''): Different versions of trans-Islamic value ideals
    - •Only (2''): Different versions of trans-outerspace value ideals

(continued on next page)

Table 4.33. Capitalism, Non-Capitalism, and Post-Capitalism (Part III)

Notes: The calling and examples in each category are solely illustrative (not exhaustive). The comparison is also relative (not absolute), nor are they mutually exclusive. As generalities, they allow exceptions. And the specific forms of each calling need to be further developed in future after-postmodern history, as they will be different from the ones we now know, while using them as the inspirational point at the beginning. The point here is to solely give an extremely rough picture of a small part of the world to come that we still do not know much about.
Source: From Ch.10 of *FCD*. Refer to the text for more info and references.

Table 4.34. Multiple Causes of the Emergence of Post-Capitalism (Part I)

- **At the Micro-Physical Level**
  —Ex: intelligent life without the human physical-chemical system
  —Ex: mastering of quantum mechanics, electromagnetism, and other fields for the understanding of a broad range of anomalous experiences and the application for artificial intelligence for spiritual quest
  —Sources: Ch.7 of *FHC*; Chs.9-10 of *FCD*; Ch.1 of *FPHC*

- **At the Chemical Level**
  —Ex: space radiation and toxins
  —Sources: Ch.7 of *FHC*; Chs.9-10 of *FCD*

- **At the Bio-Psychological Level**
  —Ex: exo-biological evolution in deep space
  —Ex: genetic engineering of new beings
  —Ex: limits of human cognition
  —Ex: the rise of unfolding unconsciousness
  —Sources: Ch.2 & Chs.9-10 of *FCD*; Ch.7 of *FHC*; *FPHU*

- **At the Institutional Level**
  —Ex: the flawed logic of the free market
  —Ex: the need of a post-autistic economics
  —Sources: Ch.10 of *FCD*

- **At the Organizational Level**
  —Ex: the dark sides of formal-legalistic routines
  —Sources: Ch.3 of *FHC*; Ch.7 of *FCD*; Ch.3 of *FPHC*

- **At the Structural Level**
  —Ex: ever new forms of inequities, at home and abroad
  —Ex: the emergence of China, women, and Islam as major actors
  —Sources: Chs.5-6 of *FHC*; Chs.7, 9 & 10 of *FCD*; Chs.4-5 of *BDPD*

(continued on next page)

Table 4.34. Multiple Causes of the Emergence of Post-Capitalism (Part II)

- **At the Cultural Level**
  —Ex: freedom/unfreedom dialectics
  —Ex: equality/inequality dialectics
  —Sources: Ch.5 of *FHC*; Chs.3 & 10 of *FCD*; Ch.4 of *FPHC*; Ch.1 of *BDPD*

- **At the Systemic Level**
  —Ex: space habitats (in zero-gravity) and colonization
  —Ex: ultra advanced future info systems
  —Ex: qualitative demography
  —Sources: Ch.7 of *FHC*; Chs. 9 & 10 of *FCD*

- **At the Cosmological Level**
  —Ex: the colonization of multiverses
  —Ex: the alteration of space-time and the creation of new matter-energy
  —Ex: the expansion of floating consciousness
  —Ex: the spread of hyper-spatial consciousness
  —Sources: Ch.7 of *FHC*; Chs. 9 & 10 of *FCD*; Ch.4 of *FPHC*; *FPHST*

Notes: The examples in each category are solely illustrative (not exhaustive), and some of the items can be reclassified somewhere else. Nor are they always mutually exclusive. Since they are generalities, exceptions are expected.
Sources: Especially from *FHC*, *FCD*, *FPHC*, *BCPC*, *BDPD*, *FPHST*, and *FPHU*. See also other books and my perspectives on civilizational holism.

Table 4.35. The Theoretical Debate on Civilization

- **The Progressive Theory of Civilization**
  —*Thesis*: The "civilizing" process is "good," as opposed to the "barbarizing" process as something "bad," relatively speaking.
  —*Discourse*: Especially, though not exclusively, in the Enlightenment era and a bit before. Example: Thomas Hobbes—in that the tribes in primitive societies were "savages."

- **The Romantic Theory of Barbarity**
  —*Thesis*: The "civilizing" process is "bad," as opposed to the "barbarizing" process as something "good," relatively speaking.
  —*Discourse*: Especially, though not exclusively, in the Counter-Enlightenment circle. Example: Jean-Jacques Rousseau—in that civilization "corrupts" men, and the "savages" are in fact "noble."

- **The Moderate Theory of Civilization**
  —*Thesis*: The "civilizing" process is "good," but there is a price to pay, especially in systematic (compulsive) self-control.
  —*Discourse*: Especially, though not exclusively, in some late modern and postmodern circles. Example: Norbert Elias—in that social manners become more refined in the civilizing process, but self-control also becomes more systematic.

- **The Theory of Post-Civilization**
  —*Thesis*: The civilizing process is as evil and good as barbarity, and each cannot exist without the other, to be eventually superseded by post-civilization unto the post-human age.
  —*Discourse*: Proposed by Peter Baofu. See the rest of *BCIV* for more analysis.

Source: From *BCIV* on the theoretical debate

Table 4.36. No Freedom Without Unfreedom in the Civilizing Processes (Part I)

- **The Rationalizing Process (at the Level of Culture)**
  —if freer from the dominance of unreason (as in barbarism) in the civilizing process, then less free from the rationalizing process (be it in the form of the principle of either transcendence or immanence)
  —if freer from the principle of immanence in the rationalizing process, then less free from the inclination to commit terror in the name of reason and the relative underdevelopment of non-reason (e.g., in relation to yoga and meditation)
  —if freer from the principle of transcendence in the rationalizing process, then less free from the relative underdevelopment of reason (e.g., in relation to systematic methodology) and the occurrence of oppression in the name of non-reason

- **The Pacifying Process (at the Level of Society)**
  —if freer from the dominance of pillage (as in savagery) in the civilizing process, then less free from the pacifying process (be it in the form of external control or self-control)
  —if freer from self-control in the pacifying process, then less free from the temptation of expansionist oppression and rebellious mindset in external control
  —if freer from external control in the pacifying process, then less free from the gruesome psychological self-torture and conformism in self-control

- **The Stewardizing Process (at the Level of Nature)**
  —if freer from the dominance of nature (as in the state of nature) in the civilizing process, then less free from the stewardizing process (be it in the form of the stewardship of creation or the covenant with nature)
  —if freer from the stewardship of creation in the stewardizing process, then less free from material underdevelopment, relatively speaking, and spiritual exclusion in the covenant with nature
  —if freer from the covenant with nature in the stewardizing process, then less free from ecological degradation and spiritual disconnection from nature in the stewardship of creation

---

(continued on next page)

Table 4.36. No Freedom Without Unfreedom in the Civilizing Processes (Part II)

- **The Subliming Process (at the Level of the Mind)**
  —if freer from the dominance of spontaneity (as in the wild state of the mind) in the civilizing process, then less free from the subliming process, be it in the form of (cyclical-centric) self-refinement or (linear-centric) self-discipline
  —if freer from (cyclical-centric) self-refinement in the subliming process, then less free from the (linear-centric) self-regimen (as a form of neurosis)
  —if freer from (linear-centric) self-discipline in the subliming process, then less free from the (cyclical-centric) self-torture (equally as a form of neurosis)

Notes: The examples in each category are solely illustrative (not exhaustive), and the comparison is relative (not absolute), nor are they necessarily mutually exclusive. And some can be easily re-classified elsewhere. As generalities, they allow exceptions.
Sources: From *BCIV*. See also *FHC*, *FCD*, *FPHC*, *BDPD*, and *BCPC*.

Table 4.37. No Equality Without Inequality in the Civilizing Processes (Part I)

- **The Rationalizing Process (at the Level of Culture)**
  —if more equal for the role of rationalization in the rationalizing process (of civilizational making), then less equal for that of mythicization (as in barbarism)
  —if more equal for the principle of transcendence in (linear-centric) rationalizing process, then less equal for the principle of immanence
  —if more equal for the principle of immanence in (cyclical-centric) rationalizing process, then less equal for the principle of transcendence

- **The Pacifying Process (at the Level of Society)**
  —if more equal for pacification in civilizational making, then less equal for the institution of pillaging and others (as in savagery)
  —if more equal for external control, relatively speaking, in pacifying process, then less equal for self-control
  —if more equal for self-control, relatively speaking, in pacifying process, then less equal for external-control

- **The Stewardizing Process (at the Level of Nature)**
  —if more equal for stewardship in the stewardizing process (of civilizational making), then less equal for reverent (submissive) existence (as in barbarism)
  —if more equal for the stewardship of creation in (linear- centric) stewardizing process, then less equal for the (cyclical-centric) covenant with nature for harmonious co-existence
  —if more equal for the (cyclical-centric) covenant with nature in the stewardizing process, then less equal for the (linear-centric) stewardship of nature for domination

(continued on next page)

Table 4.37. No Equality Without Inequality in the Civilizing Processes (Part II)

- **The Subliming Process (at the Level of the Mind)**
  —if more equal for the role of reason in the subliming process, then less equal for that of unreason (as in the natural state of wildness)
  —if more equal for the primacy of reason in (linear-centric) subliming process, then less equal for other faculties (e.g., intuition, existential feelings, and analogous thinking) in cyclical-centric one
  —if more equal for the exercise of other faculties (e.g., intuition, existential feelings, and analogous thinking) in cyclical-centric subliming process, then less equal for the role of reason in linear-centric counterpart

Notes: The examples in each category are solely illustrative (not exhaustive), and the comparison is relative (not absolute), nor are they mutually exclusive. And some can be easily reclassified else-where. As generalities, they allow exceptions.
Sources: From *BCIV*. See also *FHC*, *FCD*, *FPHC*, *BDPD*, and *BCPC*.

Table 4.38. Five Theses on Post-Civilization

• Post-civilization no longer treats civilization as good and barbarity as evil (relatively speaking), nor does it nostalgically regard barbarity as good and civilization as evil (relatively speaking again). Civilization is as evil and good as barbarity.

• Post-civilization also no longer accepts the dichotomy between civilization and barbarity. Civilization cannot exist without barbarity. It is no longer necessary to preserve civilization, any more than it is imperative to destroy barbarity. To go beyond civilization and barbarity is to acknowledge the co-existence of both, although the degree of scaling one over the over varies from case to case—but is not to be extreme in largely favoring one over the other, *on average* (subject to the constraints of existential dialectics).

• Post-civilization is thus subject to the constraints of existential dialectics. There is no freedom without unfreedom, and no equality without inequality, for instance. There will be no utopia; even should there be one, there would be dystopia embedded within it.

• Post-civilization will eventually replace civilization (as a form of life settlement), to be dominated by post-capitalist and post-democratic lifeforms here on earth and in deep space (besides other alien lifeforms that we have never known), unto the post-human age in multiverses. Those few post-humans who keep civilization will live in a "post-human civilization," while the rest (the majority), who choose post-civilization, will evolve towards the state of "post-human post-civilization." One therefore should not confuse "post-human civilization" with "post-human post-civilization," as the two are not the same.

• Post-civilization will confront psychosis as a primary problem in the culture of virtuality unto the post-human age, just as civilization has neurosis as a primary one of its own (although both neurosis and psychosis are major problems in both).

Notes: The comparison in each category is relative (not absolute), nor are they necessarily mutually exclusive. And some can be easily re-classified elsewhere. As generalities, they allow exceptions.
Sources: From *BCIV*. See also *FHC*, *FCD*, *FPHC*, *BDPD*, and *BCPC*.

Table 4.39. Barbarity, Civilization, and Post-Civilization

- **The Rationalizing Process (at the Level of Culture)**
  —*Barbarity*
    - More mythicizing than rationalizing, relatively speaking
  —*Civilization*
    - More rationalizing than mythicizing, relatively speaking
  —*Post-Civilization*
    - Beyond the dichotomy, subject to existential dialectics

- **The Pacifying Process (at the Level of Society)**
  —*Barbarity*
    - More pillaging than pacifying, relatively speaking
  —*Civilization*
    - More pacifying than pillaging, relatively speaking
  —*Post-Civilization*
    - Beyond the dichotomy, subject to existential dialectics

- **The Stewardizing Process (at the Level of Nature)**
  —*Barbarity*
    - More revering than stewardizing, relatively speaking
  —*Civilization*
    - More stewardizing than revering, relatively speaking
  —*Post-Civilization*
    - Beyond the dichotomy, subject to existential dialectics

- **The Subliming Process (at the Level of the Mind)**
  —*Barbarity*
    - More impulsing than subliming, relatively speaking
  —*Civilization*
    - More subliming than impulsing, relatively speaking
  —*Post-Civilization*
    - Beyond the dichotomy, subject to existential dialectics

Notes: The comparison in each category is relative (not absolute), nor are they necessarily mutually exclusive. And some can be easily re-classified elsewhere. As generalities, they allow exceptions.
Sources: From *BCIV*. See also *FHC*, *FCD*, *FPHC*, *BDPD*, and *BCPC*.

Table 4.40. Types of Super Civilization in the Cosmos (Part I)

- **Type I**
  —a civilization which gains control of and uses the total energy output "falling on its planet from its sun for interstellar communication" (or, in general, space colonization). For N. Kardashev, who proposed the first three types, human civilization is currently Type Zero (Type O), which is below even Type I, since its present energy consumption for all purposes, let alone for interstellar communication, is still 10,000 times less.

- **Type II**
  —a civilization which gains control of and uses directly the total energy output of its sun for interstellar communication (or, in general, space colonization).

- **Type III**
  —a civilization which gains control of and uses the total energy output of its galaxy for interstellar communication (or, in general, space colonization).

- **Type IV**
  —a civilization which gains control of and uses the total energy output of its cluster of galaxies for interstellar communication (or, in general, space colonization).

- **Type V**
  —a civilization which gains control of and uses the total energy output of its supercluster of galaxies for interstellar communica-tion (or, in general, space colonization).

(continued on next page)

Table 4.40. Types of Super Civilization in the Cosmos (Part II)

- **Type…n**
  —So continues the series in what I call the cyclical progression of hegemony in the cosmos and beyond.

Notes: The Russian astrophysicist Nikolai Kardashev proposed the first three types of super civilization in terms of total energy out-put for interstellar communication. (CSM 1979) I extend his argument further to propose Type IV, Type V, Type VI, and Type…n, in the context of my claim about the cyclical progression of he-gemony in the cosmos and beyond.
Sources: From *Table 9.4* of *FCD*. See *FHC*, *FCD*, and *FPHC* for more info.

Table 4.41. The Civilizational Project from Pre-Modernity to After-Postmodernity (Part I)

	Pre-Modern	*Modern*	*Postmodern*	*After-Postmodern*
Main narratives	•Sacralness •Courtliness •Vitalism •Animism	•Freedom •Equality •Fraternity	•Multiplicity •Hybridization	•Naked contingency •Cyclical progression of hegemony
Main institutions	•Monarchy •Aristocracy •Feudalism •Holy order •Primitivism	•Capitalism •Liberalism •Socialism •Nazism •Fascism	•Capitalism •Liberalism •Postmodern politics of difference	•Post-Capitalism •Post-Democracy •Others
Main techno-logical and economic revolutions	•Agricultural	•Service •Industrial	•Informational	•Biological •Material •Energy •Space •Others

(continued on next page)

Table 4.41. The Civilizational Project from Pre-Modernity to After-Postmodernity (Part II)

	Pre-Modern	*Modern*	*Postmodern*	*After-Postmodern*
Main agents	•Males •Upper strata •Mini-states	•Males •Upper strata •Whites •Empires	•Males •Upper strata •Whites •Others •Supra-states •IO's	•Post-humans •Humans •Others
Main impacts	•Local	•Inter-national	•Global	•Outer-space •Multiverse
Main outcomes	•Towards moderntiy •Rise of linear- & cyclical-centric civiliza-tions	•Towards post-modernity •Dominance of linear-centric civilization	•Towards after-post-moderntiy •Linear-centric civiliza-tion in crisis	•Towards human (& maybe post-human) extinction •Rise of post-civiliza-tion, especially in post-human forms of space-time

Notes: The examples in each category are solely illustrative (not exhaustive) nor necessarily mutually exclusive, and the comparison is relative (not absolute). As generalities, they allow exceptions.

Sources: From *Table 10.16* of *FCD*—and also from *BCIV* on post-civilization (and *FPHST*)

Table 4.42. Civilizational Holism (Part I)

- **At the Micro-Physical Theoretical Level**
  —Ex: Mastering of quantum mechanics, electromagnetism, and other fields for the understanding of a broad range of anomalous experiences and theapplication for artificial intelligence (*Sec.1.4.1* of *FPHC*)

- **At the Chemical Theoretical Level**
  —Ex: Unprecedented expansion of (and violence to) the mind through ever new forms of drugs (and virtual technologies, for that matter) (Ch.9 of *FCD*)

- **At the Biological Theoretical Level**
  —Ex: Humans are not biologically equal, on the basis of race, gender, ethnicity, age, and whatnot. (*Sec.2.6* & Ch.10 of *FCD*; *BNN*) And post-humans will experience the same fate, in an even more amazing way.

- **At the Psychological Theoretical Level**
  —Ex: Human cognitive impartiality and emotional neutrality are quite limited. (*Secs.2.4-2.5* of *FCD*)
  —Ex: Rise of Floating Consciousness (Ch.10 of *FCD*; Chs.1 & 4 of *FPHC*) and Unfolding Unconsciousness (*FPHU*)

- **At the Organizational Theoretical Level**
  —Ex: Administrative colonization of deep space, with less legal-formalism in some corners. (Chs.9-10 of *FCD*)

- **At the Institutional Theoretical Level**
  —Ex: Both capitalism and democracy will not last, to be superseded by different versions of post-capitalism and post-democracy in after-postmodernity. (Ch.10 of *FCD*)

(continued on next page)

Table 4.42. Civilizational Holism (Part II)

- **At the Structural Theoretical Level**
  —Ex: Social stratification reappears in ever new forms, also with new causes and new players in the cyclical progression of hegemony. (Chs.8-10 of *FCD*)
  —Ex: The world of hyper-empires, and the union of the unions (*BWT*)

- **At the Systemic Theoretical Level**
  —Ex: Outerspace expansion: local → regional → global → solar → galactic → clustery → multiversal (Ch.9 of *FCD*)
  —Ex: Demographic transition: human extinction, and the rise of post-humans (e.g., cyborgs, thinking machines, thinking robots, genetically altered superior beings, floating consciousness, hyper-spatial consciousness) (Ch.4 of *FPHC*; Ch.10 of *FCD*; & Ch.7 of *FHC*)
  —Ex: New technological forces in material sciences, electronic and communication sciences, energy sciences, biosciences, manufacturing and engineering sciences, and space sciences (Ch.10 of *FCD* & Ch.7 of *FHC*)
  —Ex: Systematic dominance towards nature for space colonization (Chs.9-10 of *FCD*; Chs.2 & 7 of *FHC*)

- **At the Cultural Theoretical Level**
  —Ex: The post-human transcendence of freedom and equality (Ch.10 of *FCD*)
  —Ex: Methodological Holism (Ch.1 of *FCD*; Ch.1 of *FPHC*; *Sec.2.1* & *Sec.2.5* of *BCPC*)
  —Ex: The Evolution from Barbarity to Post-Civilization (*BCIV*)

- **At the Cosmological Theoretical Level**
  —Ex: Mastering of dark matter and dark energy, and the exploration of multiverses (Ch.4 of *FPHC*; Ch.10 of *FCD*; & Ch.7 of *FHC*)
  —Ex: Alternation of space-time (*FPHST*)
  —Ex: The emergence of hyper-spatial consciousness (*FPHC*)

(continued on next page)

Table 4.42. Civilizational Holism (Part III)

- **At Other Levels**
  —Ex: Historical: pre-modernity → modernity → postmodernity → after-postmodernity (human distinction, and the rise of post-humans, including floating consciousness, hyper-spatial consciousness, and unfolding unconsciousness) (Ch.7 of *FHC*; Ch.10 of *FCD*; *FPHC*; *FPHU*)

Notes: These examples are solely illustrative (not exhaustive), and some of the items can be reclassified somewhere else. Nor are they always mutually exclusive. Since they are generalities, exceptions are expected. And the comparison is relative, not absolute.
Sources: From *Table 5.1* of *FPHC*—with details from *FHC*, *FCD*, and the rest of my books. Not every aspect in each category as discussed in all my books are presented here, since there are too many issues. For more info, also consult the table on theories on civilizational holism and, of course, the books themselves.

Table 4.43. Theories on Civilizational Holism (Part I)

I. Theories in Relation to Nature

—*At the Macro-Physical (Cosmological) Theoretical Level*

- • 47. Resettlement Theory of Geology (Peter Baofu) (*FPHGEOL*)
- • 46. Theory of Post-Cosmology (Peter Baofu) (*BCOS*)
- • 45. Theory of Hyper-Spatial Consciousness (Peter Baofu) (Ch.4 of *FPHC*; *FPHG*)
- (• 43). Selective Theory of Geometry (Peter Baofu) (*FPHG*)
- (• 42). Perspectival Theory of Space-Time (Peter Baofu) (*FPHST*)
- (• 41). Dialectic Theory of Complexity (Peter Baofu) (*FC*)
- (• 25). Theory of Floating Consciousness (Peter Baofu) (Ch.10 of *FCD*; Chs.1 & 4 of *FPHC*)
- • 44. Theory of the Geopower of Nature (Peter Baofu) (Ch.4 of *ALD*)

—*At the Micro-Physical Theoretical Leve*

- • 43. Selective Theory of Geometry (Peter Baofu) (*FPHG*)
- • 42. Perspectival Theory of Space-Time (Peter Baofu) (*FPHST*)
- • 41. Dialectic Theory of Complexity (Peter Baofu) (*FC*)

(continued on next page)

Table 4.43. Theories on Civilizational Holism (Part II)

II. Theories in Relation to Culture
—*At the Cultural Theoretical Level*

- 40. Mediative-Variative Theory of Chess (Peter Baofu) (*FPHCHESS*)
- 39. Theory of Post-Ethics (Peter Baofu) (*BEPE*)
- 38. Dualistic Theory of Mass Culture (Peter Baofu) (Ch.2 of *FHC*)
- 37. Comparative Theory of Religion—also known as the Comparative-Substitutive Theory of Religion (Peter Baofu) (Ch.3 of *FHC*; Ch.9 of *FCD*; Ch.1 of *FPHK*; *FPHR*)
- 36. Theory of Post-Civilization (Peter Baofu) (*BCIV*)
- 35. Theory of the Trinity of Modernity to Its After-Postmodern Counterpart (Peter Baofu) (*FHC*; Ch.10 of *FCD*)
- 34. Transformative Theory of Aesthetic Experience (Peter Baofu) (*FAE*)
- (• 17). Theory of Post-Capitalism (Peter Baofu) (Ch.10 of *FCD*; Chs.2 & 4 of *FPHC*; *BCPC*)
- (• 16). Theory of Post-Democracy (Peter Baofu) (Ch.10 of *FCD*; Chs.3 & 4 of *FPHC*; *BDPD*)
- (• 5). Theory of Existential Dialectics, or the Holistic Theory of Knowledge (Peter Baofu) (*FHC*; *FCD*; *FPHC*; *BDPD*; *FC*; *FAE*; *ALD; FIA; FPHK*; etc,)
- (• 4). Contrastive Theory of Rationality (Peter Baofu) (*FPHML*)
- (• 2). Theory of Methodological Holism (Peter Baofu) (Ch.1 of *FCD*; Ch.1of *FPHC*; *Sec.2.1* & *Sec.2.5* of *BCPC*; *FC*; *FPHK*; etc.)

(continued on next page)

Table 4.43. Theories on Civilizational Holism (Part III)

III. Theories in Relation to the Mind

—*At the Biological Theoretical Level*

- 33. Theory of Contrastive Advantages (Peter Baofu) (*Sec.2.6* & Ch.10 of *FCD; BNN*)
- (• 25). Theory of Floating Consciousness (Peter Baofu) (Ch.10 of *FCD*; Chs.1 & 4 of *FPHC*)

—*At the Psychological Theoretical Level*

- 32. Metamorphic Theory of Humor (Peter Baofu) (*FPHH*)
- 31. Contrarian Theory of Personality (Peter Baofu) (*FPHP*)
- 30. Theory of Virtual Sexuality (Peter Baofu) (*FPHS*)
- 29. Expansive-Contractive Theory of Martial Arts (Peter Baofu) (*FPHMA*)
- 28. Multilogical Theory of Learning (Peter Baofu) (*FPHL*)
- 27. Comprehensive Theory of Creative Thinking (Peter Baofu) (*FPHCT*)
- 26. Theory of Unfolding Unconsciousness—also known as the Unfolding Theory of Anomalous Experience (Peter Baofu) (*FPHU*)
- 25. Theory of Floating Consciousness (Peter Baofu) (Ch.10 of *FCD*; Chs.1 & 4 of *FPHC*)
- 24. Theory of Cognitive Partiality (Peter Baofu) (*Sec.2.4* of *FCD*; *Sec.4.5.1.1* of *BCPC*)
- 23. Theory of Emotional Non-Neutrality (Peter Baofu) (*Sec.2.5* of *FCD*; *Sec.4.5.2* of of *BCPC*)
- 22. Theory of Behavioral Alteration (Peter Baofu) (*Sec.4.5.3* of *BCPC*)

Table 4.43. Theories on Civilizational Holism (Part IV)

IV. Theories in Relation to Society

—At the Organizational Theoretical Level

- 21. Theory of E-Civic Alienation (Peter Baofu) (Ch.7 of *FCD*)
- 20. Combinational Theory of Organization (Peter Baofu) (*FPHO*; Ch.6 of *ALD*)

—At the Institutional Theoretical Level

- 19. Heterodox of Theory of Education (Peter Baofu) (*FPHEDU*)
- 18. Reconstruction of Theory of Law (Peter Baofu) (*FPHLAW*)
- 17. Theory of Post-Capitalism (Peter Baofu) (Ch.10 of *FCD*; Chs.2 & 4 of *FPHC*; *BCPC*)
- 16. Theory of Post-Democracy (Peter Baofu) (Ch.10 of *FCD*; Chs.3 & 4 of *FPHC*; *BDPD*)
- 15. Dynamic Theory of Comparative Political Systems (Peter Baofu) (*ALD*)

—At the Systemic Theoretical Level

- 14. Contingent Theory of Urban Planning (Peter Baofu) (*FPHUP*)
- 13. Totalistic Theory of Communication (Peter Baofu) (*FPHMM*; *FCD*; *FHC*)
- 12. Ambivalent Theory of Technology (Peter Baofu) (*FPHE*; *FCD*; *FHC*)
- 11. Multifaceted Theory of War and Peace (Peter Baofu) (Ch.9 of *FCD*; Ch.1 of *FPHK*)
- 10. Theory of Post-Humanity (Peter Baofu) (Ch.7 of *FHC*; Chs.3, & 10 of *FCD*; Chs.1, 3 & 4 of *FPHC*; and other books of mine)
- 9. Theory of the Cyclical Progression of System Integration and Fragmentation (Peter Baofu) (Chs.9-10 of *FCD*)
- 8. Synthetic Theory of Information Architecture (Peter Baofu) (*FIA*)

(continued on next page)

Table 4.43. Theories on Civilizational Holism (Part V)

IV. Theories in Relation to Society (*cont'd*)

—*At the Structural Theoretical Level*

- 7. Theory of the Cyclical Progression of Hegemony (Peter Baofu)
  (Chs.9-10 of *FCD*; Chs.1, 3 & 4 of *FPHC*; *BDPD*)
- 6. Theory of the Cyclical Progression of Empire-Building (Peter Baofu)
  (*BWT*)

V. Meta-Theories (in Relation to Theories)

—*At the Ontological Meta-Theoretical Level*

- 5. Theory of Existential Dialectics, or the Holistic Theory of Knowledge (Peter Baofu)
  (*FHC*; *FCD*; *FPHC*; *BDPD*; *FC*; *FAE*; *ALD; FIA; FPHK*; etc,)
- 4. Contrastive Theory of Rationality (Peter Baofu)
  (*FPHML*)

—*At the Methodological Meta-Theoretical Level*

- 3. Critical-Dialectic Theory of Formal Science (Peter Baofu)
  (*FPHFS*)
- 2. Theory of Methodological Holism (Peter Baofu)
  (Ch.1 of *FCD*; Ch.1of *FPHC*; *Sec.2.1* & *Sec.2.5* of *BCPC*; *FC*; *FPHK*; etc.)

VI. Theories in Relation to the Rest

—*At Other Levels (Historical)*

- 1. Theory of the Evolution from Pre-Modernity to After-Postmodernity (Peter Baofu)
  (*FHC*; Ch.9-10 of *FCD*; *FPHC*)

Notes: All these theories are my constructions, as some of the main contributions of my grant project on civilization and its future. These examples are solely illustrative (not exhaustive), and some of the items can be reclassified somewhere else. Nor are they always mutually exclusive. Since they are generalities, exceptions are expected.

Sources: From my previous books.

Table 4.44. Three Great Future Transformations of Mind Games

- **Virtual Games**
  —Ex: online chess
  —Ex: virtual experience

- **Novel Games**
  —Ex: new chess variants
  —Ex: new chess engines

- **Post-Human Mind Games**
  —Ex: the quest for broader/deeper mental benefits of chess playing
  —Ex: games designed for the evolution of the mind into different body-less forms (e.g., "floating consciousness," "hyper-spatial consciousness," "unfolding unconsciousness")

Notes: The examples in the categories are solely illustrative (not exhaustive), and the comparison is relative (not absolute), nor are they necessarily mutually exclusive. And some can be easily re-classified elsewhere. As generalities, they allow exceptions.
Sources: From *Sec. 4.16* of *FPHCHESS*. See text for more info. Also, consult *FCD* for strategy and tactics in warfare and *FPHO* for strategy and tactics in organization.

BIBLIOGRAPHY

Altman, N. 2006. "And Now for Something Completely Different: Humor in Psychoanalysis." *Psychoanalytic Dialogues*, 16 (5): 573-577.

Angelle, Amber. 2010. "Laugh Well, Live Well." *Discover: Expanding Your Universe*. October Issue.

Aristophanes. 2010. "The Knights" (November 30). <http://classics.mit.edu/Aristophanes/knights.pl.txt>.

______.2010a. "The Clouds" (November 30). <http://classics.mit.edu/Aristophanes/clouds.pl.txt>.

Attardo, Salvatore. 2001. *Humorous Texts: A Semantic and Pragmatic Analysis*. New YorK: Mouton de Gruyter.

______.1994. *Linguistic Theories of Humor*. New YorK: Mouton de Gruyter.

Ball, Warwick. 2001. *Rome in the East: The transformation of an Empire*. New York: Routledge.

Baofu, Peter. 2011. *Beyond Ethics to Post-Ethics: A Preface to a New Theory of Morality and Immorality*. Charlotte, NC: Information Age Publishing.

______.2011a. *The Future of Post-Human Education: A Preface to a New Theory of Teaching and Learning*. Cambridge, England: Cambridge International Science Publishing, Ltd.

______.2010. *The Future of Post-Human Religion: A Preface to a New Theory of Spirituality*. Cambridge, England: Cambridge International Science Publishing, Ltd.

______.2010a. *The Future of Post-Human Chess: A Preface to a New Theory of Tactics and Strategy*. Cambridge, England: Cambridge International Science Publishing, Ltd.

______.2010b. *The Future of Post-Human Geology: A Preface to a New Theory of Statics and Dynamics*. Cambridge, England: Cambridge International Science Publishing, Ltd.

______.2010c. *Beyond Cosmology to Post-Cosmology: A Preface to a New Theory of Different Worlds*. Cambridge, England: Cambridge International Science Publishing, Ltd.

______.2010d. *The Future of Post-Human Personaltiy: A Preface to a New Theory of Normality and Abnormality*. Cambridge, England: Cambridge International

Science Publishing, Ltd.

______.2010e. *The Future of Post-Human War and Peace: A Preface to a New Theory of Aggression and Pacificity*. Cambridge, England: Cambridge Scholars Publishing.

______.2010f. *The Future of Post-Human Formal Science: A Preface to a New Theory of Abstraction and Application*. Cambridge, England: Cambridge Scholars Publishing.

______.2010g. *The Future of Post-Human Law: A Preface to a New Theory of Necessity, Contingency, and Justice*. Cambridge, England: Cambridge Scholars Publishing.

______.2010h. *The Future of Post-Human Sexuality: A Preface to a New Theory of the Body and Spirit of Love Makers*. Cambridge, England: Cambridge Scholars Publishing.

______,2009. *The Future of Post-Human Martial Arts: A Preface to a New Theory of the Body and Spirit of Warriors*. Cambridge, England: Cambridge Scholars Publishing.

______.2009a. *The Future of Post-Human Organization: A Preface to a New Theory of Communication, Decision-Making, and Leadership*. Cambridge, England: Cambridge Scholars Publishing.

______.2009b. *The Future of Post-Human Language: A Preface to a New Theory of Structure, Context, and Learning*. Cambridge, England: Cambridge Scholars Publishing.

______.2009c. *The Future of Post-Human Urban Planning: A Preface to a New Theory of Density, Void, and Sustainability*. Cambridge, England: Cambridge Scholars Publishing.

______.2009d. *The Future of Post-Human Geometry: A Preface to a New Theory of Infinity, Symmetry, and Dimensionality*. Cambridge, England: Cambridge Scholars Publishing.

______.2009e. *The Future of Post-Human Creative Thinking: A Preface to a New Theory of Invention and Innovation*. Cambridge, England: Cambridge Scholars Publishing.

______.2009f. *The Future of Post-Human Mass Media: A Preface to a New Theory of Communication*. Cambridge, England: Cambridge Scholars Publishing.

______.2009g. *The Future of Post-Human Engineering: A Preface to a New Theory of Technology*. Cambridge, England: Cambridge Scholars Publishing.

______.2008. *The Future of Post-Human Mathematical Logic: A Preface to a New Theory of Rationality*. Cambridge, England: Cambridge Scholars Publishing.

______.2008a. *The Future of Post-Human Knowledge: A Preface to a New Theory of Methodology and Ontology*. Oxford, United Kingdom: Chandos Publishing (Oxford) Ltd.

______.2008b. *The Future of Post-Human Unconsciousness: A Preface to a New Theory of Anomalous Experience*. Cambridge, England: Cambridge Scholars Publishing.

______.2008c. *The Future of Information Architecture: Conceiving a New Way to Understand Taxonomy, Network, and Intelligence*. Oxford, United Kingdom: Chandos Publishing (Oxford) Ltd.

______.2007. *The Rise of Authoritarian Liberal Democracy: A Preface to a New Theory of Comparative Political Systems*. Cambridge, England: Cambridge Scholars Publishing.

______.2007a. *The Future of Aesthetic Experience: Conceiving a Better Way to Beauty, Ugliness, and the Rest*. Cambridge, England: Cambridge Scholars Publishing.

______.2007b. *The Future of Complexity: Conceiving a Better Way to Understand Order and Chaos*. London, United Kingdom: World Scientific Publishing Co.

______.2007c. *Beyond the World of Titans, and the Remaking of World Order: A Preface to a New Logic of Empire-Building*. Cambridge, England: Cambridge Scholars Publishing.

______.2006. *Beyond Nature and Nurture: Conceiving a Better Way to Understand Genes and Memes*. Cambridge, England: Cambridge Scholars Publishing.

______.2006a. *The Future of Post-Human Space-Time: Conceiving a Better Way to Understand Space and Time*. New York: Peter Lang Publishing, Inc.

______.2006b. *Beyond Civilization to Post-Civilization: Conceiving a Better Model of Life Settlement to Supersede Civilization*. New York: Peter Lang Publishing, Inc.

______.2005. *Beyond Capitalism to Post-Capitalism: Conceiving a Better Model of Wealth Acquisition to Supersede Capitalism*. New York: The Edwin Mellen Press.

______.2004. *The Future of Post-Human Consciousness*. New York: The Edwin Mellen Press.

______.2004a. *Beyond Democracy to Post-Democracy: Conceiving a Better Model of Governance to Supersede Democracy*. Volume 1. New York: The Edwin Mellen Press.

______.2004b. *Beyond Democracy to Post-Democracy: Conceiving a Better Model of Governance to Supersede Democracy*. Volume 2. New York: The Edwin Mellen Press.

______.2002. *The Future of Capitalism and Democracy*. Maryland: The University Press of America.

______.2000. *The Future of Human Civilization*. Volume 1. New York: The Edwin Mellen Press.

_____.2000a. *The Future of Human Civilization.* Volume 2. New York: The Edwin Mellen Press.

Barrow, John D. 1998. *Impossibility: The Limits of Science and the Science of Limits*. Oxford: Oxford University Press.

BBC News (BBC). 2009. "Tickled Apes Yield Laughter Clue" (June 4). <http://news.bbc.co.uk/2/hi/science/nature/8083230.stm>.

_____.2006. "What Makes a Happy Society?" (May 04). <http://newsforums.bbc.co.uk/nol/thread.jspa?threadID=1660&&edition=2&ttl=20060505145036>.

Beattie, J. 1776. *Essays*. Edinburg: William Creech.

Berger, Arthur Asa. 1993. *An Anatomy of Humor.* New Brunswick, NJ: Transaction Publishers.

Bergson, Henri. 1999. *Laughter: An Essay on the Meaning of the Comic.* Cloudesley Brereton and Fred Rothwell, trs. Los Angeles, CA: Green Integer.

Berger, Peter Ludwig. 1997. *Redeeming Laughter: The Comic Dimension of Human Experience.* New York : Walter de Gruyter.

Binsted, Kim; & Graeme Ritchie. 1994. "A Symbolic Description of Punning Riddles and its Computer Implementation." Research Paper 688. Edinburgh, Scotland: University of Edinburgh.

Blurton, J. N. 1992. "Categories of Child–Child Interaction." *Ethological Studies of Child Behavior.* Jones Blurton, ed. New York: Cambridge University Press.

Biletzki, Anat; & Anat Matar. 2006. "Ludwig Wittgenstein" (Nov. 17). *Stanford Encyclopedia of Philosophy*. <http://plato.stanford.edu/entries/wittgenstein/>.

Bowler, Peter; & Jonathan Green. 2002. *What a Way to Go, Deaths with a Difference*. Bounty Books.

Brooks, B. R.; R. Thisted; S. Appel, et al. 2004. "Treatment of Pseudobulbar Affect in ALS with Dextromethorphan/Quinidine: A Randomized Trial." *Neurology*, 63: 1364-1370.

Brown, Huntington. 1968. *Rabelais in English Literature*. NY: Routledge.

Bunge, Mario. 1999. *Dictionary of philosophy*. Amherst, MA: Prometheus Books.

Camazine, Scott, et al. 2003. *Self-Organization in Biological Systems*. Princeton, NJ: Princeton University Press.

Canongate (CG). 2009. "9 People Who Died Laughing." <http://web.archive.org/web/20080412072030/http://www.canongate.net/Lists/Death/9PeopleWhoDiedLaughing>.

Cardoso, S. H. 2010. "Our Ancient Laughing Brain" (December 02). <http://www.cerebromente.org.br/n13/mente/laughter/laughter1.html>.

Carlin, George. 2010. *George Carlin Reads to You: Brain Droppings, Napalm & Silly Putty, and More Napalm & Silly Putty*. Highbridge Company.

Chase, Scott. 1993. "Tachyons" (March). *Physics FAQ.* <http://math.ucr.edu/home/baez/physics/ParticleAndNuclear/tachyons.html>.

Chislenko, Alexander. 2010. "Theory of Humor" (November 14). <http://www.lucifer.com/~sasha/articles/humor.html>.

Christine, G. 2010. "The Social Function of Humor" (December 03). <http://www.helium.com/items/1549733-social-function-of-humor>.

Collinson, D. L. 2002. "Managing Humour." *Journal of Management Studies*, 39: 269-288.

Comerford, Jason. 2005. "Author Profile: Arthur Koestler" (August 26). <http://oneletteratatime.blogspot.com/2005/08/author-profile-arthur-koestler.html>.

Corazzon, Raul. 2007. "Definitions of Ontology: From Nicolai Hartmann to the Present Time." <http://www.formalontology.it/section_4_two.htm>.

Corbett, Dan. 2008. "Introduction to String Theory" (November 23). *ThinkQuest.* <http://library.thinkquest.org/27930/stringtheory1.htm>.

Davis, Jeanie Lerche. 2010. "Why Do We Laugh? No Laughing Matter" (November 25). *WebMD Feature.* <http://men.webmd.com/features/why-do-we-laugh>.

Dawson, Jim. 1999. *Who Cut the Cheese? A Cultural History of the Fart.* CA: Ten Speed Press.

De Bono, Edward. 1991. *I am Right, You are Wrong: From This to the New Renaissance: From Rock Logic to Water Logic.* New York: Penguin.

_____.1990. *The Mechanism of Mind.* London: Penguin.

Eiseley, Loren. 1964. "Book Review: The Genesis of Genius; The Act of Creation" (October 18). *The New York Times.* <http://select.nytimes.com/gst/abstract.html?res=F10C12FC3E541B728DDDA10994D8415B848AF1D3>.

Ellinson, Ter. 2001. *The Myth of the Noble Sav*age. Berkley, CA: University of California Press.

Elliott, Robert. 2004. "Satire." *Encyclopaedia Britannica.*

Encyclopedia.com (EC). 2010. "Black Humor" (November 27). <http://www.encyclopedia.com/doc/1E1-blackhum.html>.

_____.2010a. "Humor Therapy" (December 02). <http://www.encyclopedia.com/doc/1G2-3435100402.html>.

Everett, Hugh. 1957. "'Relative State' Formulation of Quantum Mechanics" (July). *Reviews of Modern Physics*, vol. 29, no.3. <http://www.univer.omsk.su/omsk/Sci/Everett/paper1957.html>.

Famularo, G.; F. Corsi; G. Minisola; C. De Simone; & G. Nicotra. 2007. "Cerebellar Tumour Presenting with Pathological Laughter and Gelastic Syncope." *European Journal of Neurology*, 14 (8): 940–3. <http://www.blackwell-synergy.com/openurl?genre=article&sid=nlm:pubmed&issn=1351-5101&date=2007&volume=14&issue=8&spage=940>.

Firehammer, Reginald. 2005. "Basic Principles of Ontology" (January 05). <http://usabig.com/autonomist/philosophy/ontology2.html>.

Free Dictionary, the (FD). 2010. "Black Humor" (November 27). <http://encyclopedia.farlex.com/black+humor>.

Freud, Sigmund. 1966. "Civilization and Its Discontents." *The Standard Edition of the Complete Psychological Works of Sigmund Freud.* J. Strachey & A. Tyson. Trs. London: Hogarth Press.

_____.1960. *Jokes and their Relation to the Unconscious.* J. Strachey, Tr. New York: W. W. Norton.

_____.1928. "Humor." *International Journal of Psychoanalysis*, 9: 1-6.

Gondim, F.; B. Parks; & S. Cruz-Flores. 2001. "'Fou Rire Prodromique' as the Presentation of Pontine Ischaemia Secondary to Vertebrobasilar Stenosis." *Journal of Neurology, Neurosurgery, and Psychiatry*, 71 (6): 802–804. <http://www.ncbi.nlm.nih.gov/pmc/articles/PMC1737630/?tool=pmcentrez>.

Gott, J. Richard. 2002. *Time Travel in Einstein's Universe.* Boston : Houghton Mifflin.

Gregory, J. C. 1924. *The Nature of Laughter.* New York: Harcourt Brace.

Guth, Alan. 1997. *The Inflationary Universe: The Quest for a New Theory Of Cosmic Origins.* New York: Helix Books.

Hallett, R. W. 1971. "The Laughter of Gogol." *Russian Review*, 30 (4): 373-384.

Henderson, J. 1993. "Comic Hero versus Political Elite." *Tragedy, Comedy and the Polis.* A. Sommerstein, S. Halliwell, J. Henderson, and B. Zimmerman, eds. Bari: Levante Editori.

Hewitt, J. A. 2010. "Theory of Humor as an IFF" (November 28). <http://www.sexandphilosophy.co.uk/humour.htm>.

Heyd, David. 1982. "The Place of Laughter in Hobbes's Theory of Emotions." *Journal of the History of Ideas*, 43 (2): 285-295.

Hulstijn, J.; & A. Nijholt, eds. 1996. *Proceedings of the International Workshop on Computational Humor.* Enschede, Netherlands: University of Twente.

Ibagere, Eniwoke. 2005. "Nigeria's Soyinka back on Stage" (August 6). *BBC News.* <http://news.bbc.co.uk/2/hi/africa/1476167.stm>.

Jabberwock (JW). 2010. "Recos: Woody Allen Stories" (December 01). <http://jaiarjun.blogspot.com/2006/06/recos-woody-allen-stories.html>.

Joseph, John. 2008. "World's Oldest Joke Traced Back to 1900 BC" (July 31). <http://www.reuters.com/article/idUSKUA14785120080731>.

Kaku, Michio. 1994. *Hyperspace: A Scientific Odyssey Through Parallel Universes, Time Warps, and The Tenth Dimension.* Illustrations by Robert O'Keefe. Oxford: Oxford University Press.

Kawakami, Kiyobumi; Kiyoko Takai-Kawakami; Masaki Tomonaga; Juri Suzuki; Tomiyo Kusaka; and Takashi Okai. 2006. "Origins of Smile and Laughter: A Preliminary Study." *Early Human Development*,

82: 61-66. <http://www.pri.kyoto-u.ac.jp/ai/papers/ref3/kawakami2006.pdf>.

Kharpertian, Theodore D. 1990. *A Hand to Turn the Rime: The Menippean Satires of Thomas Pynchon*. Rutherford, NJ: Fairleigh Dickinson University Press.

Kincaid, J. R. 2001. "Falstaff as an Example for Freud's 'comic.'" <http://www.victorianweb.org/authors/dickens/kincaid2>.

Koestler, Arthur. 1964. *The Act of Creation*. New York: Macmillan.

Lateiner, Donald. 1977. "No Laughing Matter: A Literary Tactic in Herodotus." *Transactions of the American Philological Association*, vol. 107. <http://www.jstor.org/pss/284034>.

Leclair, Thomas. 1975. *Death and Black Humour in Critique*, Vol. 17.

Lessard, G.; & M. Levison. 1992. "Computational Modeling of Linguistic Humour: Tom Swifties." *ALLC/ACH Joint Annual Conference*: 175–178.

Levin, Max. 1931. "Inability to Laugh Audibly: Aphonogelia." *Archives of Neurology and Psychiatry*, 25(1):157-159.

Lezard, Nicholas. 2009. "From the Sublime to the Surreal" (February 21). *The Guardian*. <http://www.guardian.co.uk/books/2009/feb/21/anthology-of-black-humour>.

Lo, R.; & T. Cohen. 2007. "Laughter-Induced Syncope: No Laughing Matter." *American Journal of Medicine*, 120 (11): <http://linkinghub.elsevier.com/retrieve/pii/S0002-9343(06)00898-9>.

Lynch, O. H. 2002. "Humorous Communication: Finding a Place for Humor in Communication Research." *Communication Theory*, 4: 423-445.

MacDonald, C. 2004. "A Chuckle a Day Keeps the Doctor Away: Therapeutic Humor & Laughter." *Journal of Psychosocial Nursing and Mental Health Services*, 3: 18-25.

Maddox, Angelo Vildasol. 2006. *The Alphabet of Manliness*. <http://books.google.com/books?id=Ud58Z64QwjMC&pg=PA66&dq=dutch+oven+fart#v=onepage&q=dutch%20oven%20fart&f=false>.

Magstadt, Thomas; & Peter M.Schotten. 1999. *Understanding Politics: Ideas, Institutions, and Issues*. NY: Worth Publishers.

Marteinson, P. 2006. *On the Problem of the Comic*. Ottawa, Canada: Legas Press.

Martin J. 2006. "Studies in American Humor." CA: University of Southern California. <http://www.compedit.com/introduction.htm>.

Matte, G. 2001. "Humor." *A Psychoanalytical Perspective of Humor*, 14 (3): 223-241.

McAleer, Neil. 1987. *The Mind-Boggling Universe*. New York: Doubleday & Co.

McCullagh, S., M. Moore; M. Gawel; & A. Feinstein. 1999. "Pathological Laughing and Crying in Amyotrophic Lateral Sclerosis: An Association with Prefrontal Cognitive Dysfunction." *Journal of Neurological Sciences*, 169: 43–48.

Meineck, Peter, tr.; & Ian Storey, intr. 2000. *Aristophanes I: Clouds, Wasps, Birds*.

Hackett Publishing.

Meredith, George. 1897. "Essay on Comedy, Comic Spirit." *The Encyclopedia of the Self.* Mark Zimmerman. Archibald Constable and Company. <http://emotional-literacy-education.com/classic-books-online-b/esycm10.htm>.

Merriam-Webster's Collegiate Dictionary Online (MWD). 2010. "Metamorphism" (November 26). <http://www.m-w.com/dictionary/Metamorphism>.

_____.2007. "Agency" (March 20). <http://www.m-w.com/dictionary/agency>.

Merton, Robert. 1968. "Manifest and Latent Functions." *Social Theory and Social Structure*. New York: Free Press.

Mikkelson, Barbara. 2009. "The Last Laugh's on Him." <http://www.snopes.com/horrors/freakish/laughing.asp>.

Miller, Geoffrey. 2001. *The Mating Mind: How Sexual Choice Shaped the Evolution of Human Nature*. New York: Doubleday.

Miller, M.; C. Mangano; Y. Park; R. Goel, G. Plotnick; & R. Vogel. 2006. "Impact of Cinematic Viewing on Endothelial Function." *Heart*, 92 (2): 261-2.

Mulder, M. P.; & A. Nijholt. 2002. "Humour Research: State of the Art." <http://citeseer.ist.psu.edu/580062.html>.

New Oxford American Dictionary (NOAD). 2010. "Herodotos." England: Oxford University Press.

Newirth, J. 2006. "Jokes and their Relation to the Unconscious: Humor as a Fundamental Emotional experience." *Psychoanalytic Dialogues*, 16 (5): 557-571.

Nishida, K.; S. Hirota; & J. Tokeshi. 2008. "Laugh Syncope as a Rare Sub-Type of the Situational Syncopes: A Case Report." *Journal of Medical Case Reports*, 2: 197. <http://www.jmedicalcasereports.com/content/2//197>.

Nova Online (NO). 2000. "Time Can Vary." <http://www.pbs.org/wgbh/nova/time/thinktime.html>.

Panitch, H. S.; R. Thisted; R. Smith, et al. 2006. "Pseudobulbar Affect in Multiple Sclerosis Study Group. Randomized, Controlled Trial of Dextromethorphan/Quinidine for Pseudobulbar Affect in Multiple Sclerosis." *Annals of Neurology*, 59: 780-787.

Pankseppa, Jaak; & Jeff Burgdorf. 2003. "'Laughing' Rats and the Evolutionary Antecedents of Human Joy?" *Physiology & Behavior*, 79: 533-547. <http://www.psych.umn.edu/courses/fall06/macdonalda/psy4960/Readings/PankseppRatLaugh_P&B03.pdf>.

Parvizi, J., D. Arciniegas; G. Bernardini; M. Hoffmann; J. Mohr; M. Rapoport; J. Schmahmann; J. Silver; & S. Tuhrim. 2006 "Diagnosis and Management of Pathological Laughter and Crying." *Mayo Clinic Proceedings*, 811482-1486.

_____. S. Anderson; C. Martin; H. Damasio; & A. Damasio. 2001. "Pathological Laughter and Crying: A Link to the Cerebellum." *Brain*, 124:1708-1719.

Piscitelli, Emil. 1993. "Before Socrates-Diotima. Phaedrus: The Efficient Selfishness of the Utilitarian." The Second Boston College Lecture on the Symposium. <http://mysite.verizon.net/thelogos/lect-2.htm>.

Power, Jonathan. 2003. "Nigeria: Happiest Nation on Earth?" *The Toronto Star*

(Monday, December 29). Republished in <http://www.commondreams.org/views 03/1229-09.htm>.

Provine, Robert. 1999. "A Big Mystery: Why Do we Laugh? Contrary to Folk Wisdom, Most Laughter Is Not about Humor" (May 27). <http://www.msnbc.msn.com/id/3077386/>.

QuoteWorld.Org (QW). 2010. "Justin Brooks Atkinson" (November 14). <http://www.quoteworld.org/categories/humor/>.

_____.2010a. "Aristotle" (November 14). <http://www.quoteworld.org/categories/humor/1/>.

Rabelais, François. 1990. *Gargantua and Pantagruel*. W.W. Norton & Co.

Raman, Shankar. 1997. Lectures on Literary Theory. Cambridge, MA: MIT (spring).

Reiss A. L.; F. Hoeft; A. Tenforde; W. Chen; D. Mobbs; E. Mignot. 2008. "Anomalous Hypothalamic Responses to Humor in Cataplexy." *PLoS ONE*, 3 (5): e2225. <http://www.plosone.org/article/info:doi/10.1371/journal.pone.0002225>.

Ritchie, Graeme; Ruli Manurung; Helen Pain; Annalu Waller; Rolf Black; & Dave O'Mara. 2007. "A Practical Application of Computational Humour." *Proceedings of the 4th. International Joint Workshop on Computational Creativity*. A. Cardoso and G. Wiggins, eds.

Ritzer, George. 2003. *Contemporary Sociological Theory and Its Classical Roots*. New York: McGraw-Hill.

Robinson, R. G.; R. Parikh; J. Lipsey; S. Starkstein; & T. Price. 1993. "Pathological Laughing and Crying Following Stroke: Validation of a Measurement Scale and a Double-Blind Treatment Study." *American Journal of Psychiatry*, 150: 286-293.

Ross, Robert. 2000. *The Complete Goodies*. London, England: B T Batsford.

Rousseau, Jean-Jacques. 1984. *A Discourse on Inequality*. Maurice Cranston, trs. New York: Penguin Books.

Salingar, Leo. 1976. *Shakespeare and the Traditions of Comedy*. England: Cambridge University Press.

Schiffer, R. B.; R. Herndon; & R. Rudick. 1985. "Treatment of Pathologic Laughing and Weeping with Amitriptyline." *New England Journal of Medicine,* 312: 1480-1482.

Schott, Ben. 2003. *Schott's Original Miscellany*. New York: Holtzbrinck Publishers.

Science News (SN). 2001. "Don't Look Now, but Is that Dog Laughing?" (July 28). <http://www.sciencenews.org/view/generic/id/1847/title/Dont_look_now%2C_but_is_that_dog_laughing%3F>.

Seneca, Lucius Annaeus. 1920. *Apocolocyntosis*. W. H. D. Rouse, tr. Project Gutenberg: E-text No. 10001. <http://www.gutenberg.org/ebooks/ 10001>.

Shlain, Leonard. 1991. *Art and Physics: Parallel Visions in Space,Time, and Light*. New York: William Morrow and Co., Inc.

Simonet, Patricia; Donna Versteeg; & Dan Storie. 2005. "Dog-Laughter: Recorded Playback Reduces Stress Related Behavior in Shelter Dogs." *Proceedings of the 7th International Conference on Environmental Enrichment* (July 31-August 5). <http://www.petalk.org/LaughingDog.pdf>.

Smuts, A. 2006. "Humor" (April 20). *The Internet Encyclopedia of Philosophy.* <http://www.iep.utm.edu/h/humor.htm#H3

Staveacre, Tony. 1987. *Slapstick!: The Illustrated Story of Knockabout Comedy* . North Ryde, NWS, Australia: Angus & Robertson Publishers.

Suslov, I. M. 1992. "Computer Model of 'a Sense of Humour'. I. General Algorithm." *Biofizika SSSR*, 37 [*Biophysics,* 37]. <http://arxiv.org/abs/0711.2058>.

_____.1992a. "Computer Model of "a Sense of Humour". II. Realization in Neural Networks." *Biofizika SSSR*, 37 [*Biophysics*, 37]. <http://arxiv.org/abs/0711.2061>.

Tateno, A.; R. Jorge; & R. Robinson. 2004. "Pathological Laughing and Crying Following Traumatic Brain Injury." *Journal of Neuropsychiatry and Clinical Neuroscience*, 16:426-434.

Tomlinson, Sarah. 2006. "African Spirit: A film Festival and a Photo Exhibit Present Africa's New Urban Reality—and the Humor, Resourcefulness, and Heart of Its People" (February 15). <http://www.boston.com/ae/events/articles/2006/02/15/ african_spirit/>.

Totah, A. R; & S. Benbadis. 2002. "Gelastic Syncope Mistaken for Cataplexy." *Sleep Med.*, 3 (1): 77–8. <http://linkinghub.elsevier.com/retrieve/pii/S1389945701001137>.

Tracy, S. J.; K. K. Myers; & C. W. Scott. 2006. "Cracking Jokes and Crafting Selves: Sensemaking and Identity Management among Human Service Workers." *Communication Monographs*, 73: 283-308.

Turner, Mark, ed. 2006. *The Artful Mind: Cognitive Science and the Riddle of Human Creativity*. New York: Oxford University Press.

Twain, Mark. 1880. "1601: Conversation as it was by the Social Fireside in the Time of the Tudors." <http://www.gutenberg.org/files/3190/3190.txt>.

van Wattum, P.J.; & C. Chiles. 2001. "Rapid Response to Low Dose Citalopram in Pathological Crying." *General Hospital Psychiatry*, 23: 167-168.

Vlachopoulos, C.; P. Xaplanteris; N. Alexopoulos; K. Aznaouridis; C. Vasiliadou; K. Baou; E. Stefanadi; & C. Stefanadis. 2009. "Divergent Effects of Laughter and Mental Stress on Arterial Stiffness and Central Hemodynamics." *Psychosomatic Medicine*, 71 (4): 446-53.

Waterfield, Gordon, ed. 1966. *First Footsteps in East Africa*. New York: Praeger Publishers.

Weber, Max. 1930. *The Protestant Ethic and the Spirit of Capitalism.* Talcott Parsons, tr. New York: Scribner.

Wikipedia (WK). 2010. "Humor" (November 14). <http://en.wikipedia.org/wiki/Humor>.

______.2010a. "Joke" (November 25). <http://en.wikipedia.org/wiki/Joke>.

______.2010b. "Laughter" (November 25). <http://en.wikipedia.org/wiki/Laughter>.

______.2010c. "Theories of Humor" (November 25). <http://en.wikipedia.org/wiki/Theories_of_humor>.

______.2010d. "Geoffrey Miller (Evolutionary Psychologist" (November 26). <http://en.wikipedia.org/wiki/Geoffrey_Miller_(evolutionary_psychologist)>.

______.2010e. "The Act of Creation" (November 26). <http://en.wikipedia.org/wiki/The_Act_of_Creation>.

______.2010f. "Humor in Freud" (November 26). <http://en.wikipedia.org/wiki/Jokes_and_their_Relation_to_the_Unconsciou>.

______.2010g. "Black Comedy" (November 27). <http://en.wikipedia.org/wiki/Black_comedy>.

______.2010h. "Jean-Jacques Rousseau" (November 27). <http://en.wikipedia.org/wiki/Rousseau>.

______.2010i. "Satire" (November 28). <http://en.wikipedia.org/wiki/Satire>.

______.2010j. "Political Satire" (November 28). <http://en.wikipedia.org/wiki/Political_satire>.

______.2010k. "Comedy" (November 29). <http://en.wikipedia.org/wiki/Comedy>.

______.2010l. "Ethnic Jokes" (November 29). <http://en.wikipedia.org/wiki/Ethnic_jokes>.

______.2010m. "Burlesque" (November 29). <http://en.wikipedia.org/wiki/Burlesque>.

______.2010n. "Parody" (November 29). <http://en.wikipedia.org/wiki/Parody>.

______.2010o. "Farce" (November 29). <http://en.wikipedia.org/wiki/Farce>.

______.2010p. "Flatulence Humor" (November 30). <http://en.wikipedia.org/wiki/Flatulent_humor>.

______.2010q. "Wit" (November 30). <http://en.wikipedia.org/wiki/Wit>.

______.2010r. "Comic Timing" (December 01). <http://en.wikipedia.org/wiki/Comic_timing>.

______.2010s. "Double Entendre" (December 01). <http://en.wikipedia.org/wiki/Double_entendre>.

______.2010t. "Irony" (December 01). <http://en.wikipedia.org/wiki/Irony>.

______.2010u. "Paradox" (December 01). <http://en.wikipedia.org/wiki/Paradox>.

______.2010v. "Pathological Laughing and Crying" (December 01). <http://en.wikipedia.org/wiki/Pathological_laughing_and_crying>.

______.2010w. "Wole Soyinka" (December 01). <http://en.wikipedia.org/wiki/Wole_Soyinka>.

______.2010x. "Gelotology" (December 02). <http://en.wikipedia.org/wiki/

Gelotology>.

_____.2010y. "Michel Foucault" (December 02). <http://en.wikipedia.org/wiki/Michel_Foucault>.

_____.2010z. "The Birth of the Clinic" (December 02). <http://en.wikipedia.org/wiki/The_Birth_of_the_Clinic>.

_____.2010aa. "Laughter in Animals" (December 02). <http://en.wikipedia.org/wiki/Laughter_in_animals>.

_____.2010bb. "Laughter in Literature" (December 04). <http://en.wikipedia.org/wiki/Laughter_in_literature>.

_____.2010cc. "Herodotus" (December 04). <http://en.wikipedia.org/wiki/Herodotus>.

_____.2010dd. "Nikolai Gogol" (December 04). <http://en.wikipedia.org/wiki/Nikolai_Gogol>.

_____.2010ee. "Friedrich Nietzsche" (December 04). <http://en.wikipedia.org/wiki/Friedrich_Nietzsche >.

_____.2010ff. "Henri Bergson" (December 04). <http://en.wikipedia.org/wiki/Henri_Bergson>.

_____.2010gg. "Death from Laughter" (December 04). <http://en.wikipedia.org/wiki/Death_from_laughter>.

_____.2010hh. "Computational Humor" (December 05). <http://en.wikipedia.org/wiki/Computational_humor>.

_____.2008. "Posthumanism" (October 20). <http://en.wikipedia.org/wiki/Posthumanism>.

_____.2008a. "Transhumanism" (October 20). <http://en.wikipedia.org/wiki/Transhumanism>.

_____.2008b. "Lowest Common Denominator" (March 26). <http://en.wikipedia.org/ wiki/Least_common_denominator>.

_____.2008c. "Infinity" (November 11). <http://en.wikipedia.org/wiki/Infinity>.

_____.2008d. "Transfinite Number" (November 10). <http://en.wikipedia.org/wiki/Transfinite_ number>.

_____.2008e. "Quantum Mechanics" (November 26). <http://en.wikipedia.org/wiki/Quantum_mechanics>.

_____.2008f. "Copenhagen Interpretation" (November 26). <http://en.wikipedia.org/wiki/Copenhagen_interpretation >.

_____.2008g. "Many Worlds Interpretation" (November 26). <http://en.wikipedia.org/wiki/Many_Worlds_Interpretation>.

_____.2008h. "Hyperspace (Science Fiction)" (November 23). <http://en.wikipedia.org/wiki/Hyperspace_(science_fiction)>.

_____.2008i. "Time Travel" (November 26). <http://en.wikipedia.org/

wiki/Time_travel#Time_dilation>.

_____.2008j. "Wormhole" (November 25). <http://en.wikipedia.org/wiki/Wormhole>.

_____.2007. "Linguistics" (March 04). <http://en.wikipedia.org/wiki/Linguistics>.

Wikiversity (WKV). 2008. "Why 10 Dimensions" (November 23). <ttp://en.wikiversity.org/wiki/Why_10_dimensions>

Wilson, Sak. 1924. "Some Problems in Neurology II: Pathological Laughing and Crying." *Journal of Neurology and Psychopathology*, 6:299-333.

Wittgenstein, Ludwig.1953. *Philosophical Investigations*. G. E. M. Anscombe and R. Rhees, eds. G.E.M. Anscombe, tr. Oxford: Blackwell.

Wortzel, H. S.; T. Oster; C. Anderson; & D. Arciniegas. 2008. "Pathological Laughing and Crying: Epidemiology, Pathophysiology and Treatment." *CNS Drugs*, 22 (7): 531–45.

Zakaria, Fareed. 1997. "An Optimist's Lament" (March 30). *The New York Times Book Review Online*. <http://www.nytimes.com/books>.

INDEX

•A•

•B•

•C•

•D•

•E•

•F•

•I•

•J•

•K•

•L•

•N•

•O•

•P•

•Q•

•R•

•S•

•U•